MY HERO ACADEMIA vol.21

Why He Gets Back Up

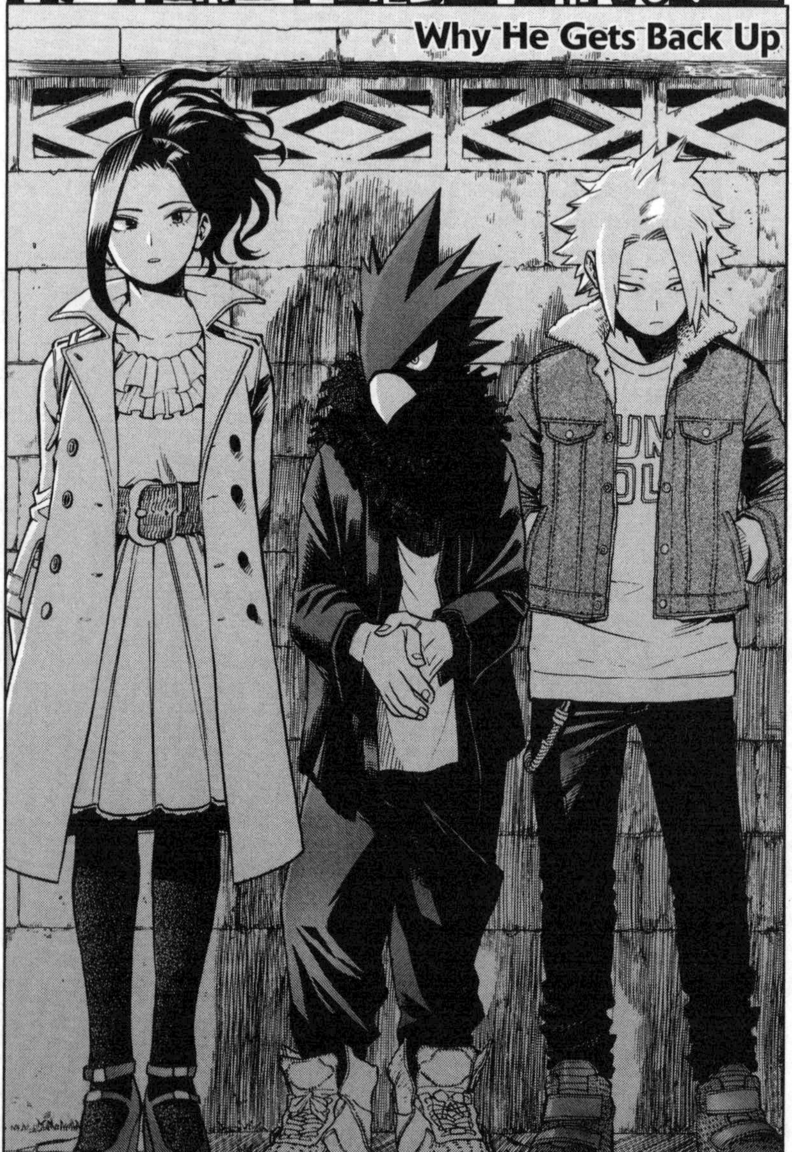

KOHEI HORIKOSHI

INTRODUCING: IRIS VISION

World-renowned fashion designer Iris Vision has come to town, and her Quirk can give anyone hyper-eyesight!! Bow down, world, for none can resist this eye-opening power!!

IRIS VISION

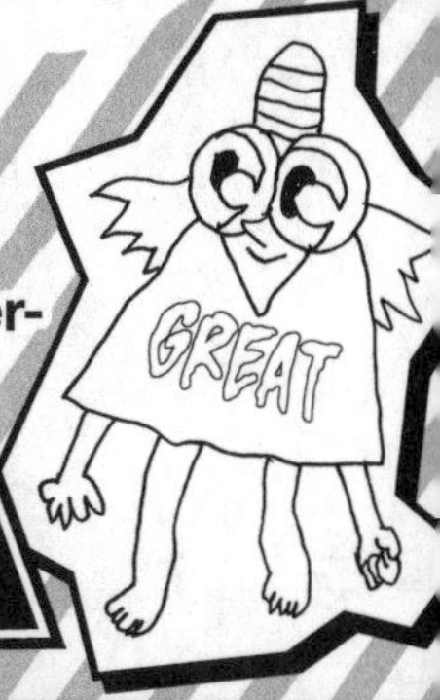
GREAT

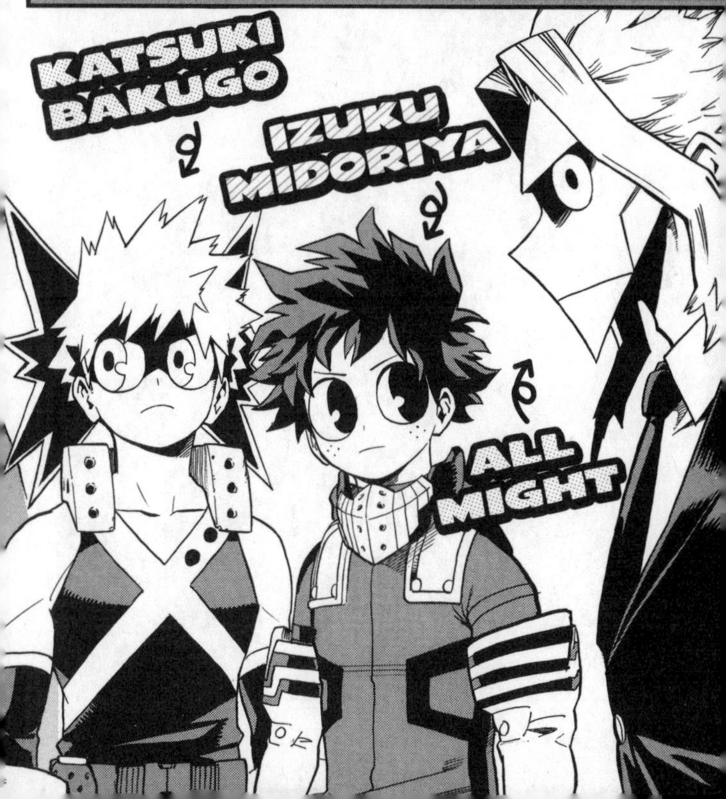
KATSUKI BAKUGO
IZUKU MIDORIYA
ALL MIGHT

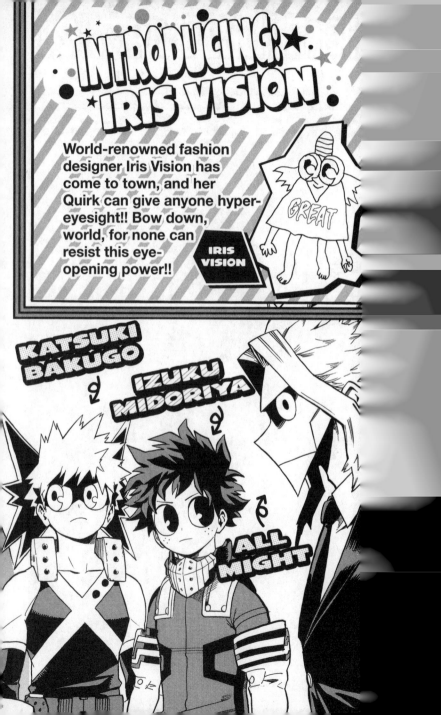

STORY

One day, people began manifesting special abilities that came to be known as "Quirks," and before long, the world was full of superpowered humans. But with the advent of these exceptional individuals came an increase in crime, and governments alone were unable to deal with the situation. At the same time, others emerged to oppose the spread of evil! As if straight from the comic books, these heroes keep the peace and are even officially authorized to fight crime. Our story begins when a certain Quirkless boy and lifelong hero fan meets the world's number one hero, starting him on his path to becoming the greatest hero ever!

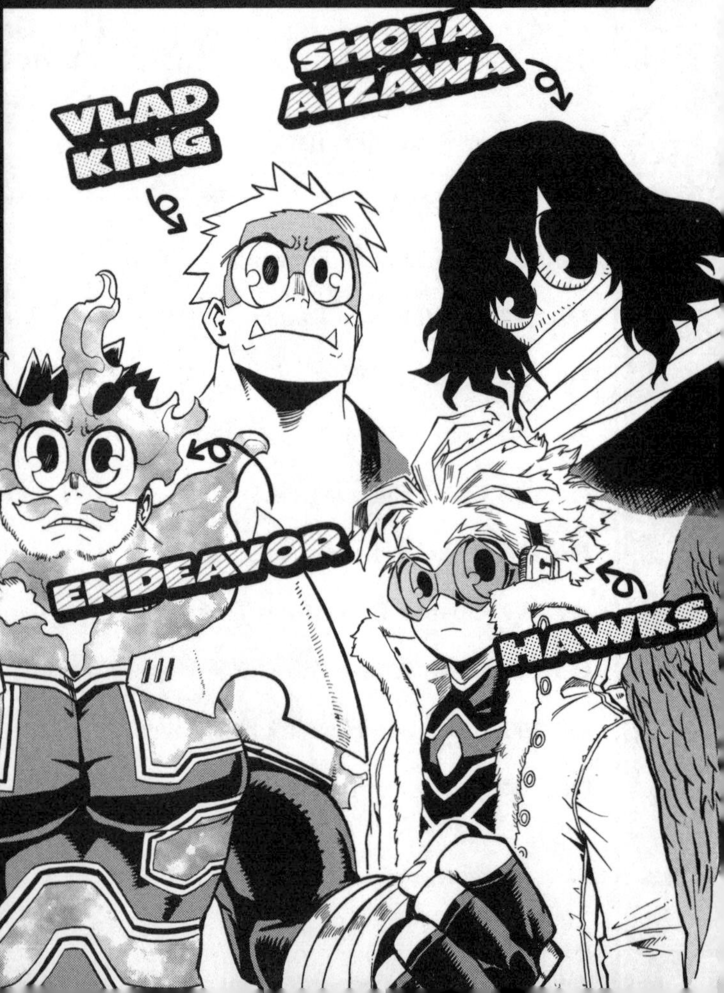
SHOTA AIZAWA
VLAD KING
ENDEAVOR
HAWKS

MY HERO ACADEMIA

Vol. 21

CONTENTS

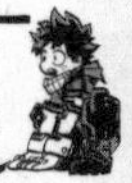

Why He Gets Back Up

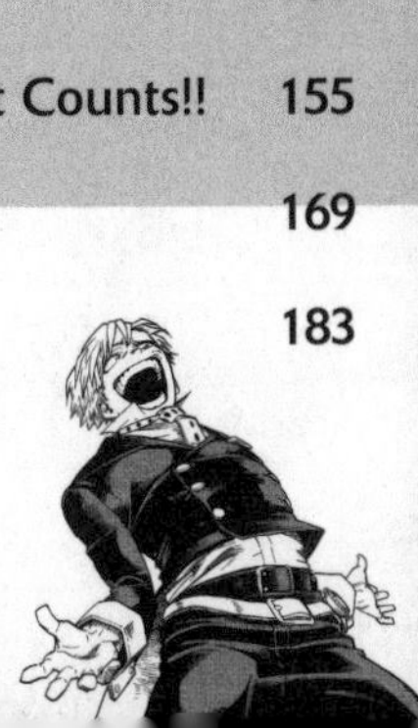

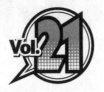

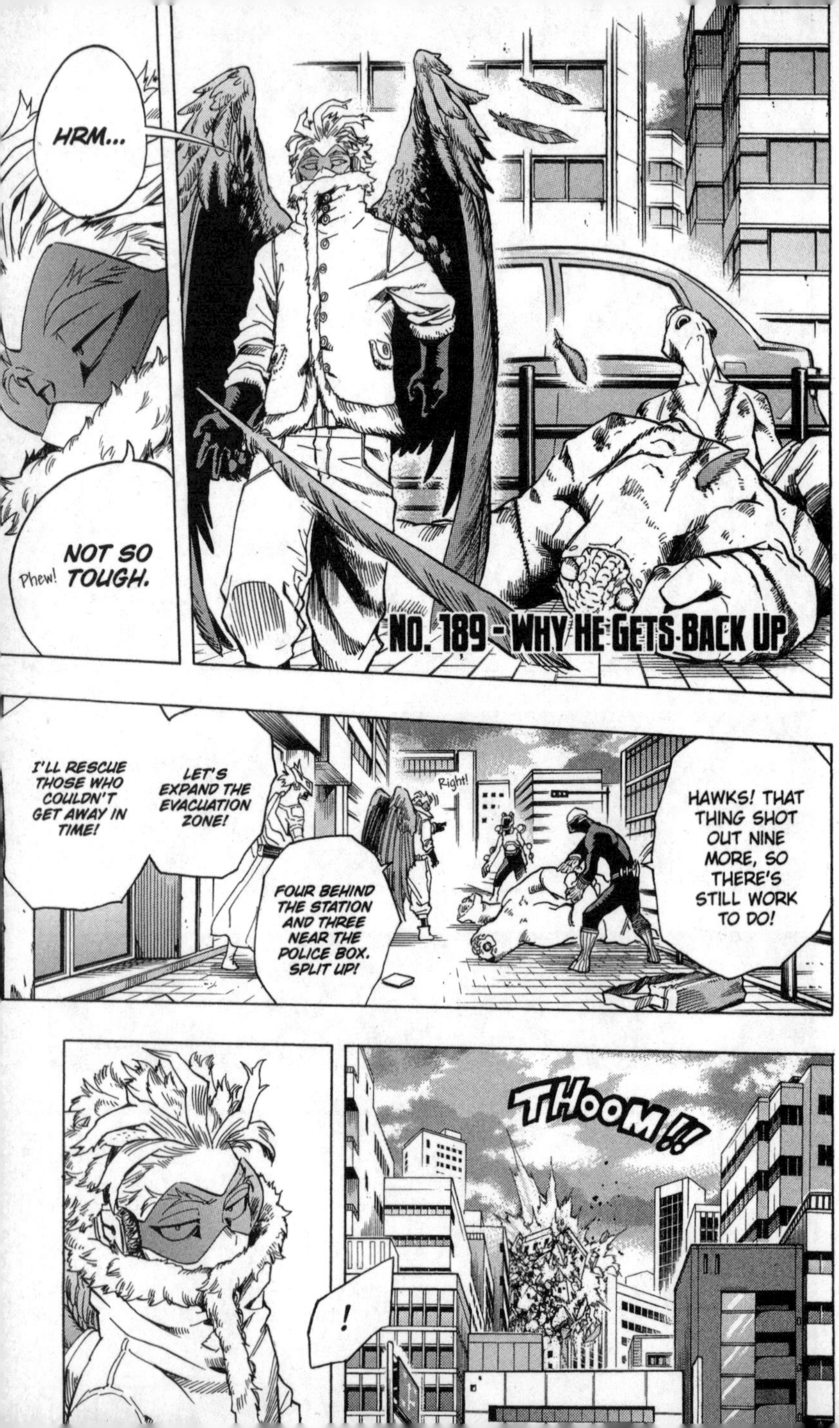
No. 189 - Why He Gets Back Up
HRM...
Phew! NOT SO TOUGH.
HAWKS! THAT THING SHOT OUT NINE MORE, SO THERE'S STILL WORK TO DO!
Right!
FOUR BEHIND THE STATION AND THREE NEAR THE POLICE BOX. SPLIT UP!
LET'S EXPAND THE EVACUATION ZONE!
I'LL RESCUE THOSE WHO COULDN'T GET AWAY IN TIME!
THOOM!!
!

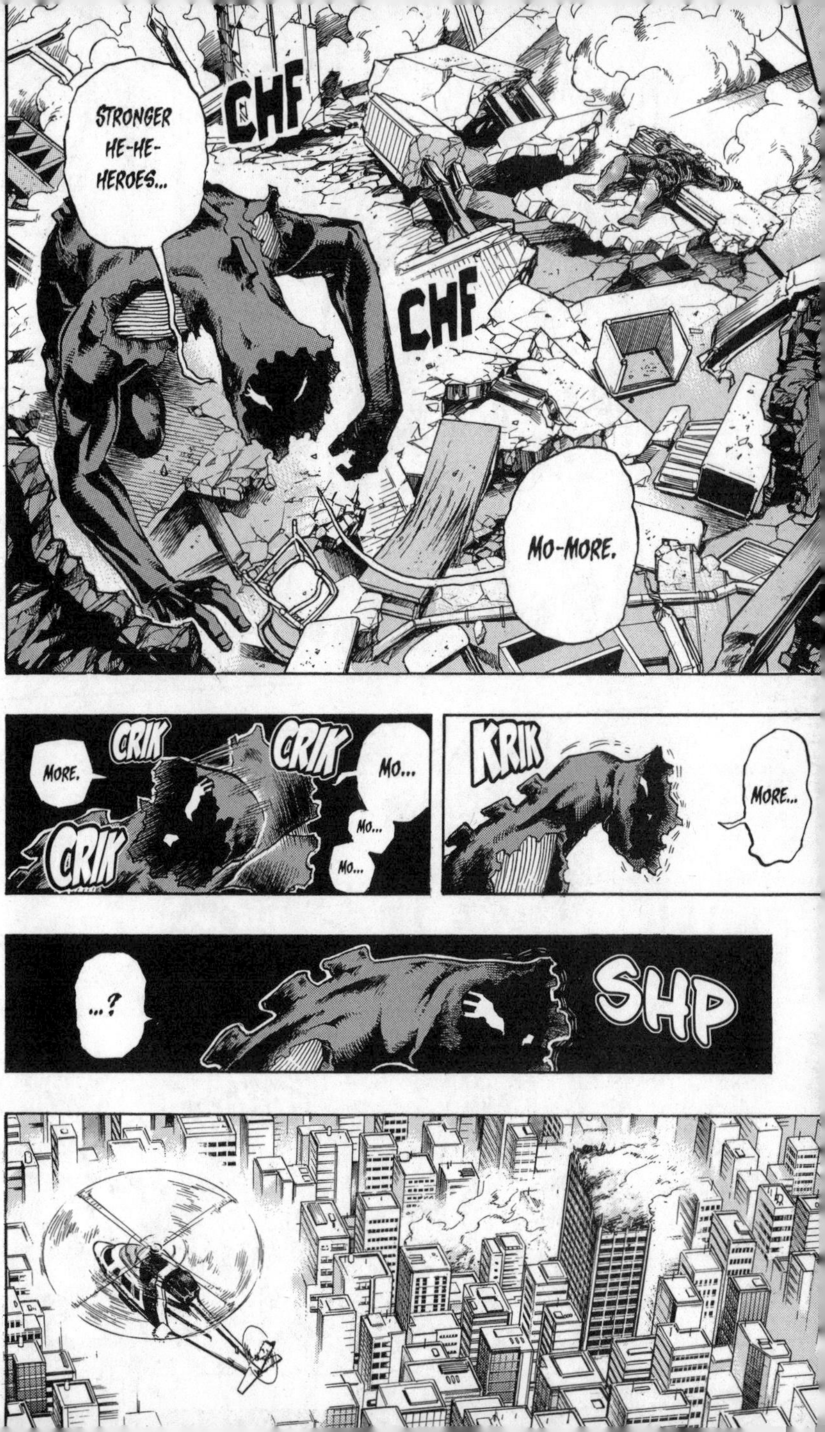
CHF
STRONGER HE-HE-HEROES...
CHF
MO-MORE.
KRIK
MORE...
MO...
MO...
MO...
CRIK
CRIK
MORE.
CRIK
SHP
...?

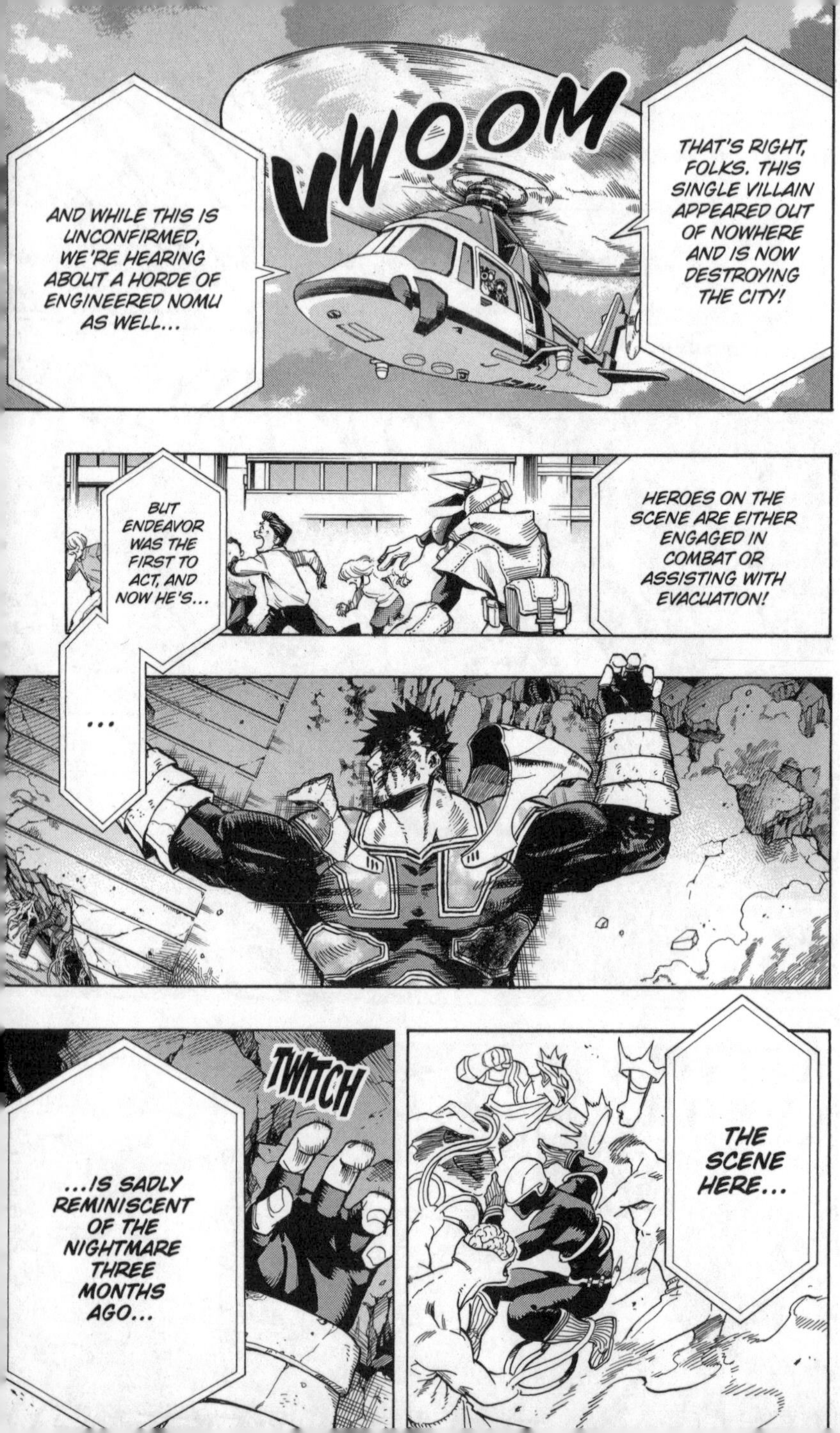
THAT'S RIGHT, FOLKS. THIS SINGLE VILLAIN APPEARED OUT OF NOWHERE AND IS NOW DESTROYING THE CITY!
VWOOM
AND WHILE THIS IS UNCONFIRMED, WE'RE HEARING ABOUT A HORDE OF ENGINEERED NOMU AS WELL...
HEROES ON THE SCENE ARE EITHER ENGAGED IN COMBAT OR ASSISTING WITH EVACUATION!
BUT ENDEAVOR WAS THE FIRST TO ACT, AND NOW HE'S...
...
THE SCENE HERE...
TWITCH
...IS SADLY REMINISCENT OF THE NIGHTMARE THREE MONTHS AGO...

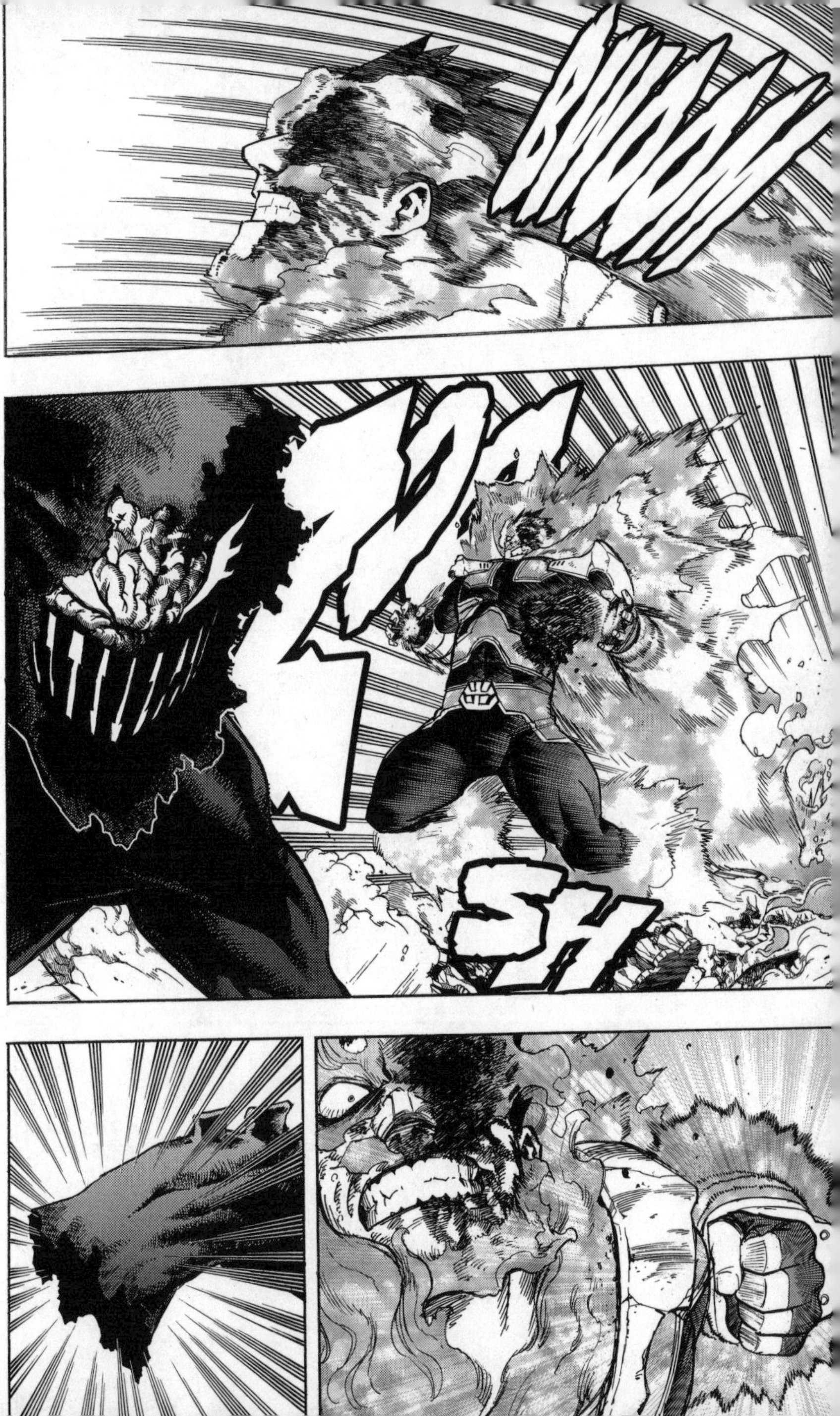
BWOOOM

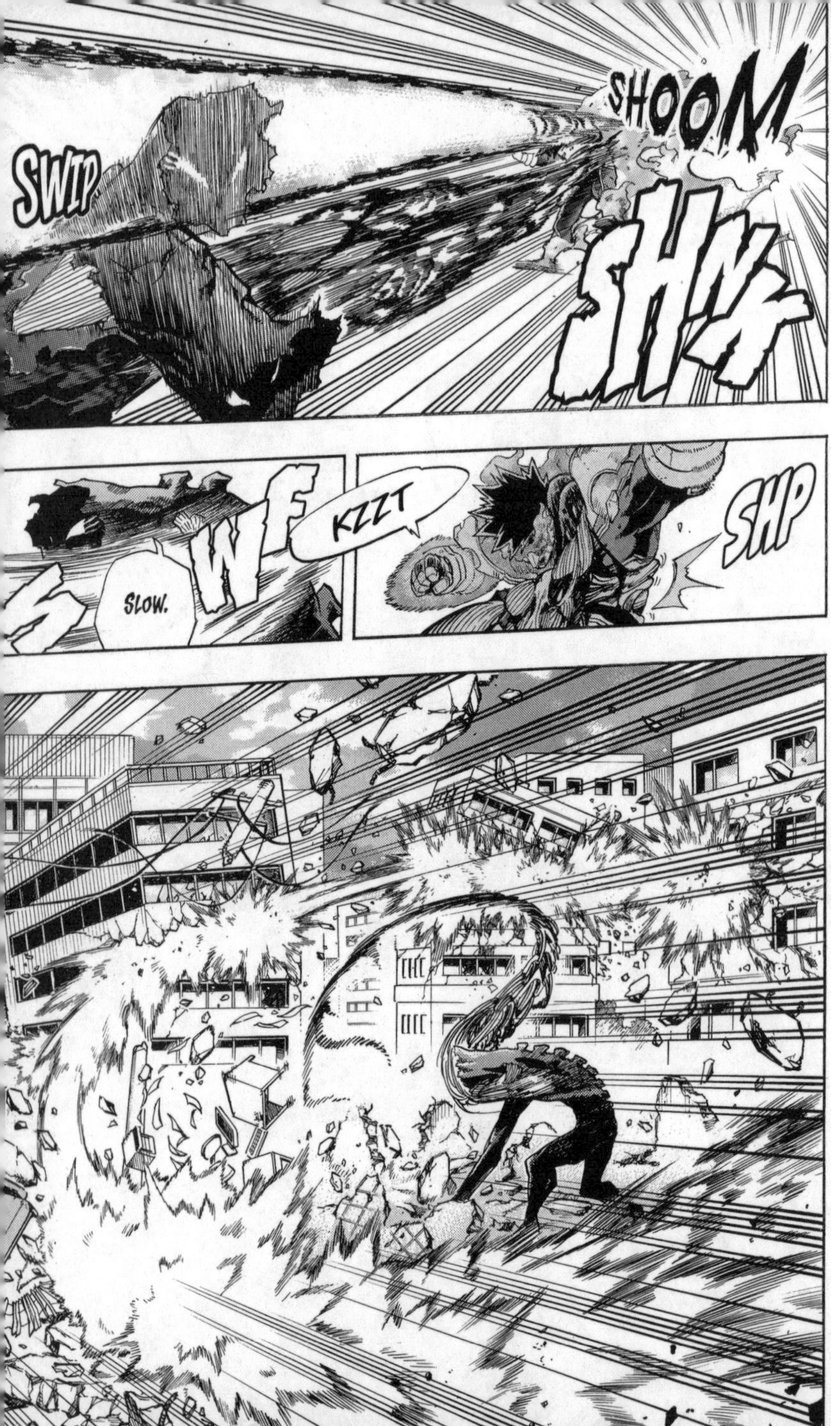
SHOOM
SHNK
SWIP
SHP
KZZT
SWF
SLOW.

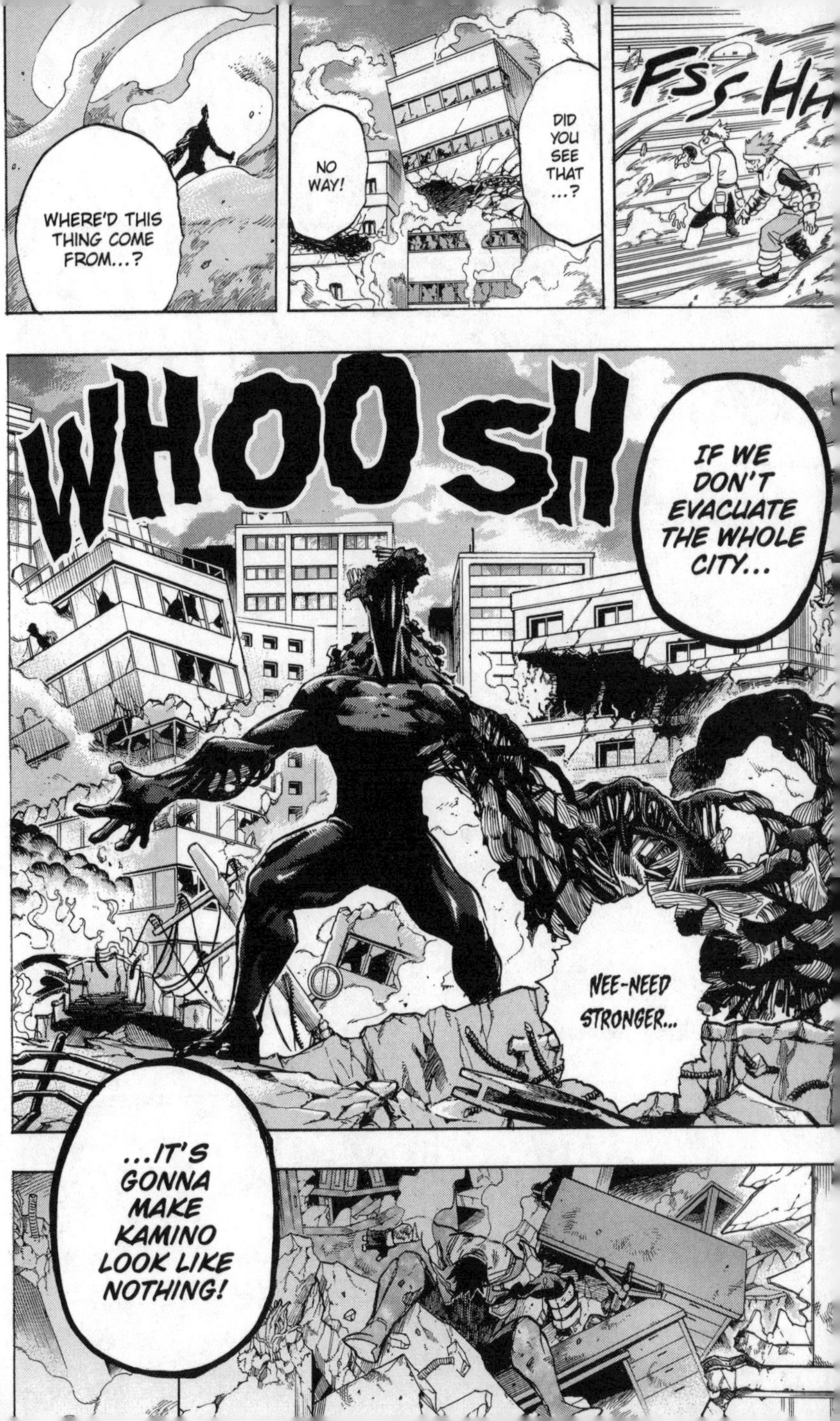
FSS-HH
DID YOU SEE THAT...?
NO WAY!
WHERE'D THIS THING COME FROM...?
WHOOSH
IF WE DON'T EVACUATE THE WHOLE CITY...
NEE-NEED STRONGER...
...IT'S GONNA MAKE KAMINO LOOK LIKE NOTHING!

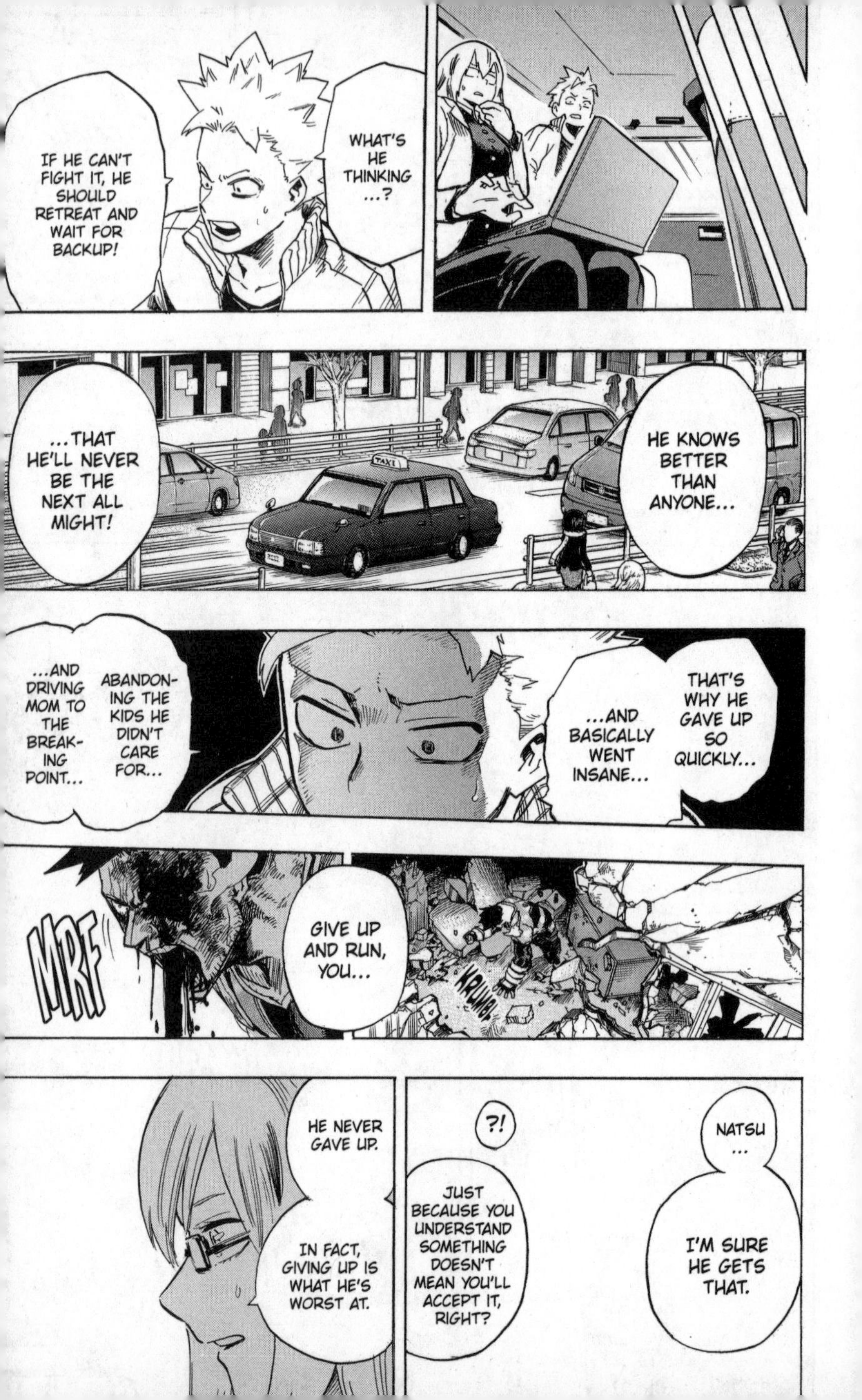

WHAT'S HE THINKING ...?
IF HE CAN'T FIGHT IT, HE SHOULD RETREAT AND WAIT FOR BACKUP!
HE KNOWS BETTER THAN ANYONE...
...THAT HE'LL NEVER BE THE NEXT ALL MIGHT!
TAXI
THAT'S WHY HE GAVE UP SO QUICKLY...
...AND BASICALLY WENT INSANE...
ABANDONING THE KIDS HE DIDN'T CARE FOR...
...AND DRIVING MOM TO THE BREAKING POINT...
KRUMB!
GIVE UP AND RUN, YOU...
MRF
NATSU ...
I'M SURE HE GETS THAT.
?!
JUST BECAUSE YOU UNDERSTAND SOMETHING DOESN'T MEAN YOU'LL ACCEPT IT, RIGHT?
HE NEVER GAVE UP.
IN FACT, GIVING UP IS WHAT HE'S WORST AT.

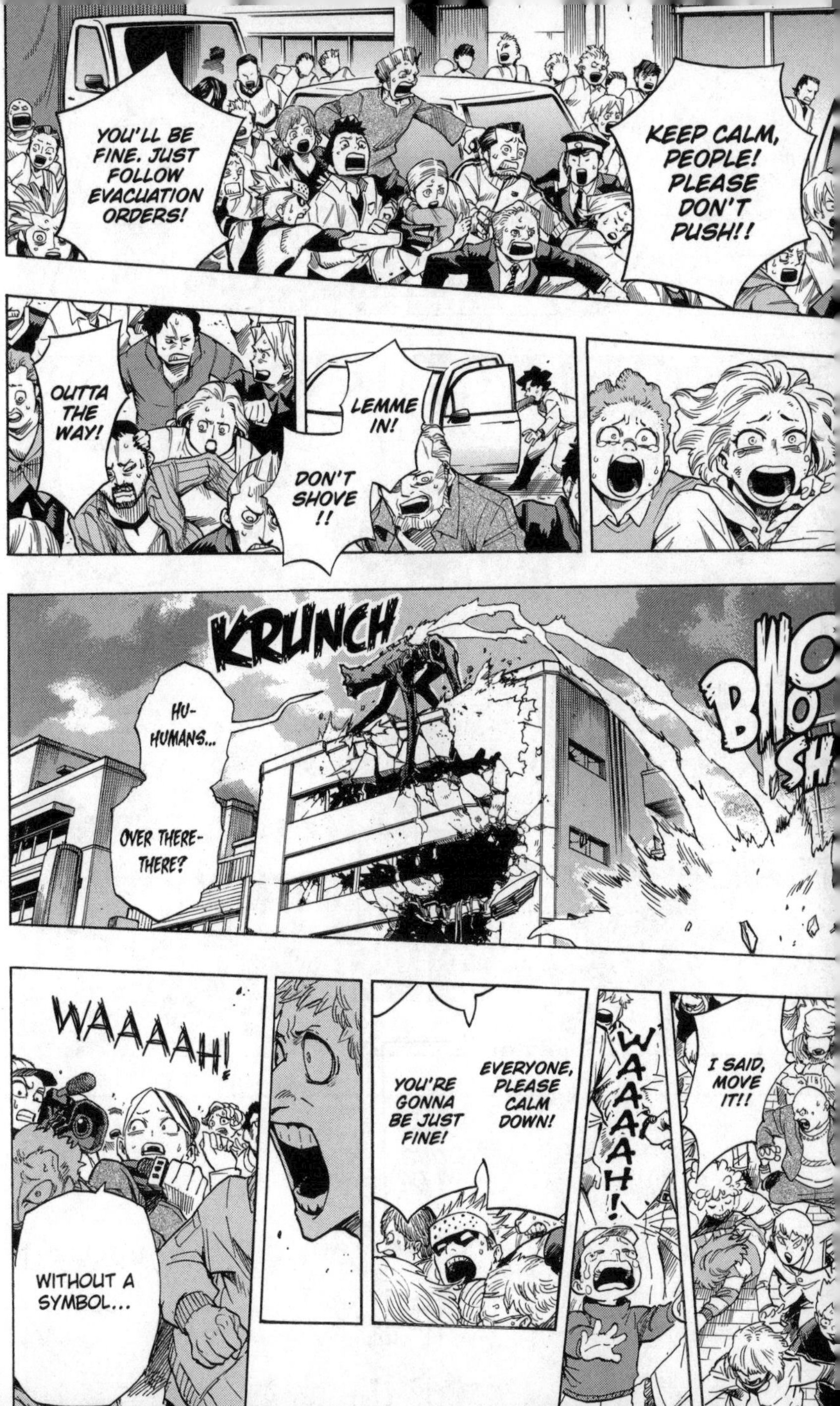
KEEP CALM, PEOPLE! PLEASE DON'T PUSH!!
YOU'LL BE FINE. JUST FOLLOW EVACUATION ORDERS!
LEMME IN!
DON'T SHOVE!!
OUTTA THE WAY!
BOOSH
KRUNCH
HU-HUMANS... OVER THERE-THERE?
I SAID, MOVE IT!!
WAAAAH!
EVERYONE, PLEASE CALM DOWN!
YOU'RE GONNA BE JUST FINE!
WAAAAH!
WITHOUT A SYMBOL...

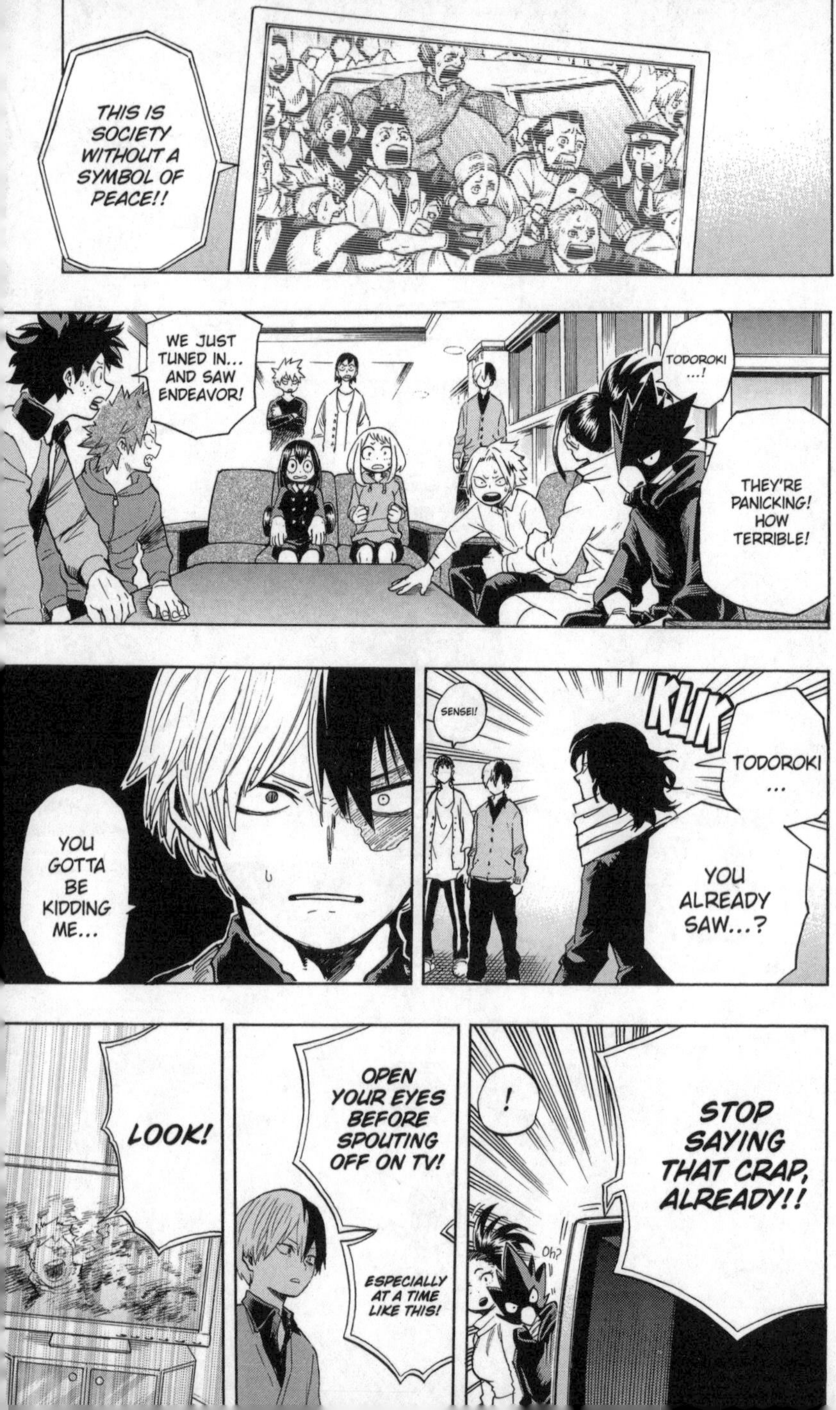

THIS IS SOCIETY WITHOUT A SYMBOL OF PEACE!!
TODOROKI ...!
WE JUST TUNED IN... AND SAW ENDEAVOR!
THEY'RE PANICKING! HOW TERRIBLE!
KLIK
SENSEI!
TODOROKI ...
YOU ALREADY SAW...?
YOU GOTTA BE KIDDING ME...
!
STOP SAYING THAT CRAP, ALREADY!!
Oh?
OPEN YOUR EYES BEFORE SPOUTING OFF ON TV!
ESPECIALLY AT A TIME LIKE THIS!
LOOK!

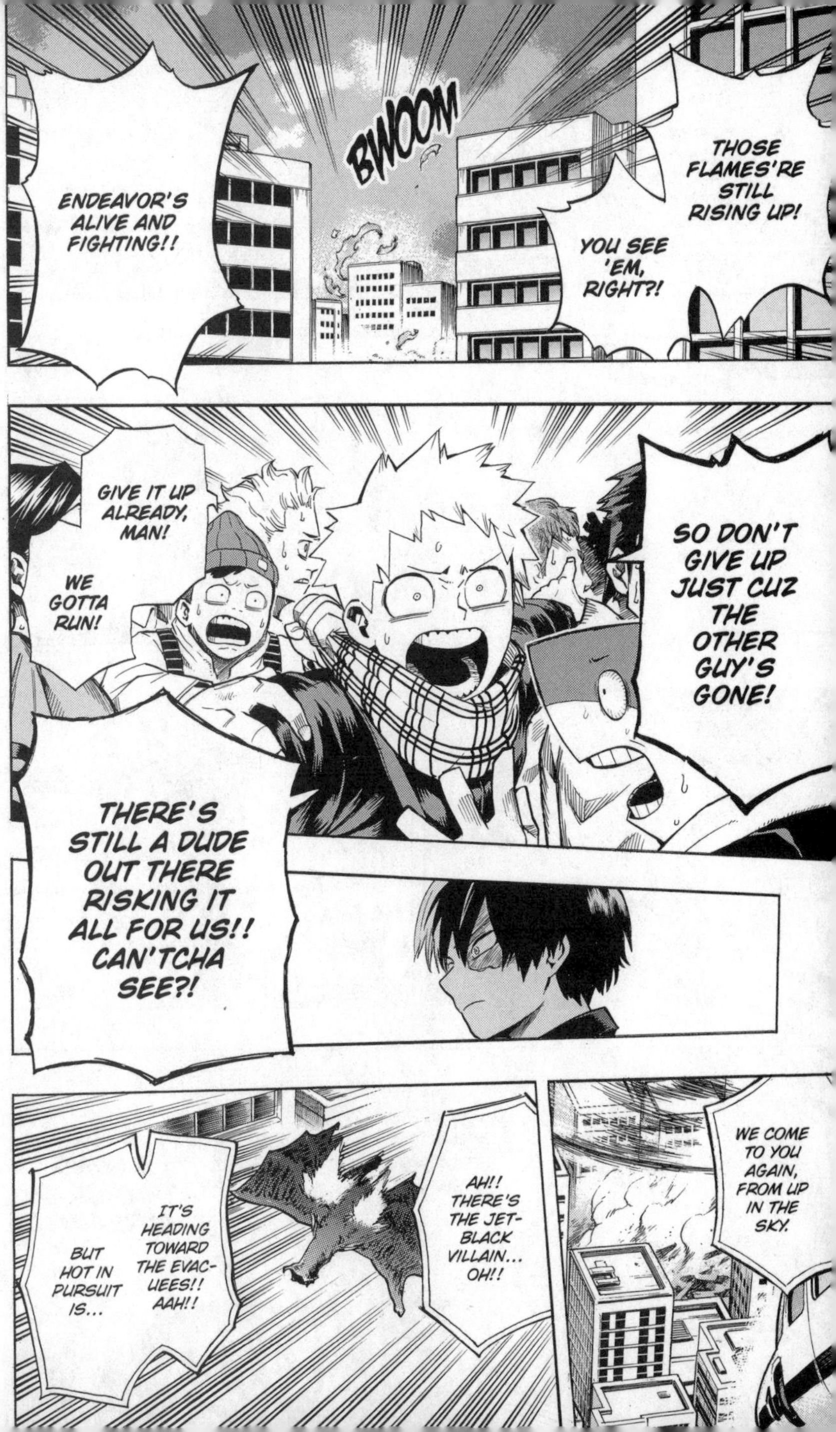
THOSE FLAMES'RE STILL RISING UP!
BWOOM
YOU SEE 'EM, RIGHT?!
ENDEAVOR'S ALIVE AND FIGHTING!!
SO DON'T GIVE UP JUST CUZ THE OTHER GUY'S GONE!
GIVE IT UP ALREADY, MAN!
WE GOTTA RUN!
THERE'S STILL A DUDE OUT THERE RISKING IT ALL FOR US!! CAN'TCHA SEE?!
WE COME TO YOU AGAIN, FROM UP IN THE SKY.
AH!! THERE'S THE JET-BLACK VILLAIN... OH!!
IT'S HEADING TOWARD THE EVACUEES!! AAH!!
BUT HOT IN PURSUIT IS...

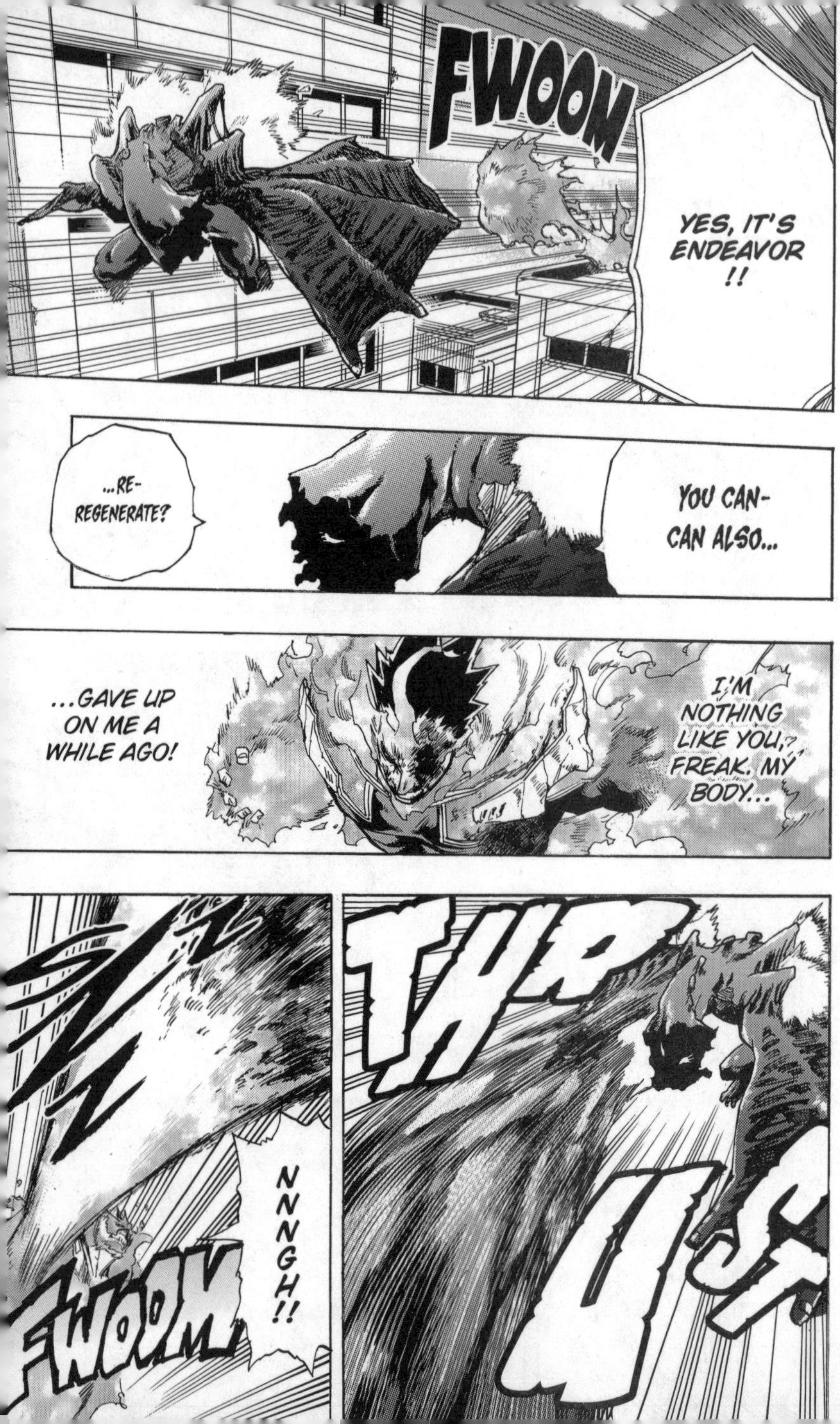
FWOOM
YES, IT'S ENDEAVOR !!
YOU CAN- CAN ALSO...
...RE- REGENERATE?
I'M NOTHING LIKE YOU, FREAK. MY BODY...
...GAVE UP ON ME A WHILE AGO!
THRUST
NNNNGH!!
FWOOM

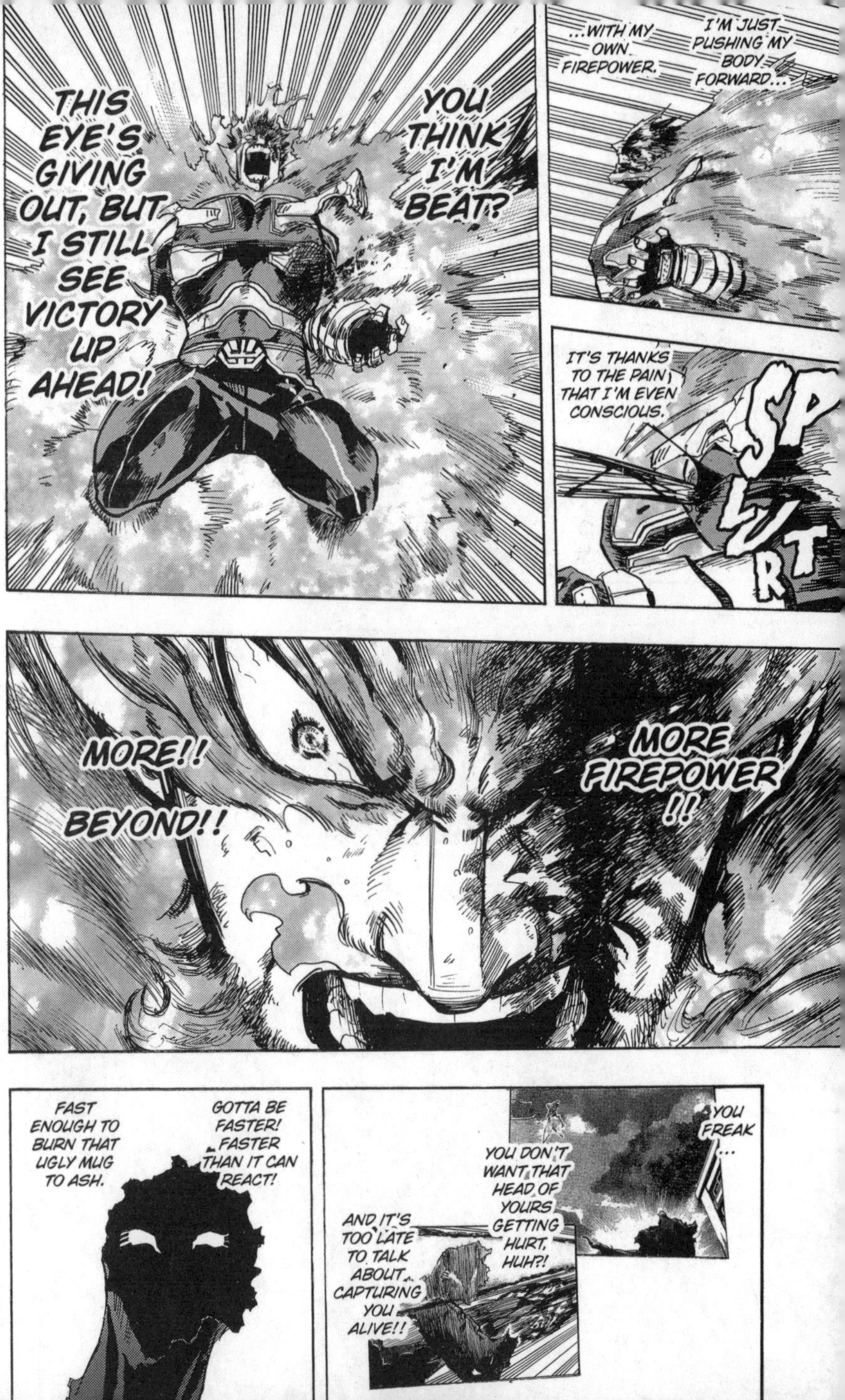
I'M JUST PUSHING MY BODY FORWARD...
...WITH MY OWN FIREPOWER.
IT'S THANKS TO THE PAIN THAT I'M EVEN CONSCIOUS.
SPLURT
YOU THINK I'M BEAT?
THIS EYE'S GIVING OUT, BUT I STILL SEE VICTORY UP AHEAD!
MORE FIREPOWER!!
MORE!!
BEYOND!!
YOU FREAK...
YOU DON'T WANT THAT HEAD OF YOURS GETTING HURT, HUH?!
AND IT'S TOO LATE TO TALK ABOUT CAPTURING YOU ALIVE!!
GOTTA BE FASTER! FASTER THAN IT CAN REACT!
FAST ENOUGH TO BURN THAT UGLY MUG TO ASH.

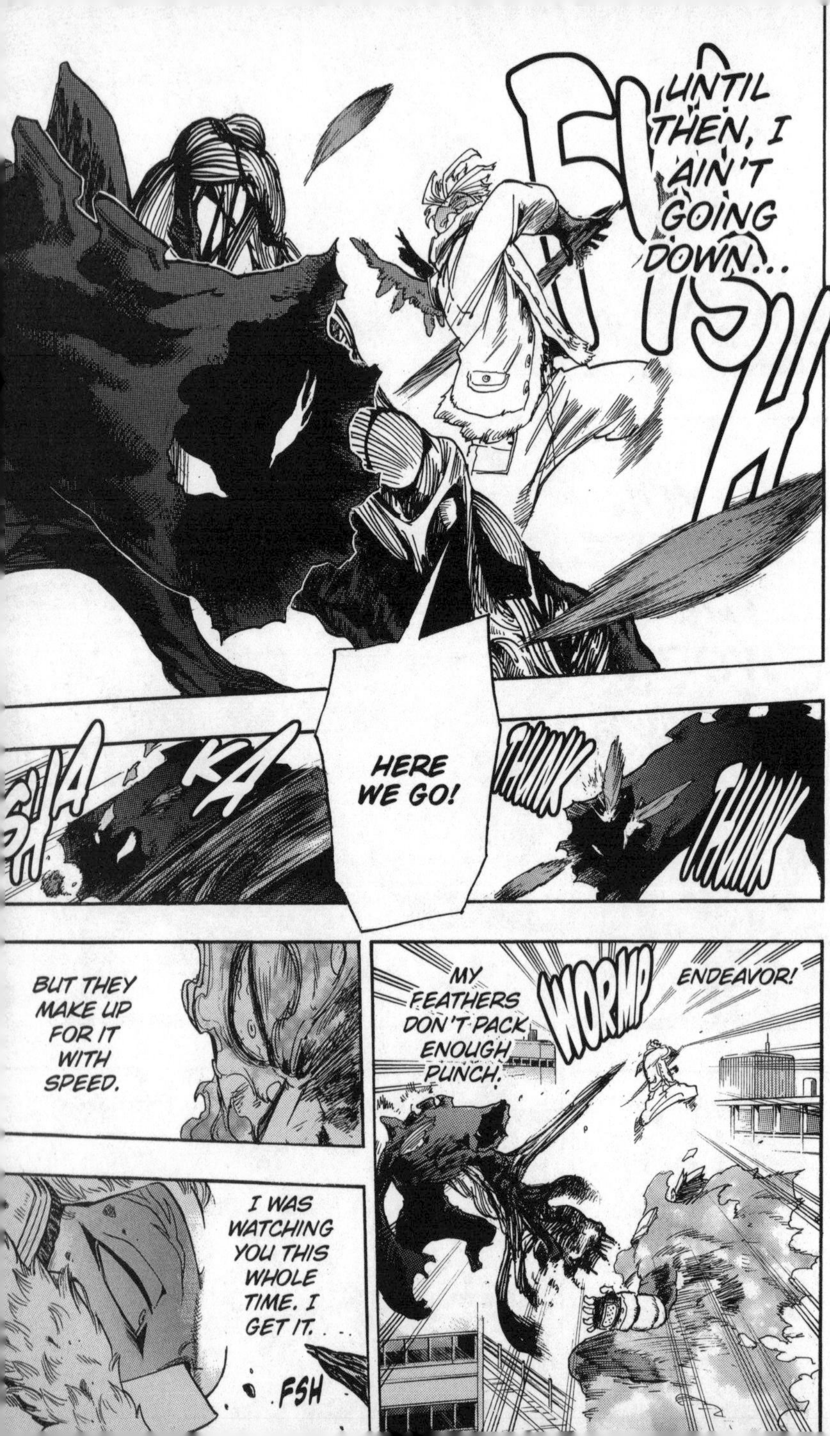
UNTIL THEN, I AIN'T GOING DOWN...
THUNK
THUNK
HERE WE GO!
KA
ENDEAVOR!
WORMP
MY FEATHERS DON'T PACK ENOUGH PUNCH.
BUT THEY MAKE UP FOR IT WITH SPEED.
I WAS WATCHING YOU THIS WHOLE TIME. I GET IT...
FSH

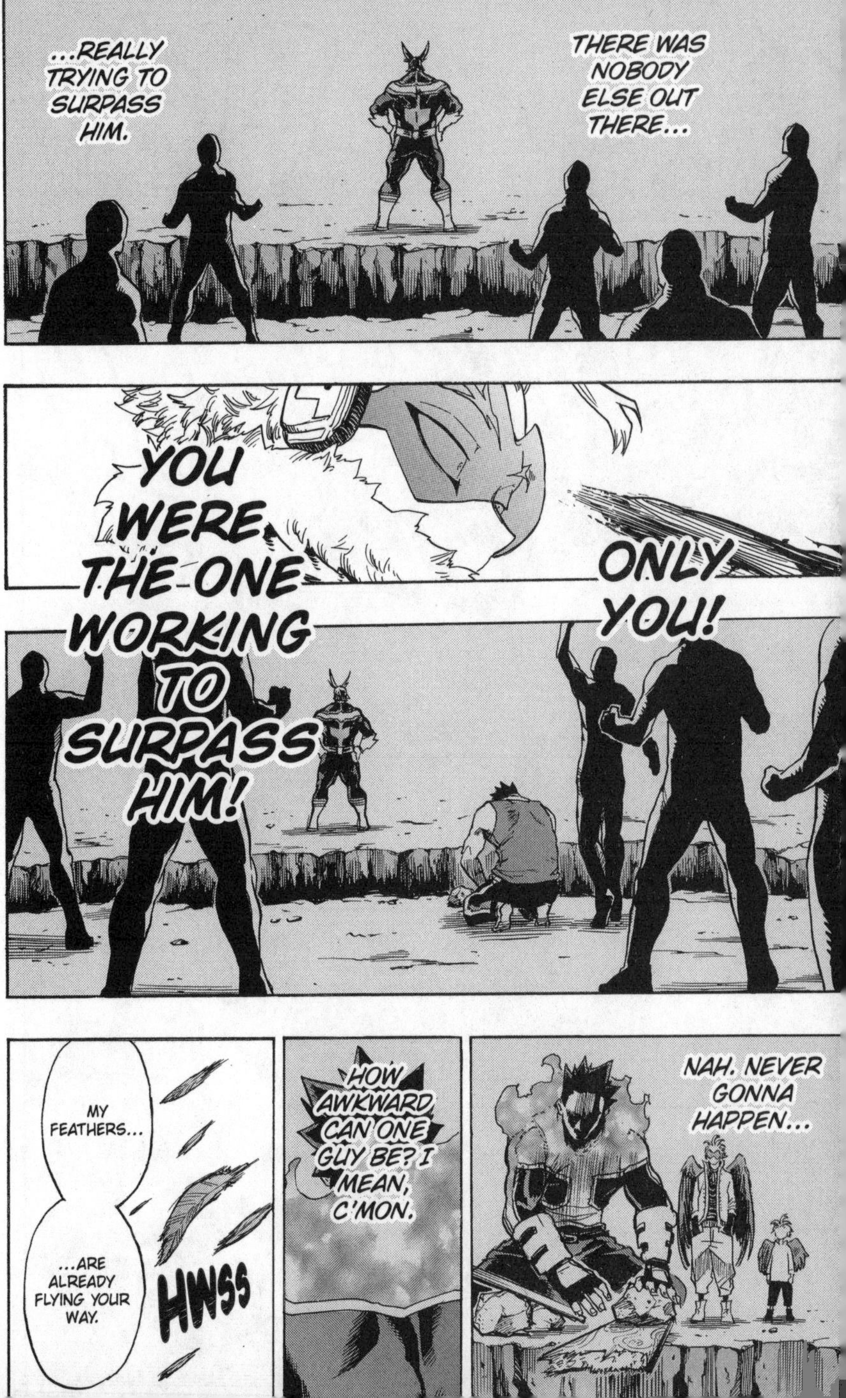
THERE WAS NOBODY ELSE OUT THERE...
...REALLY TRYING TO SURPASS HIM.
YOU WERE THE ONE WORKING TO SURPASS HIM!
ONLY YOU!
NAH. NEVER GONNA HAPPEN...
HOW AWKWARD CAN ONE GUY BE? I MEAN, C'MON.
MY FEATHERS...
...ARE ALREADY FLYING YOUR WAY.
HWSS

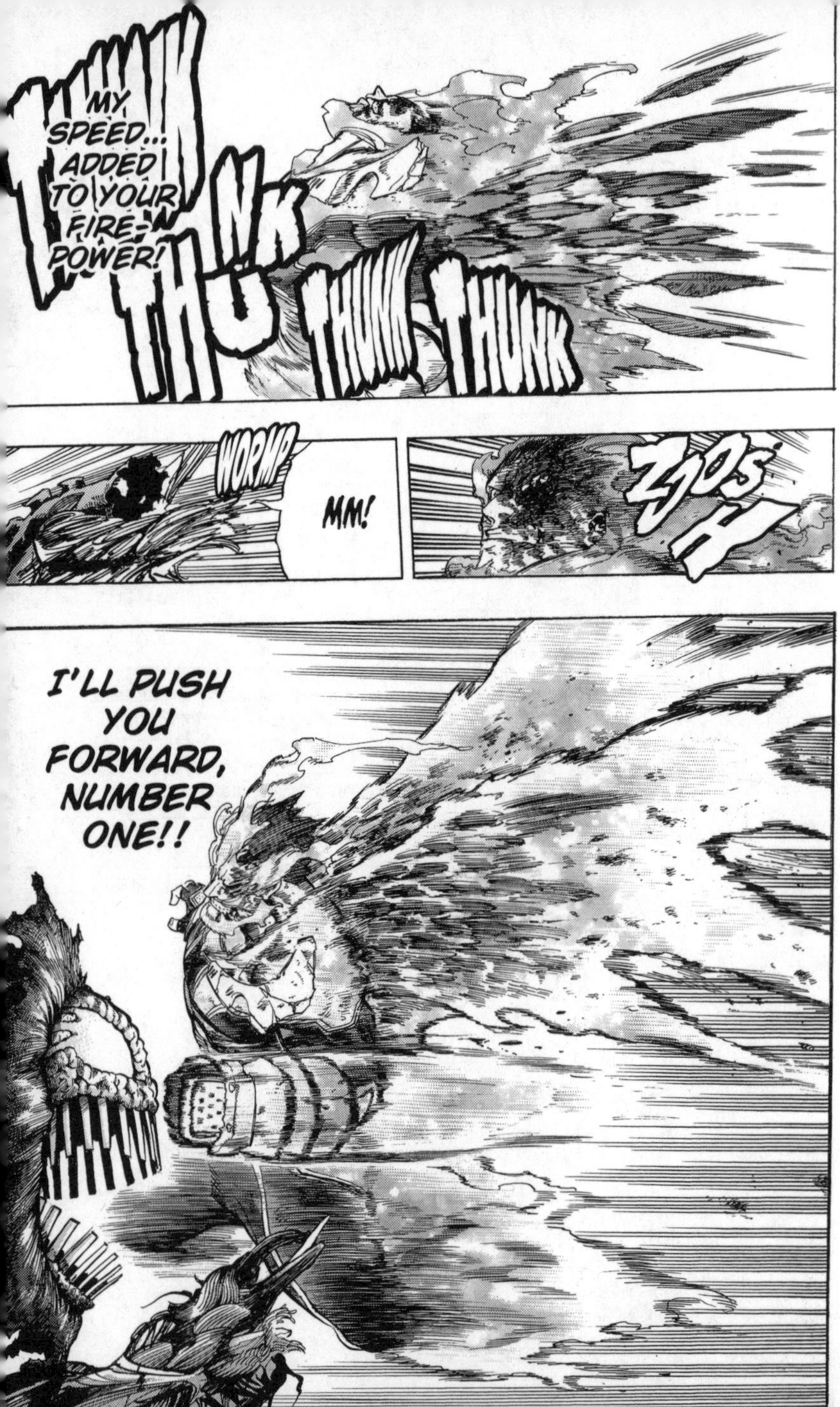
THUNK
THUNK
THUNK
MY SPEED... ADDED TO YOUR FIRE-POWER!
ZOOSH
MM!
WORMP
I'LL PUSH YOU FORWARD, NUMBER ONE!!

轟

NATSUO TODOROKI (19)

STREET CLOTHES

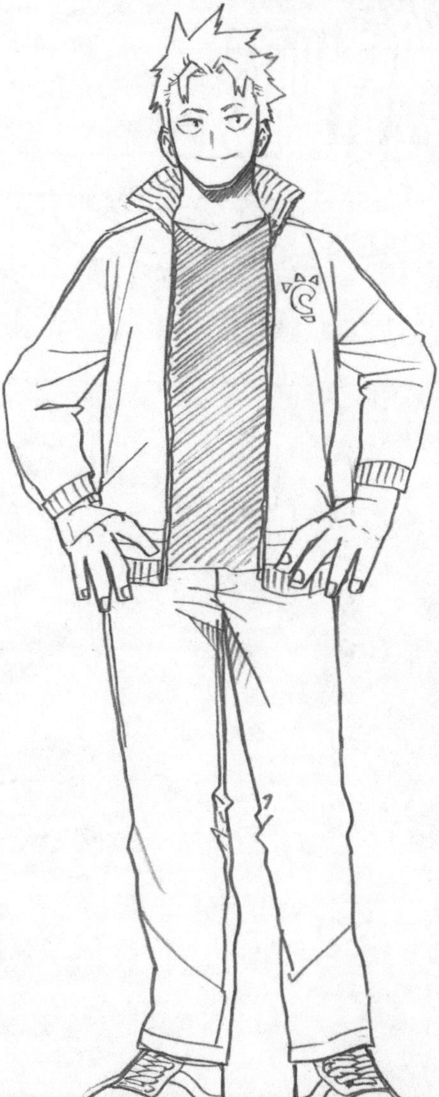

Birthday: 7/1
Height: 181 cm
Favorite Things: Sashimi, the sea

NATSUO IN A NUTSHELL

His family's past weighs on him just as heavily as it does his sister, but she told him, "Let me take care of things at home. You try to move on with your life, okay?" So he decided to go to college after all.

He's studying for a degree in health and welfare.

He's totally not head over heels for his current girlfriend.

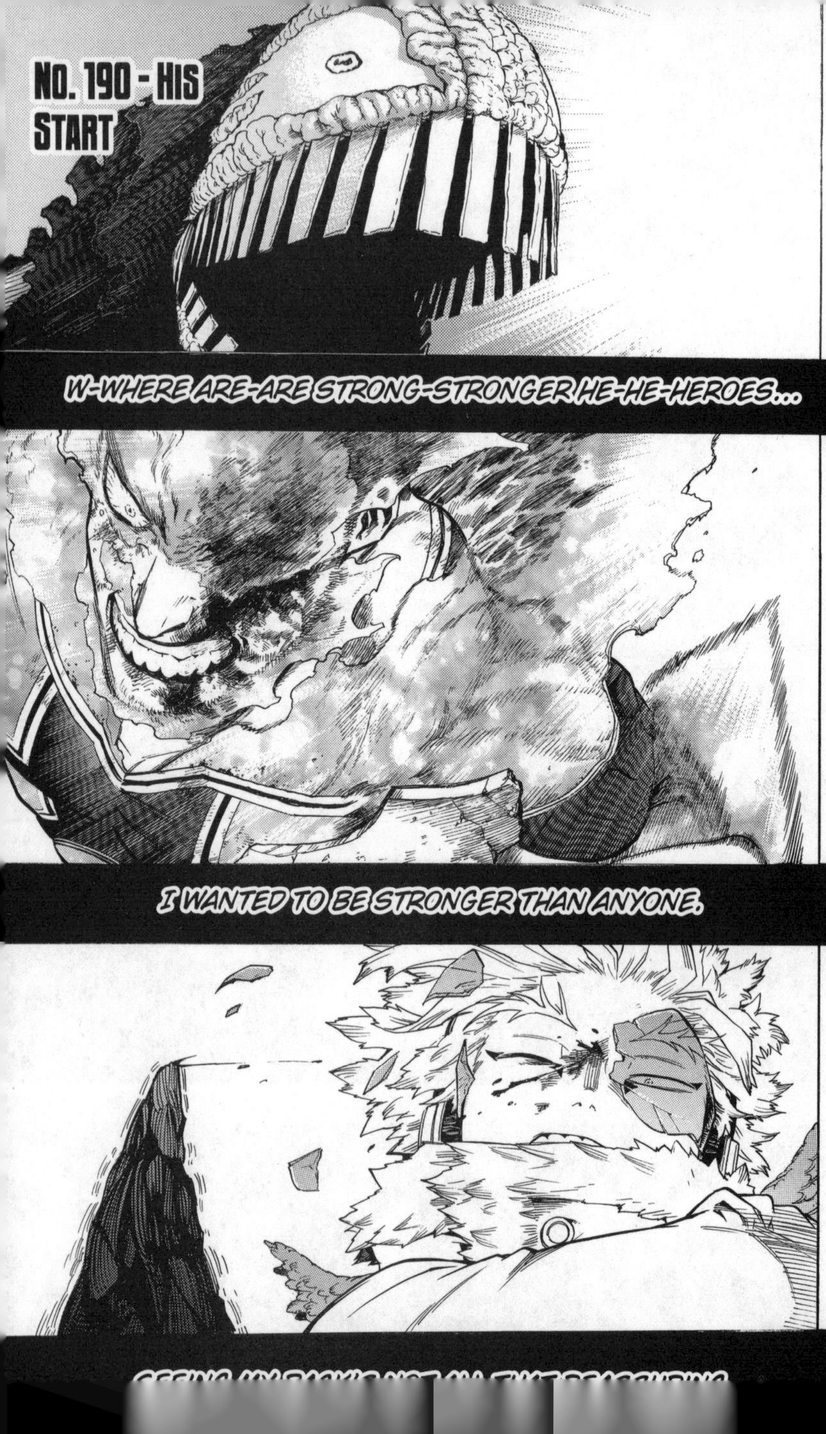
NO. 190 - HIS START
W-WHERE ARE-ARE STRONG-STRONGER HE-HE-HEROES...
I WANTED TO BE STRONGER THAN ANYONE.

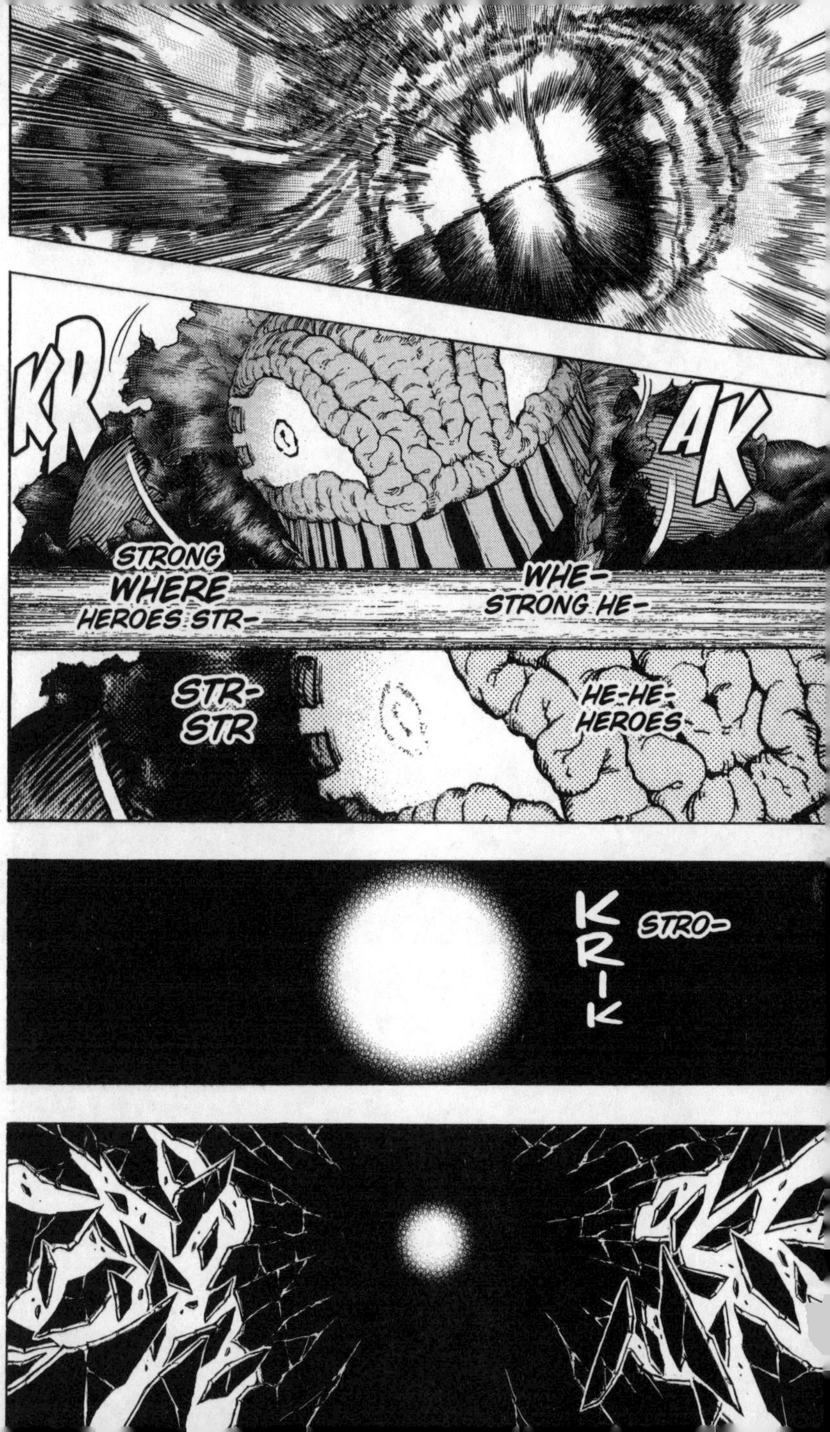
KR
AK
WHE- STRONG HE-
STRONG WHERE HEROES STR-
HE-HE-HEROES
STR- STR
STRO-
KRIK

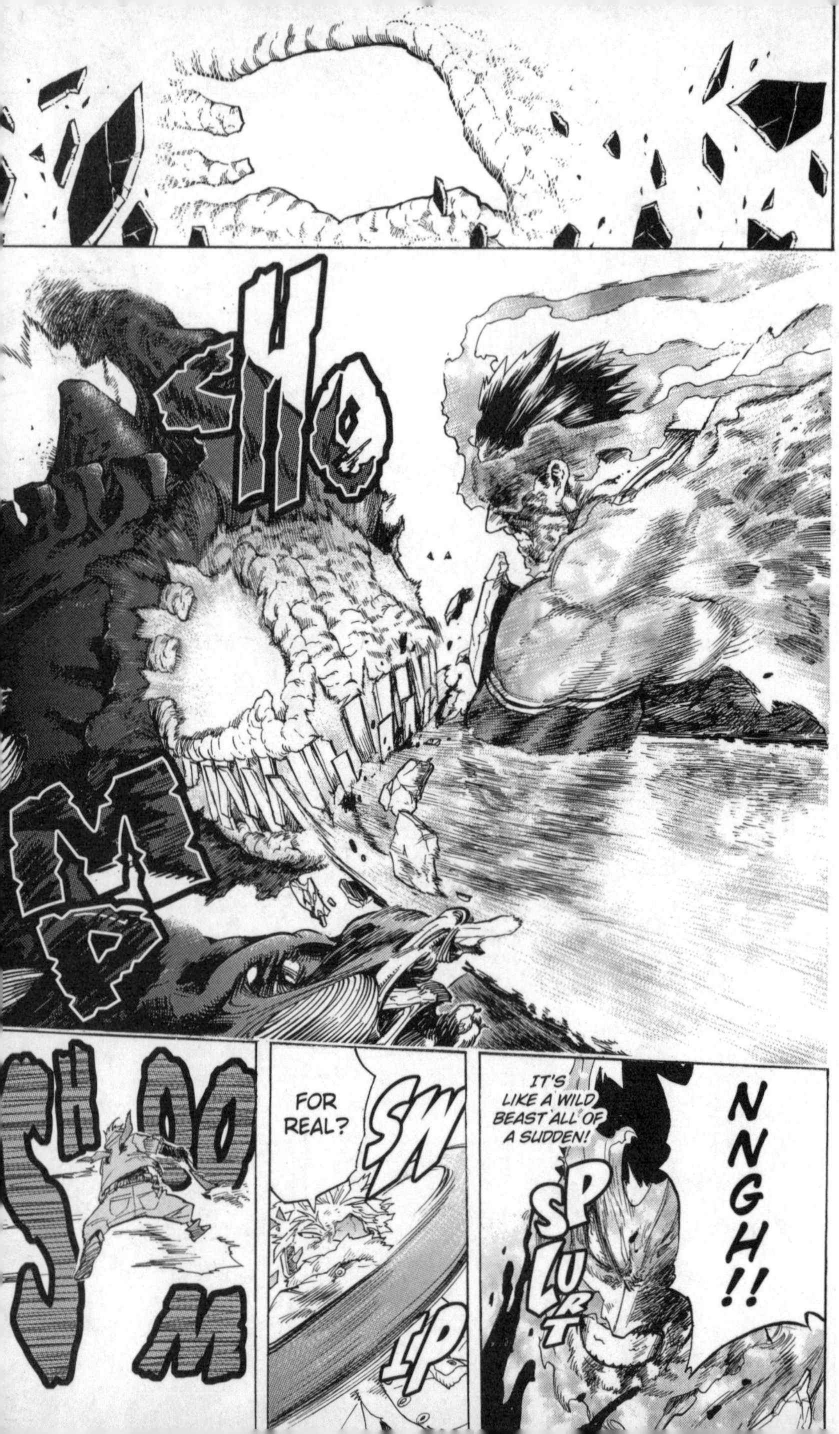

CHOMP
IT'S LIKE A WILD BEAST ALL OF A SUDDEN!
NNGH!!
SPLURT
FOR REAL?
SWIP
SHOOM

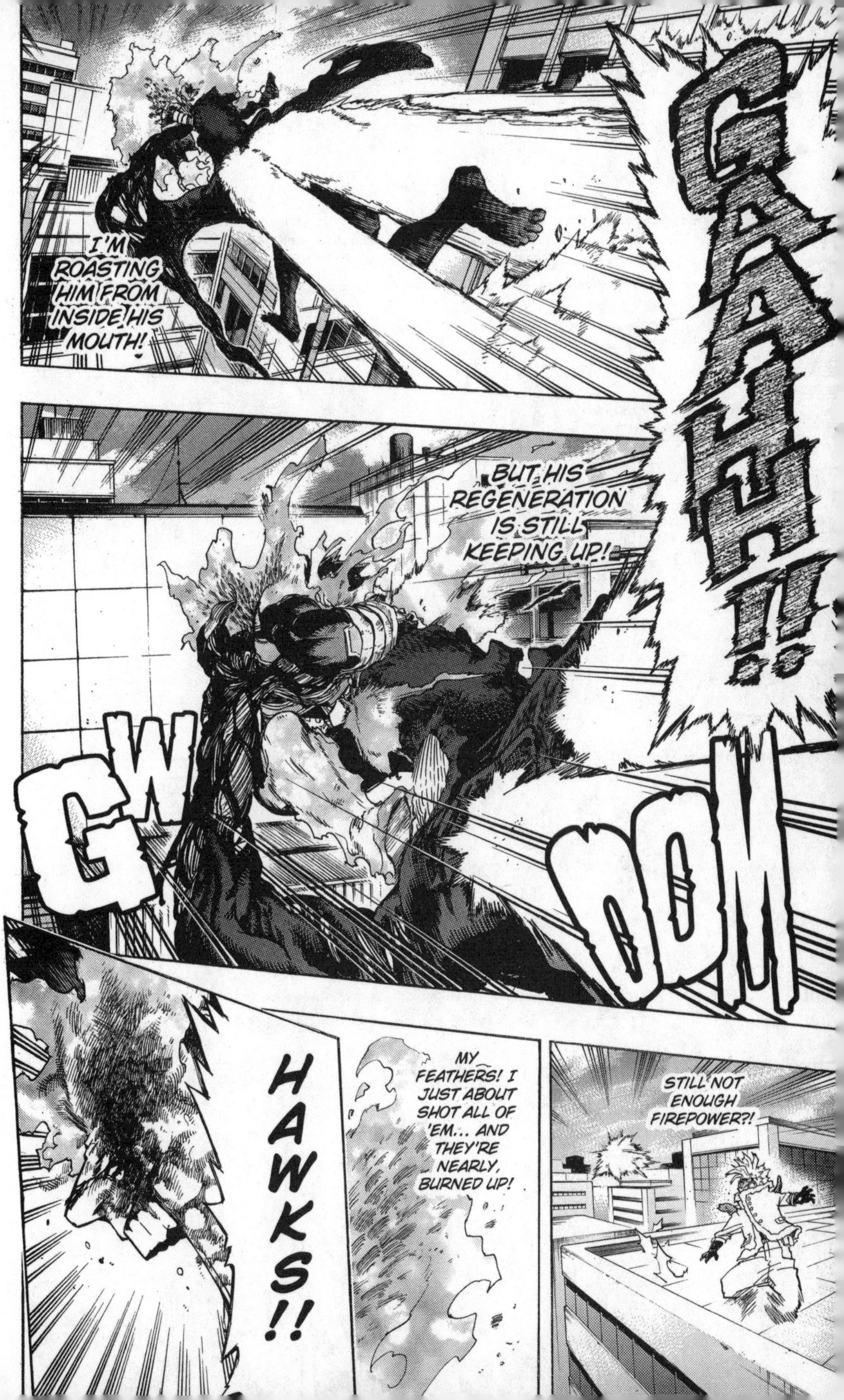
GAAUGH!!
I'M ROASTING HIM FROM INSIDE HIS MOUTH!
BUT HIS REGENERATION IS STILL KEEPING UP!
GWOOM
STILL NOT ENOUGH FIREPOWER?!
MY FEATHERS! I JUST ABOUT SHOT ALL OF 'EM... AND THEY'RE NEARLY BURNED UP!
HAWKS!!

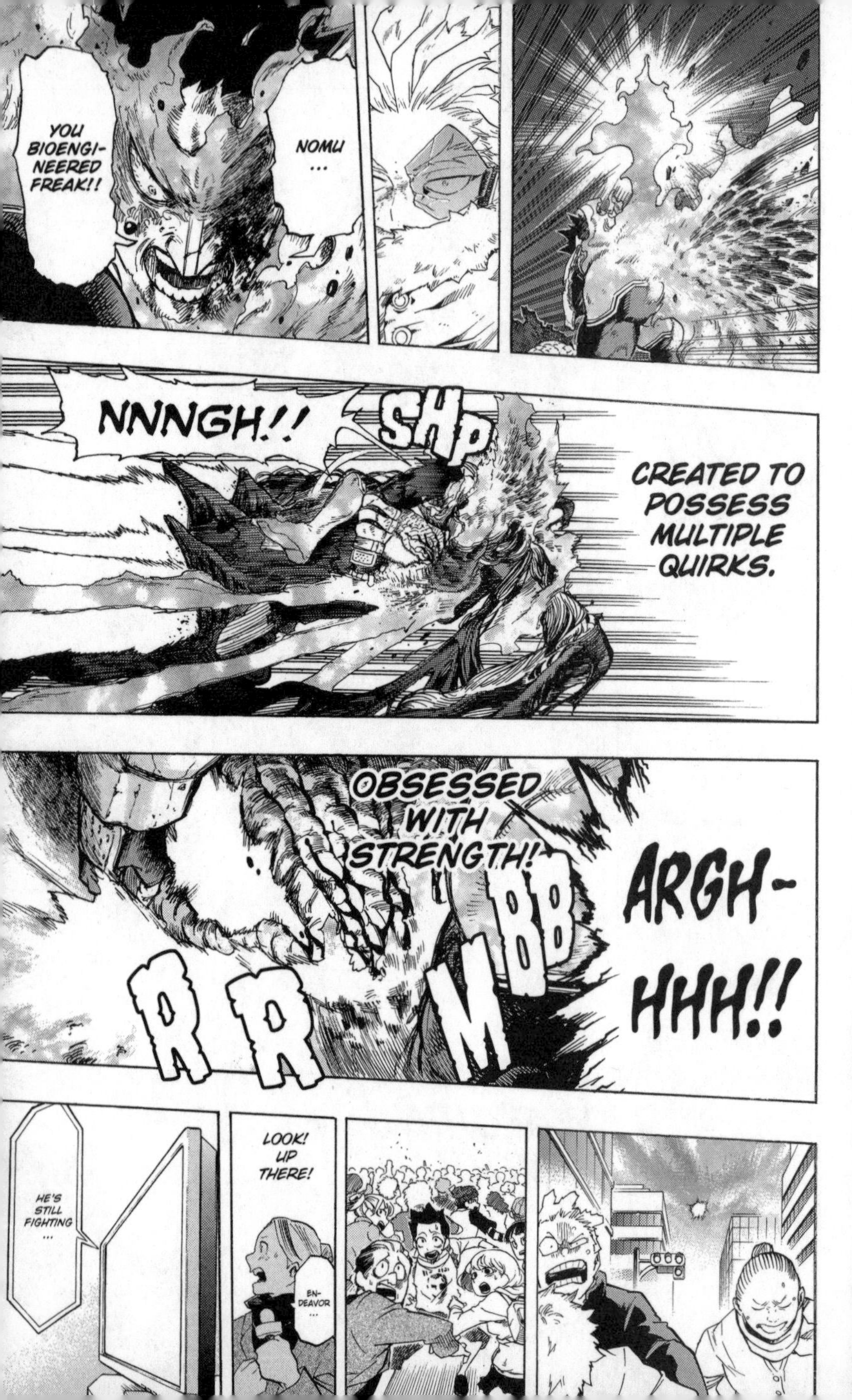
NOMU ...
YOU BIOENGI-NEERED FREAK!!
CREATED TO POSSESS MULTIPLE QUIRKS.
SHP
NNNGH!!
ARGH-HHH!!
OBSESSED WITH STRENGTH!
RRMBB
LOOK! UP THERE!
EN-DEAVOR ...
HE'S STILL FIGHTING ...

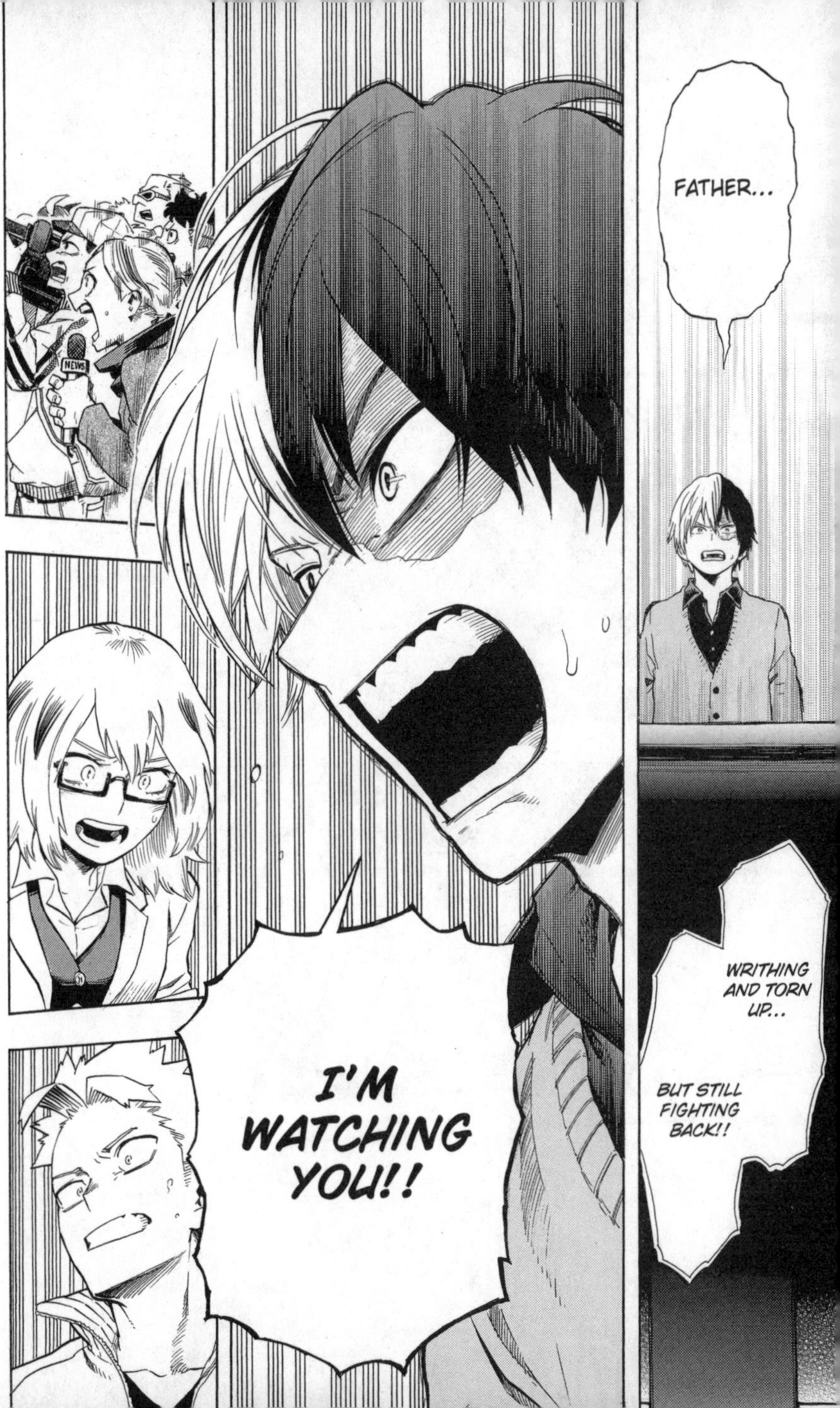
FATHER...
WRITHING AND TORN UP...
BUT STILL FIGHTING BACK!!
I'M WATCHING YOU!!

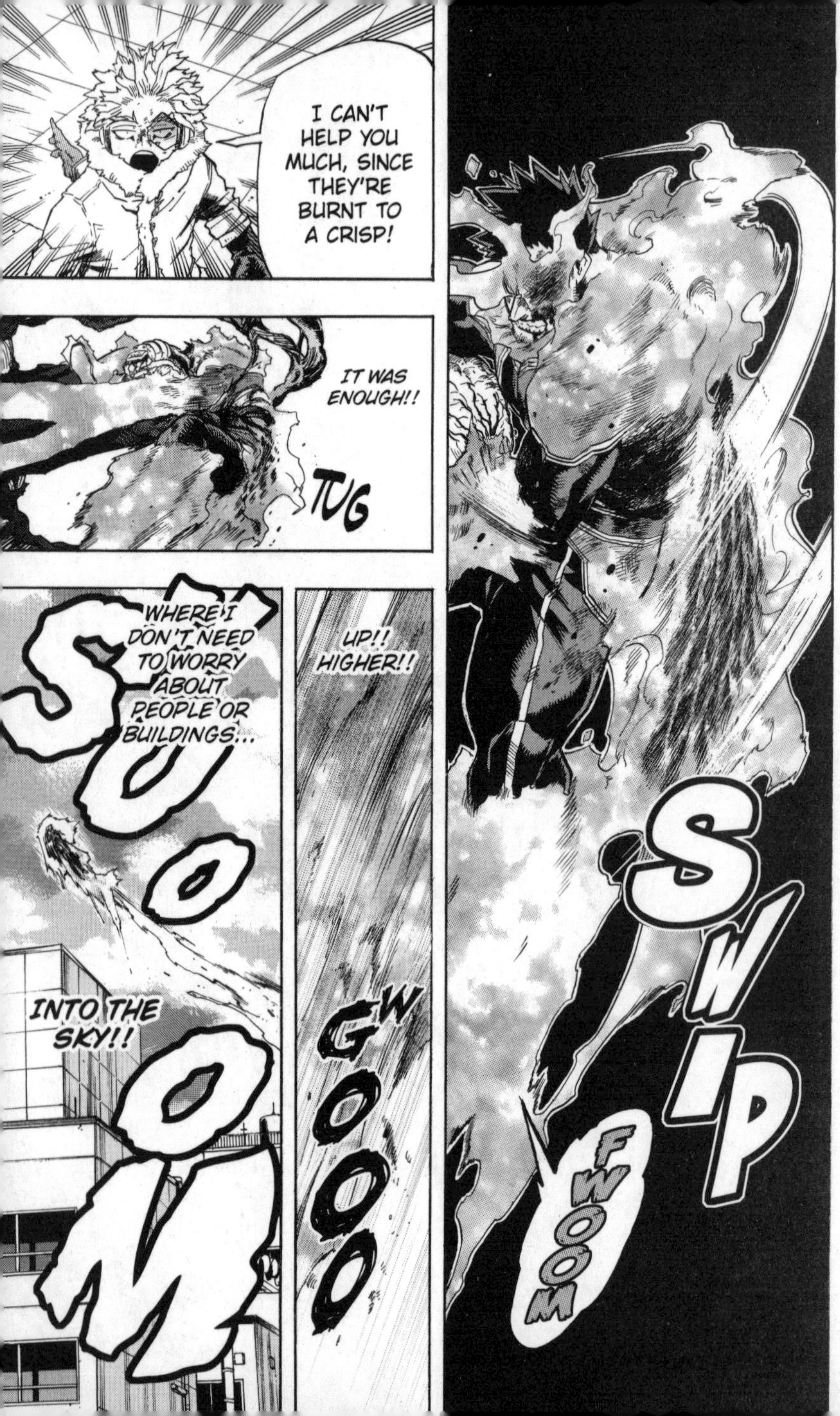
SWIP
FWOOM
I CAN'T HELP YOU MUCH, SINCE THEY'RE BURNT TO A CRISP!
IT WAS ENOUGH!!
TUG
UP!! HIGHER!!
GWOOOO
WHERE I DON'T NEED TO WORRY ABOUT PEOPLE OR BUILDINGS...
SOOOM
INTO THE SKY!!

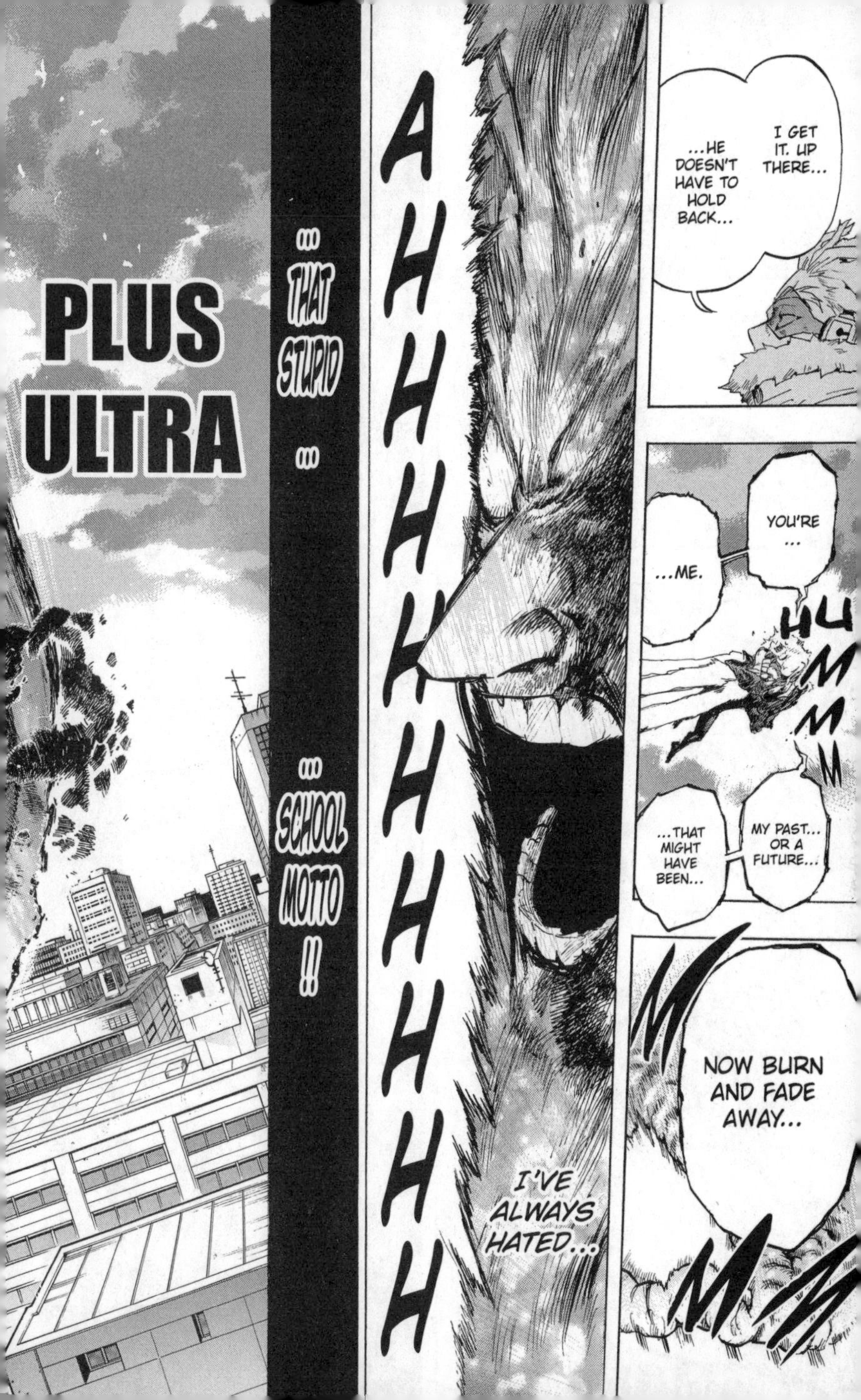
I GET IT. UP THERE...
...HE DOESN'T HAVE TO HOLD BACK...
YOU'RE...
...ME.
HUMMM
MY PAST... OR A FUTURE...
...THAT MIGHT HAVE BEEN...
NOW BURN AND FADE AWAY...
MMM
AHHHHHHHHHH
I'VE ALWAYS HATED...
...THAT STUPID...
...SCHOOL MOTTO!!
PLUS ULTRA

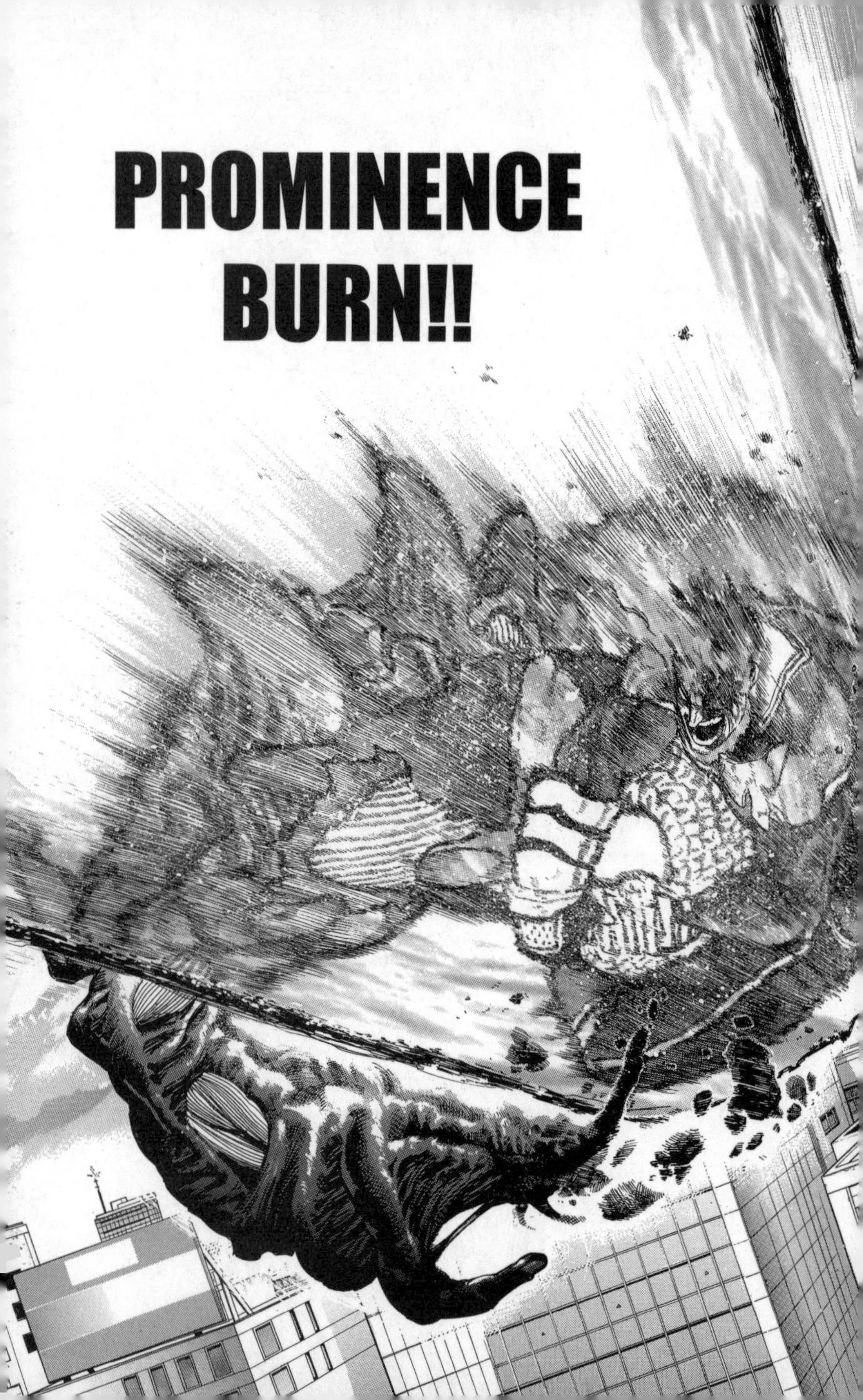
PROMINENCE
BURN!!

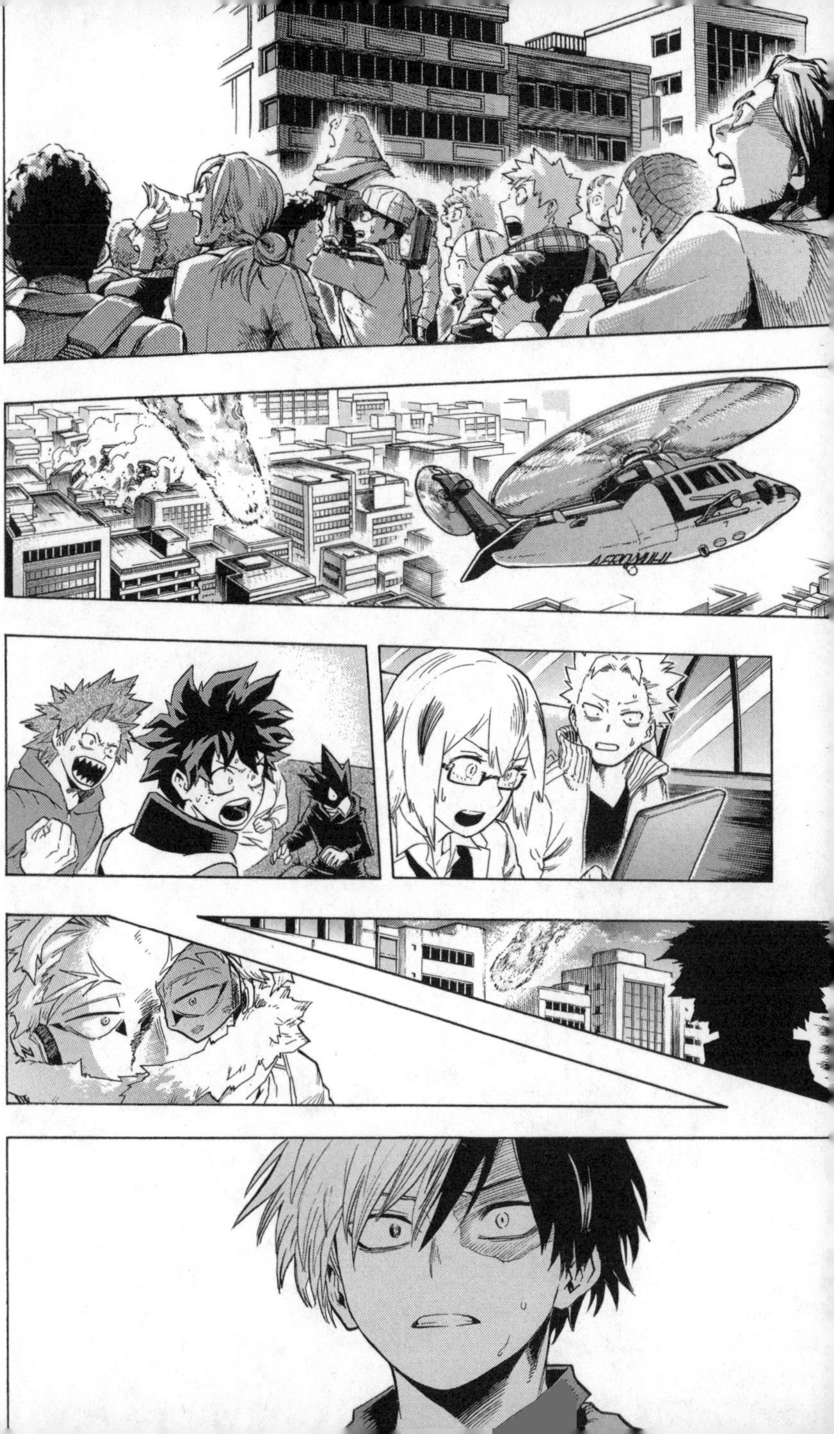

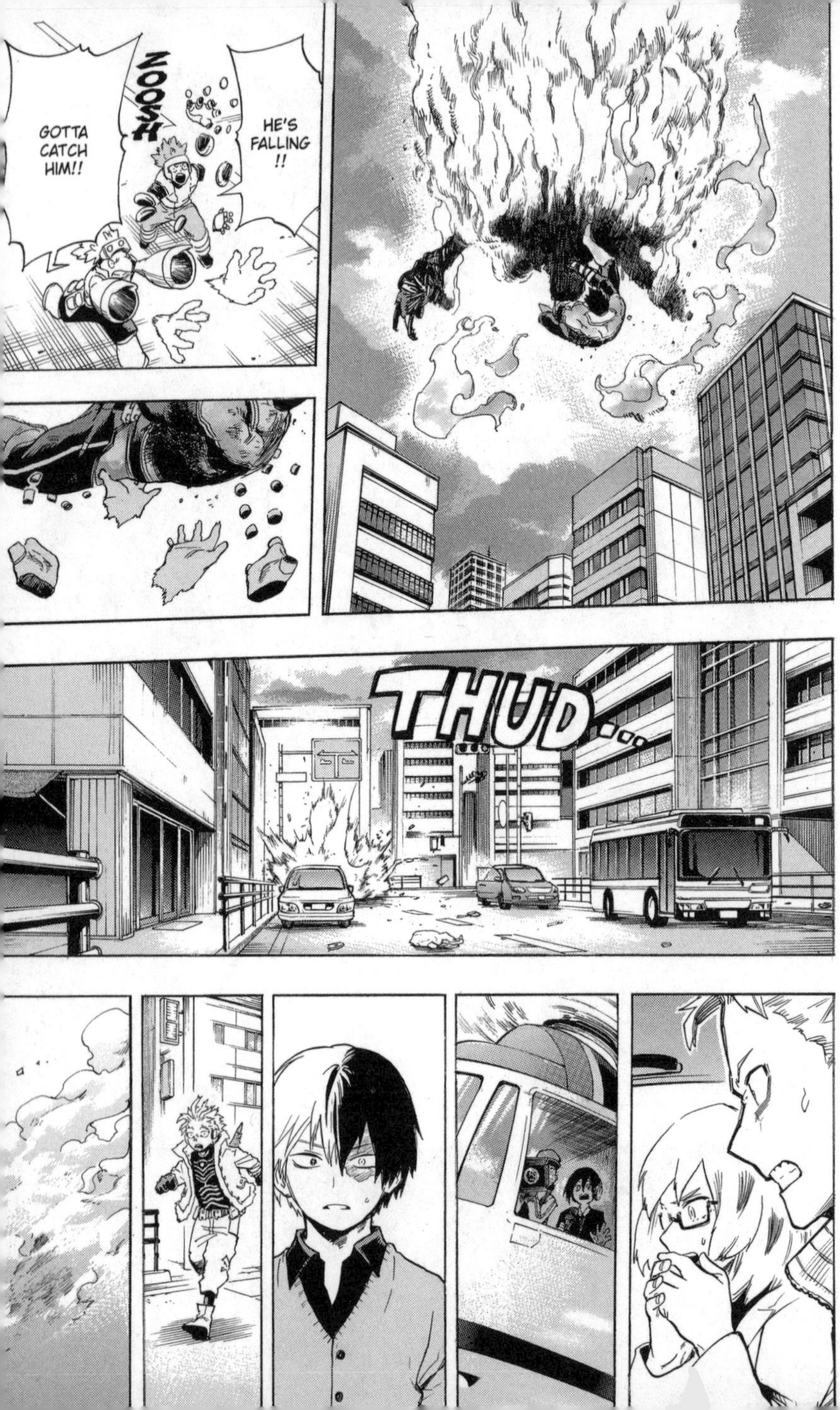
HE'S FALLING!!
ZOOSH
GOTTA CATCH HIM!!
THUD...

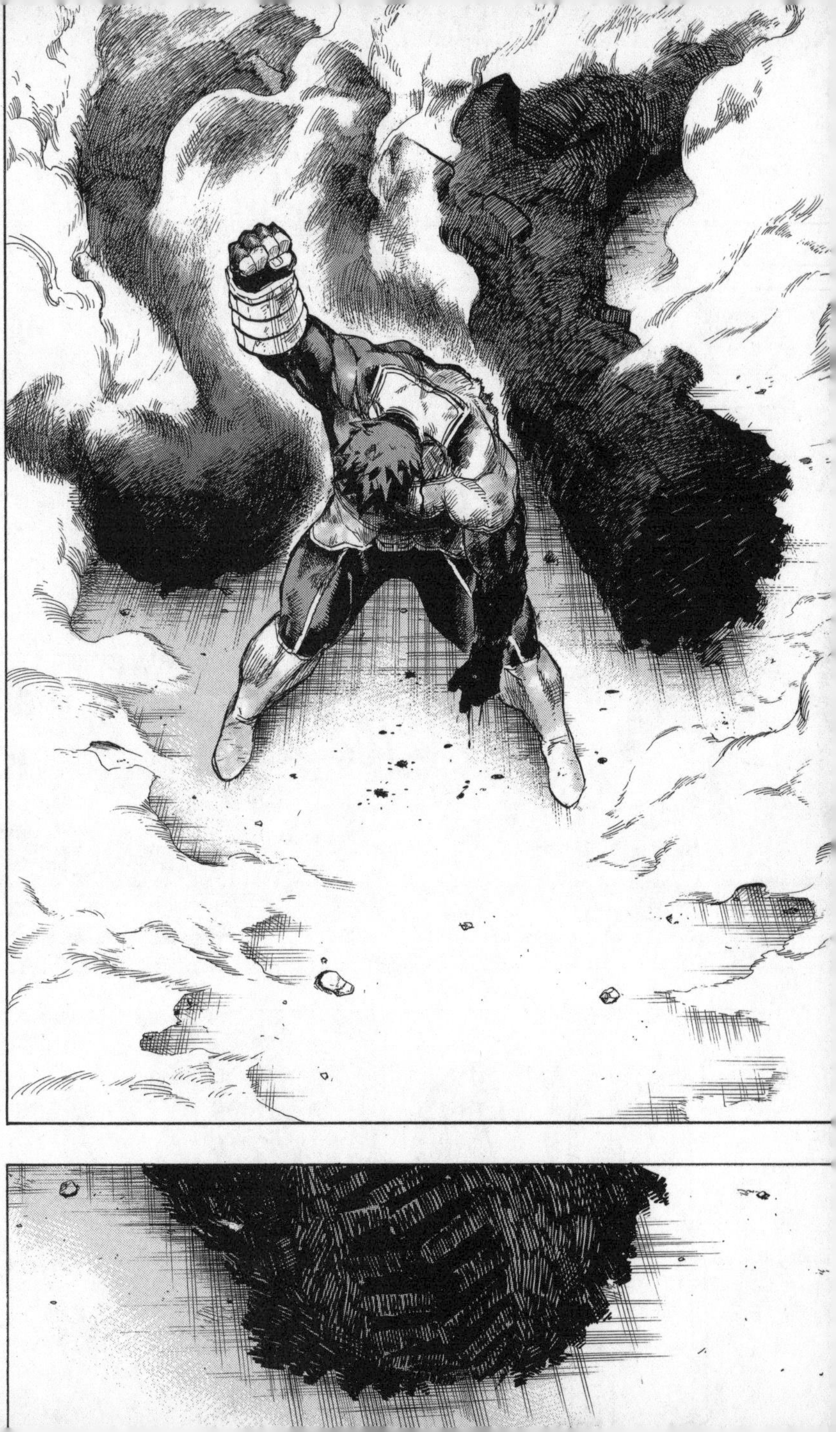

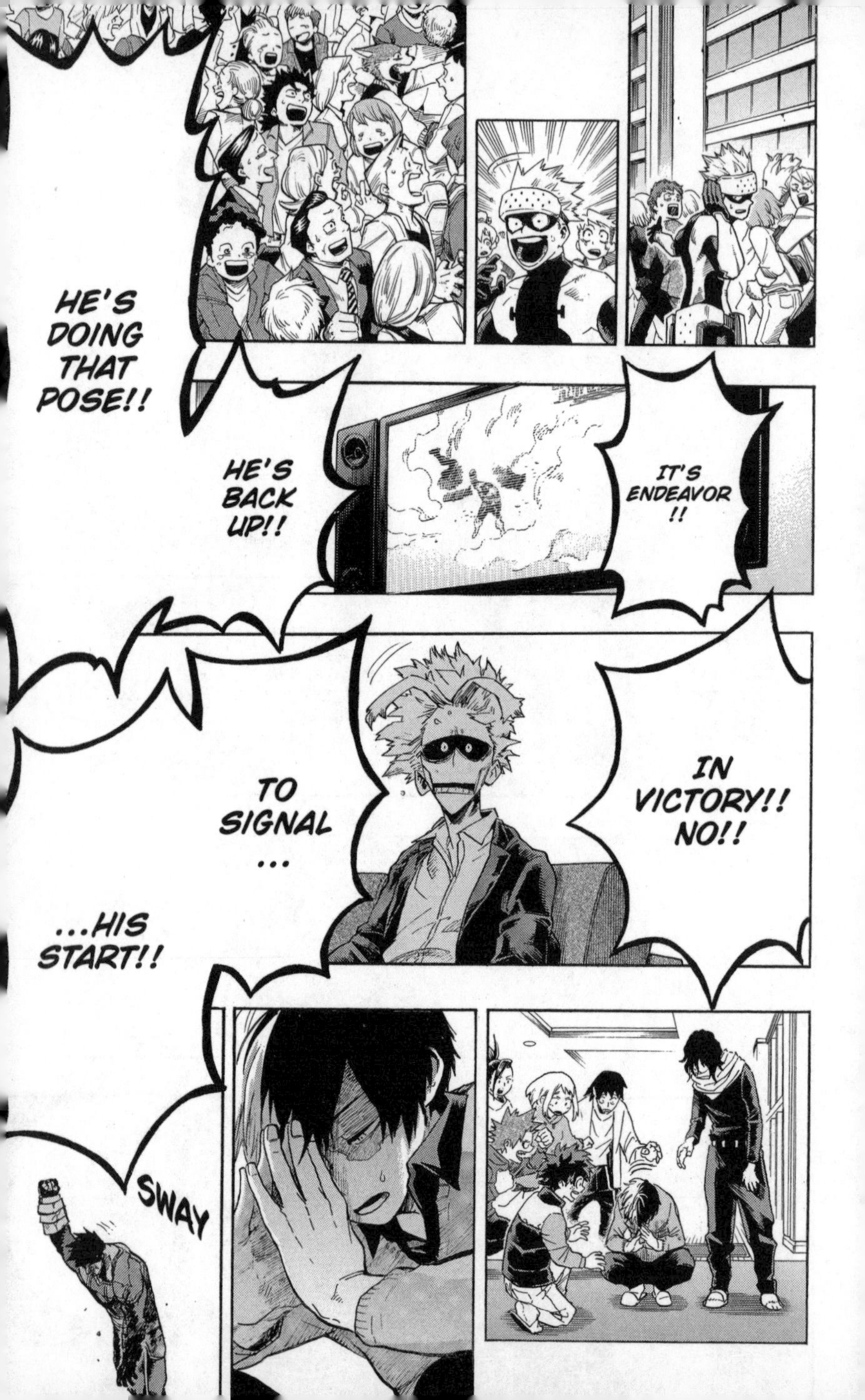
HE'S DOING THAT POSE!!
IT'S ENDEAVOR!!
HE'S BACK UP!!
IN VICTORY!! NO!!
TO SIGNAL...
...HIS START!!
SWAY

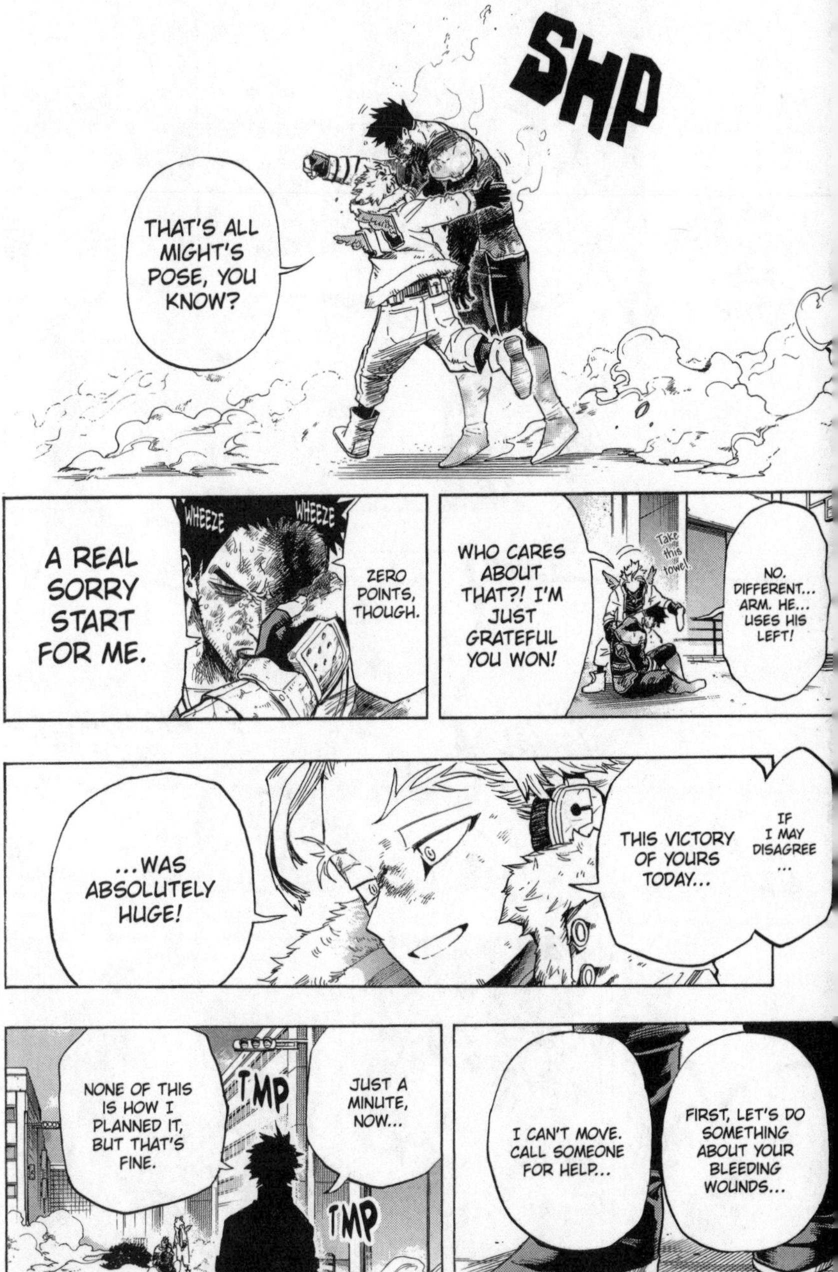
SHP
THAT'S ALL MIGHT'S POSE, YOU KNOW?
NO. DIFFERENT... ARM. HE... USES HIS LEFT!
Take this towel!
WHO CARES ABOUT THAT?! I'M JUST GRATEFUL YOU WON!
WHEEZE
WHEEZE
ZERO POINTS, THOUGH.
A REAL SORRY START FOR ME.
IF I MAY DISAGREE...
THIS VICTORY OF YOURS TODAY...
...WAS ABSOLUTELY HUGE!
FIRST, LET'S DO SOMETHING ABOUT YOUR BLEEDING WOUNDS...
I CAN'T MOVE. CALL SOMEONE FOR HELP...
JUST A MINUTE, NOW...
TMP
TMP
NONE OF THIS IS HOW I PLANNED IT, BUT THAT'S FINE.

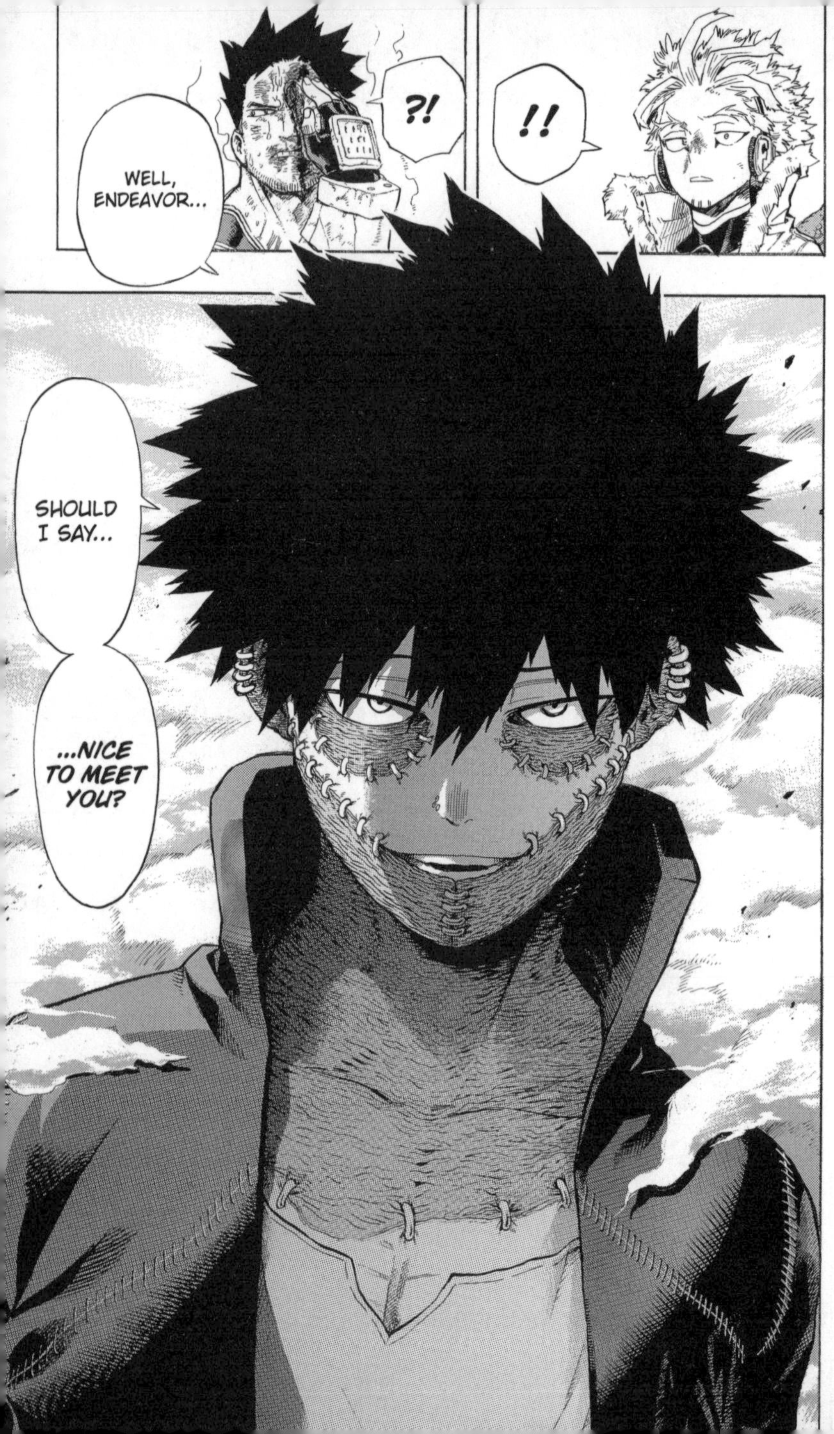
!!
?!
WELL, ENDEAVOR...
SHOULD I SAY...
...NICE TO MEET YOU?

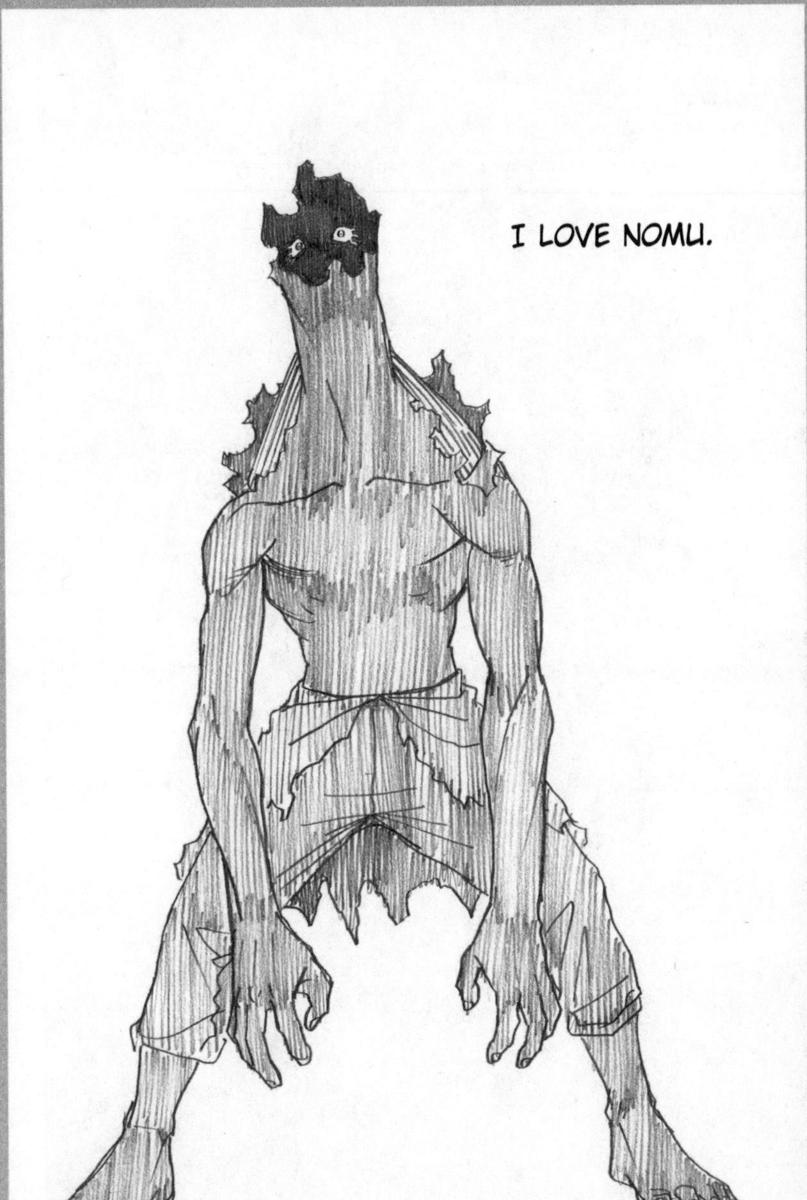
I LOVE NOMU.

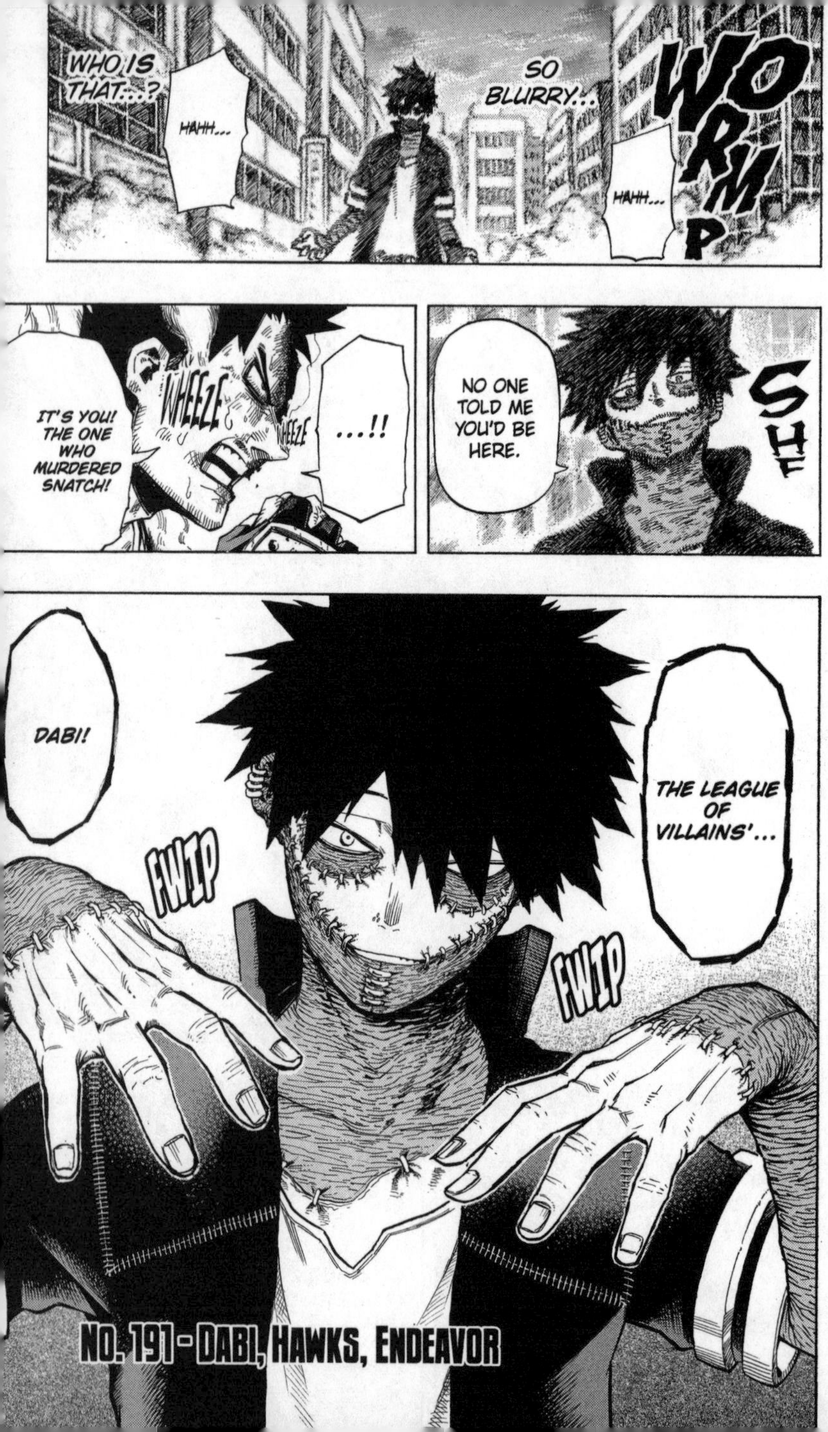
WORMP
HAHH...
SO BLURRY...
HAHH...
WHO IS THAT...?
NO ONE TOLD ME YOU'D BE HERE.
SHF
...!!
WHEEZE
WHEEZE
IT'S YOU! THE ONE WHO MURDERED SNATCH!
THE LEAGUE OF VILLAINS'...
DABI!
FWIP
FWIP

No. 191 - Dabi, Hawks, Endeavor

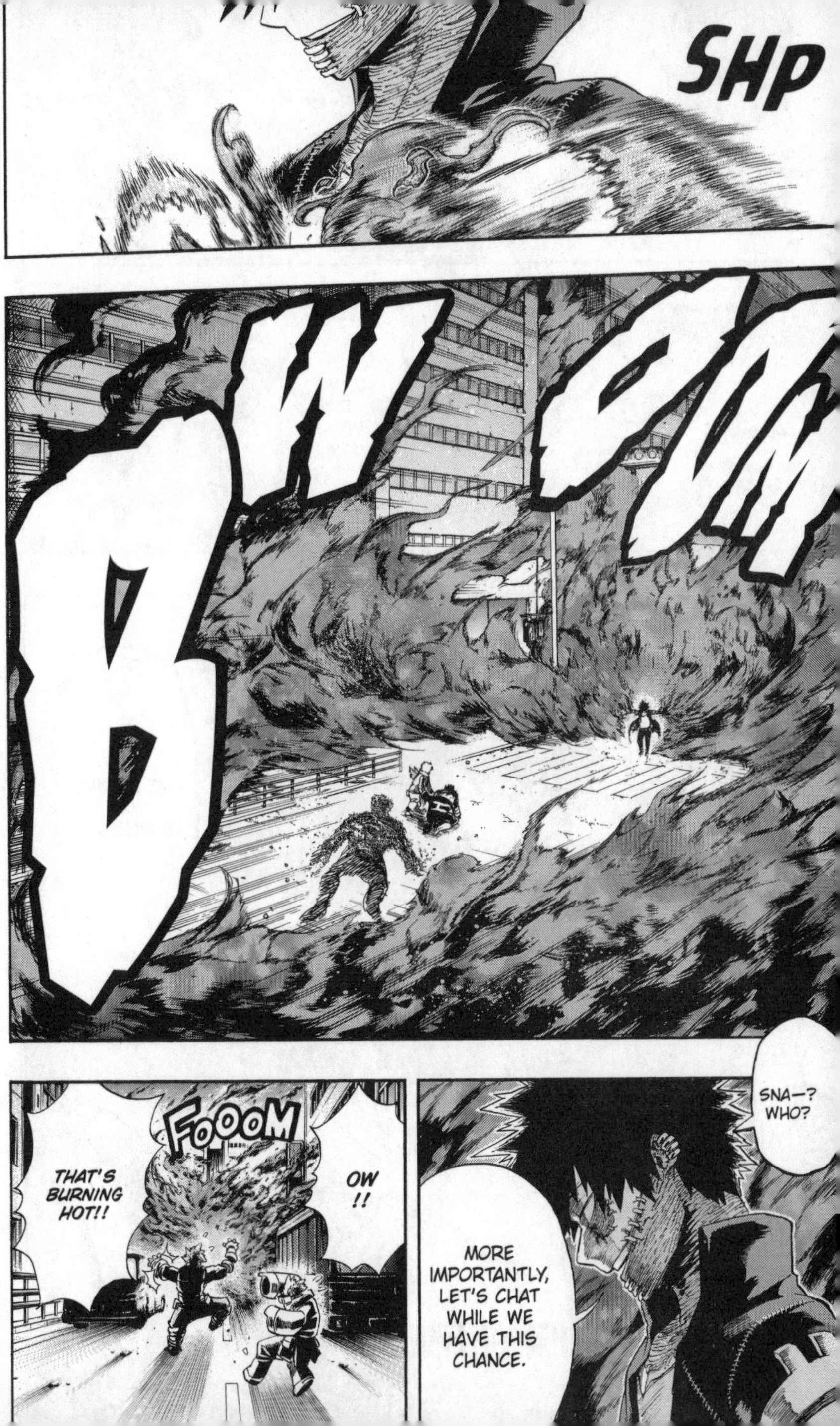
SHP
SNA—? WHO?
MORE IMPORTANTLY, LET'S CHAT WHILE WE HAVE THIS CHANCE.
FOOOM
OW!!
THAT'S BURNING HOT!!

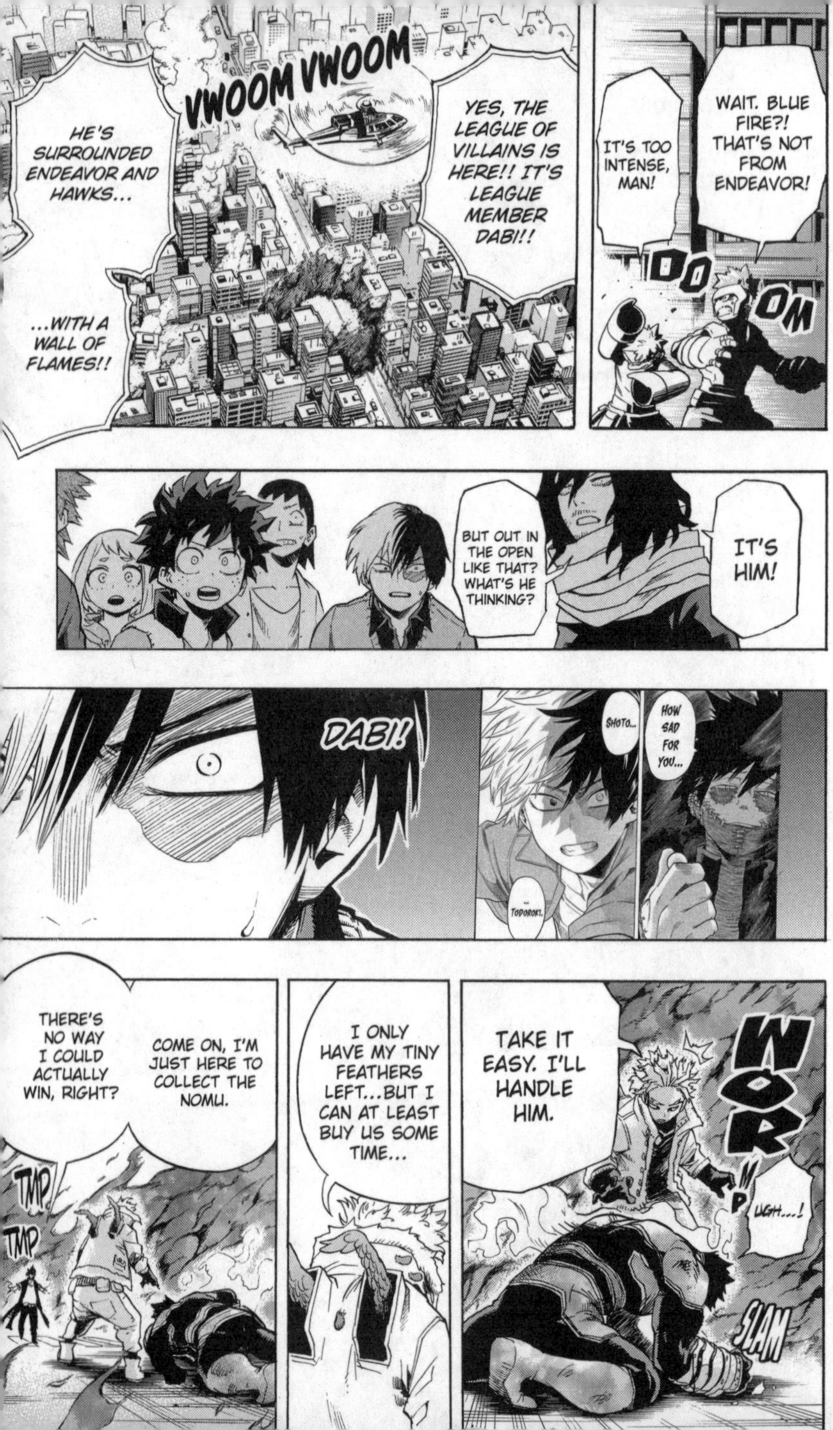
WAIT. BLUE FIRE?! THAT'S NOT FROM ENDEAVOR!
IT'S TOO INTENSE, MAN!
DOOM
YES, THE LEAGUE OF VILLAINS IS HERE!! IT'S LEAGUE MEMBER DABI!!
VWOOM VWOOM
HE'S SURROUNDED ENDEAVOR AND HAWKS...
...WITH A WALL OF FLAMES!!
IT'S HIM!
BUT OUT IN THE OPEN LIKE THAT? WHAT'S HE THINKING?
HOW SAD FOR YOU...
SHOTO...
...TODOROKI.
DABI!
TAKE IT EASY. I'LL HANDLE HIM.
WORMP
UGH...!
SLAM
I ONLY HAVE MY TINY FEATHERS LEFT...BUT I CAN AT LEAST BUY US SOME TIME...
COME ON, I'M JUST HERE TO COLLECT THE NOMU.
THERE'S NO WAY I COULD ACTUALLY WIN, RIGHT?
TMP
TMP

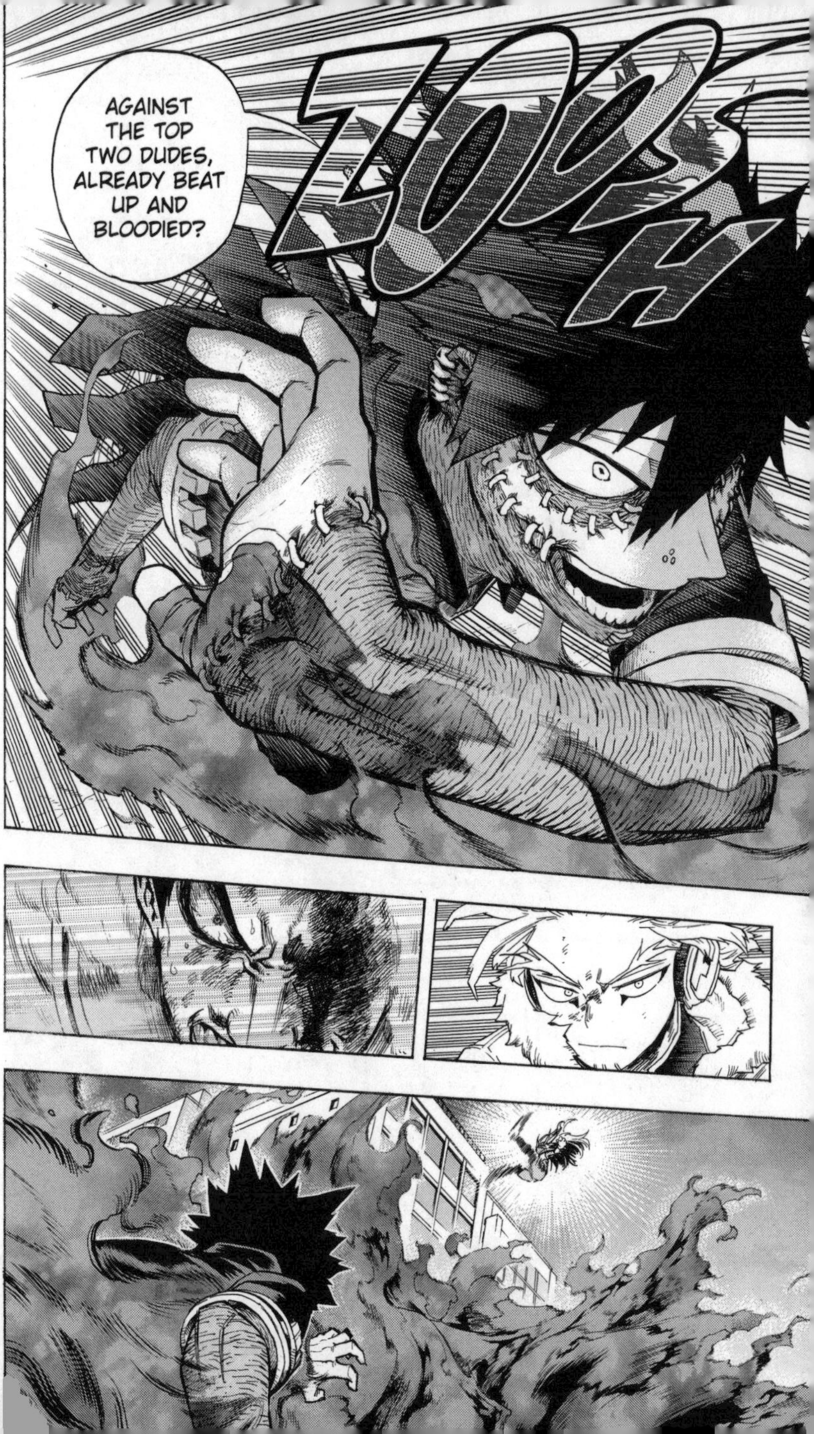
ZOOSH
AGAINST THE TOP TWO DUDES, ALREADY BEAT UP AND BLOODIED?

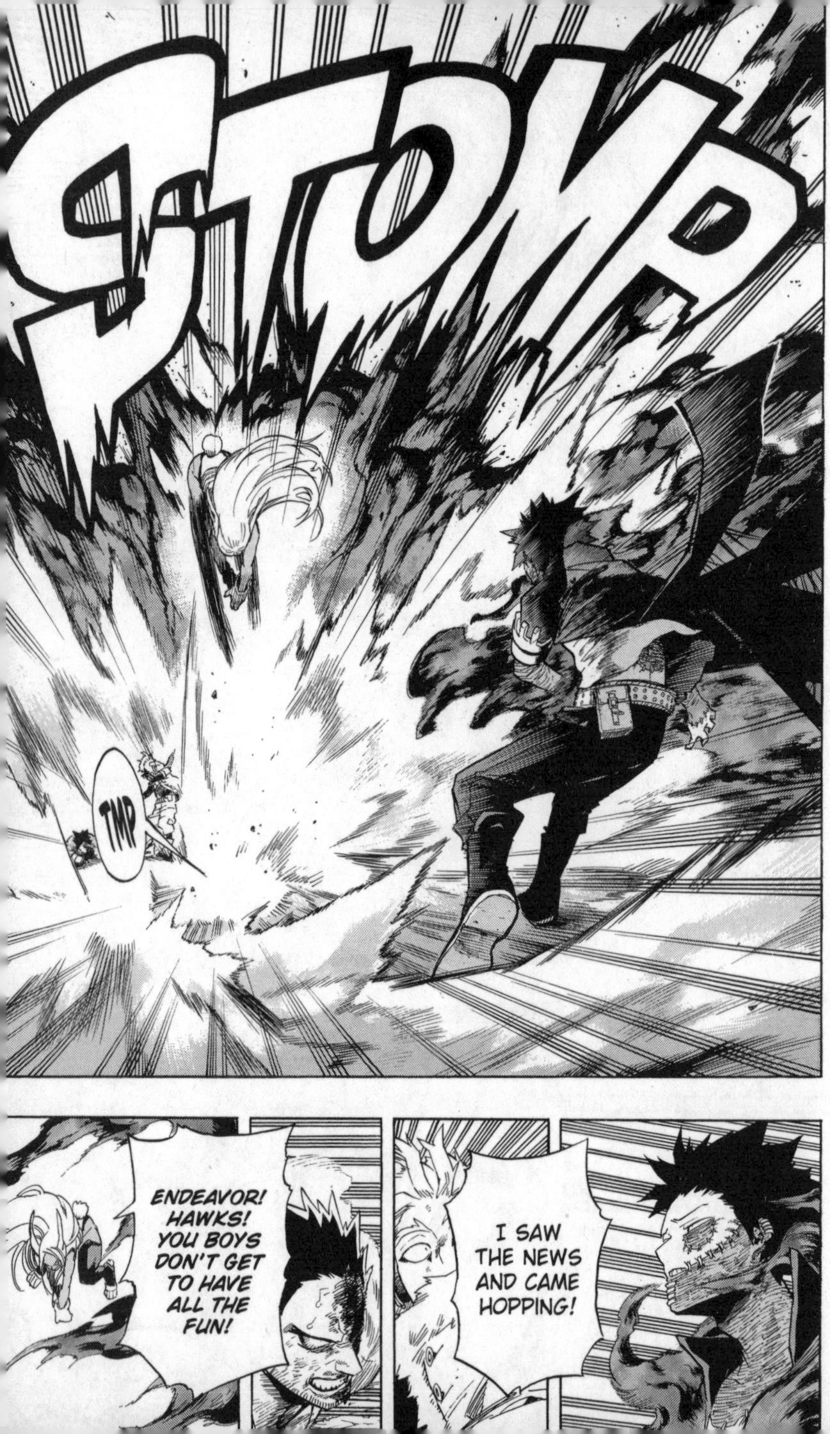
STOMP
TMP
I SAW THE NEWS AND CAME HOPPING!
ENDEAVOR! HAWKS! YOU BOYS DON'T GET TO HAVE ALL THE FUN!

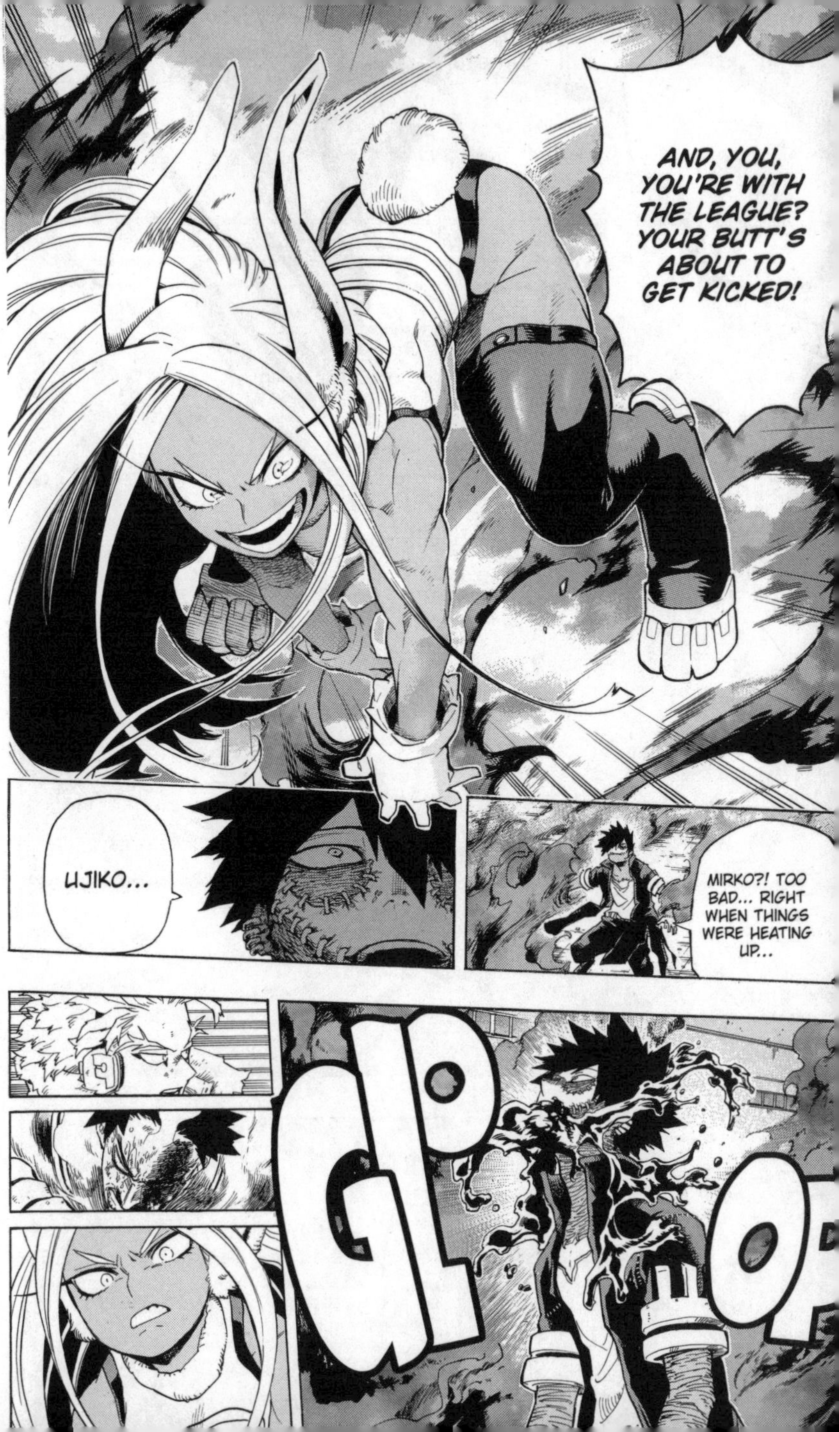
AND, YOU, YOU'RE WITH THE LEAGUE? YOUR BUTT'S ABOUT TO GET KICKED!
MIRKO?! TOO BAD... RIGHT WHEN THINGS WERE HEATING UP...
UJIKO...
GLOP

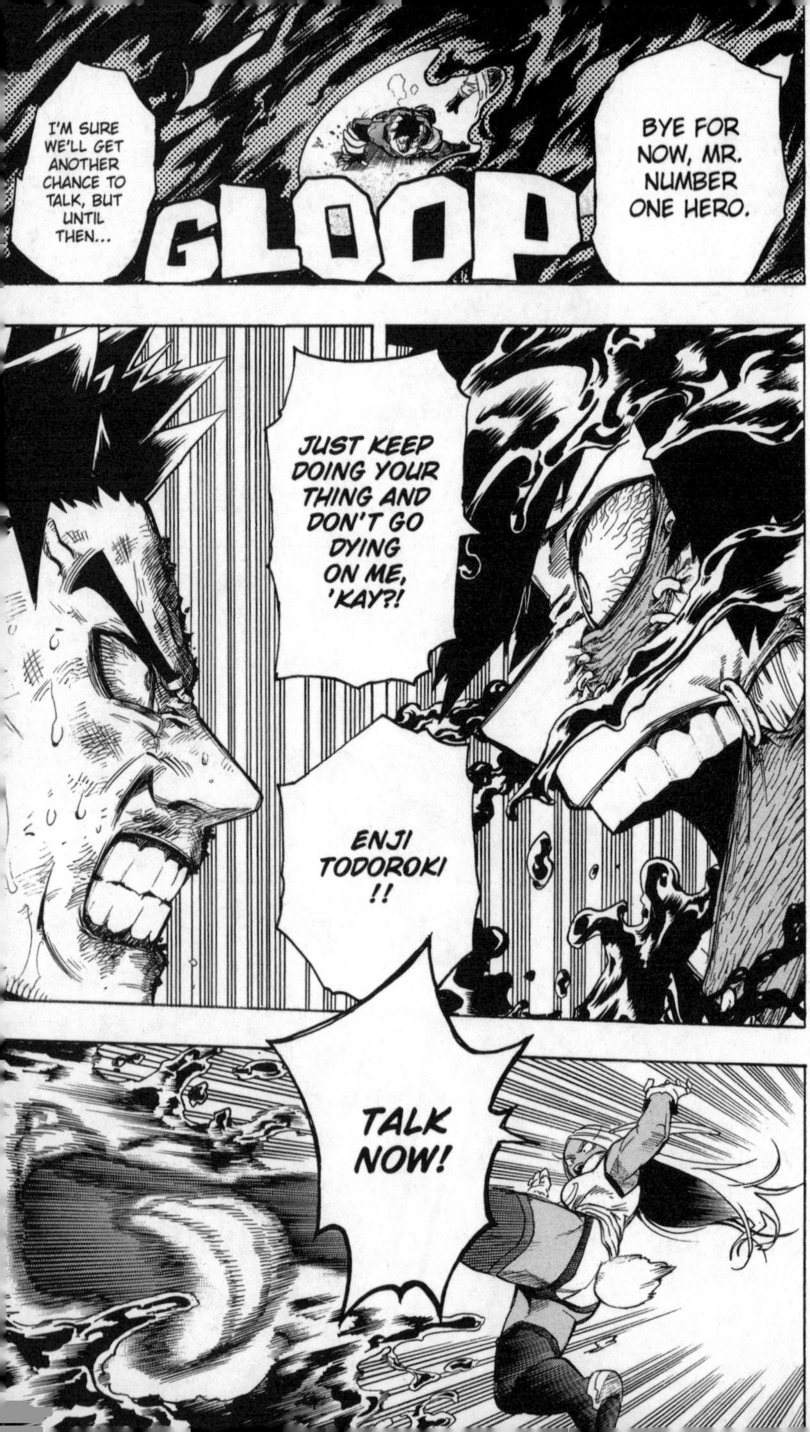
I'M SURE WE'LL GET ANOTHER CHANCE TO TALK, BUT UNTIL THEN...
BYE FOR NOW, MR. NUMBER ONE HERO.
GLOOP
JUST KEEP DOING YOUR THING AND DON'T GO DYING ON ME, 'KAY?!
ENJI TODOROKI !!
TALK NOW!

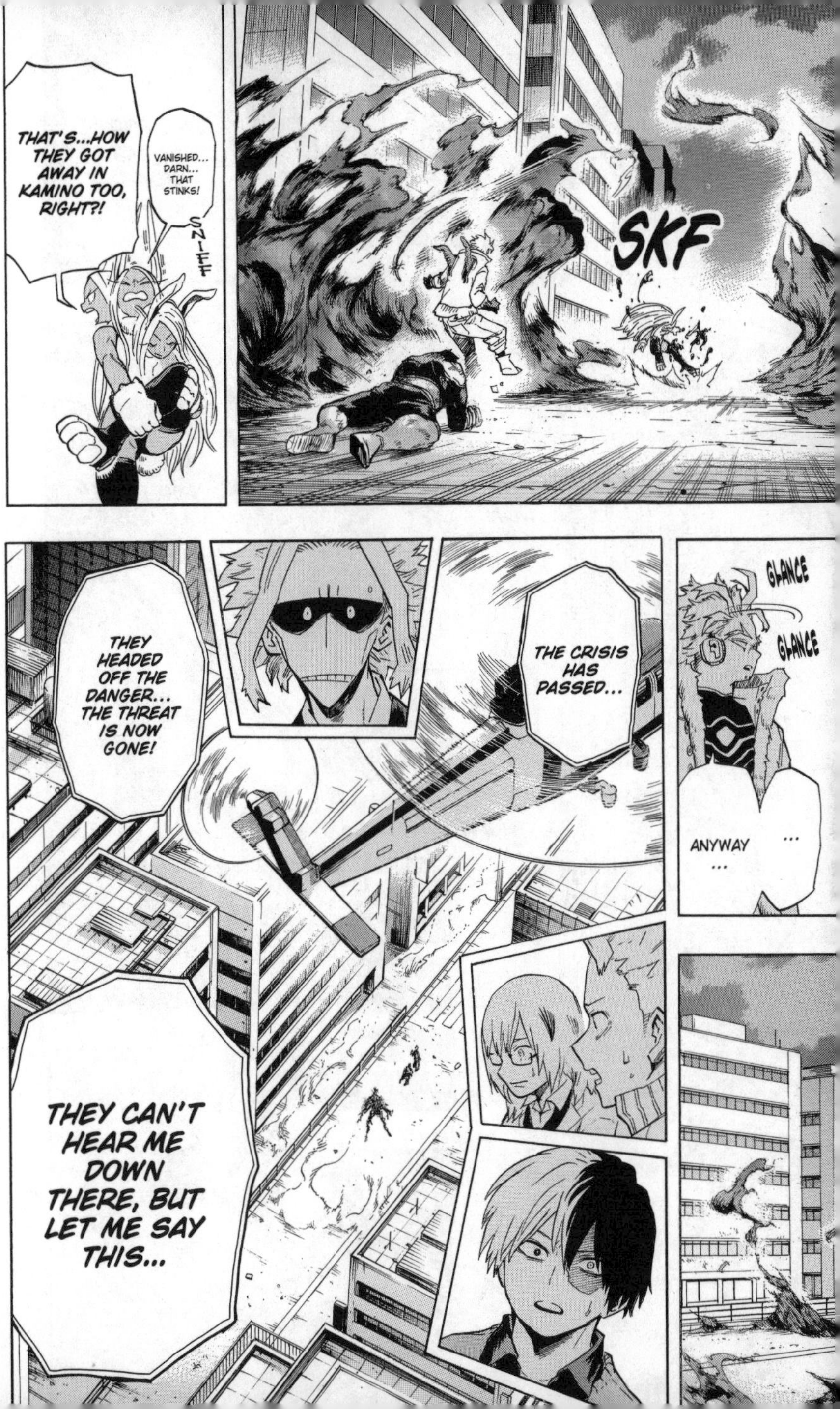
SKF
VANISHED... DARN... THAT STINKS!
SNIFF
THAT'S...HOW THEY GOT AWAY IN KAMINO TOO, RIGHT?!
GLANCE
GLANCE
ANYWAY ...
...
THE CRISIS HAS PASSED...
THEY HEADED OFF THE DANGER... THE THREAT IS NOW GONE!
THEY CAN'T HEAR ME DOWN THERE, BUT LET ME SAY THIS...

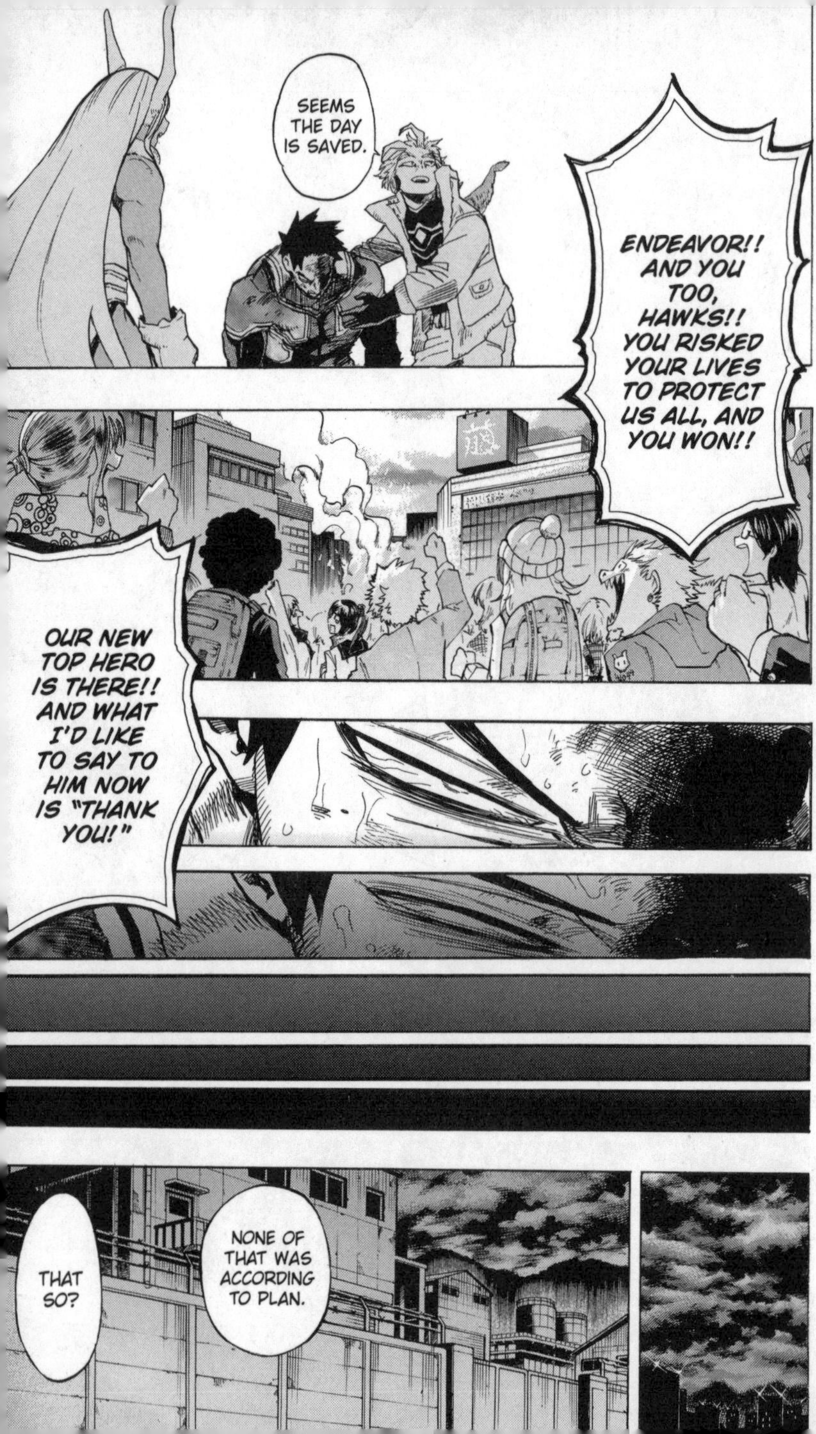
SEEMS THE DAY IS SAVED.
ENDEAVOR!! AND YOU TOO, HAWKS!! YOU RISKED YOUR LIVES TO PROTECT US ALL, AND YOU WON!!
OUR NEW TOP HERO IS THERE!! AND WHAT I'D LIKE TO SAY TO HIM NOW IS "THANK YOU!"
NONE OF THAT WAS ACCORDING TO PLAN.
THAT SO?

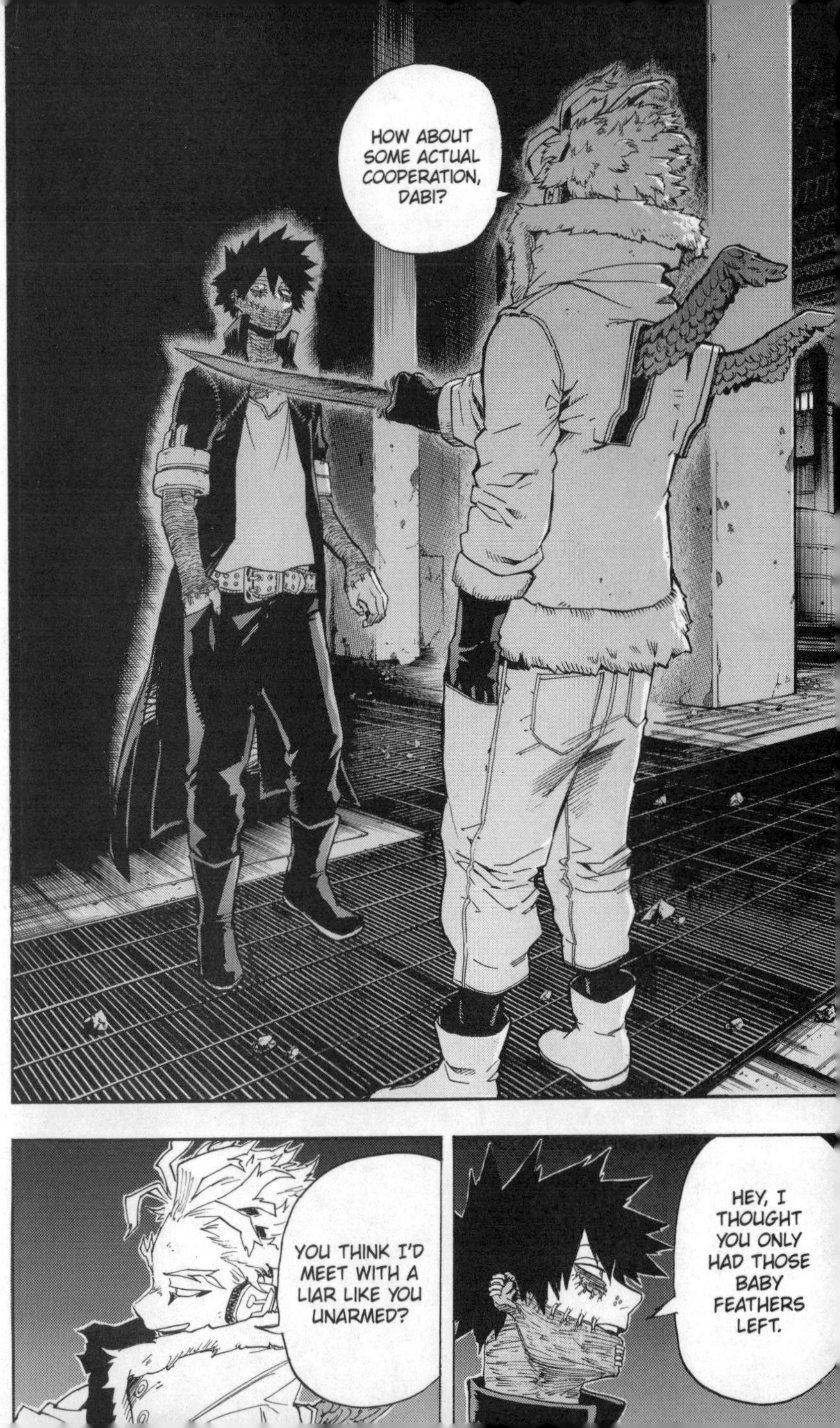
HOW ABOUT SOME ACTUAL COOPERATION, DABI?
HEY, I THOUGHT YOU ONLY HAD THOSE BABY FEATHERS LEFT.
YOU THINK I'D MEET WITH A LIAR LIKE YOU UNARMED?

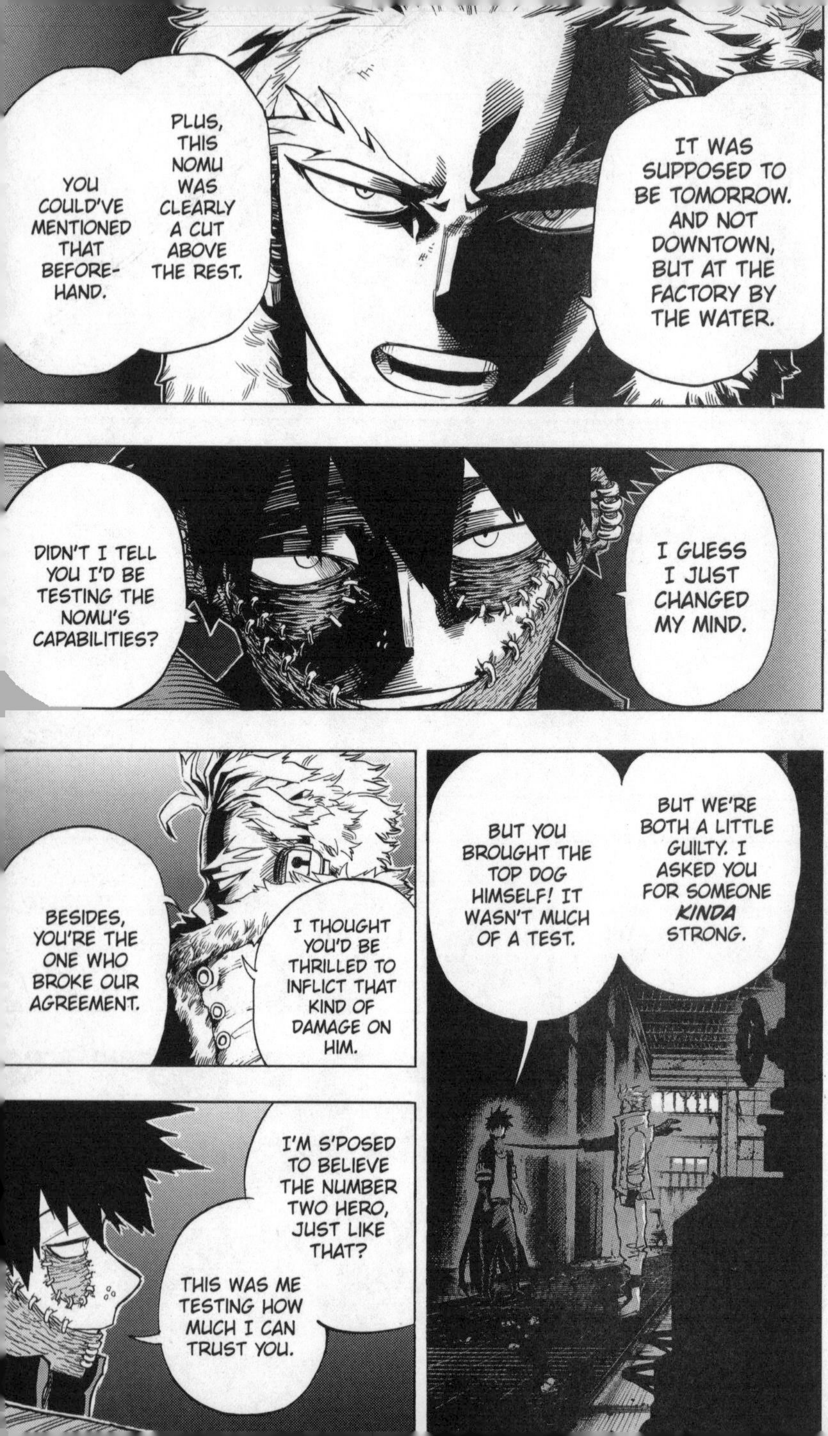
IT WAS SUPPOSED TO BE TOMORROW. AND NOT DOWNTOWN, BUT AT THE FACTORY BY THE WATER.
PLUS, THIS NOMU WAS CLEARLY A CUT ABOVE THE REST.
YOU COULD'VE MENTIONED THAT BEFORE-HAND.
I GUESS I JUST CHANGED MY MIND.
DIDN'T I TELL YOU I'D BE TESTING THE NOMU'S CAPABILITIES?
BUT WE'RE BOTH A LITTLE GUILTY. I ASKED YOU FOR SOMEONE *KINDA* STRONG.
BUT YOU BROUGHT THE TOP DOG HIMSELF! IT WASN'T MUCH OF A TEST.
I THOUGHT YOU'D BE THRILLED TO INFLICT THAT KIND OF DAMAGE ON HIM.
BESIDES, YOU'RE THE ONE WHO BROKE OUR AGREEMENT.
I'M S'POSED TO BELIEVE THE NUMBER TWO HERO, JUST LIKE THAT?
THIS WAS ME TESTING HOW MUCH I CAN TRUST YOU.

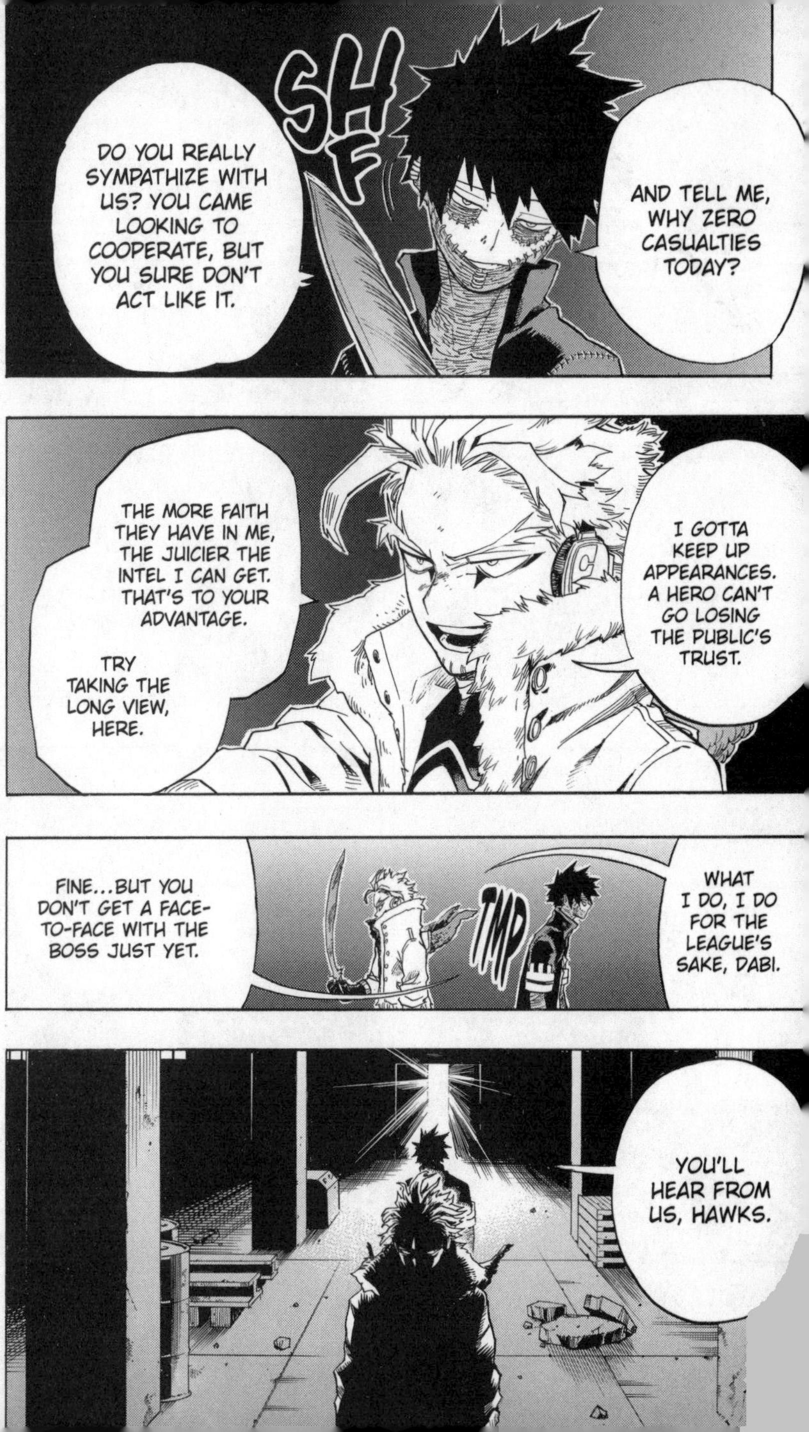
AND TELL ME, WHY ZERO CASUALTIES TODAY?
SHF
DO YOU REALLY SYMPATHIZE WITH US? YOU CAME LOOKING TO COOPERATE, BUT YOU SURE DON'T ACT LIKE IT.
I GOTTA KEEP UP APPEARANCES. A HERO CAN'T GO LOSING THE PUBLIC'S TRUST.
THE MORE FAITH THEY HAVE IN ME, THE JUICIER THE INTEL I CAN GET. THAT'S TO YOUR ADVANTAGE.
TRY TAKING THE LONG VIEW, HERE.
WHAT I DO, I DO FOR THE LEAGUE'S SAKE, DABI.
TMP
FINE...BUT YOU DON'T GET A FACE-TO-FACE WITH THE BOSS JUST YET.
YOU'LL HEAR FROM US, HAWKS.

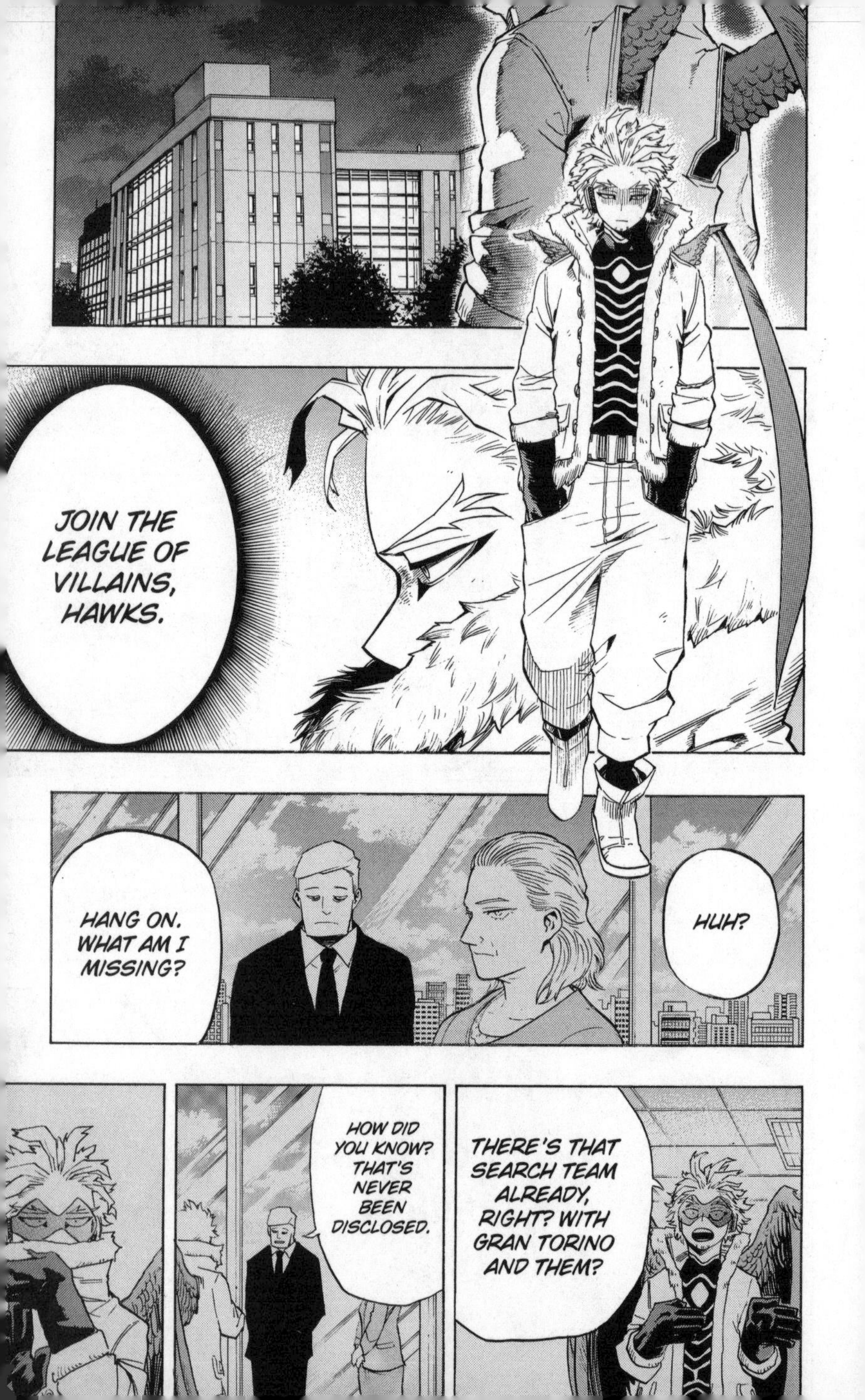
JOIN THE LEAGUE OF VILLAINS, HAWKS.
HUH?
HANG ON. WHAT AM I MISSING?
THERE'S THAT SEARCH TEAM ALREADY, RIGHT? WITH GRAN TORINO AND THEM?
HOW DID YOU KNOW? THAT'S NEVER BEEN DISCLOSED.

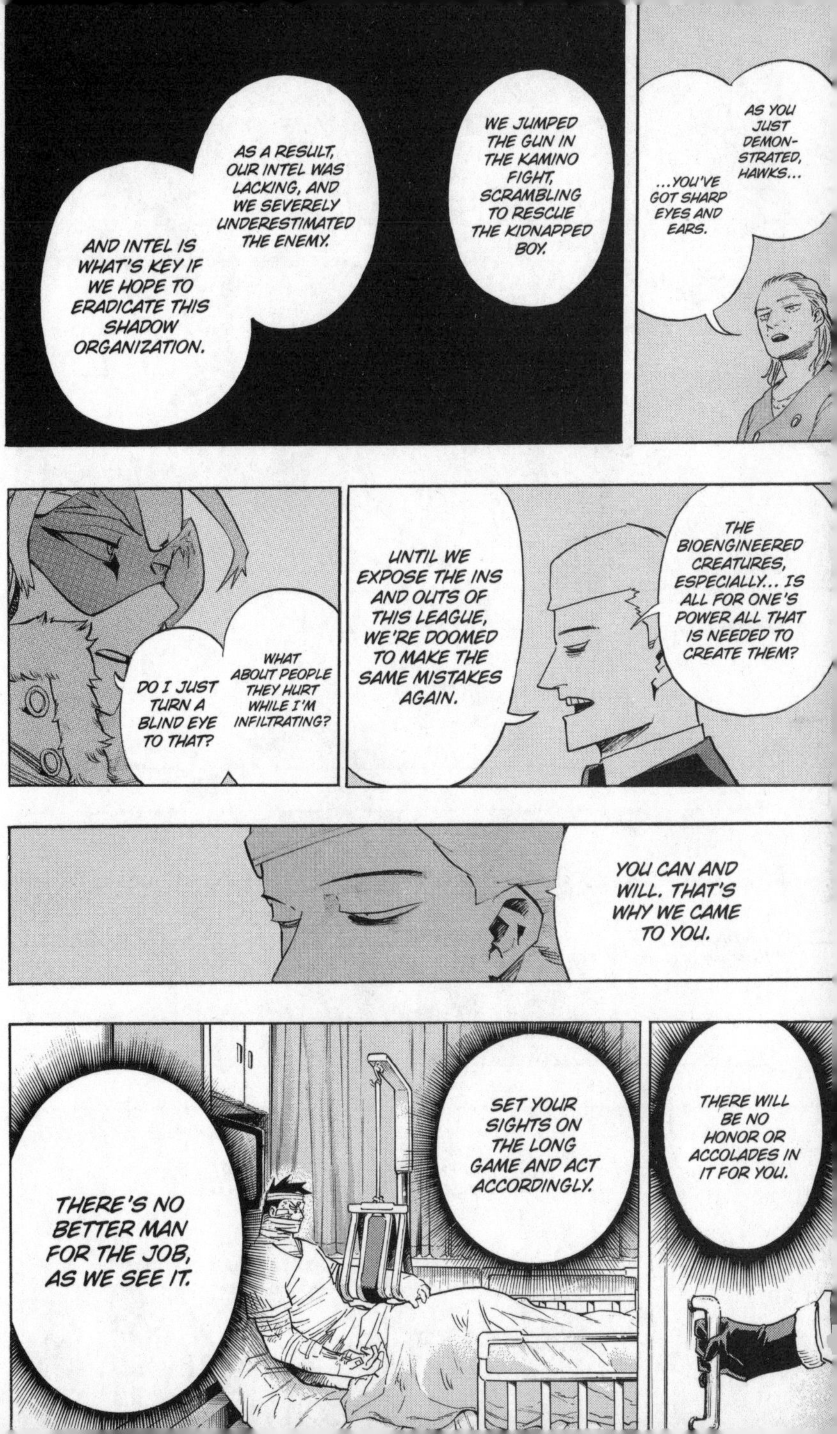
AS YOU JUST DEMON-STRATED, HAWKS...
...YOU'VE GOT SHARP EYES AND EARS.
WE JUMPED THE GUN IN THE KAMINO FIGHT, SCRAMBLING TO RESCUE THE KIDNAPPED BOY.
AS A RESULT, OUR INTEL WAS LACKING, AND WE SEVERELY UNDERESTIMATED THE ENEMY.
AND INTEL IS WHAT'S KEY IF WE HOPE TO ERADICATE THIS SHADOW ORGANIZATION.
THE BIOENGINEERED CREATURES, ESPECIALLY... IS ALL FOR ONE'S POWER ALL THAT IS NEEDED TO CREATE THEM?
UNTIL WE EXPOSE THE INS AND OUTS OF THIS LEAGUE, WE'RE DOOMED TO MAKE THE SAME MISTAKES AGAIN.
WHAT ABOUT PEOPLE THEY HURT WHILE I'M INFILTRATING?
DO I JUST TURN A BLIND EYE TO THAT?
YOU CAN AND WILL. THAT'S WHY WE CAME TO YOU.
THERE WILL BE NO HONOR OR ACCOLADES IN IT FOR YOU.
SET YOUR SIGHTS ON THE LONG GAME AND ACT ACCORDINGLY.
THERE'S NO BETTER MAN FOR THE JOB, AS WE SEE IT.

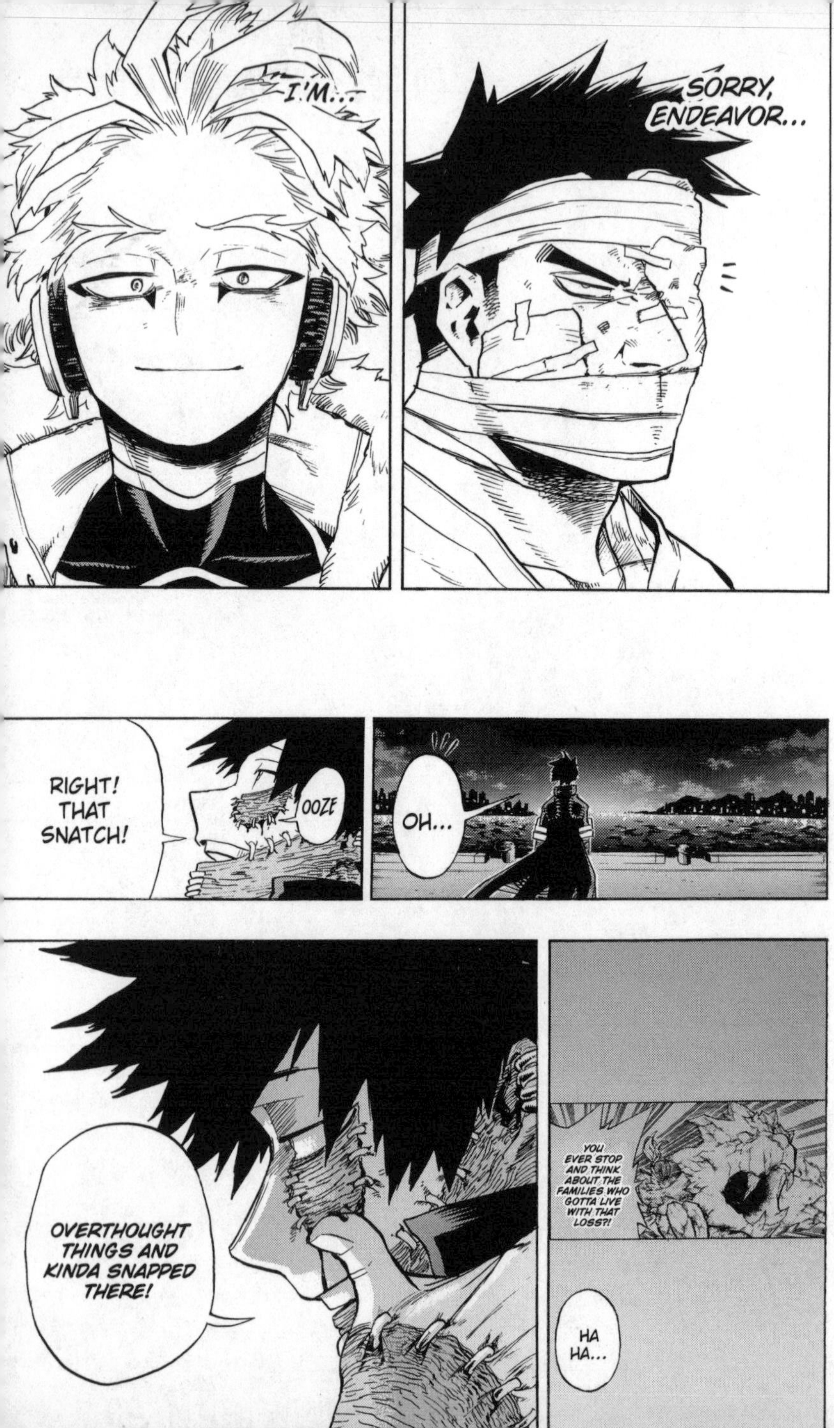
SORRY, ENDEAVOR...
I'M...
OH...
OOZE
RIGHT! THAT SNATCH!
YOU EVER STOP AND THINK ABOUT THE FAMILIES WHO GOTTA LIVE WITH THAT LOSS?!
HA HA...
OVERTHOUGHT THINGS AND KINDA SNAPPED THERE!

No. 192 - The Todoroki Family

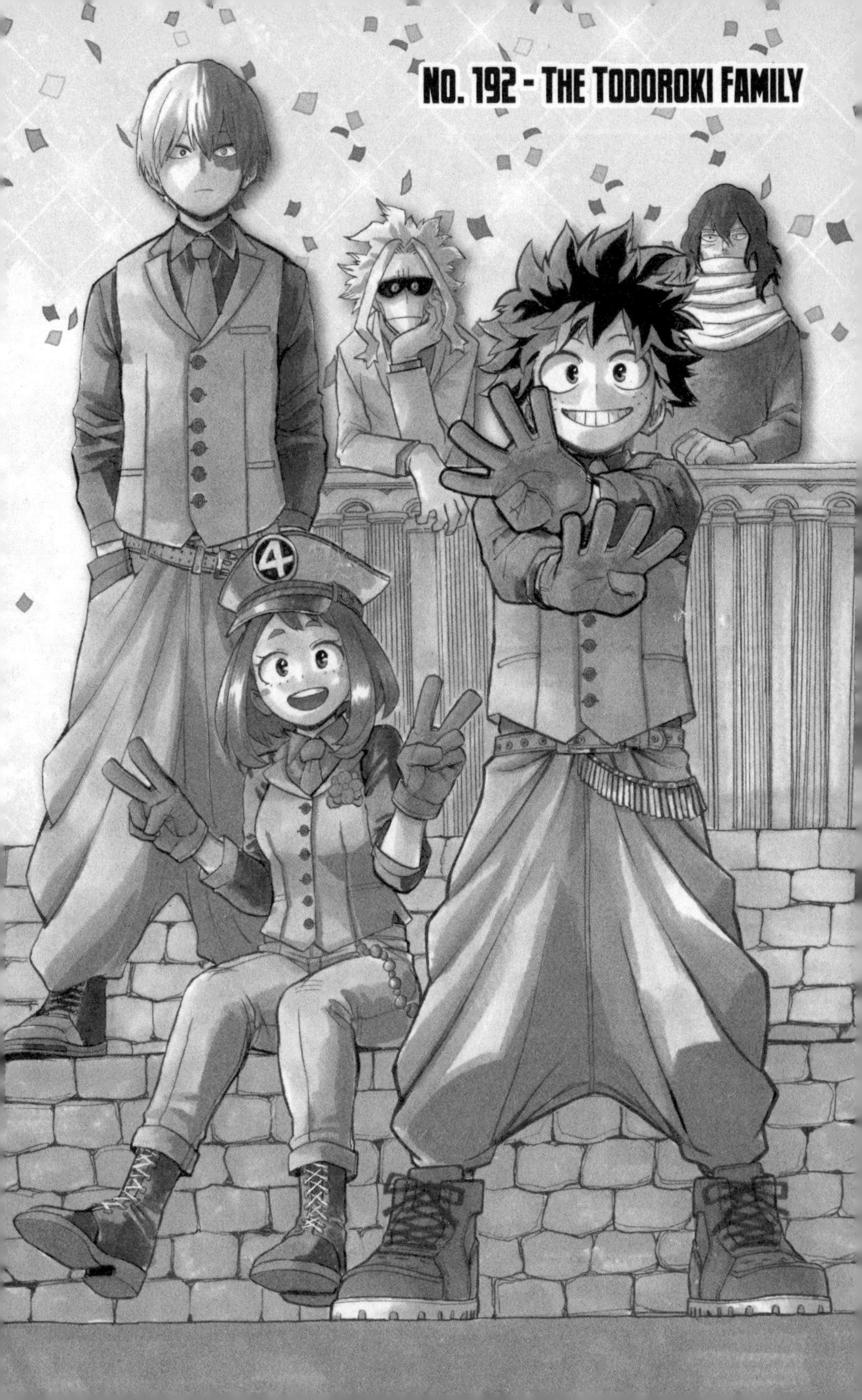

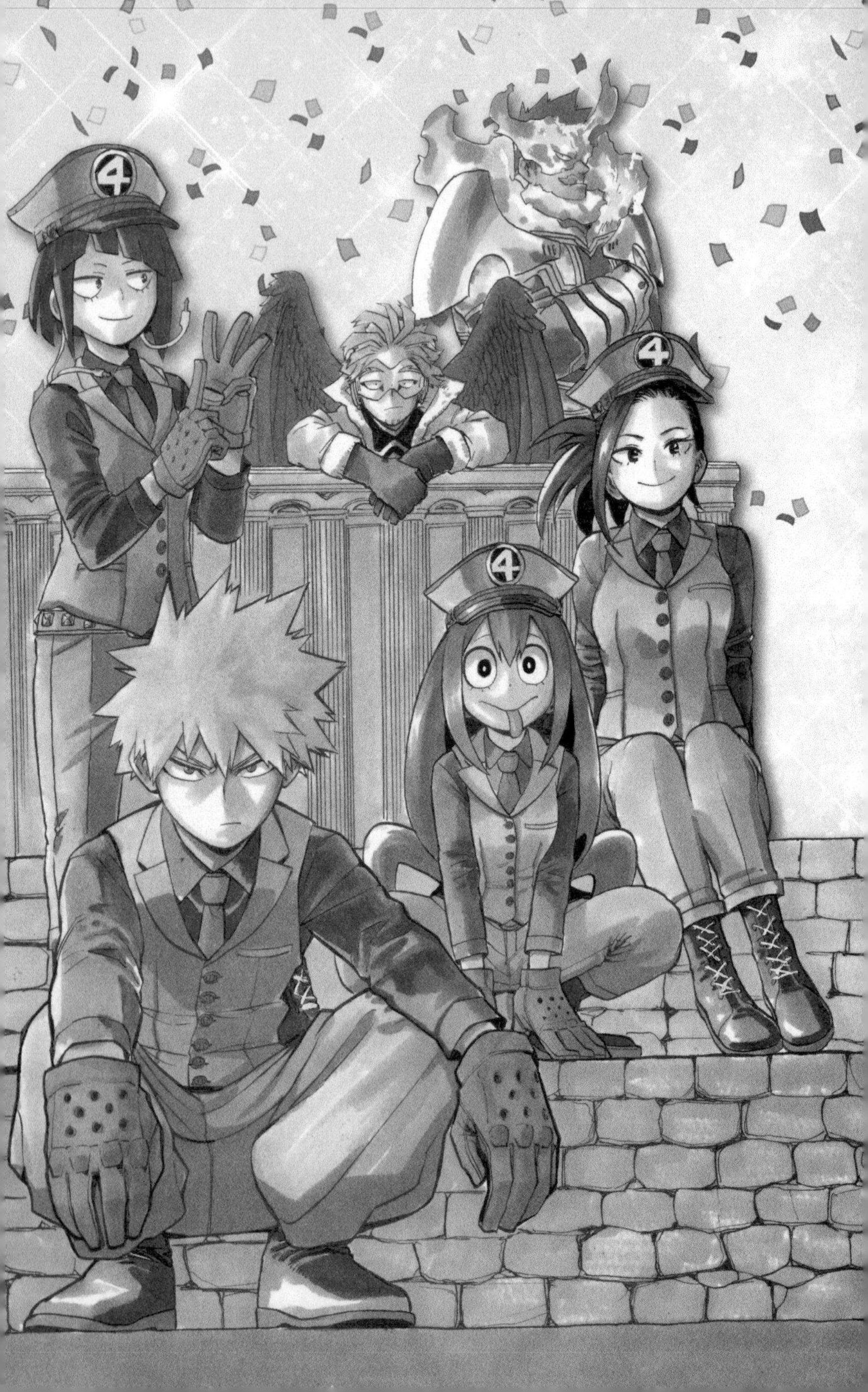

MY HERO ACADEMIA

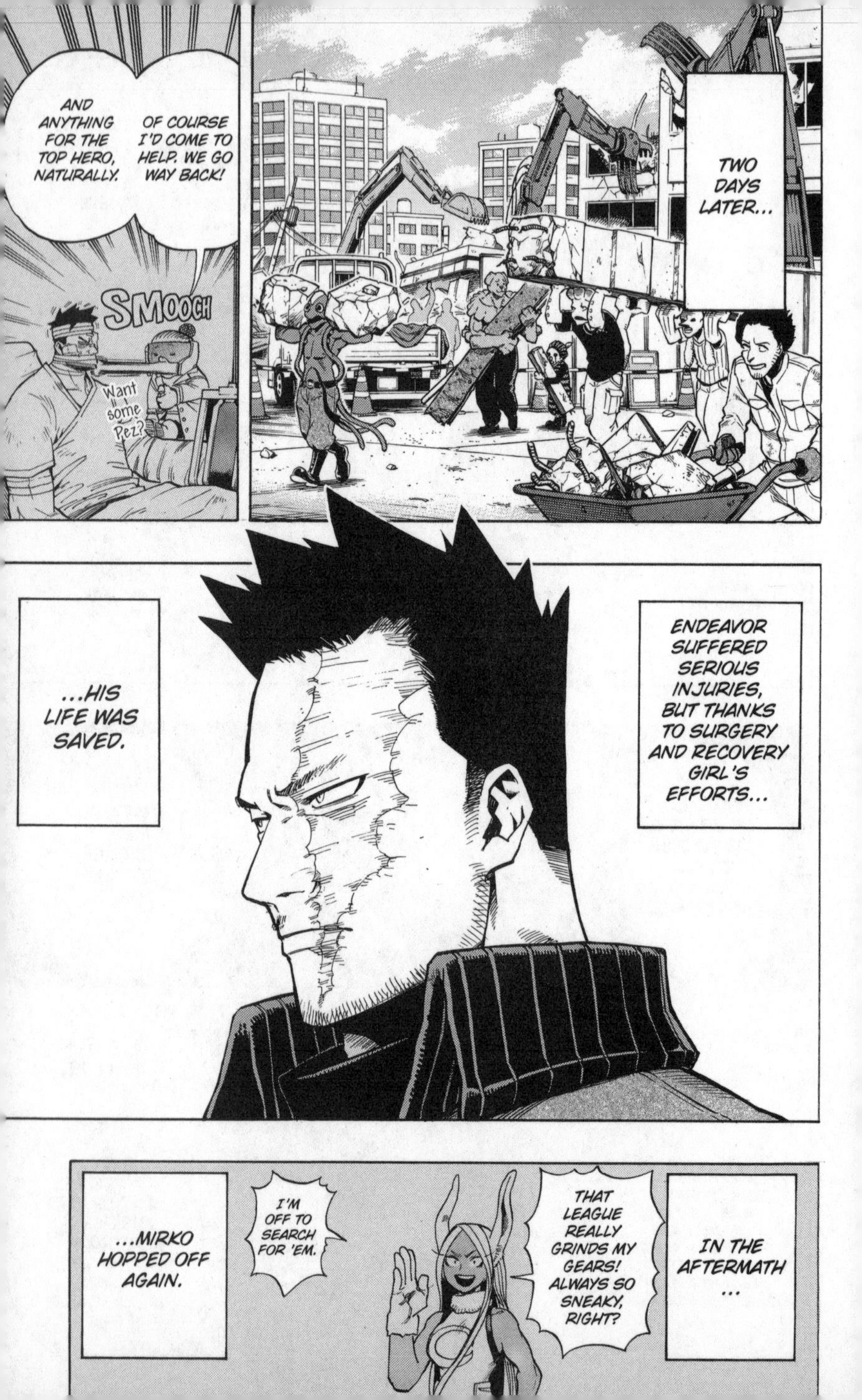
TWO DAYS LATER...
OF COURSE I'D COME TO HELP. WE GO WAY BACK!
AND ANYTHING FOR THE TOP HERO, NATURALLY.
SMOOCH
Want some Pez?
ENDEAVOR SUFFERED SERIOUS INJURIES, BUT THANKS TO SURGERY AND RECOVERY GIRL'S EFFORTS...
...HIS LIFE WAS SAVED.
IN THE AFTERMATH...
THAT LEAGUE REALLY GRINDS MY GEARS! ALWAYS SO SNEAKY, RIGHT?
I'M OFF TO SEARCH FOR 'EM.
...MIRKO HOPPED OFF AGAIN.

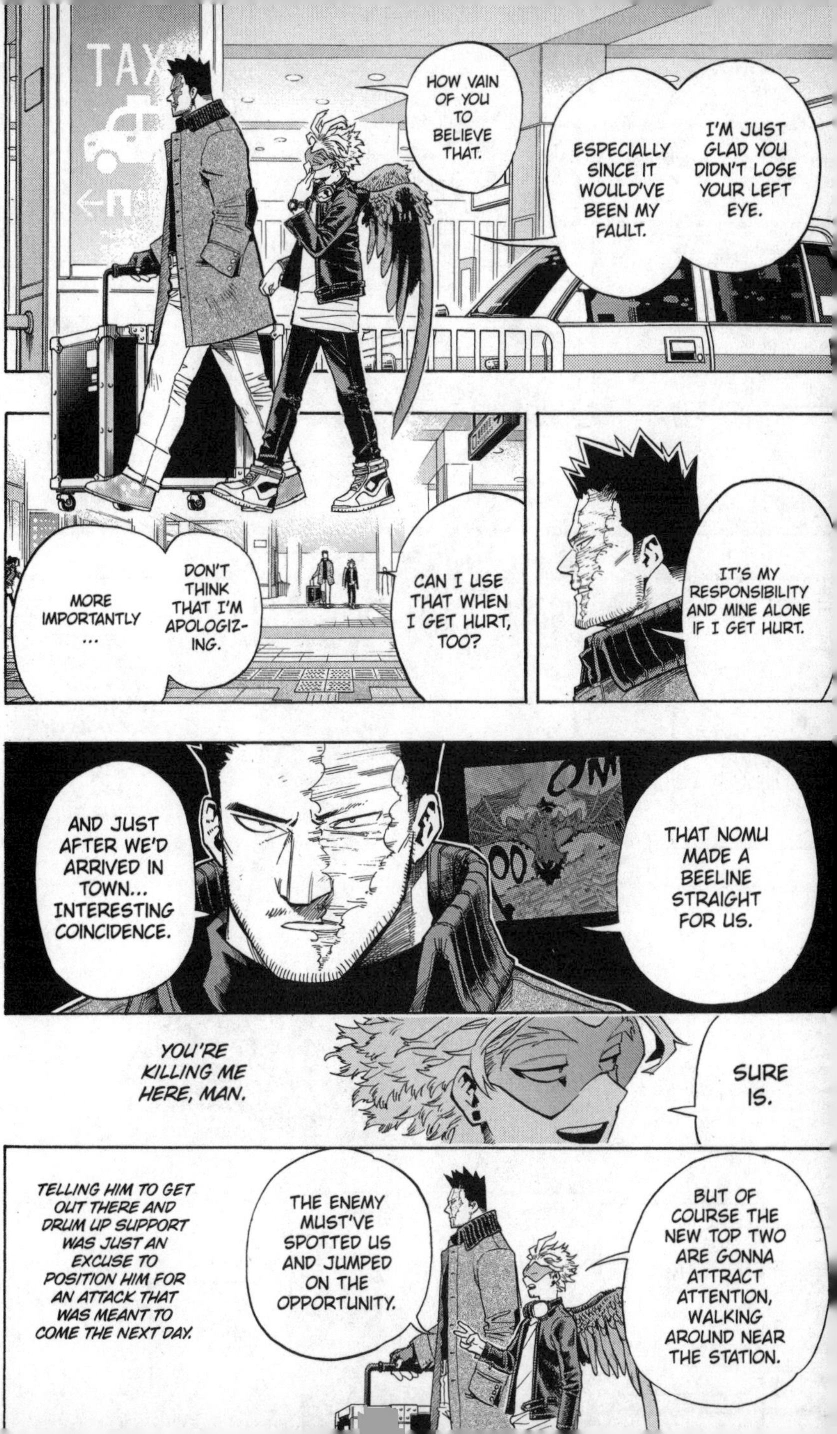
I'M JUST GLAD YOU DIDN'T LOSE YOUR LEFT EYE.
ESPECIALLY SINCE IT WOULD'VE BEEN MY FAULT.
HOW VAIN OF YOU TO BELIEVE THAT.
IT'S MY RESPONSIBILITY AND MINE ALONE IF I GET HURT.
CAN I USE THAT WHEN I GET HURT, TOO?
DON'T THINK THAT I'M APOLOGIZING.
MORE IMPORTANTLY...
THAT NOMU MADE A BEELINE STRAIGHT FOR US.
AND JUST AFTER WE'D ARRIVED IN TOWN... INTERESTING COINCIDENCE.
SURE IS.
YOU'RE KILLING ME HERE, MAN.
BUT OF COURSE THE NEW TOP TWO ARE GONNA ATTRACT ATTENTION, WALKING AROUND NEAR THE STATION.
THE ENEMY MUST'VE SPOTTED US AND JUMPED ON THE OPPORTUNITY.
TELLING HIM TO GET OUT THERE AND DRUM UP SUPPORT WAS JUST AN EXCUSE TO POSITION HIM FOR AN ATTACK THAT WAS MEANT TO COME THE NEXT DAY.

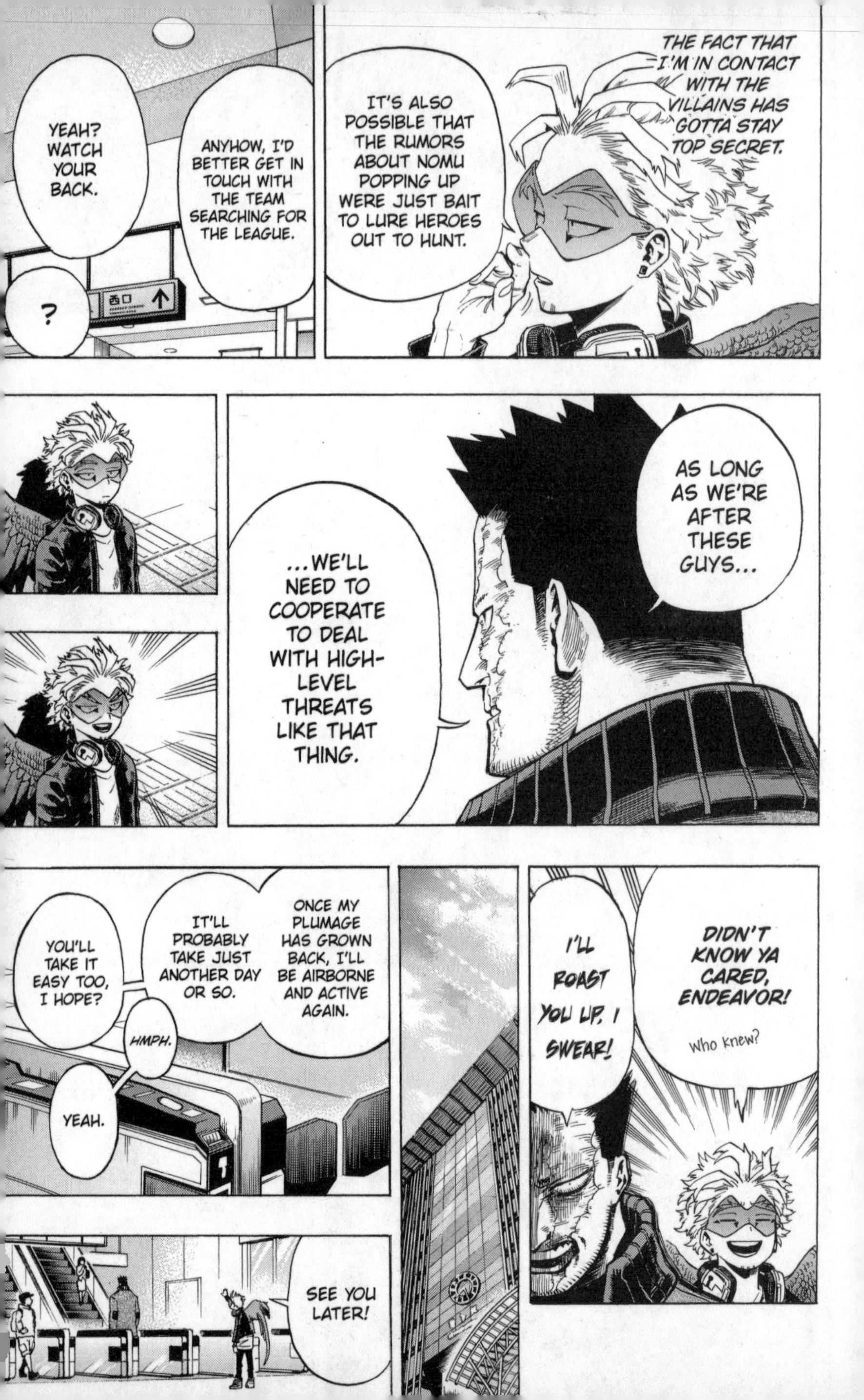
THE FACT THAT I'M IN CONTACT WITH THE VILLAINS HAS GOTTA STAY TOP SECRET.
IT'S ALSO POSSIBLE THAT THE RUMORS ABOUT NOMU POPPING UP WERE JUST BAIT TO LURE HEROES OUT TO HUNT.
ANYHOW, I'D BETTER GET IN TOUCH WITH THE TEAM SEARCHING FOR THE LEAGUE.
YEAH? WATCH YOUR BACK.
?
西口
AS LONG AS WE'RE AFTER THESE GUYS...
...WE'LL NEED TO COOPERATE TO DEAL WITH HIGH-LEVEL THREATS LIKE THAT THING.
DIDN'T KNOW YA CARED, ENDEAVOR!
Who knew?
I'LL ROAST YOU UP, I SWEAR!
ONCE MY PLUMAGE HAS GROWN BACK, I'LL BE AIRBORNE AND ACTIVE AGAIN.
IT'LL PROBABLY TAKE JUST ANOTHER DAY OR SO.
YOU'LL TAKE IT EASY TOO, I HOPE?
HMPH.
YEAH.
SEE YOU LATER!

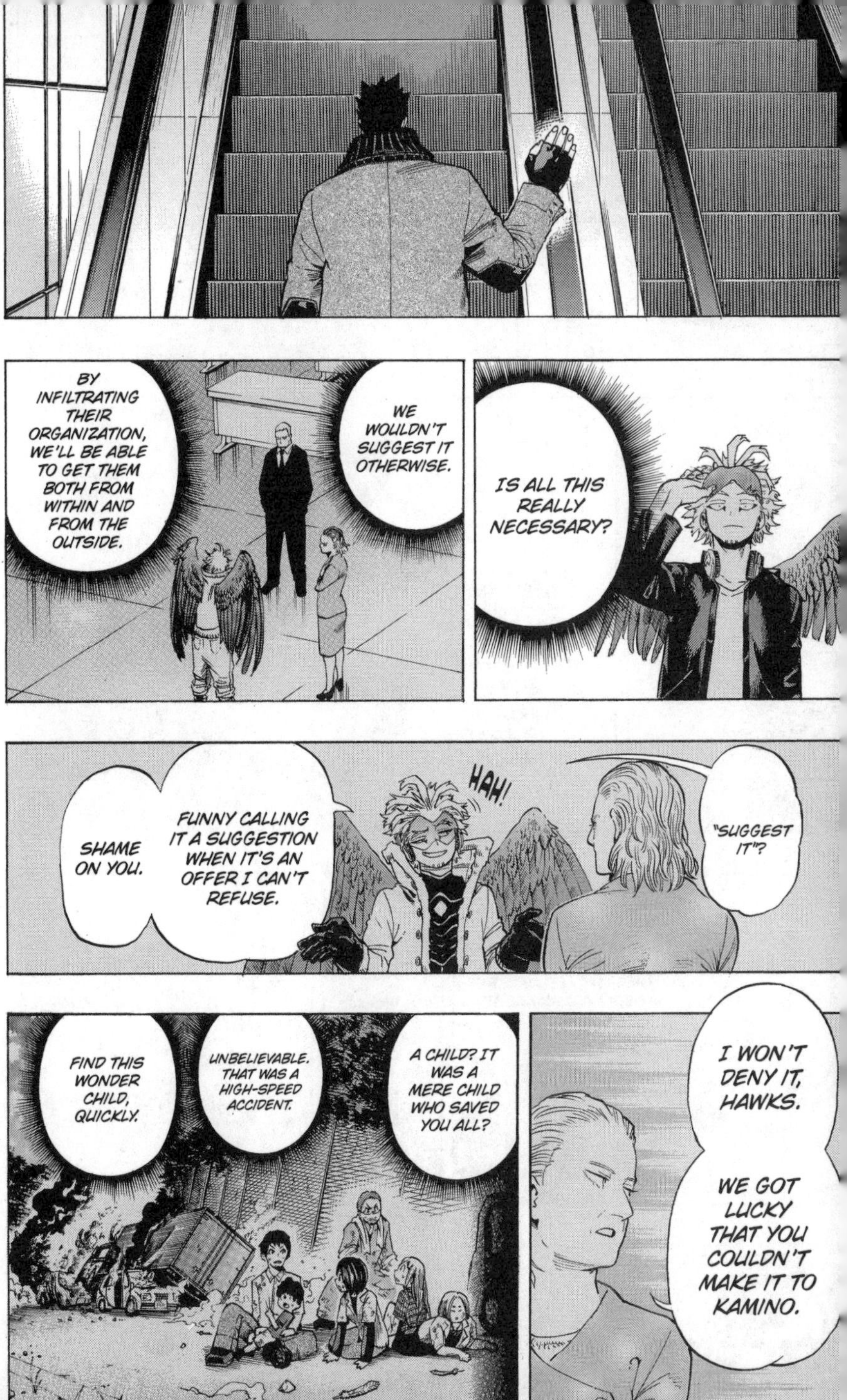
IS ALL THIS REALLY NECESSARY?
WE WOULDN'T SUGGEST IT OTHERWISE.
BY INFILTRATING THEIR ORGANIZATION, WE'LL BE ABLE TO GET THEM BOTH FROM WITHIN AND FROM THE OUTSIDE.
"SUGGEST IT"?
HAH!
FUNNY CALLING IT A SUGGESTION WHEN IT'S AN OFFER I CAN'T REFUSE.
SHAME ON YOU.
I WON'T DENY IT, HAWKS.
WE GOT LUCKY THAT YOU COULDN'T MAKE IT TO KAMINO.
A CHILD? IT WAS A MERE CHILD WHO SAVED YOU ALL?
UNBELIEVABLE. THAT WAS A HIGH-SPEED ACCIDENT.
FIND THIS WONDER CHILD, QUICKLY.

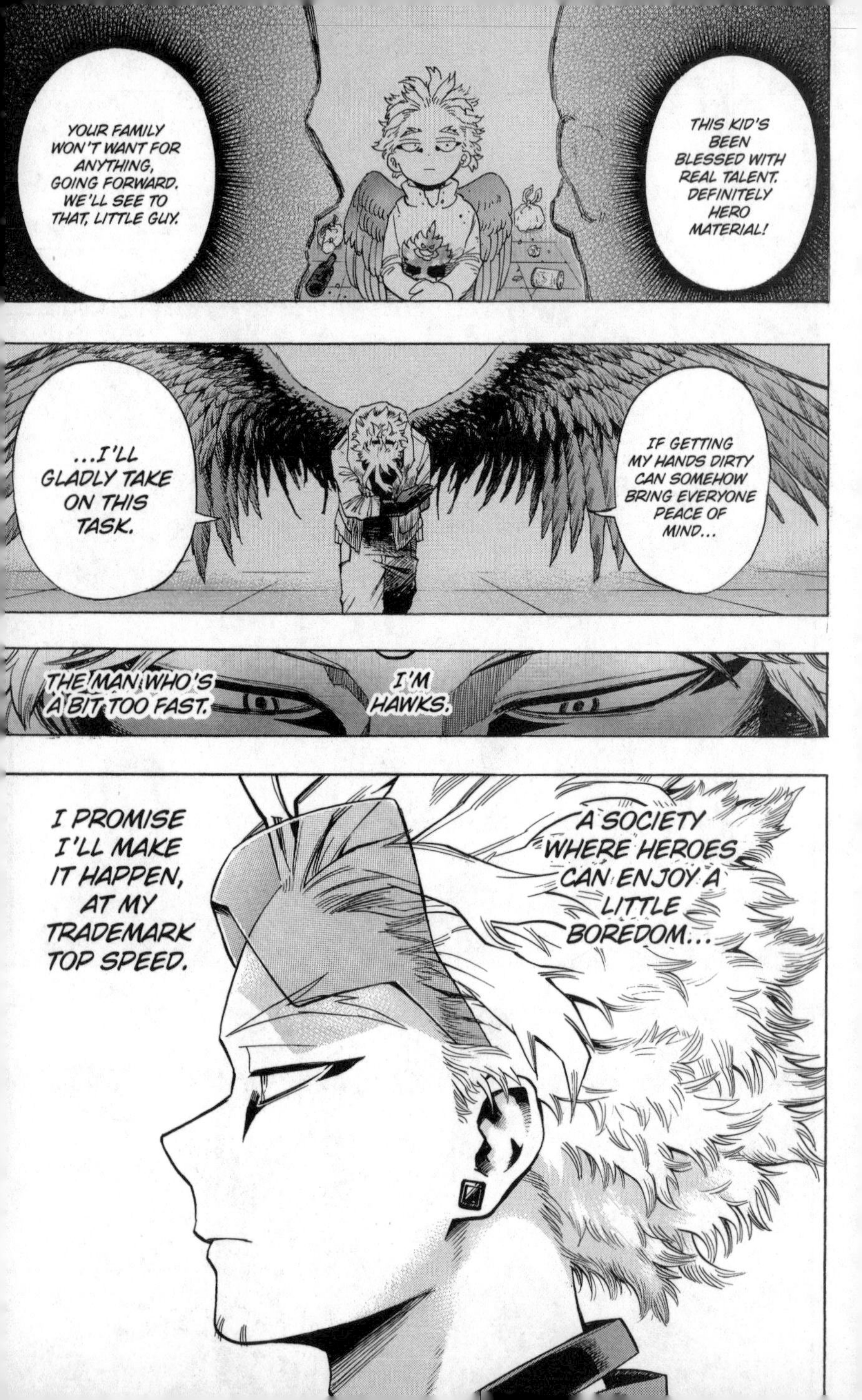
THIS KID'S BEEN BLESSED WITH REAL TALENT. DEFINITELY HERO MATERIAL!
YOUR FAMILY WON'T WANT FOR ANYTHING, GOING FORWARD. WE'LL SEE TO THAT, LITTLE GUY.
IF GETTING MY HANDS DIRTY CAN SOMEHOW BRING EVERYONE PEACE OF MIND...
...I'LL GLADLY TAKE ON THIS TASK.
I'M HAWKS.
THE MAN WHO'S A BIT TOO FAST.
A SOCIETY WHERE HEROES CAN ENJOY A LITTLE BOREDOM...
I PROMISE I'LL MAKE IT HAPPEN, AT MY TRADEMARK TOP SPEED.

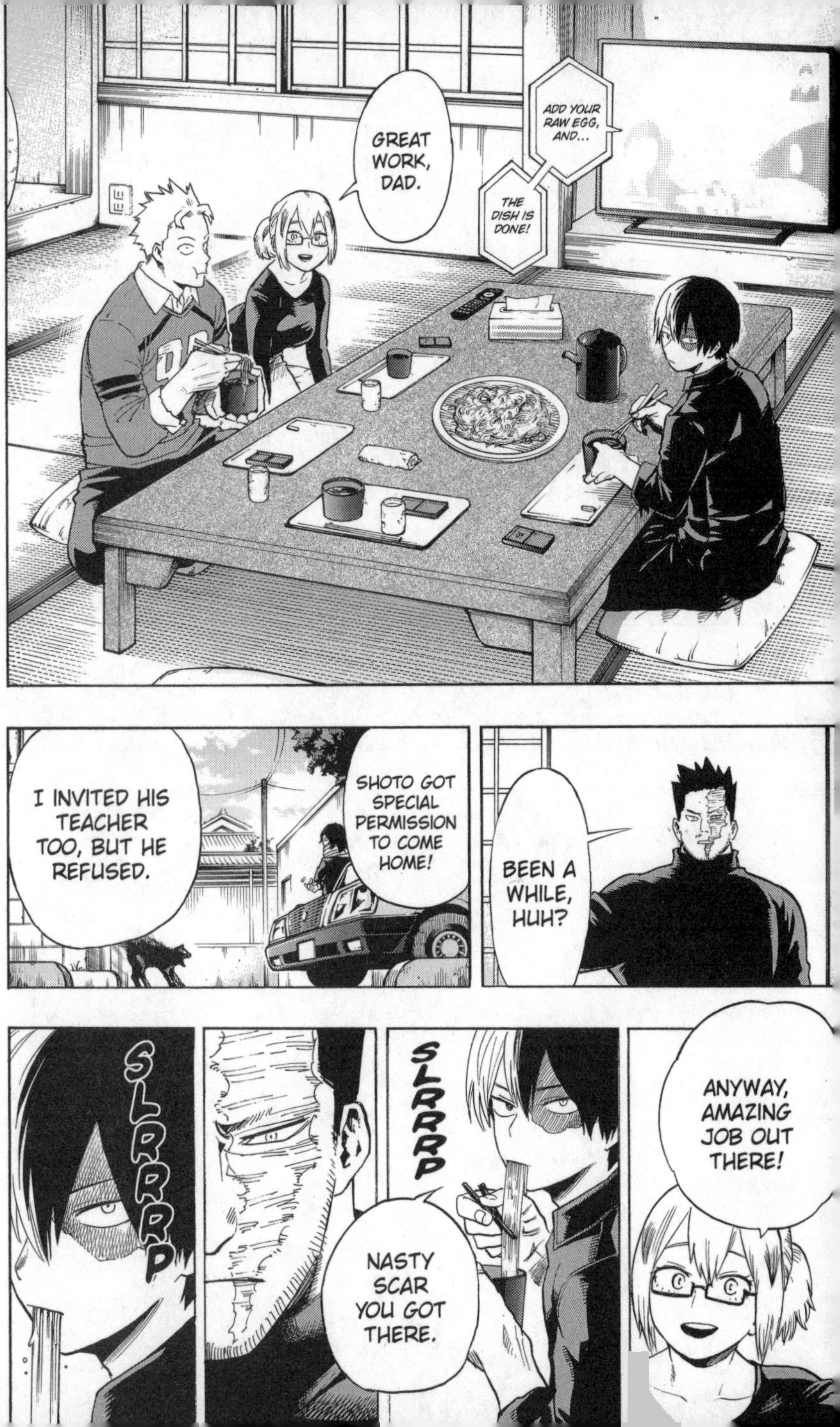
ADD YOUR RAW EGG, AND...
THE DISH IS DONE!
GREAT WORK, DAD.
BEEN A WHILE, HUH?
SHOTO GOT SPECIAL PERMISSION TO COME HOME!
I INVITED HIS TEACHER TOO, BUT HE REFUSED.
ANYWAY, AMAZING JOB OUT THERE!
SLRRRP
NASTY SCAR YOU GOT THERE.
SLRRRP

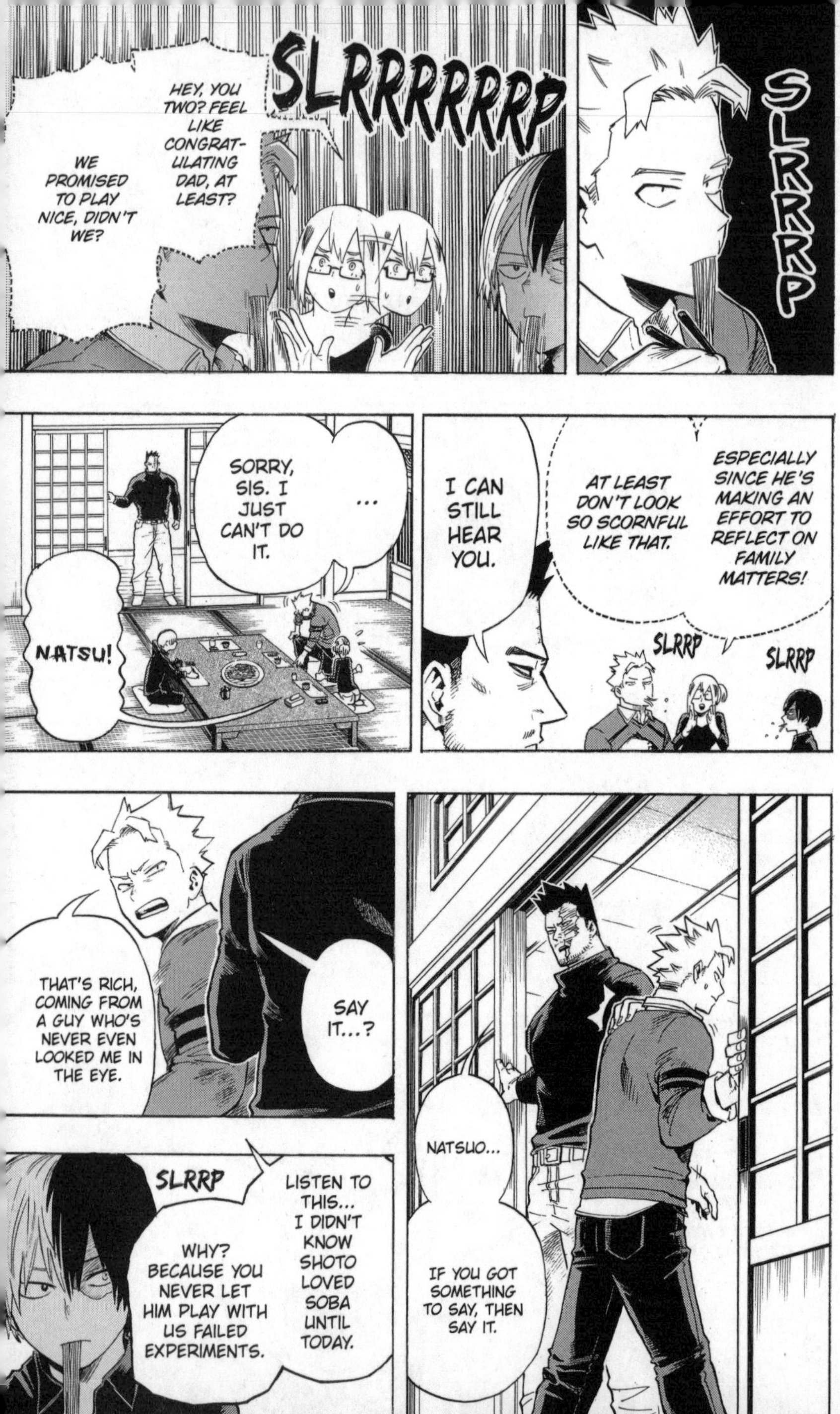
SLRRRRP
SLRRRRRRRP
HEY, YOU TWO? FEEL LIKE CONGRAT-ULATING DAD, AT LEAST?
WE PROMISED TO PLAY NICE, DIDN'T WE?
AT LEAST DON'T LOOK SO SCORNFUL LIKE THAT.
ESPECIALLY SINCE HE'S MAKING AN EFFORT TO REFLECT ON FAMILY MATTERS!
SLRRP
SLRRP
I CAN STILL HEAR YOU.
...
SORRY, SIS. I JUST CAN'T DO IT.
NATSU!
NATSUO...
IF YOU GOT SOMETHING TO SAY, THEN SAY IT.
SAY IT...?
THAT'S RICH, COMING FROM A GUY WHO'S NEVER EVEN LOOKED ME IN THE EYE.
LISTEN TO THIS... I DIDN'T KNOW SHOTO LOVED SOBA UNTIL TODAY.
SLRRP
WHY? BECAUSE YOU NEVER LET HIM PLAY WITH US FAILED EXPERIMENTS.

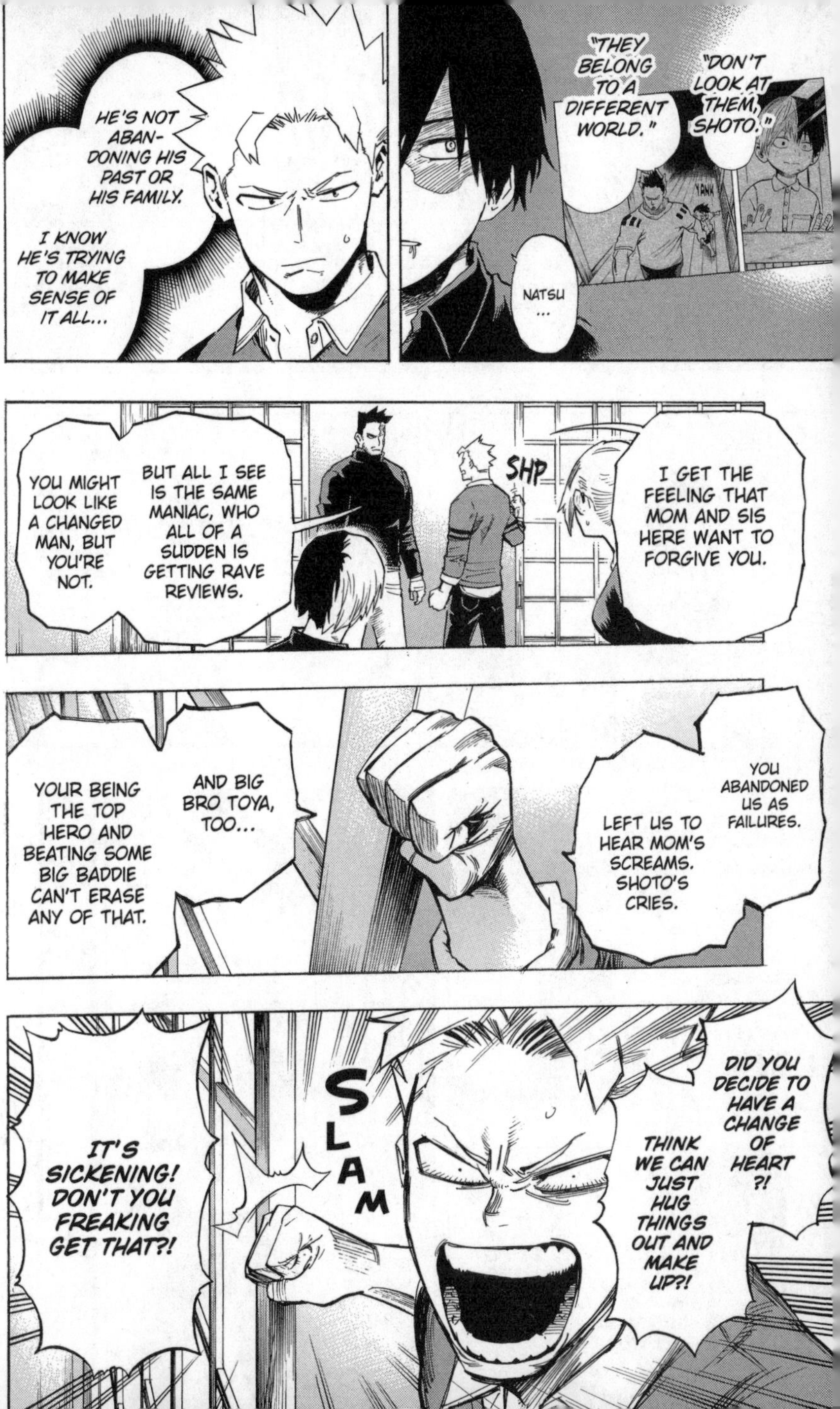
"DON'T LOOK AT THEM, SHOTO."
"THEY BELONG TO A DIFFERENT WORLD."
YANK
NATSU...
HE'S NOT ABANDONING HIS PAST OR HIS FAMILY.
I KNOW HE'S TRYING TO MAKE SENSE OF IT ALL...
I GET THE FEELING THAT MOM AND SIS HERE WANT TO FORGIVE YOU.
SHP
BUT ALL I SEE IS THE SAME MANIAC, WHO ALL OF A SUDDEN IS GETTING RAVE REVIEWS.
YOU MIGHT LOOK LIKE A CHANGED MAN, BUT YOU'RE NOT.
YOU ABANDONED US AS FAILURES.
LEFT US TO HEAR MOM'S SCREAMS. SHOTO'S CRIES.
AND BIG BRO TOYA, TOO...
YOUR BEING THE TOP HERO AND BEATING SOME BIG BADDIE CAN'T ERASE ANY OF THAT.
DID YOU DECIDE TO HAVE A CHANGE OF HEART?!
THINK WE CAN JUST HUG THINGS OUT AND MAKE UP?!
SLAM
IT'S SICKENING! DON'T YOU FREAKING GET THAT?!

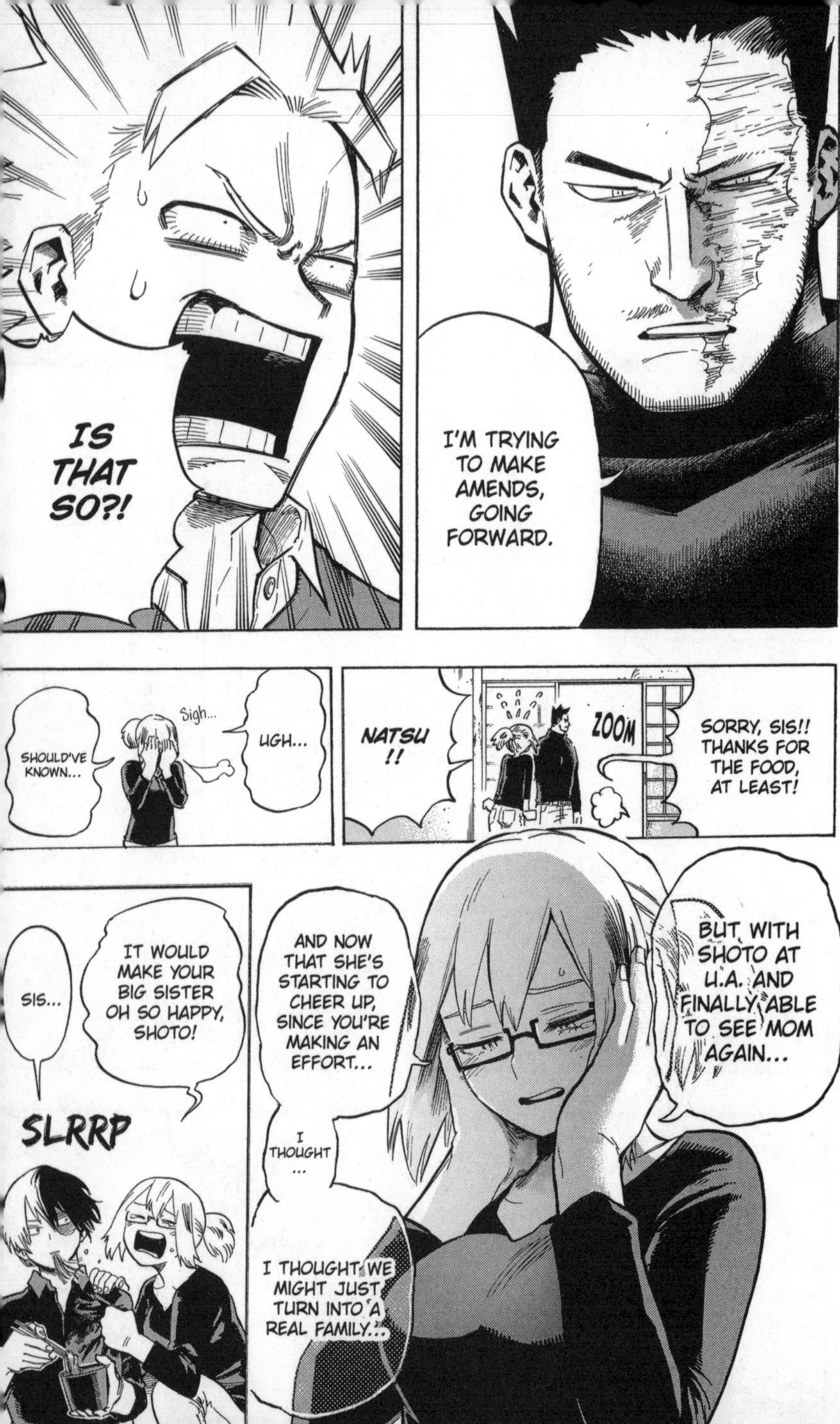
I'M TRYING TO MAKE AMENDS, GOING FORWARD.
IS THAT SO?!
SORRY, SIS!! THANKS FOR THE FOOD, AT LEAST!
ZOOM
NATSU!!
UGH...
Sigh...
SHOULD'VE KNOWN...
BUT WITH SHOTO AT U.A. AND FINALLY ABLE TO SEE MOM AGAIN...
AND NOW THAT SHE'S STARTING TO CHEER UP, SINCE YOU'RE MAKING AN EFFORT...
I THOUGHT...
I THOUGHT WE MIGHT JUST TURN INTO A REAL FAMILY...
IT WOULD MAKE YOUR BIG SISTER OH SO HAPPY, SHOTO!
SIS...
SLRRP

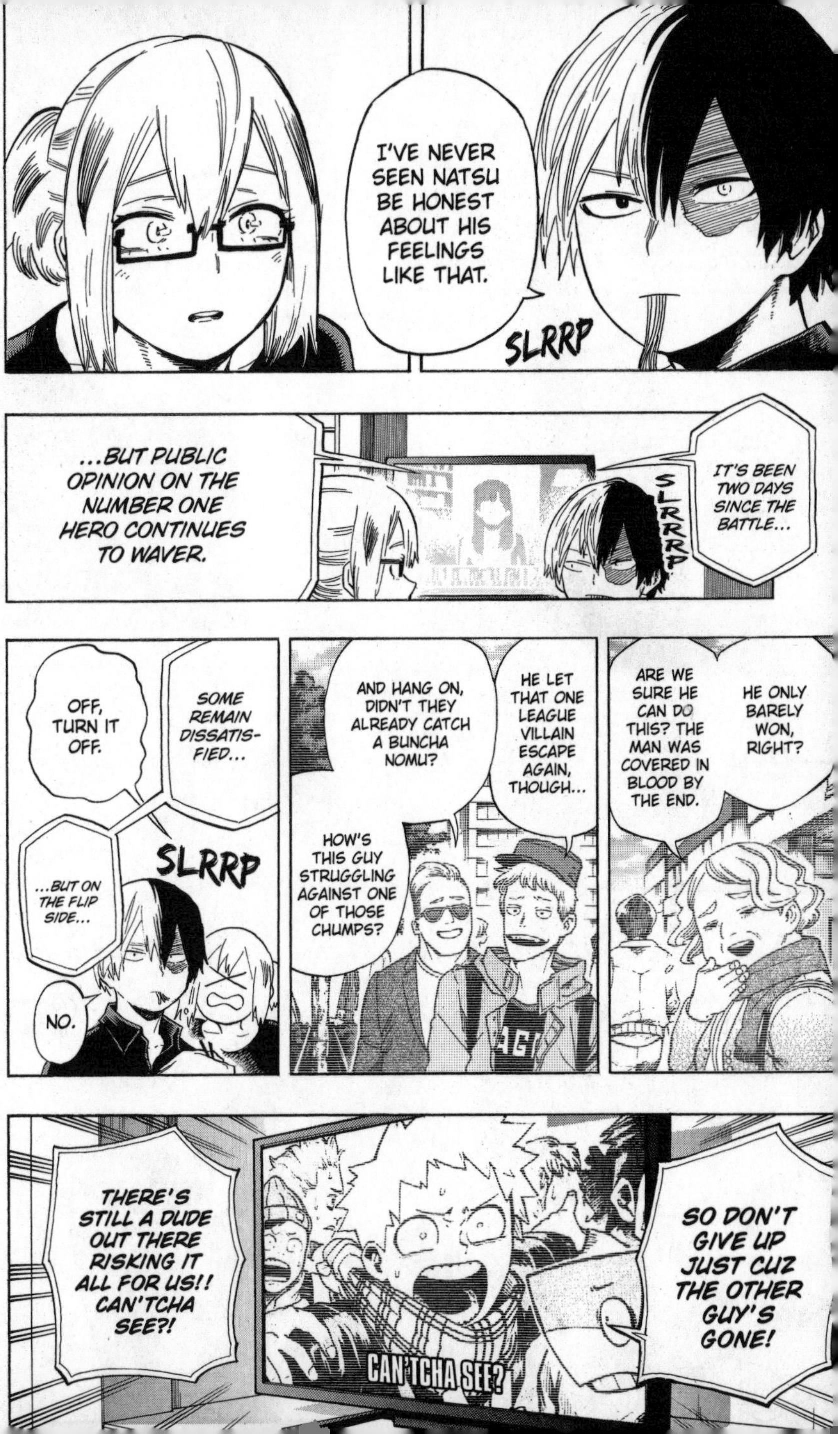
I'VE NEVER SEEN NATSU BE HONEST ABOUT HIS FEELINGS LIKE THAT.
SLRRP
IT'S BEEN TWO DAYS SINCE THE BATTLE...
SLRRRRP
...BUT PUBLIC OPINION ON THE NUMBER ONE HERO CONTINUES TO WAVER.
HE ONLY BARELY WON, RIGHT?
ARE WE SURE HE CAN DO THIS? THE MAN WAS COVERED IN BLOOD BY THE END.
HE LET THAT ONE LEAGUE VILLAIN ESCAPE AGAIN, THOUGH...
AND HANG ON, DIDN'T THEY ALREADY CATCH A BUNCHA NOMU?
HOW'S THIS GUY STRUGGLING AGAINST ONE OF THOSE CHUMPS?
SOME REMAIN DISSATIS-FIED...
OFF, TURN IT OFF.
SLRRP
...BUT ON THE FLIP SIDE...
NO.
SO DON'T GIVE UP JUST CUZ THE OTHER GUY'S GONE!
THERE'S STILL A DUDE OUT THERE RISKING IT ALL FOR US!! CAN'TCHA SEE?!
CAN'TCHA SEE?

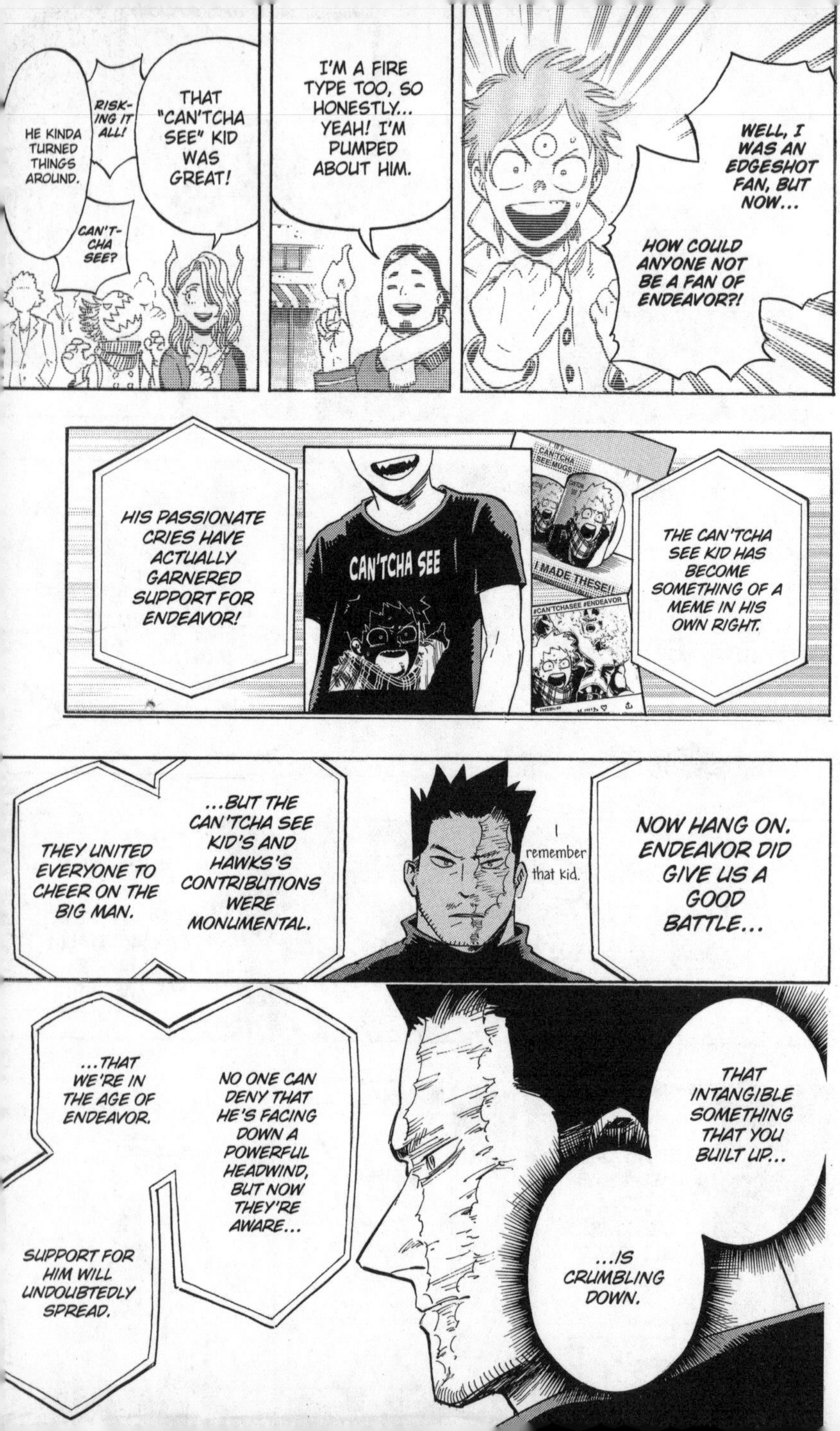
WELL, I WAS AN EDGESHOT FAN, BUT NOW...
HOW COULD ANYONE NOT BE A FAN OF ENDEAVOR?!
I'M A FIRE TYPE TOO, SO HONESTLY... YEAH! I'M PUMPED ABOUT HIM.
THAT "CAN'TCHA SEE" KID WAS GREAT!
RISK-ING IT ALL!
HE KINDA TURNED THINGS AROUND.
CAN'T-CHA SEE?
THE CAN'TCHA SEE KID HAS BECOME SOMETHING OF A MEME IN HIS OWN RIGHT.
CAN'TCHA SEE MUGS
I MADE THESE!!
#CAN'TCHASEE #ENDEAVOR
CAN'TCHA SEE
HIS PASSIONATE CRIES HAVE ACTUALLY GARNERED SUPPORT FOR ENDEAVOR!
NOW HANG ON. ENDEAVOR DID GIVE US A GOOD BATTLE...
I remember that kid.
...BUT THE CAN'TCHA SEE KID'S AND HAWKS'S CONTRIBUTIONS WERE MONUMENTAL.
THEY UNITED EVERYONE TO CHEER ON THE BIG MAN.
THAT INTANGIBLE SOMETHING THAT YOU BUILT UP...
...IS CRUMBLING DOWN.
NO ONE CAN DENY THAT HE'S FACING DOWN A POWERFUL HEADWIND, BUT NOW THEY'RE AWARE...
...THAT WE'RE IN THE AGE OF ENDEAVOR.
SUPPORT FOR HIM WILL UNDOUBTEDLY SPREAD.

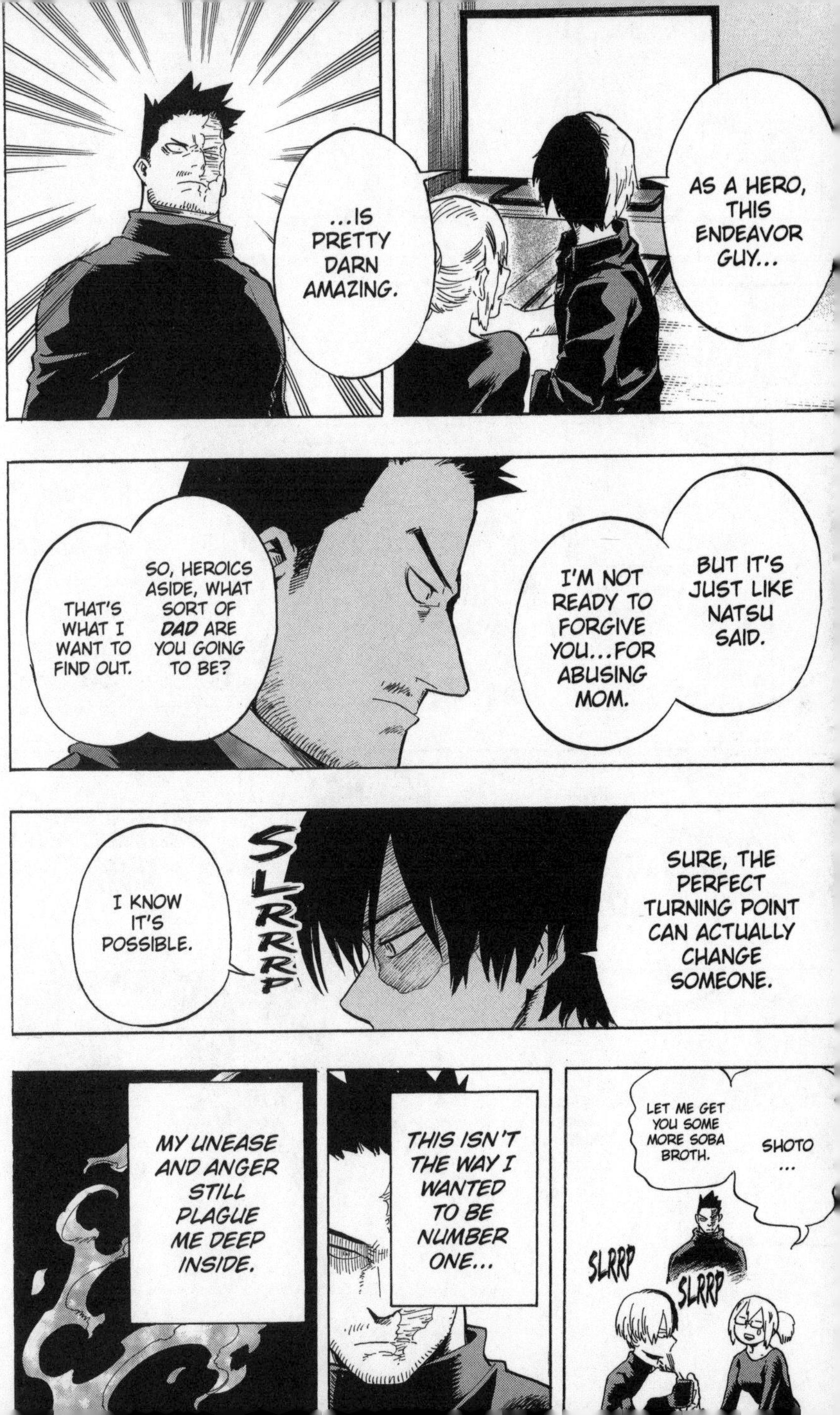
AS A HERO, THIS ENDEAVOR GUY...
...IS PRETTY DARN AMAZING.
BUT IT'S JUST LIKE NATSU SAID.
I'M NOT READY TO FORGIVE YOU...FOR ABUSING MOM.
SO, HEROICS ASIDE, WHAT SORT OF *DAD* ARE YOU GOING TO BE?
THAT'S WHAT I WANT TO FIND OUT.
SURE, THE PERFECT TURNING POINT CAN ACTUALLY CHANGE SOMEONE.
SLRRRRP
I KNOW IT'S POSSIBLE.
SHOTO ...
LET ME GET YOU SOME MORE SOBA BROTH.
SLRRP
SLRRP
THIS ISN'T THE WAY I WANTED TO BE NUMBER ONE...
MY UNEASE AND ANGER STILL PLAGUE ME DEEP INSIDE.

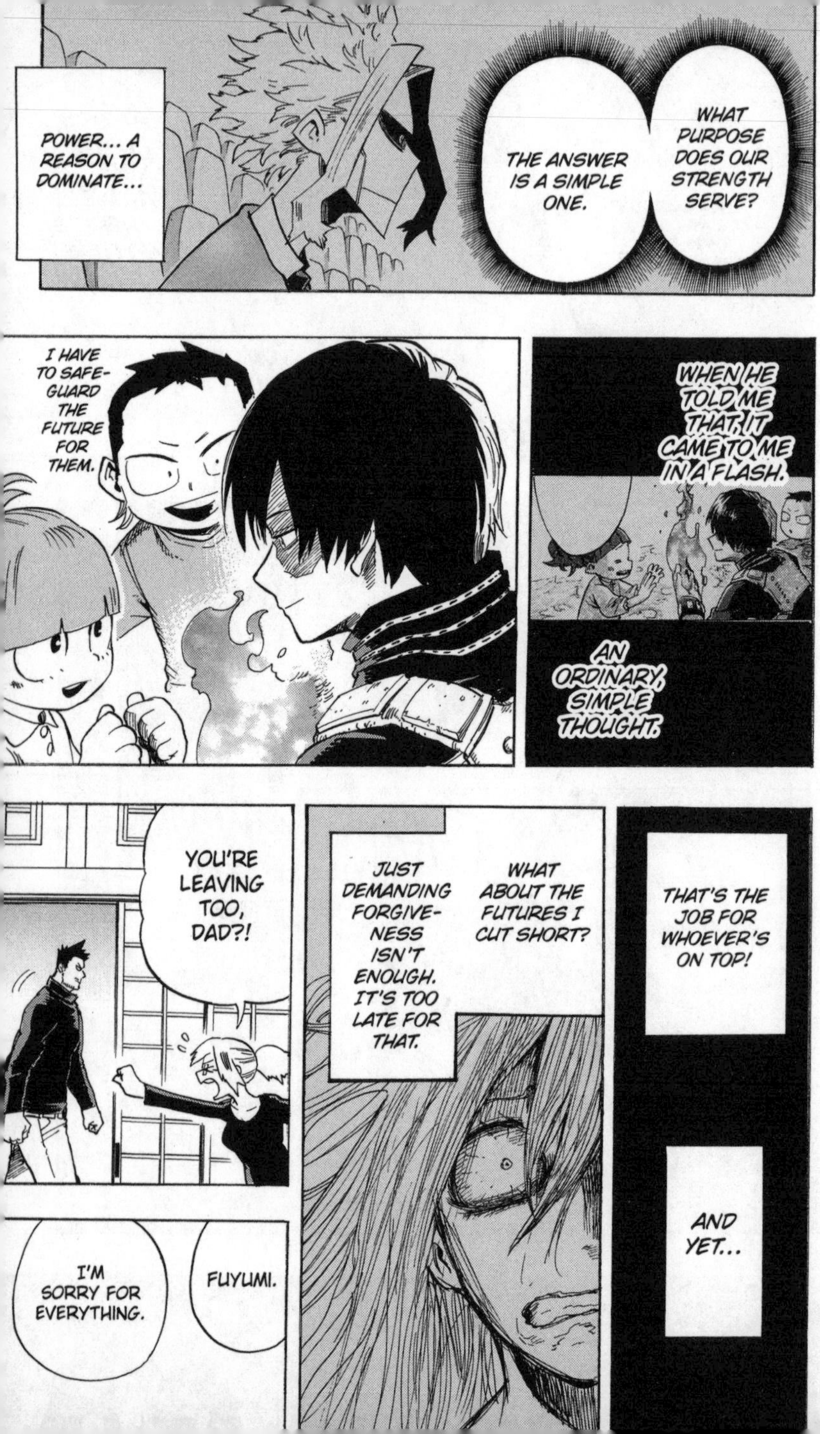
WHAT PURPOSE DOES OUR STRENGTH SERVE?
THE ANSWER IS A SIMPLE ONE.
POWER... A REASON TO DOMINATE...
WHEN HE TOLD ME THAT, IT CAME TO ME IN A FLASH.
AN ORDINARY, SIMPLE THOUGHT.
I HAVE TO SAFE-GUARD THE FUTURE FOR THEM.
THAT'S THE JOB FOR WHOEVER'S ON TOP!
AND YET...
WHAT ABOUT THE FUTURES I CUT SHORT?
JUST DEMANDING FORGIVE-NESS ISN'T ENOUGH. IT'S TOO LATE FOR THAT.
YOU'RE LEAVING TOO, DAD?!
FUYUMI.
I'M SORRY FOR EVERYTHING.

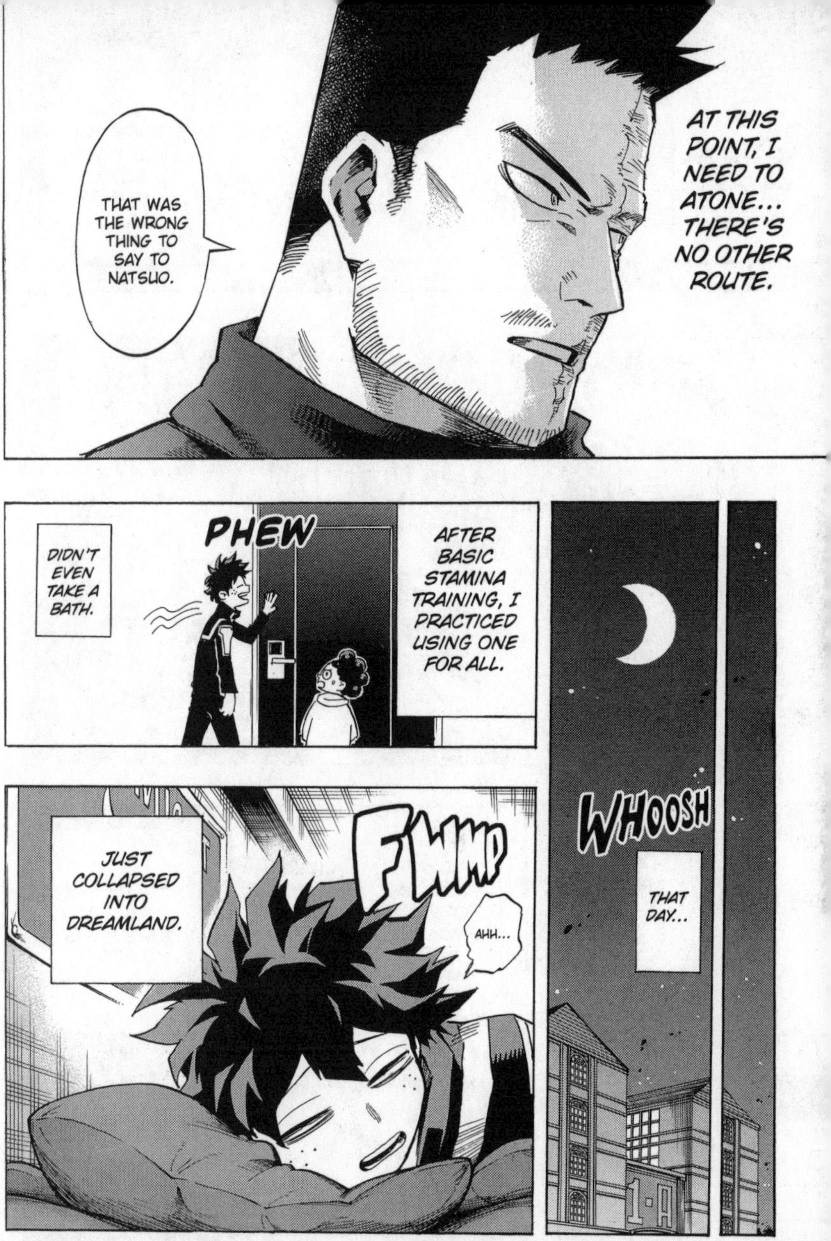
AT THIS POINT, I NEED TO ATONE... THERE'S NO OTHER ROUTE.
THAT WAS THE WRONG THING TO SAY TO NATSUO.
WHOOSH
THAT DAY...
AFTER BASIC STAMINA TRAINING, I PRACTICED USING ONE FOR ALL.
PHEW
DIDN'T EVEN TAKE A BATH.
FWMP
AHH...
JUST COLLAPSED INTO DREAMLAND.

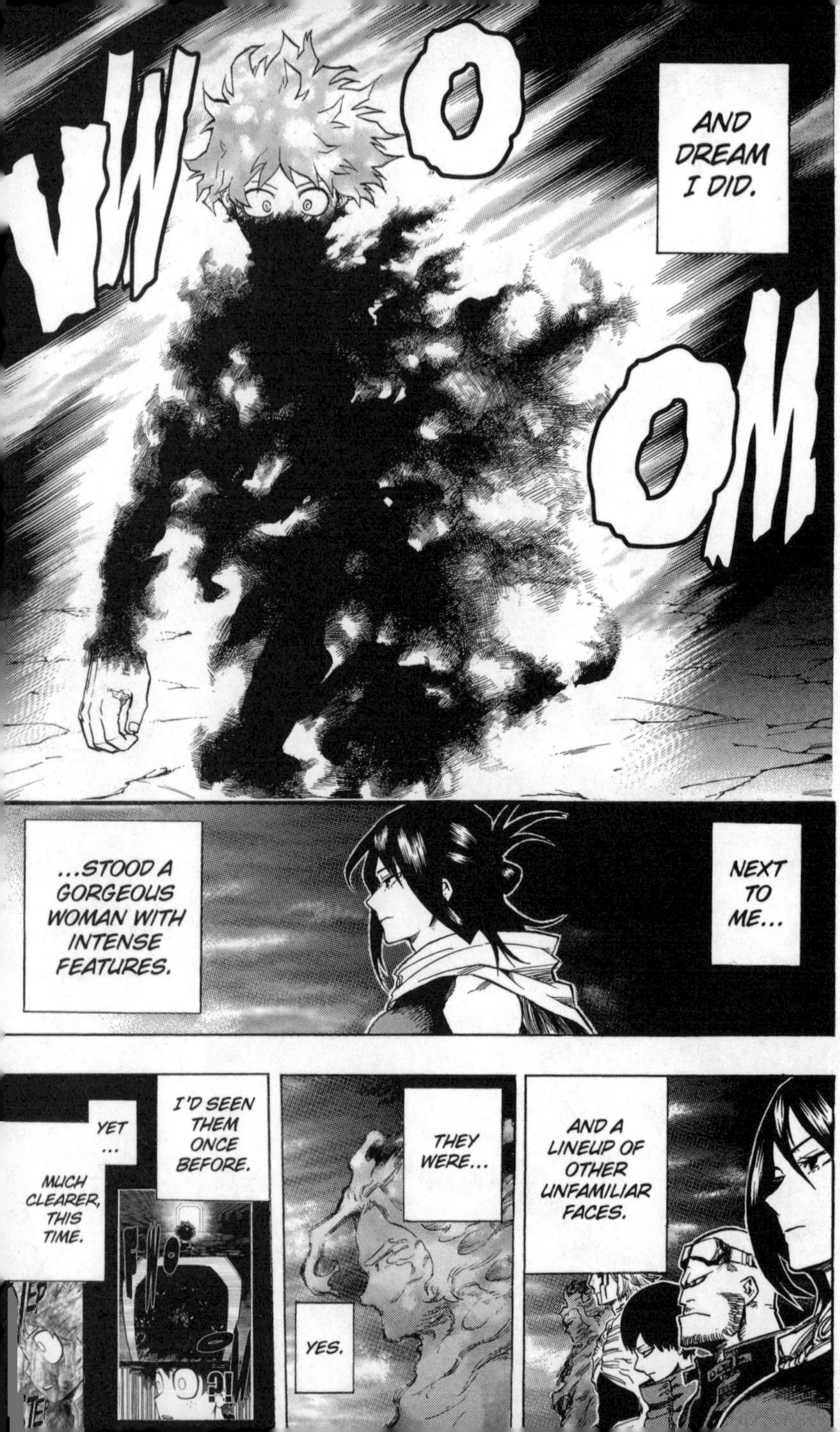
AND DREAM I DID.
VWOOM
NEXT TO ME...
...STOOD A GORGEOUS WOMAN WITH INTENSE FEATURES.
AND A LINEUP OF OTHER UNFAMILIAR FACES.
THEY WERE...
YES.
I'D SEEN THEM ONCE BEFORE.
YET...
MUCH CLEARER, THIS TIME.

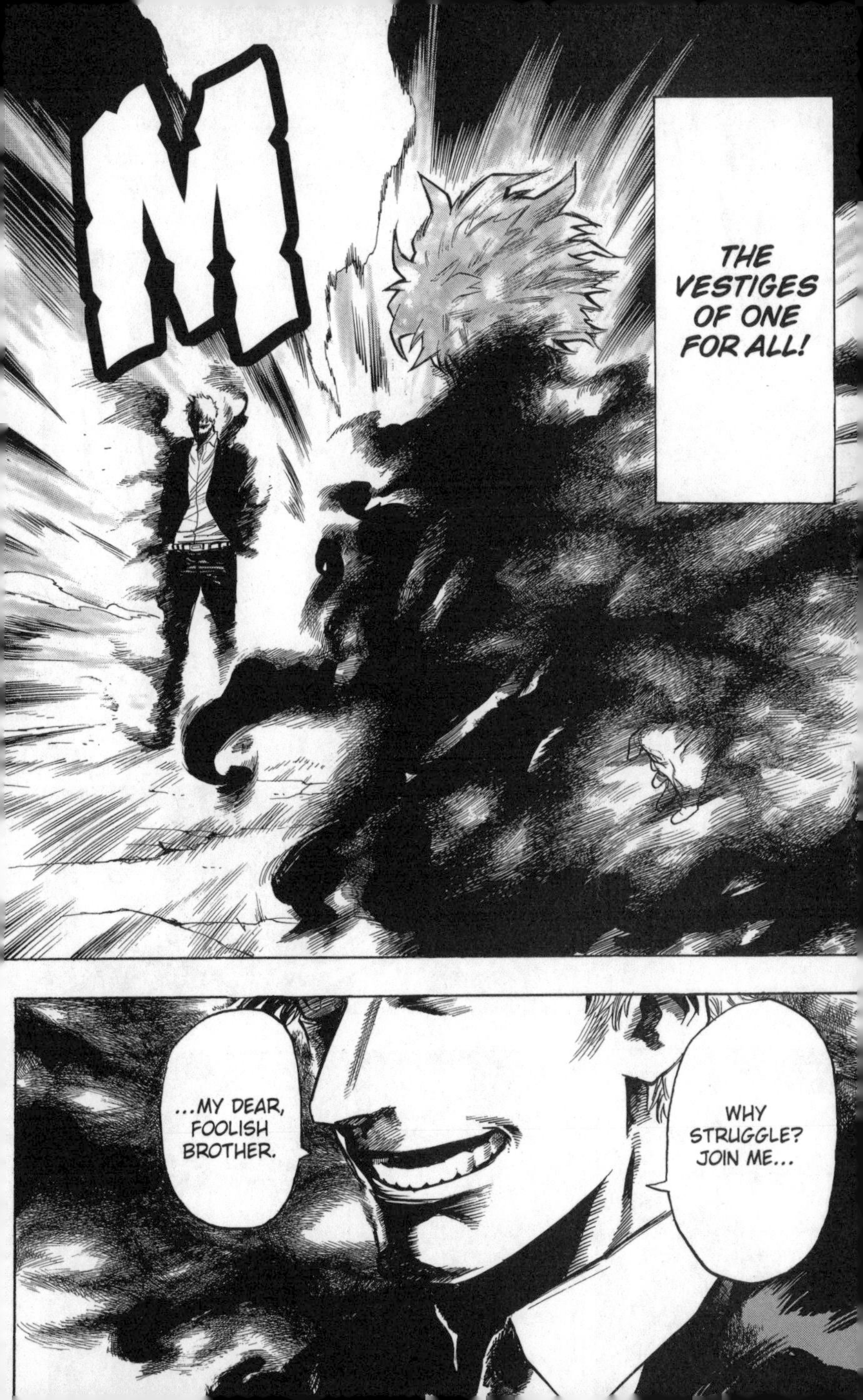
THE VESTIGES OF ONE FOR ALL!
M
WHY STRUGGLE? JOIN ME...
...MY DEAR, FOOLISH BROTHER.

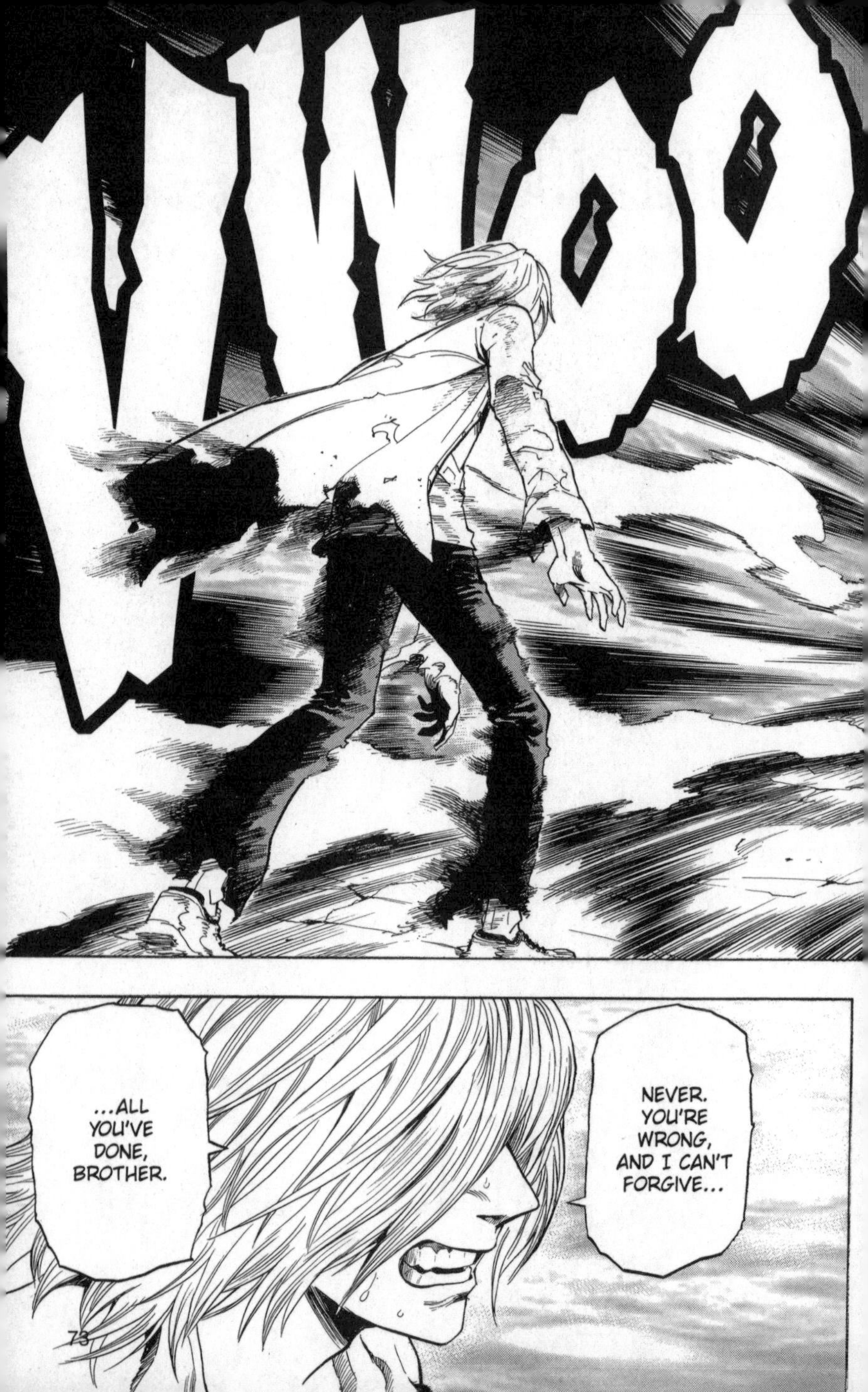
VWOO
NEVER. YOU'RE WRONG, AND I CAN'T FORGIVE...
...ALL YOU'VE DONE, BROTHER.

FUYUMI TODOROKI (22)

STREET CLOTHES

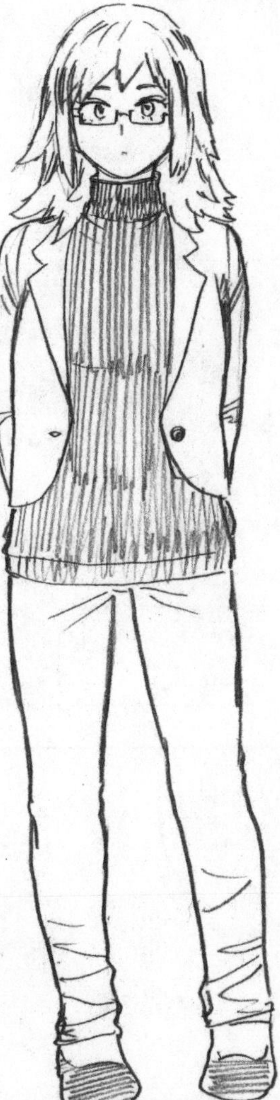

Birthday: 12/6
Height: 160 cm
Favorite Thing: Soap operas

THE SUPPLEMENT

She's never quite gotten over the fact that she couldn't do anything to help Shoto.

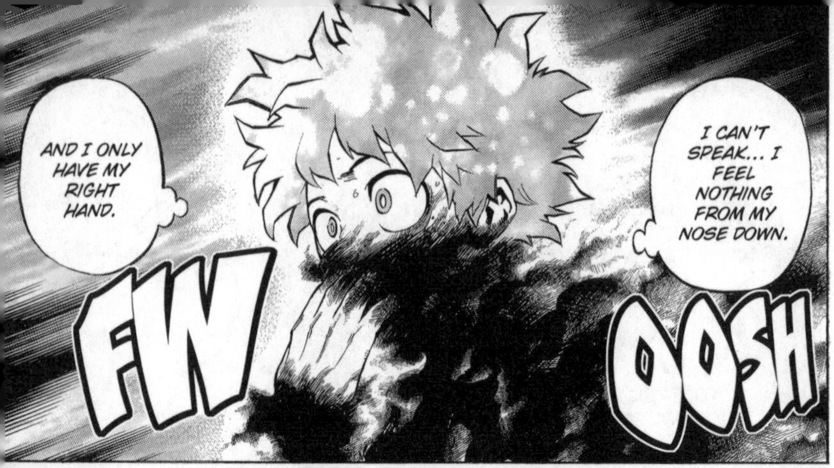
I CAN'T SPEAK... I FEEL NOTHING FROM MY NOSE DOWN.
AND I ONLY HAVE MY RIGHT HAND.
FWOOSH

NO. 193 - VESTIGES

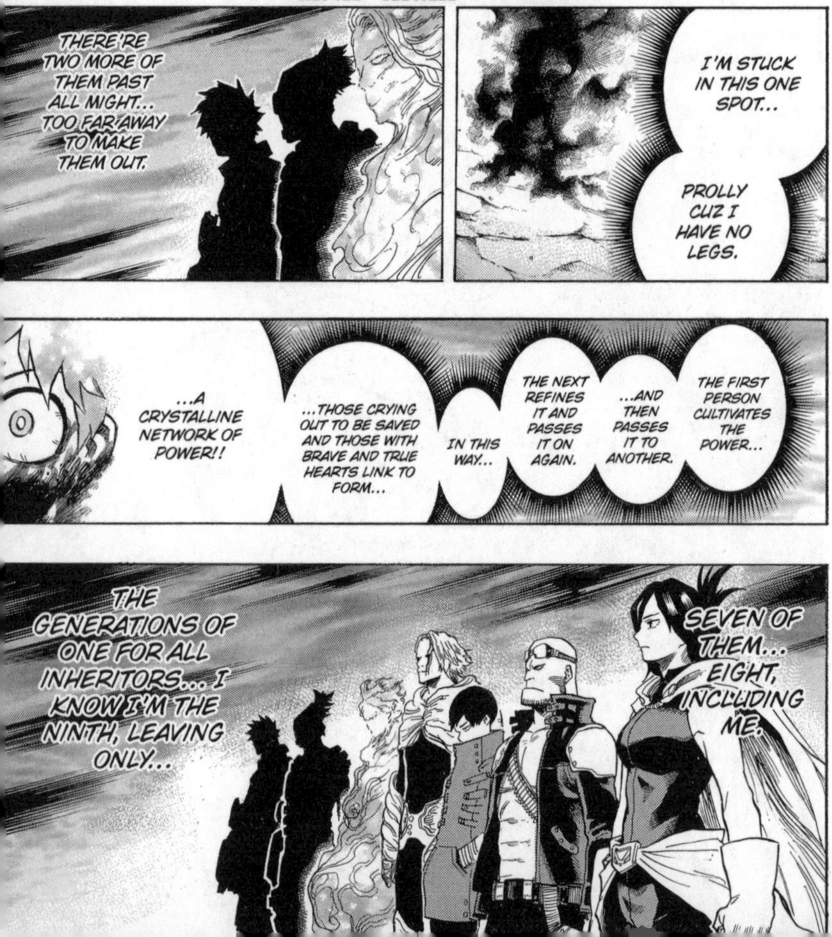
I'M STUCK IN THIS ONE SPOT...
PROLLY CUZ I HAVE NO LEGS.
THERE'RE TWO MORE OF THEM PAST ALL MIGHT... TOO FAR AWAY TO MAKE THEM OUT.
THE FIRST PERSON CULTIVATES THE POWER...
...AND THEN PASSES IT TO ANOTHER.
THE NEXT REFINES IT AND PASSES IT ON AGAIN.
IN THIS WAY...
...THOSE CRYING OUT TO BE SAVED AND THOSE WITH BRAVE AND TRUE HEARTS LINK TO FORM...
...A CRYSTALLINE NETWORK OF POWER!!
SEVEN OF THEM... EIGHT, INCLUDING ME.
THE GENERATIONS OF ONE FOR ALL INHERITORS... I KNOW I'M THE NINTH, LEAVING ONLY...

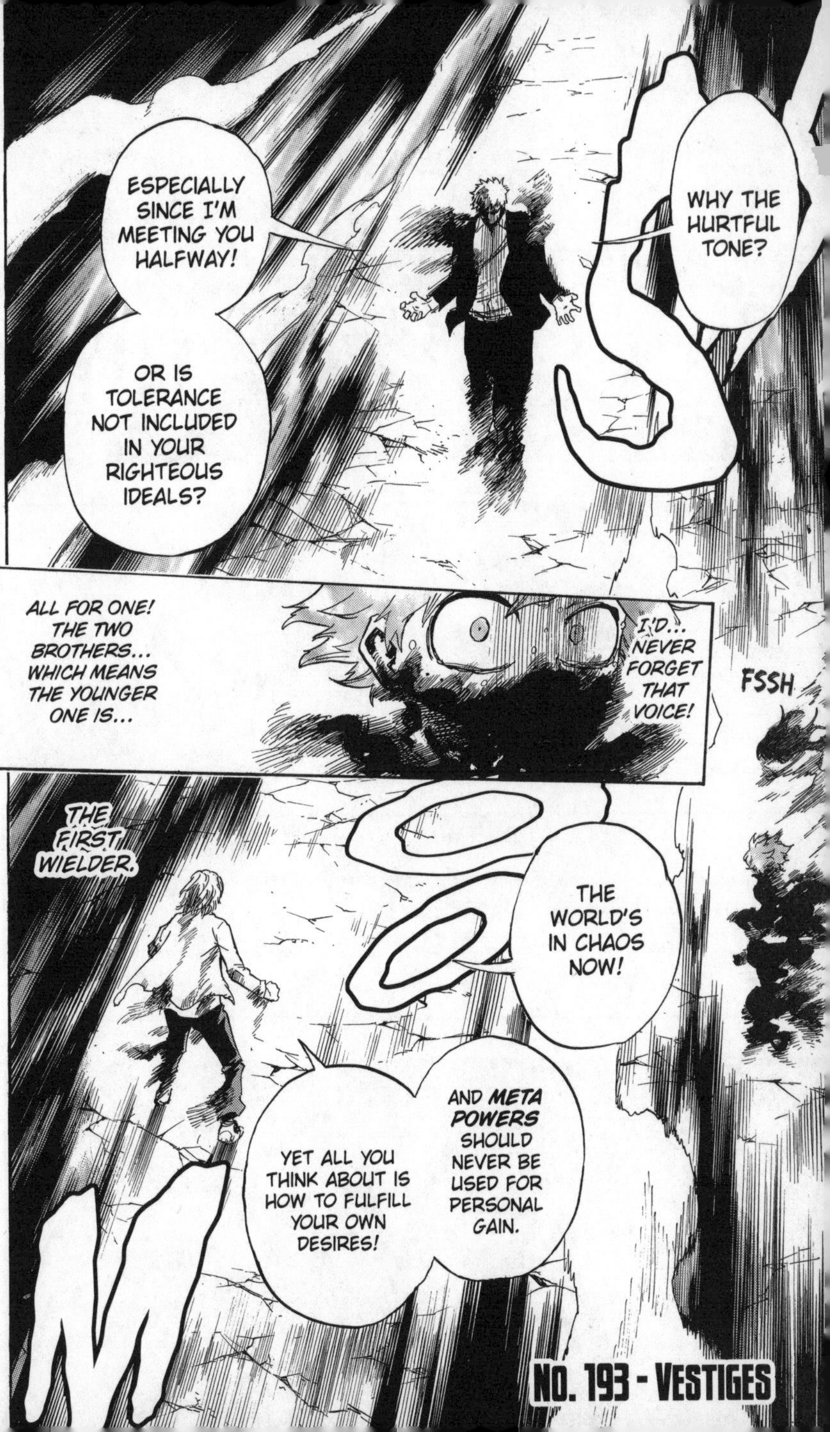
WHY THE HURTFUL TONE?
ESPECIALLY SINCE I'M MEETING YOU HALFWAY!
OR IS TOLERANCE NOT INCLUDED IN YOUR RIGHTEOUS IDEALS?
FSSH
I'D... NEVER FORGET THAT VOICE!
ALL FOR ONE! THE TWO BROTHERS... WHICH MEANS THE YOUNGER ONE IS...
THE WORLD'S IN CHAOS NOW!
AND **META POWERS** SHOULD NEVER BE USED FOR PERSONAL GAIN.
YET ALL YOU THINK ABOUT IS HOW TO FULFILL YOUR OWN DESIRES!
THE FIRST WIELDER.

NO. 193 - VESTIGES

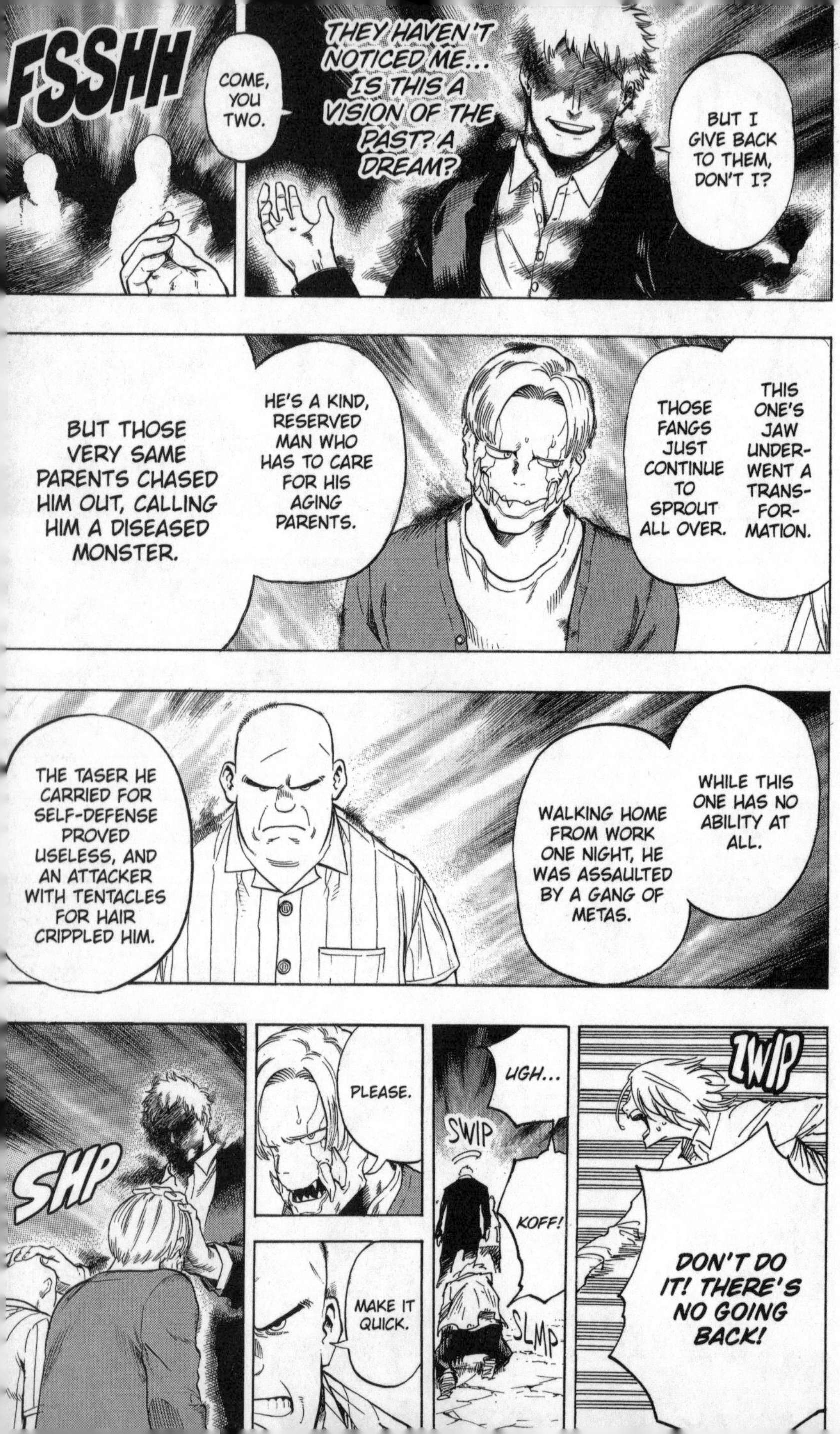
THEY HAVEN'T NOTICED ME... IS THIS A VISION OF THE PAST? A DREAM?
BUT I GIVE BACK TO THEM, DON'T I?
FSSHH
COME, YOU TWO.
THIS ONE'S JAW UNDERWENT A TRANSFORMATION.
THOSE FANGS JUST CONTINUE TO SPROUT ALL OVER.
HE'S A KIND, RESERVED MAN WHO HAS TO CARE FOR HIS AGING PARENTS.
BUT THOSE VERY SAME PARENTS CHASED HIM OUT, CALLING HIM A DISEASED MONSTER.
WHILE THIS ONE HAS NO ABILITY AT ALL.
WALKING HOME FROM WORK ONE NIGHT, HE WAS ASSAULTED BY A GANG OF METAS.
THE TASER HE CARRIED FOR SELF-DEFENSE PROVED USELESS, AND AN ATTACKER WITH TENTACLES FOR HAIR CRIPPLED HIM.
ZWIP
DON'T DO IT! THERE'S NO GOING BACK!
UGH...
SWIP
KOFF!
SLMP
PLEASE.
MAKE IT QUICK.
SHP

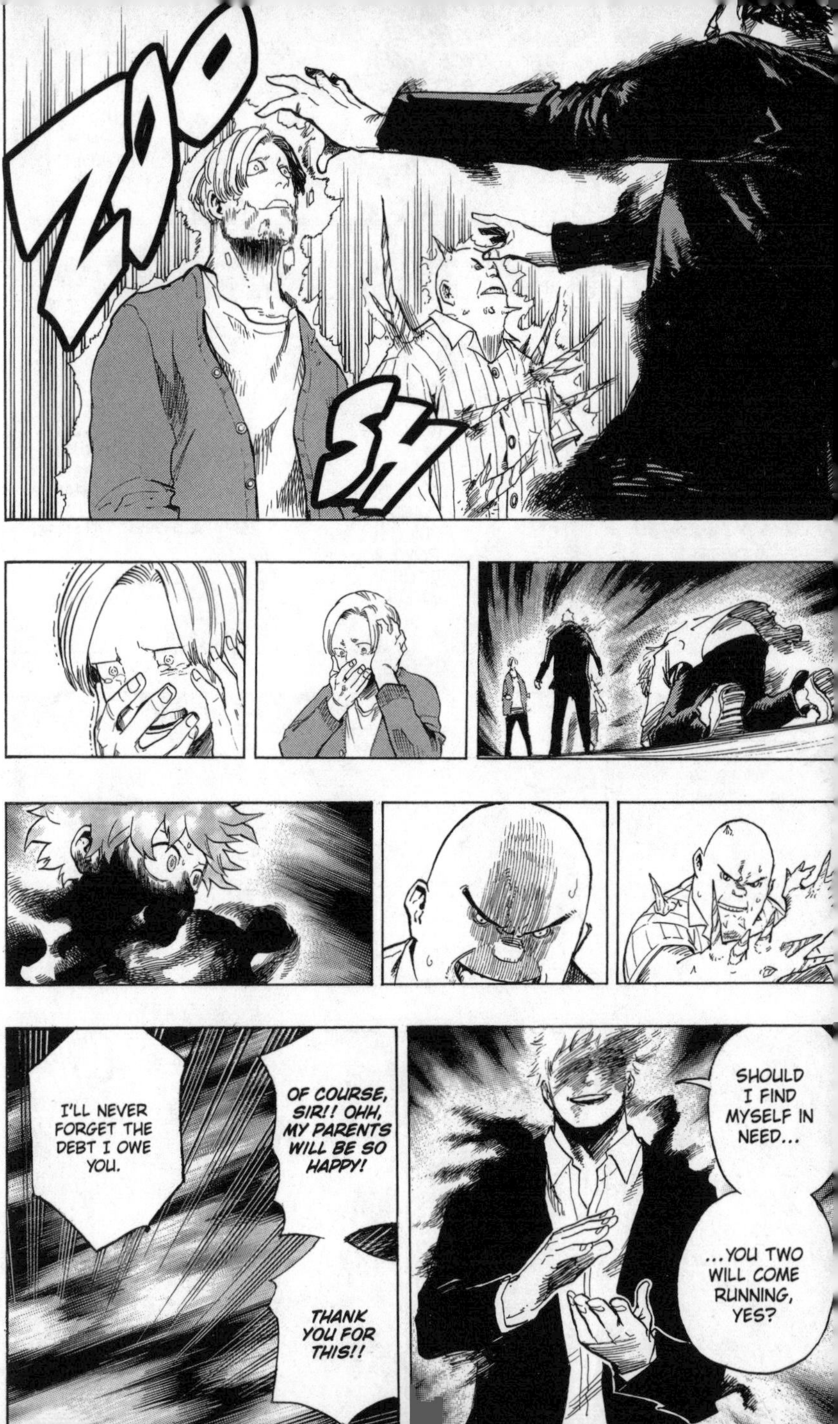
ZOO
SH
SHOULD I FIND MYSELF IN NEED...
...YOU TWO WILL COME RUNNING, YES?
OF COURSE, SIR!! OHH, MY PARENTS WILL BE SO HAPPY!
I'LL NEVER FORGET THE DEBT I OWE YOU.
THANK YOU FOR THIS!!

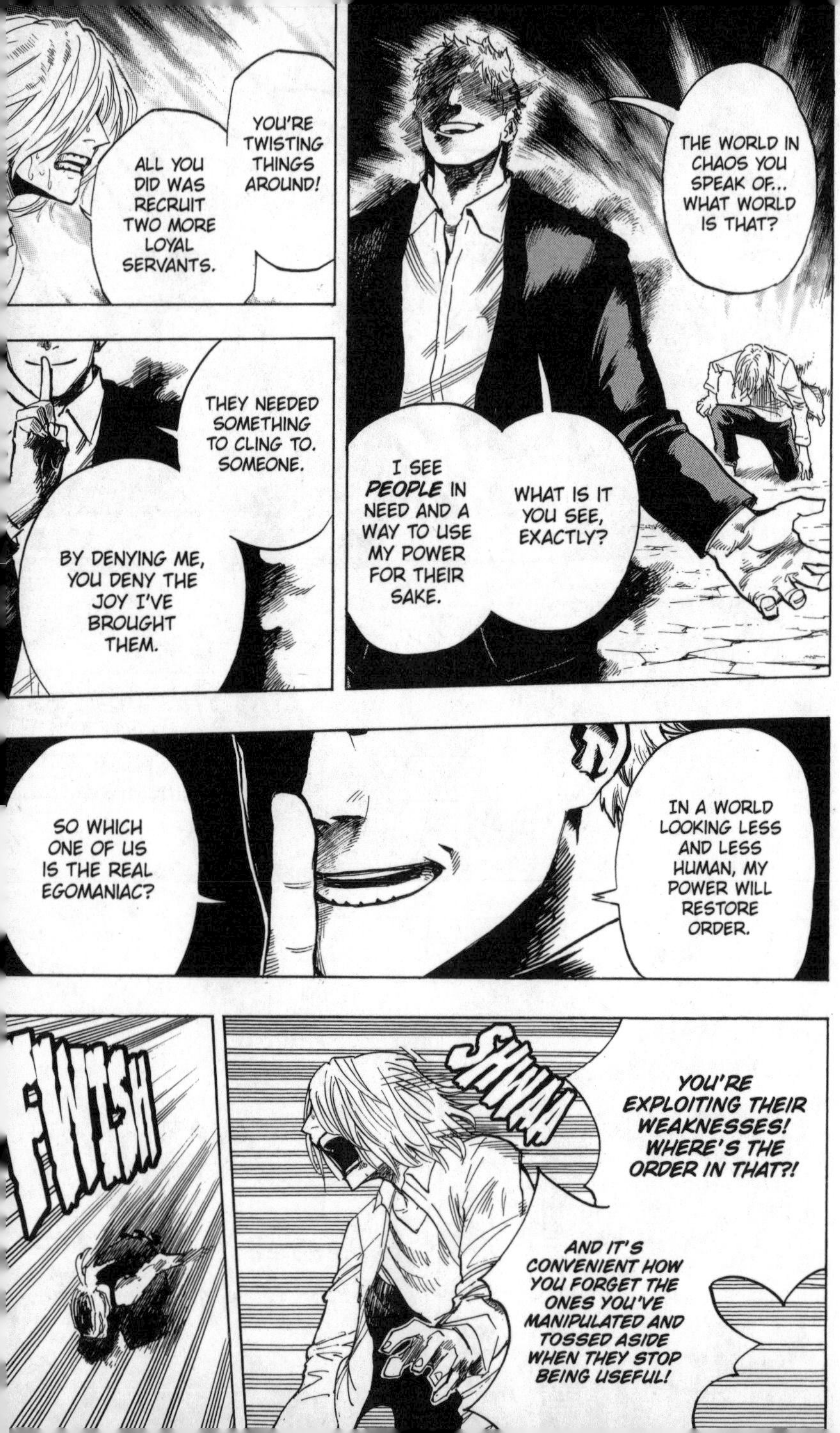
THE WORLD IN CHAOS YOU SPEAK OF... WHAT WORLD IS THAT?
WHAT IS IT YOU SEE, EXACTLY?
I SEE *PEOPLE* IN NEED AND A WAY TO USE MY POWER FOR THEIR SAKE.
YOU'RE TWISTING THINGS AROUND!
ALL YOU DID WAS RECRUIT TWO MORE LOYAL SERVANTS.
THEY NEEDED SOMETHING TO CLING TO. SOMEONE.
BY DENYING ME, YOU DENY THE JOY I'VE BROUGHT THEM.
IN A WORLD LOOKING LESS AND LESS HUMAN, MY POWER WILL RESTORE ORDER.
SO WHICH ONE OF US IS THE REAL EGOMANIAC?
SHWAA
YOU'RE EXPLOITING THEIR WEAKNESSES! WHERE'S THE ORDER IN THAT?!
AND IT'S CONVENIENT HOW YOU FORGET THE ONES YOU'VE MANIPULATED AND TOSSED ASIDE WHEN THEY STOP BEING USEFUL!
FWTSH

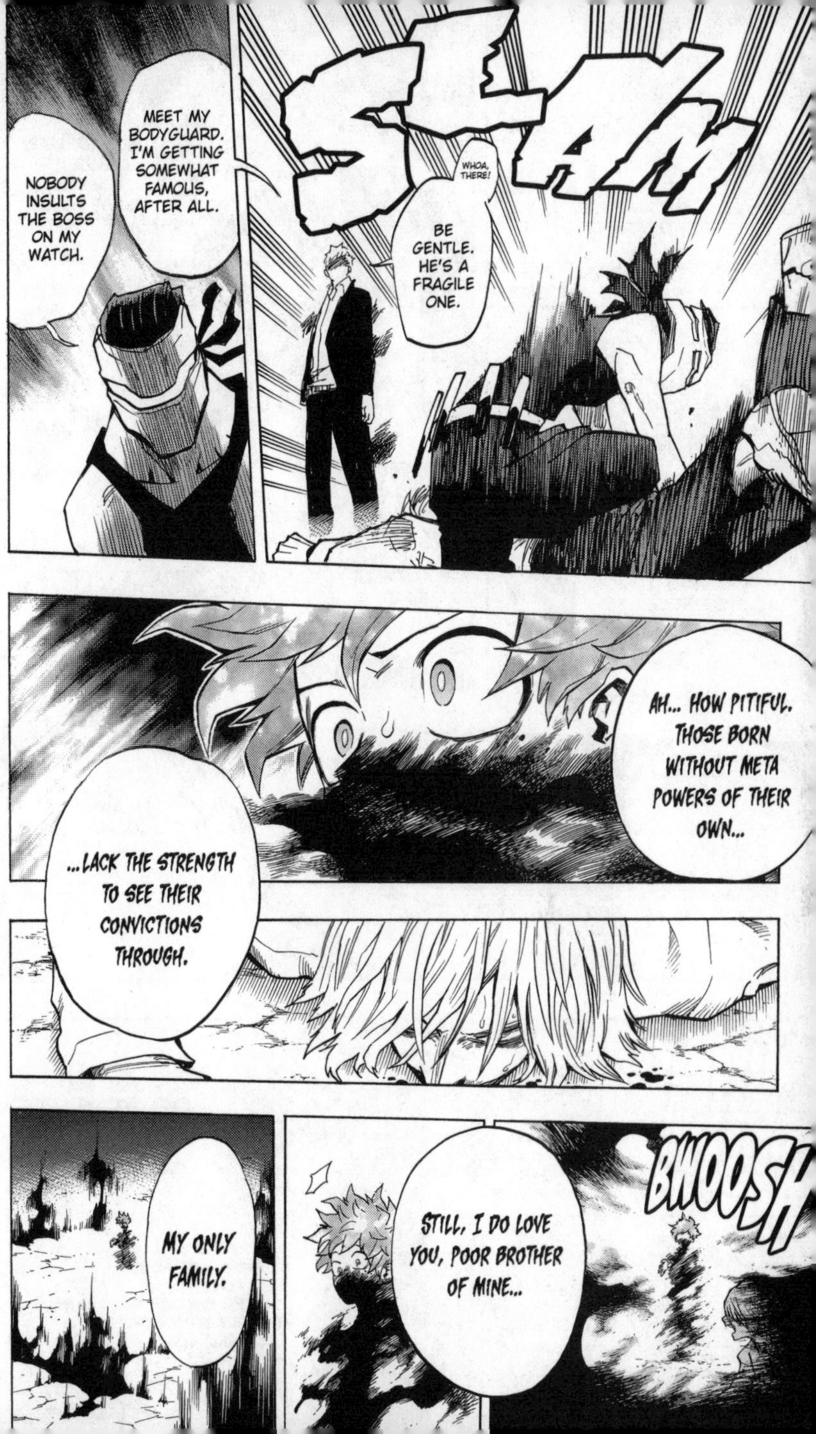
SLAM
WHOA, THERE!
BE GENTLE. HE'S A FRAGILE ONE.
MEET MY BODYGUARD. I'M GETTING SOMEWHAT FAMOUS, AFTER ALL.
NOBODY INSULTS THE BOSS ON MY WATCH.
AH... HOW PITIFUL. THOSE BORN WITHOUT META POWERS OF THEIR OWN...
...LACK THE STRENGTH TO SEE THEIR CONVICTIONS THROUGH.
BWOOSH
STILL, I DO LOVE YOU, POOR BROTHER OF MINE...
MY ONLY FAMILY.

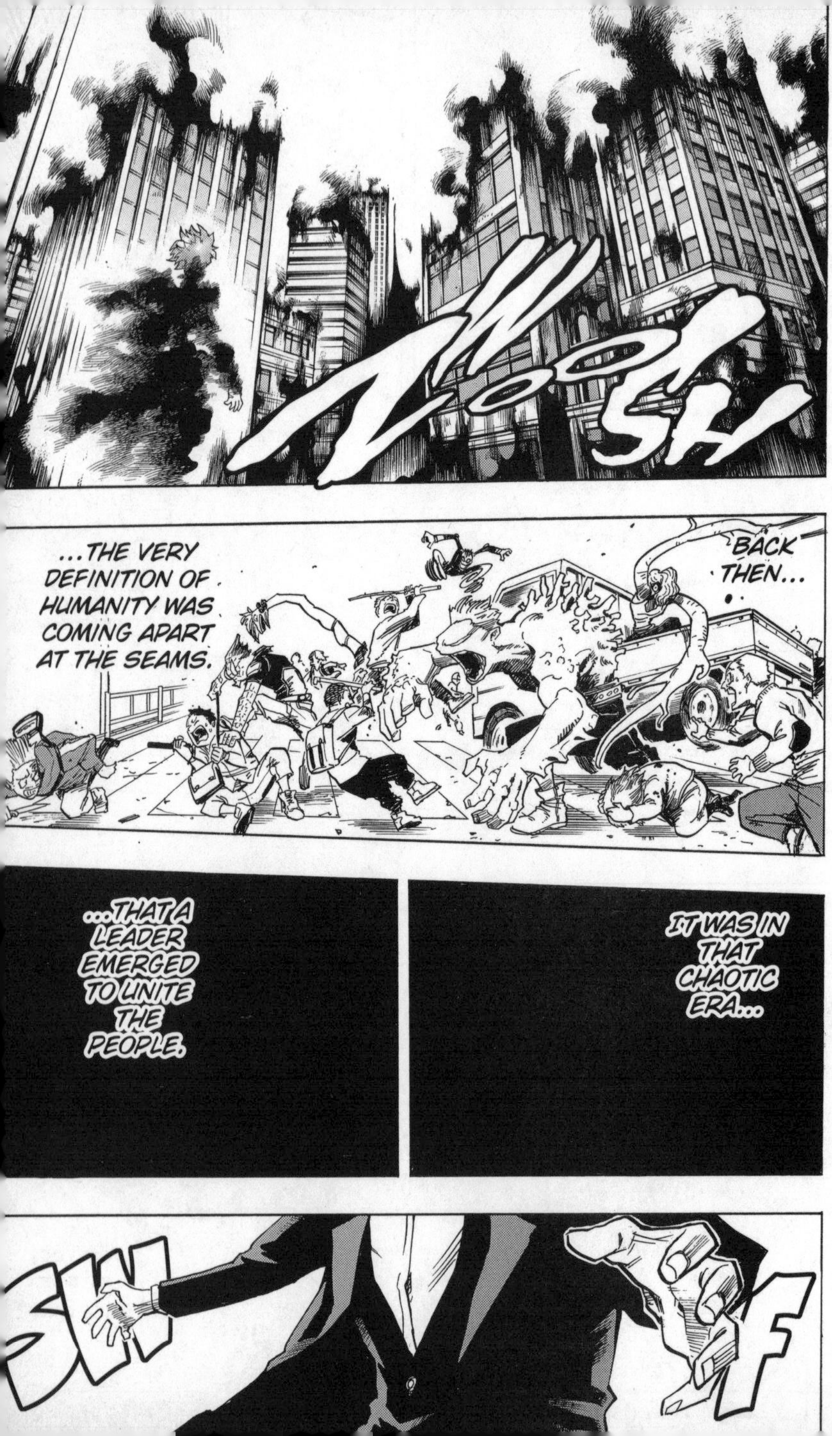
WHOOSH
BACK THEN...
...THE VERY DEFINITION OF HUMANITY WAS COMING APART AT THE SEAMS.
IT WAS IN THAT CHAOTIC ERA...
...THAT A LEADER EMERGED TO UNITE THE PEOPLE.
SHF

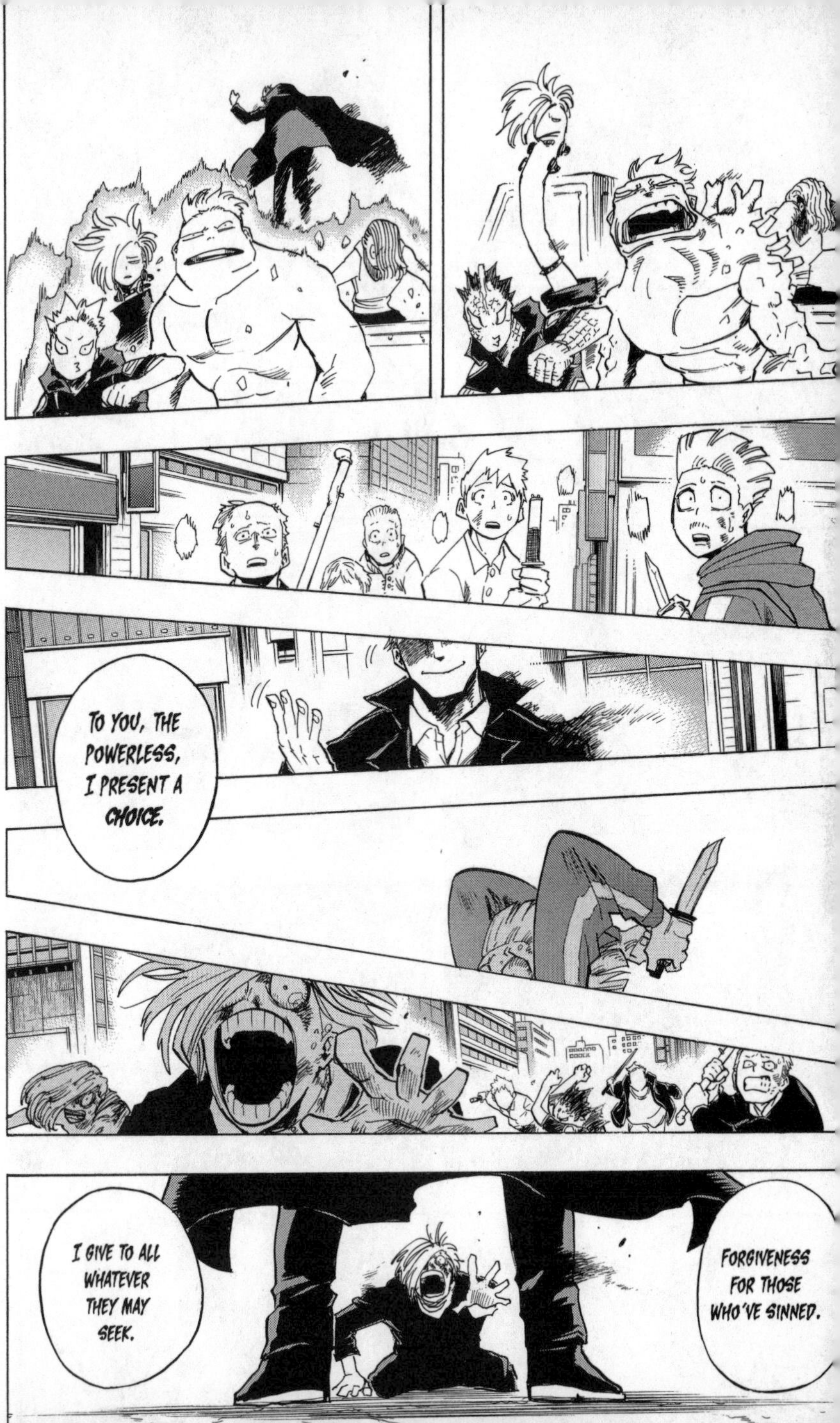
TO YOU, THE POWERLESS, I PRESENT A CHOICE.
FORGIVENESS FOR THOSE WHO'VE SINNED.
I GIVE TO ALL WHATEVER THEY MAY SEEK.

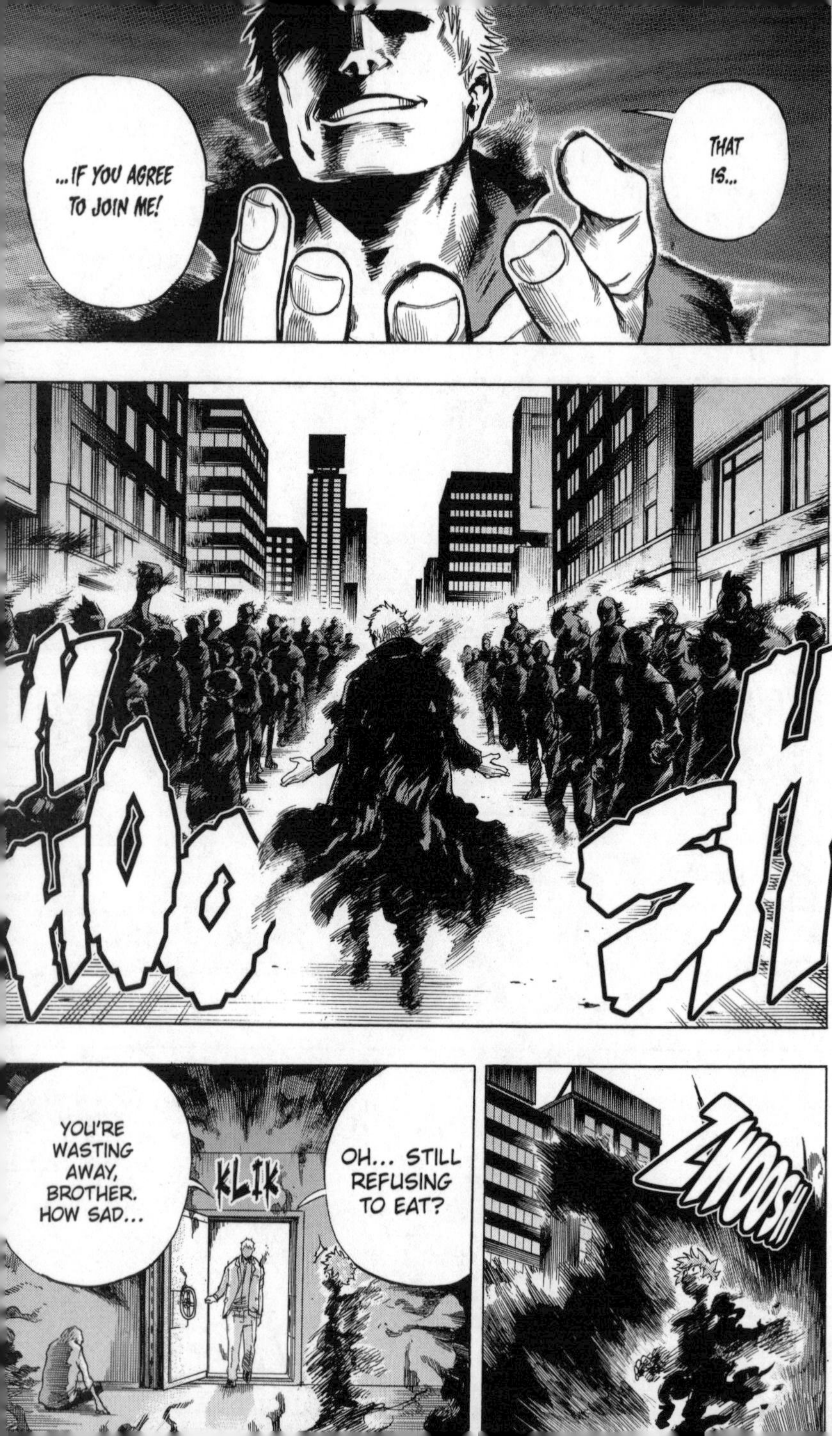
THAT IS...
...IF YOU AGREE TO JOIN ME!
WHOOSH
ZWOOSH
OH... STILL REFUSING TO EAT?
KLIK
YOU'RE WASTING AWAY, BROTHER. HOW SAD...

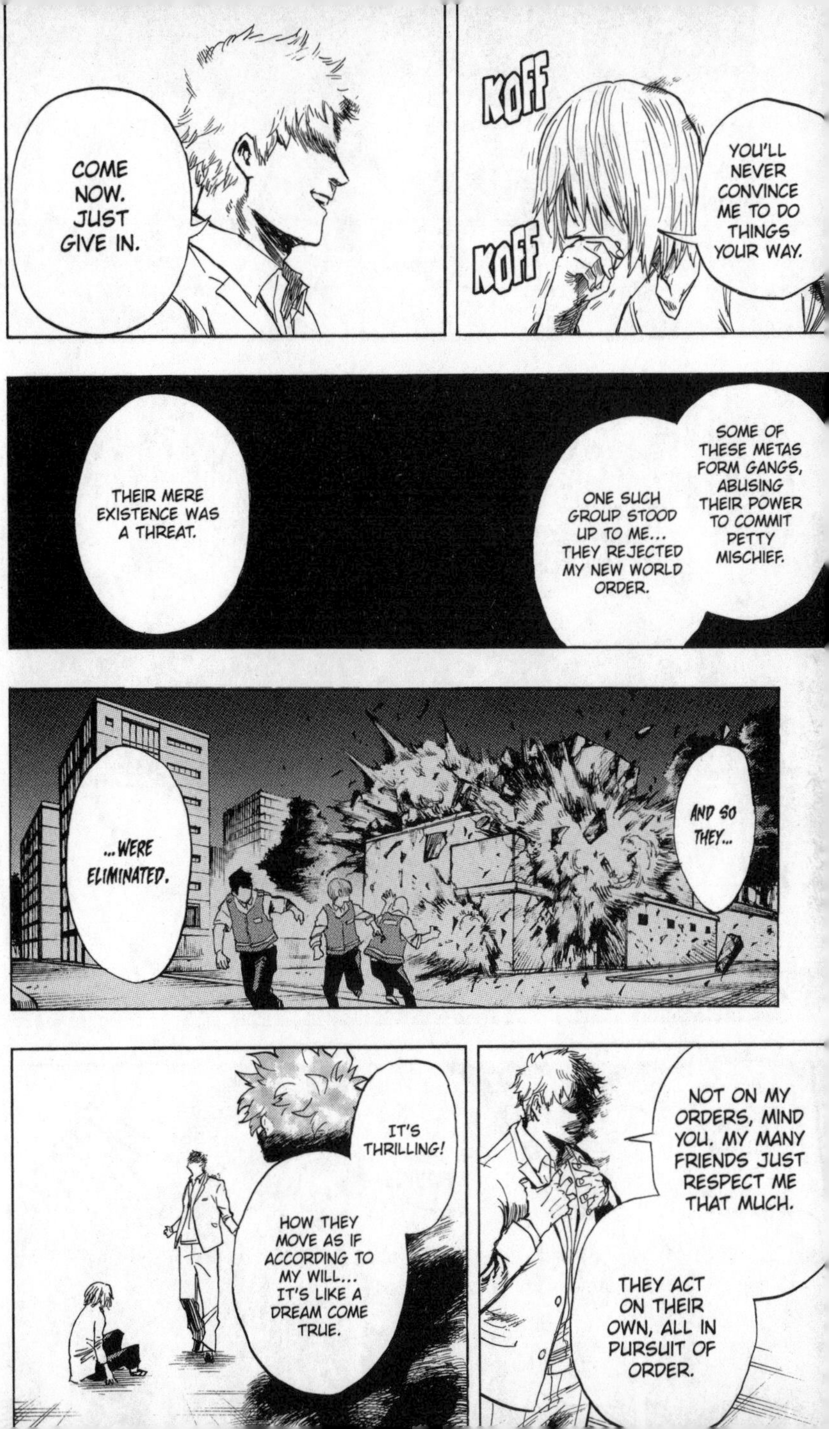
YOU'LL NEVER CONVINCE ME TO DO THINGS YOUR WAY.
KOFF
KOFF
COME NOW. JUST GIVE IN.
SOME OF THESE METAS FORM GANGS, ABUSING THEIR POWER TO COMMIT PETTY MISCHIEF.
ONE SUCH GROUP STOOD UP TO ME... THEY REJECTED MY NEW WORLD ORDER.
THEIR MERE EXISTENCE WAS A THREAT.
AND SO THEY...
...WERE ELIMINATED.
NOT ON MY ORDERS, MIND YOU. MY MANY FRIENDS JUST RESPECT ME THAT MUCH.
THEY ACT ON THEIR OWN, ALL IN PURSUIT OF ORDER.
IT'S THRILLING!
HOW THEY MOVE AS IF ACCORDING TO MY WILL... IT'S LIKE A DREAM COME TRUE.

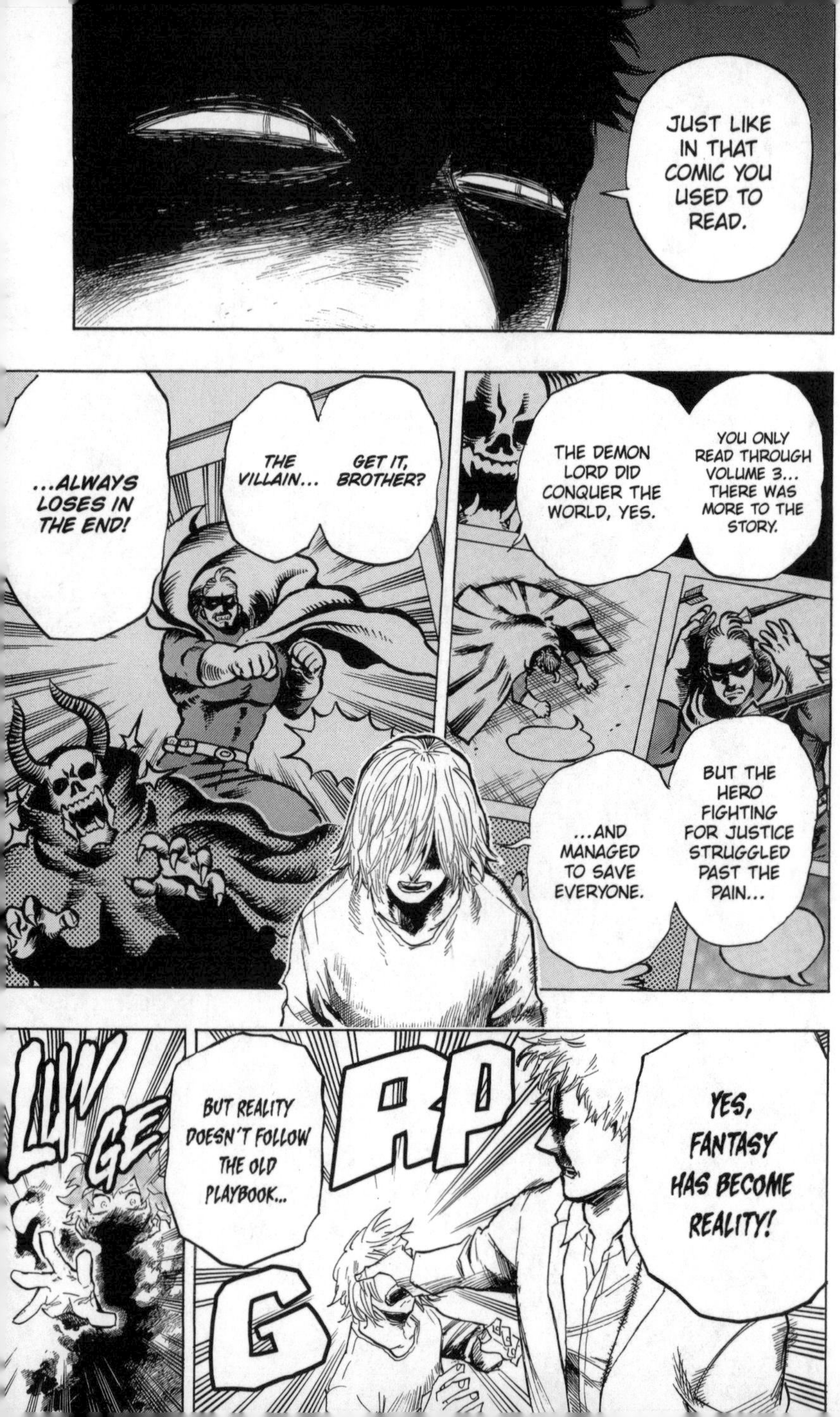
JUST LIKE IN THAT COMIC YOU USED TO READ.
YOU ONLY READ THROUGH VOLUME 3... THERE WAS MORE TO THE STORY.
THE DEMON LORD DID CONQUER THE WORLD, YES.
BUT THE HERO FIGHTING FOR JUSTICE STRUGGLED PAST THE PAIN...
...AND MANAGED TO SAVE EVERYONE.
GET IT, BROTHER?
THE VILLAIN...
...ALWAYS LOSES IN THE END!
YES, FANTASY HAS BECOME REALITY!
RP
G
BUT REALITY DOESN'T FOLLOW THE OLD PLAYBOOK...
LUNGE

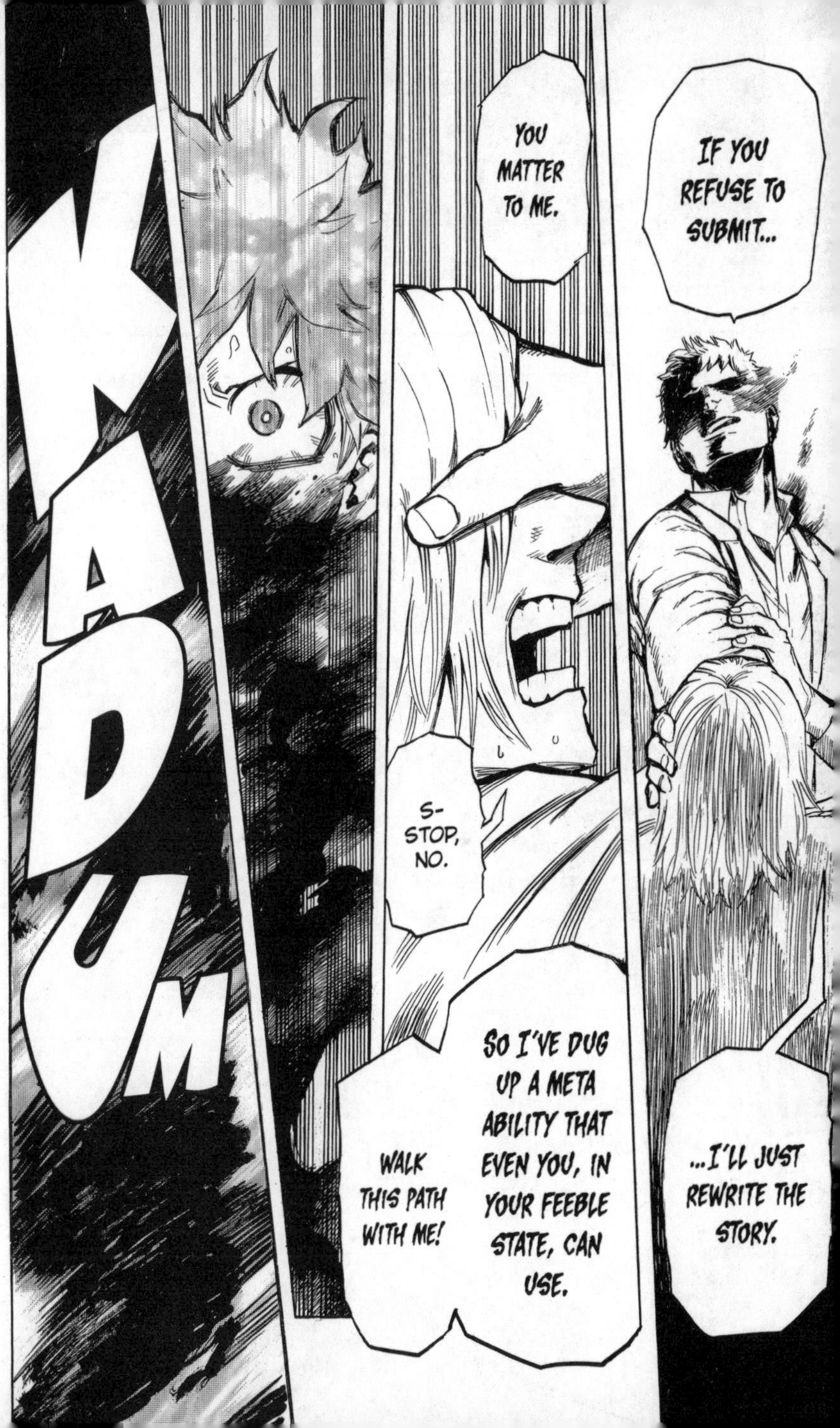
IF YOU REFUSE TO SUBMIT...
...I'LL JUST REWRITE THE STORY.
YOU MATTER TO ME.
S-STOP, NO.
SO I'VE DUG UP A META ABILITY THAT EVEN YOU, IN YOUR FEEBLE STATE, CAN USE.
WALK THIS PATH WITH ME!
KADUMM

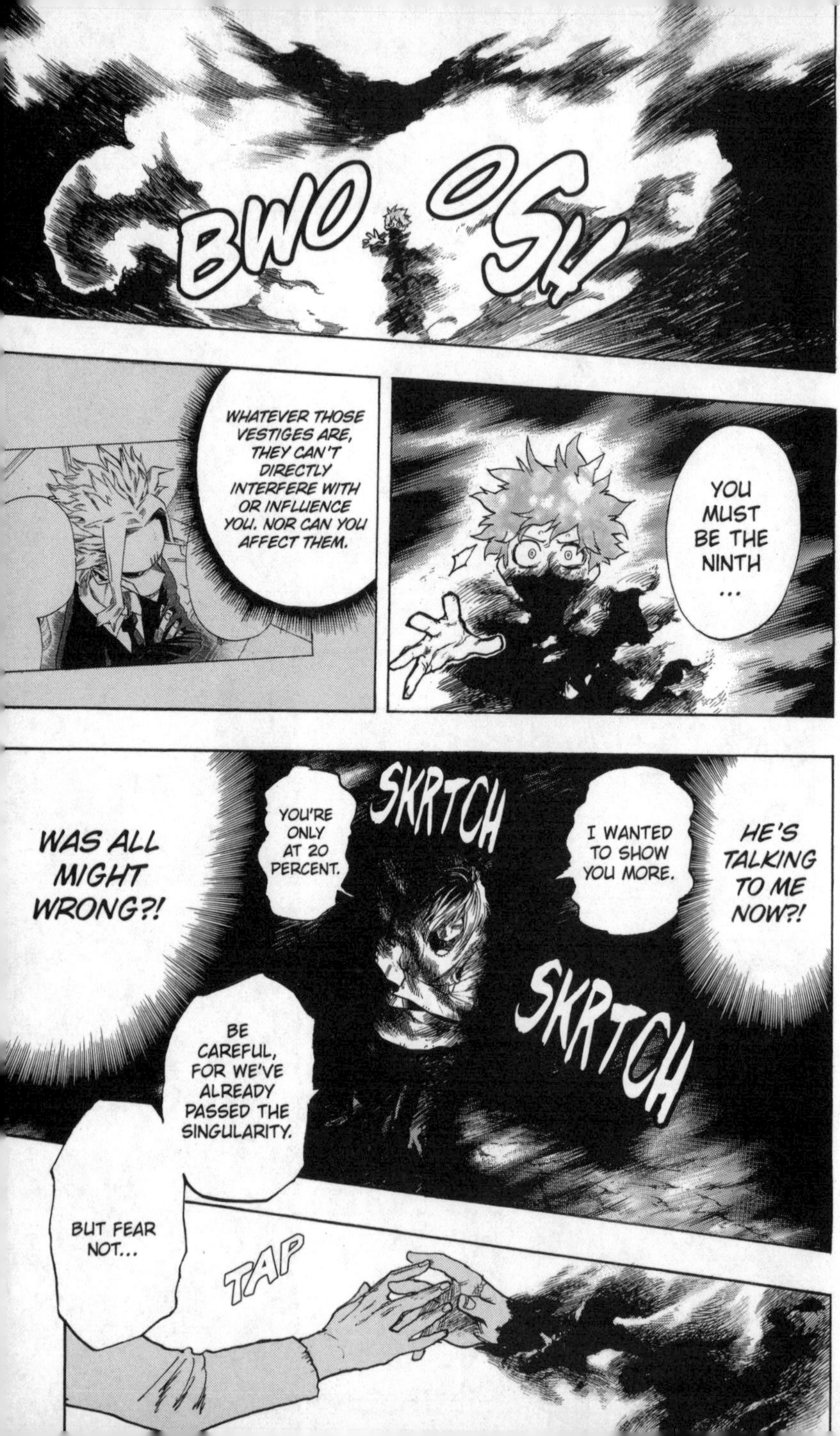
BWOOSH
YOU MUST BE THE NINTH ...
WHATEVER THOSE VESTIGES ARE, THEY CAN'T DIRECTLY INTERFERE WITH OR INFLUENCE YOU. NOR CAN YOU AFFECT THEM.
HE'S TALKING TO ME NOW?!
I WANTED TO SHOW YOU MORE.
SKRTCH
YOU'RE ONLY AT 20 PERCENT.
WAS ALL MIGHT WRONG?!
SKRTCH
BE CAREFUL, FOR WE'VE ALREADY PASSED THE SINGULARITY.
BUT FEAR NOT...
TAP

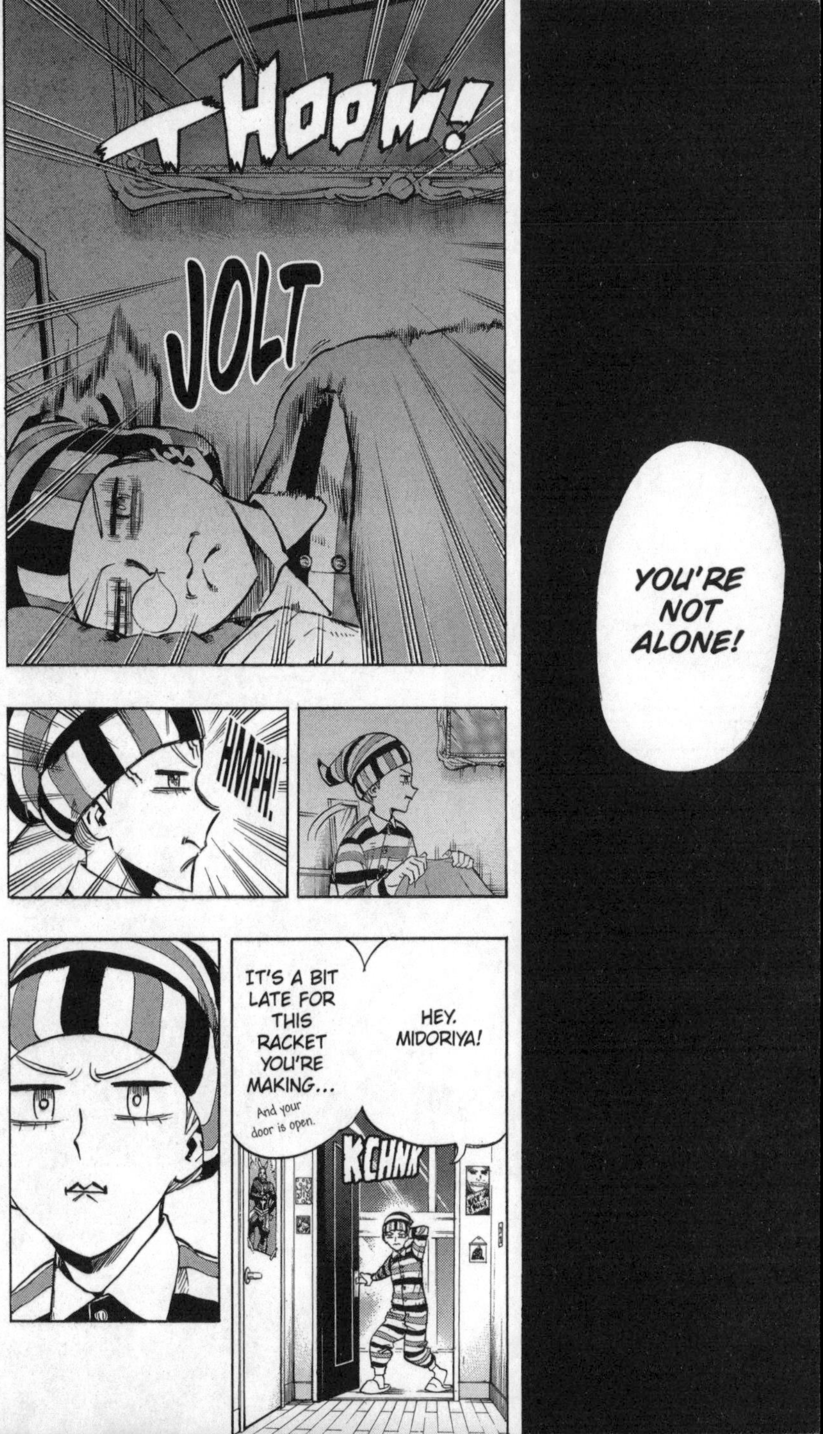
YOU'RE NOT ALONE!
THOOM!
JOLT
HMPH!
HEY. MIDORIYA!
IT'S A BIT LATE FOR THIS RACKET YOU'RE MAKING...
And your door is open.
KCHNK

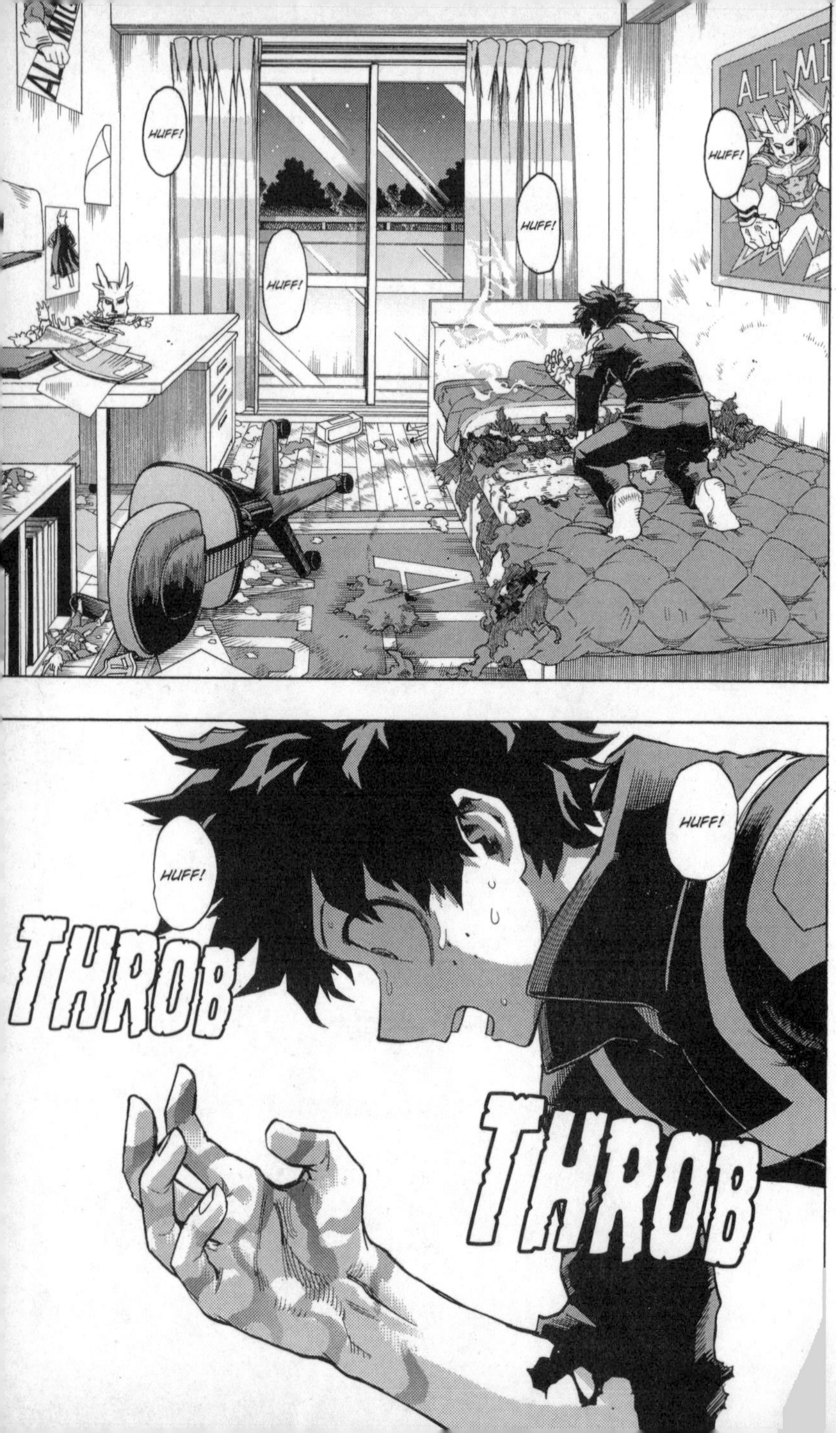
HUFF!
HUFF!
HUFF!
HUFF!
HUFF!
HUFF!
THROB
THROB

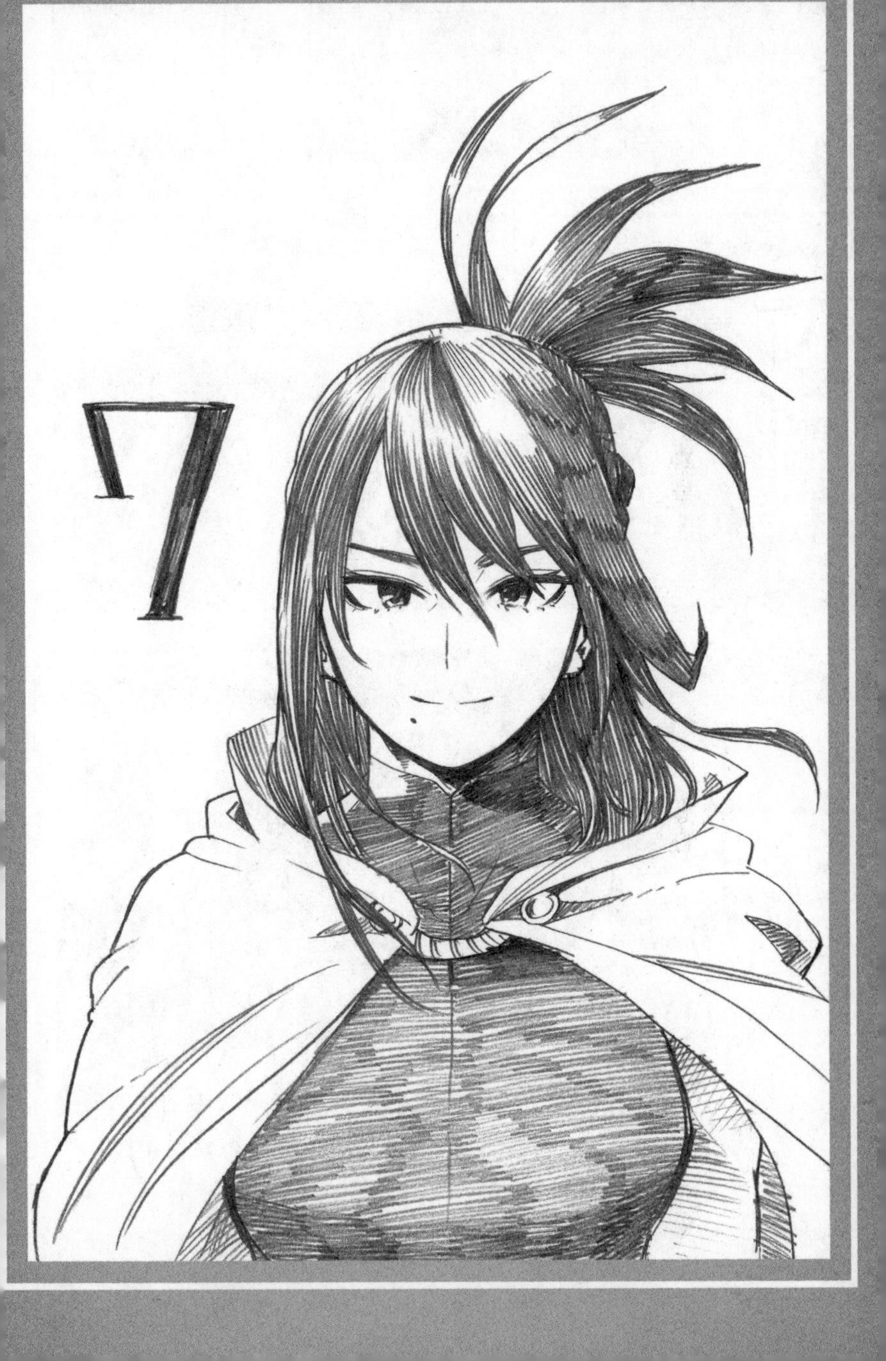
7

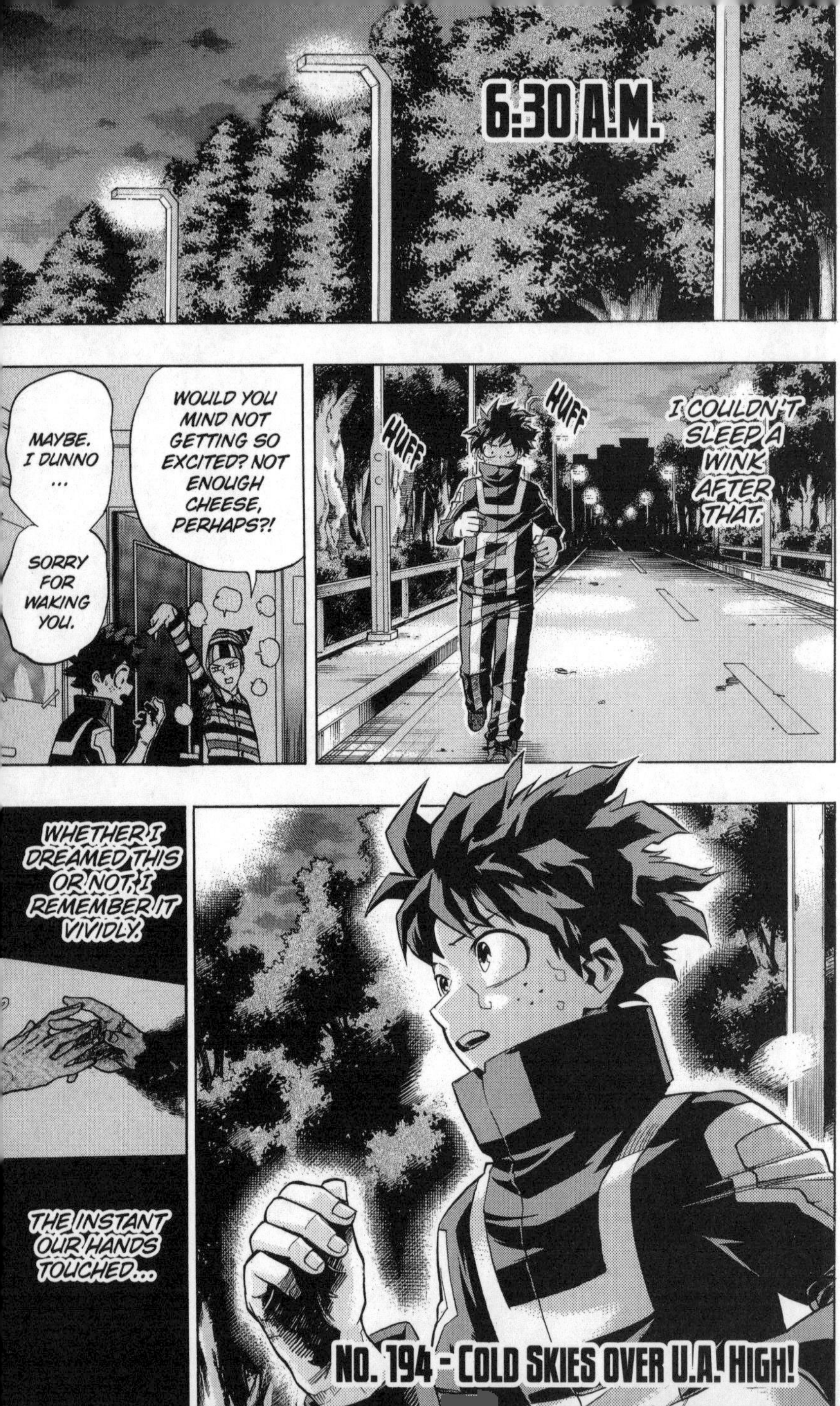
6:30 A.M.
HUFF
HUFF
I COULDN'T SLEEP A WINK AFTER THAT.
WOULD YOU MIND NOT GETTING SO EXCITED? NOT ENOUGH CHEESE, PERHAPS?!
MAYBE. I DUNNO ...
SORRY FOR WAKING YOU.
NO. 194 - COLD SKIES OVER U.A. HIGH!
WHETHER I DREAMED THIS OR NOT, I REMEMBER IT VIVIDLY.
THE INSTANT OUR HANDS TOUCHED...

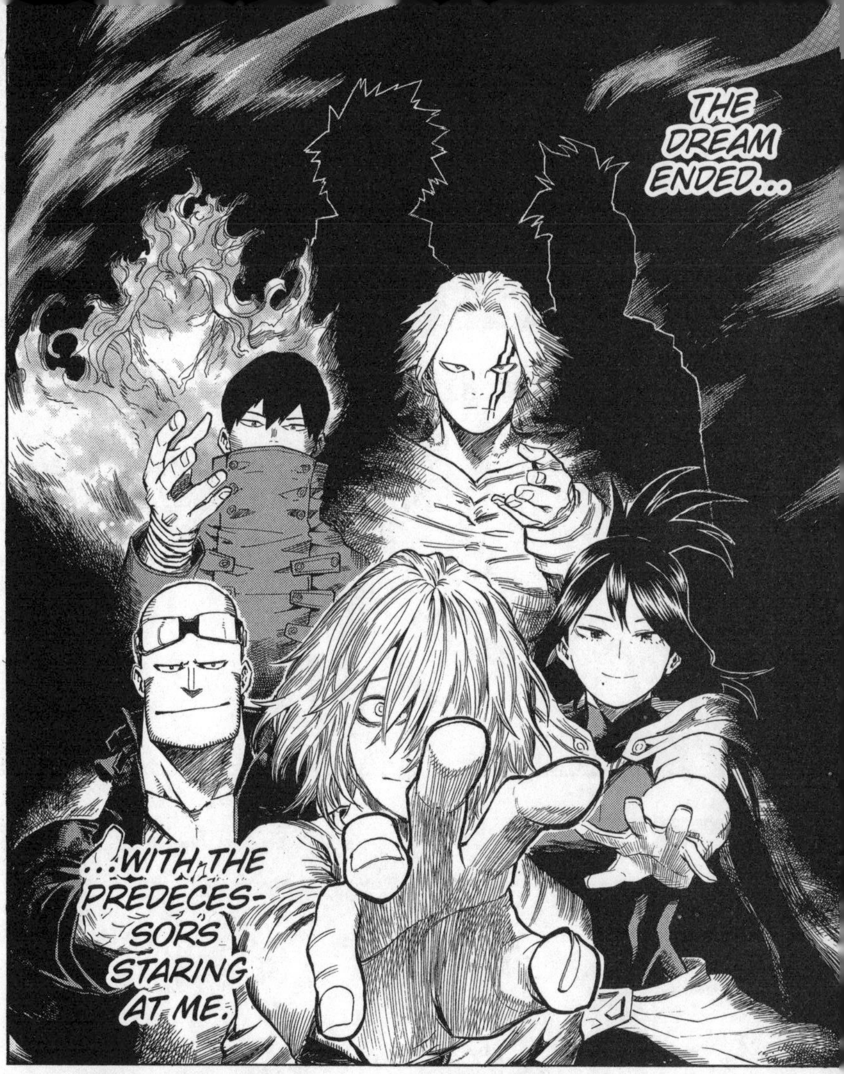
THE DREAM ENDED...
...WITH THE PREDECES-SORS STARING AT ME.
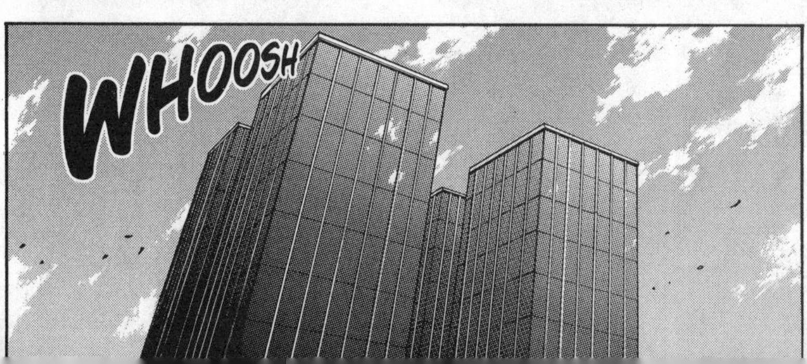
WHOOSH

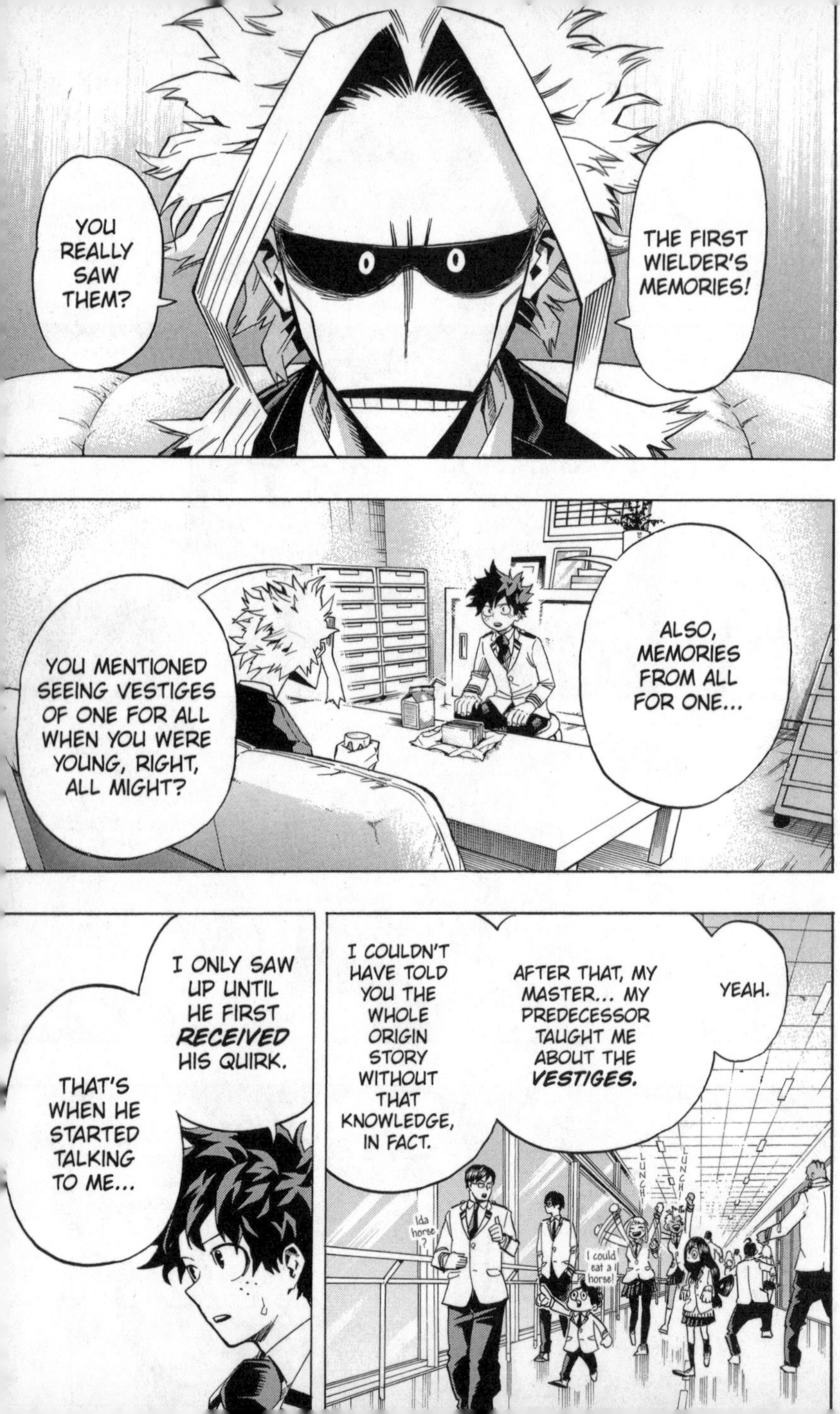
THE FIRST WIELDER'S MEMORIES!
YOU REALLY SAW THEM?
ALSO, MEMORIES FROM ALL FOR ONE...
YOU MENTIONED SEEING VESTIGES OF ONE FOR ALL WHEN YOU WERE YOUNG, RIGHT, ALL MIGHT?
YEAH.
AFTER THAT, MY MASTER... MY PREDECESSOR TAUGHT ME ABOUT THE ***VESTIGES.***
I COULDN'T HAVE TOLD YOU THE WHOLE ORIGIN STORY WITHOUT THAT KNOWLEDGE, IN FACT.
LUNCH!
LUNCH!
Ida horse?
I could eat a horse!
I ONLY SAW UP UNTIL HE FIRST ***RECEIVED*** HIS QUIRK.
THAT'S WHEN HE STARTED TALKING TO ME...

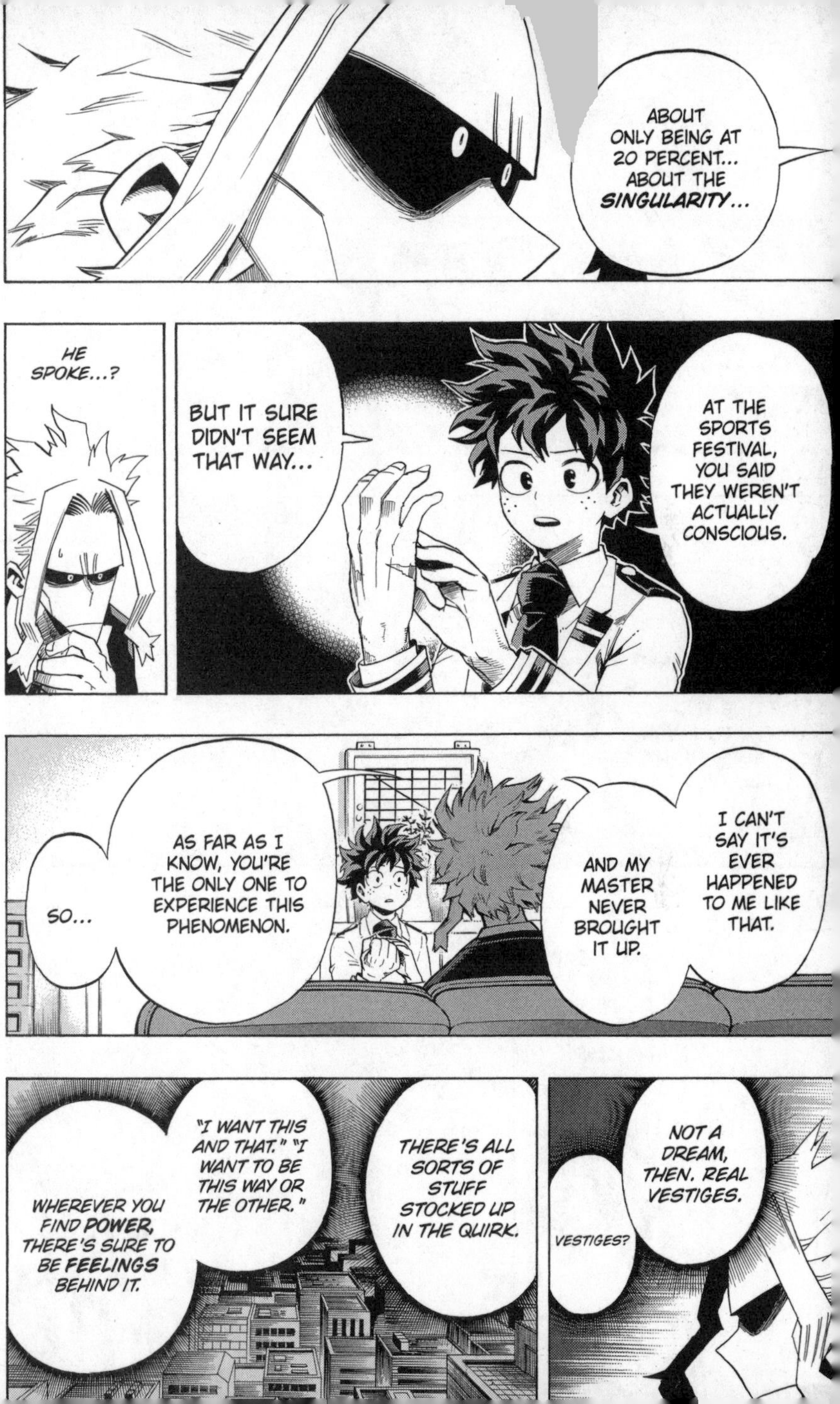
ABOUT ONLY BEING AT 20 PERCENT... ABOUT THE SINGULARITY...
AT THE SPORTS FESTIVAL, YOU SAID THEY WEREN'T ACTUALLY CONSCIOUS.
BUT IT SURE DIDN'T SEEM THAT WAY...
HE SPOKE...?
I CAN'T SAY IT'S EVER HAPPENED TO ME LIKE THAT.
AND MY MASTER NEVER BROUGHT IT UP.
AS FAR AS I KNOW, YOU'RE THE ONLY ONE TO EXPERIENCE THIS PHENOMENON.
SO...
NOT A DREAM, THEN. REAL VESTIGES.
VESTIGES?
THERE'S ALL SORTS OF STUFF STOCKED UP IN THE QUIRK.
"I WANT THIS AND THAT." "I WANT TO BE THIS WAY OR THE OTHER."
WHEREVER YOU FIND POWER, THERE'S SURE TO BE FEELINGS BEHIND IT.

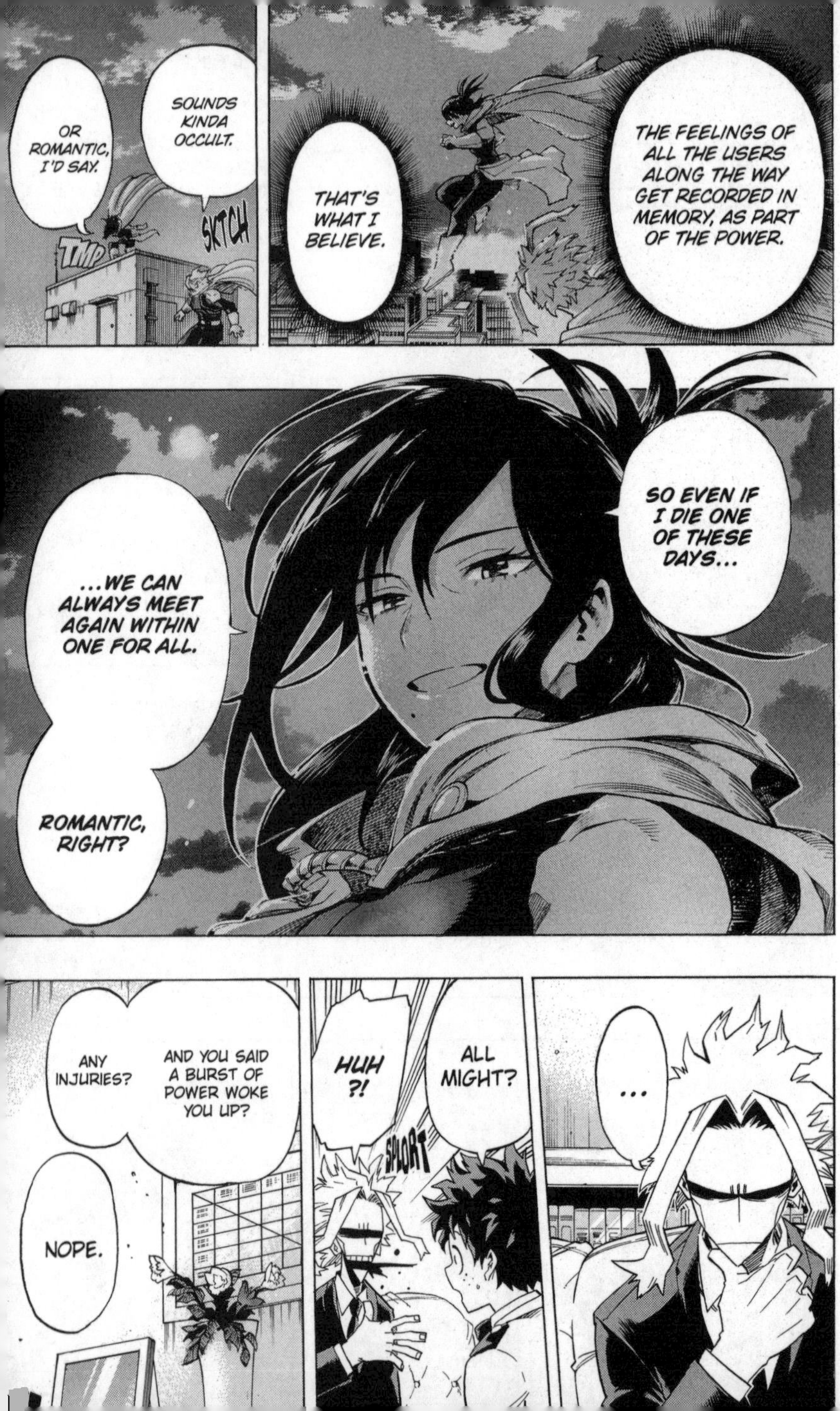
THE FEELINGS OF ALL THE USERS ALONG THE WAY GET RECORDED IN MEMORY, AS PART OF THE POWER.
THAT'S WHAT I BELIEVE.
SOUNDS KINDA OCCULT.
SKTCH
OR ROMANTIC, I'D SAY.
TMP
SO EVEN IF I DIE ONE OF THESE DAYS...
...WE CAN ALWAYS MEET AGAIN WITHIN ONE FOR ALL.
ROMANTIC, RIGHT?
...
ALL MIGHT?
HUH ?!
SPLORT
AND YOU SAID A BURST OF POWER WOKE YOU UP?
ANY INJURIES?
NOPE.

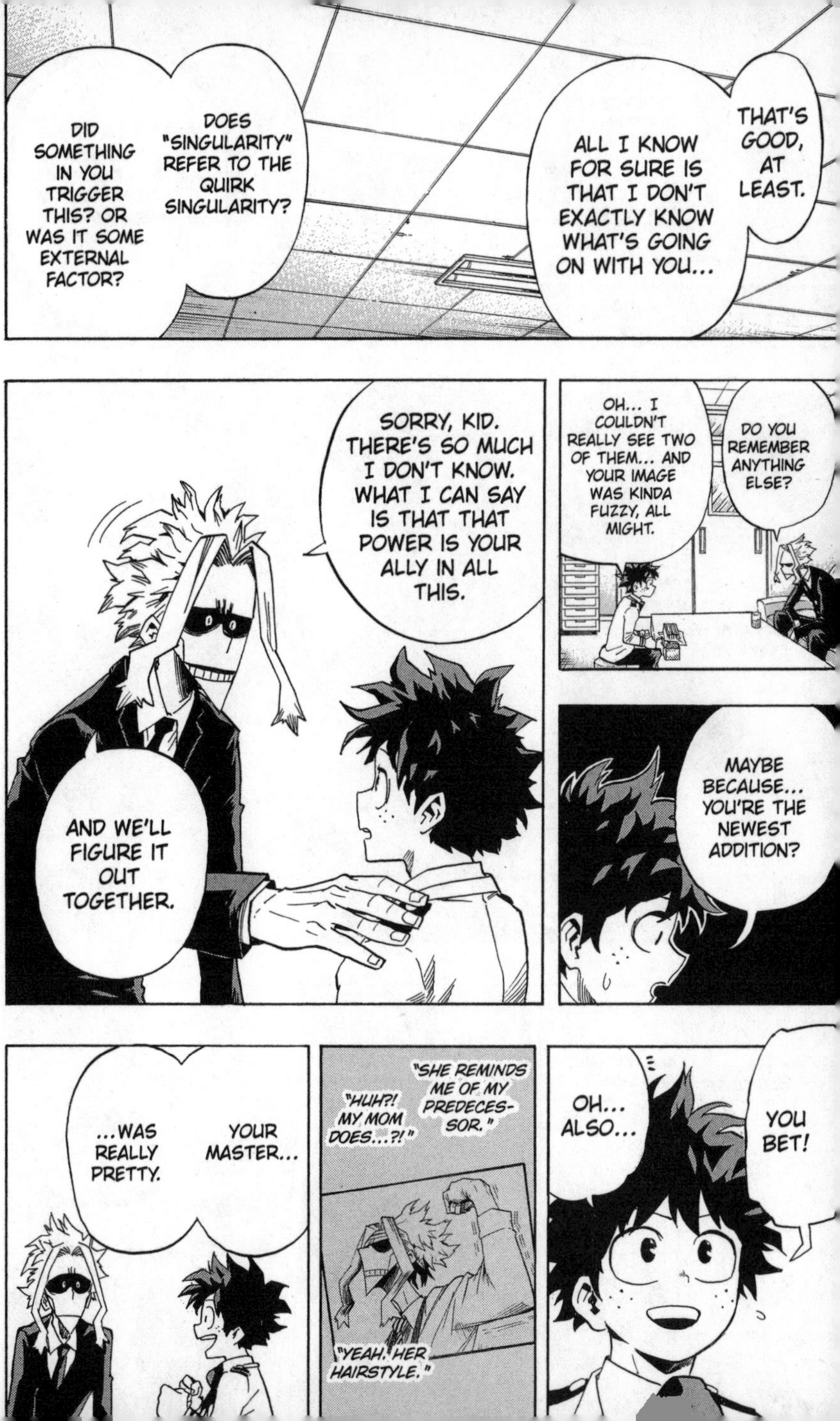
THAT'S GOOD, AT LEAST.
ALL I KNOW FOR SURE IS THAT I DON'T EXACTLY KNOW WHAT'S GOING ON WITH YOU...
DOES "SINGULARITY" REFER TO THE QUIRK SINGULARITY?
DID SOMETHING IN YOU TRIGGER THIS? OR WAS IT SOME EXTERNAL FACTOR?
DO YOU REMEMBER ANYTHING ELSE?
OH... I COULDN'T REALLY SEE TWO OF THEM... AND YOUR IMAGE WAS KINDA FUZZY, ALL MIGHT.
MAYBE BECAUSE... YOU'RE THE NEWEST ADDITION?
SORRY, KID. THERE'S SO MUCH I DON'T KNOW. WHAT I CAN SAY IS THAT THAT POWER IS YOUR ALLY IN ALL THIS.
AND WE'LL FIGURE IT OUT TOGETHER.
YOU BET!
OH... ALSO...
"SHE REMINDS ME OF MY PREDECES-SOR."
"HUH?! MY MOM DOES...?!"
"YEAH. HER HAIRSTYLE."
YOUR MASTER...
...WAS REALLY PRETTY.

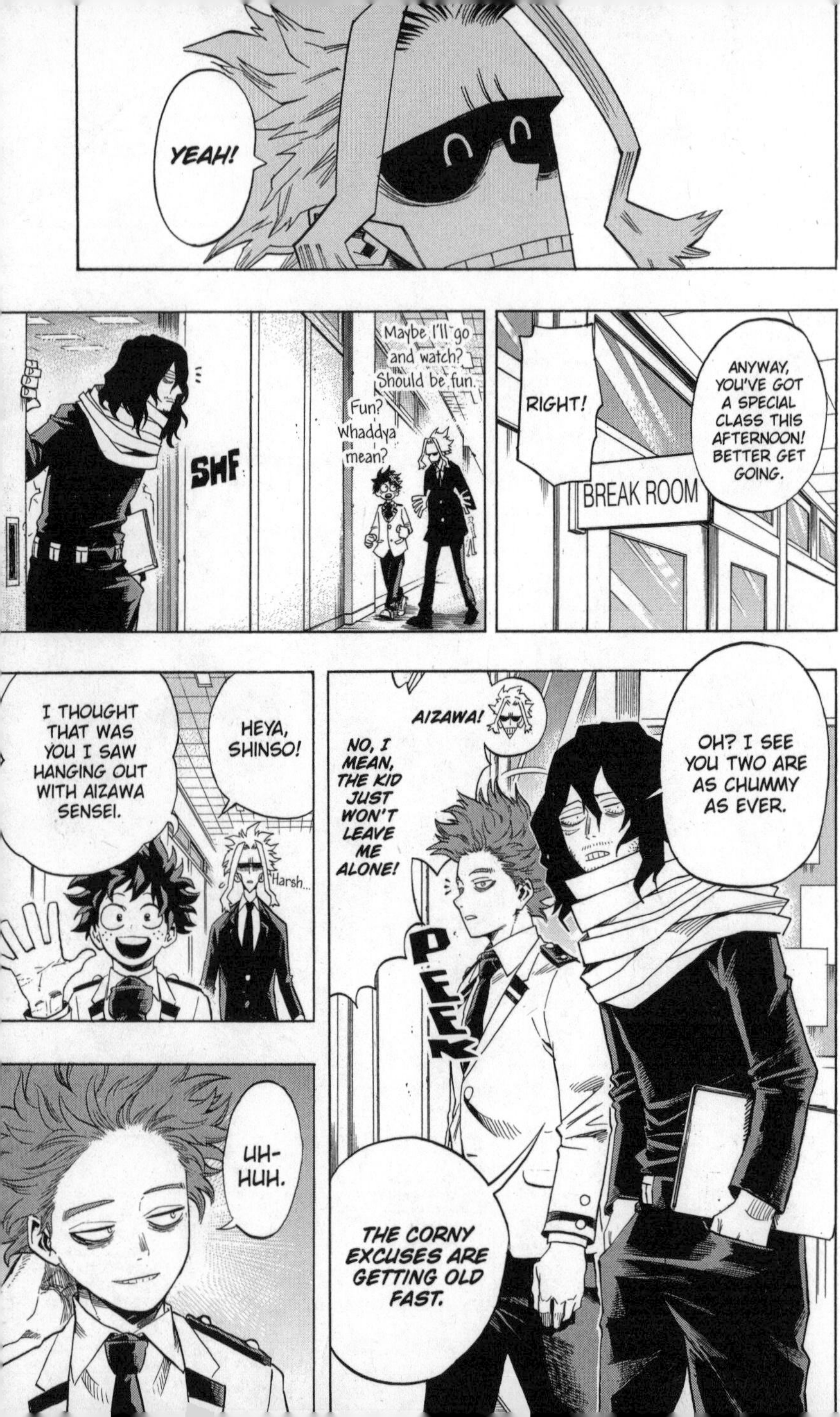
YEAH!
ANYWAY, YOU'VE GOT A SPECIAL CLASS THIS AFTERNOON! BETTER GET GOING.
RIGHT!
BREAK ROOM
Maybe I'll go and watch? Should be fun.
Fun? Whaddya mean?
SHF
OH? I SEE YOU TWO ARE AS CHUMMY AS EVER.
AIZAWA!
NO, I MEAN, THE KID JUST WON'T LEAVE ME ALONE!
PEEK
THE CORNY EXCUSES ARE GETTING OLD FAST.
HEYA, SHINSO!
I THOUGHT THAT WAS YOU I SAW HANGING OUT WITH AIZAWA SENSEI.
Harsh...
UH-HUH.

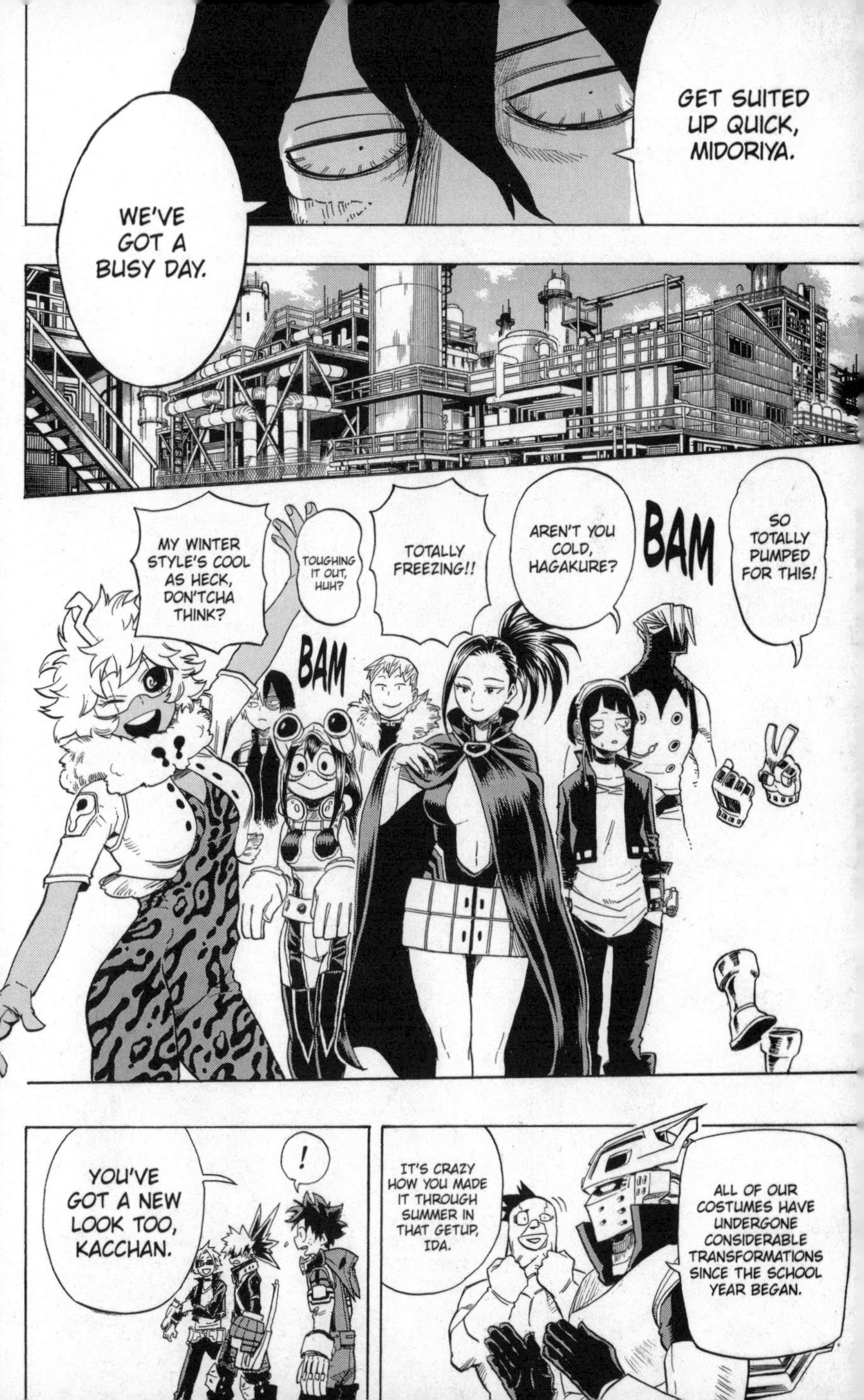
GET SUITED UP QUICK, MIDORIYA.
WE'VE GOT A BUSY DAY.
SO TOTALLY PUMPED FOR THIS!
BAM
AREN'T YOU COLD, HAGAKURE?
TOTALLY FREEZING!!
TOUGHING IT OUT, HUH?
MY WINTER STYLE'S COOL AS HECK, DON'TCHA THINK?
BAM
ALL OF OUR COSTUMES HAVE UNDERGONE CONSIDERABLE TRANSFORMATIONS SINCE THE SCHOOL YEAR BEGAN.
IT'S CRAZY HOW YOU MADE IT THROUGH SUMMER IN THAT GETUP, IDA.
!
YOU'VE GOT A NEW LOOK TOO, KACCHAN.

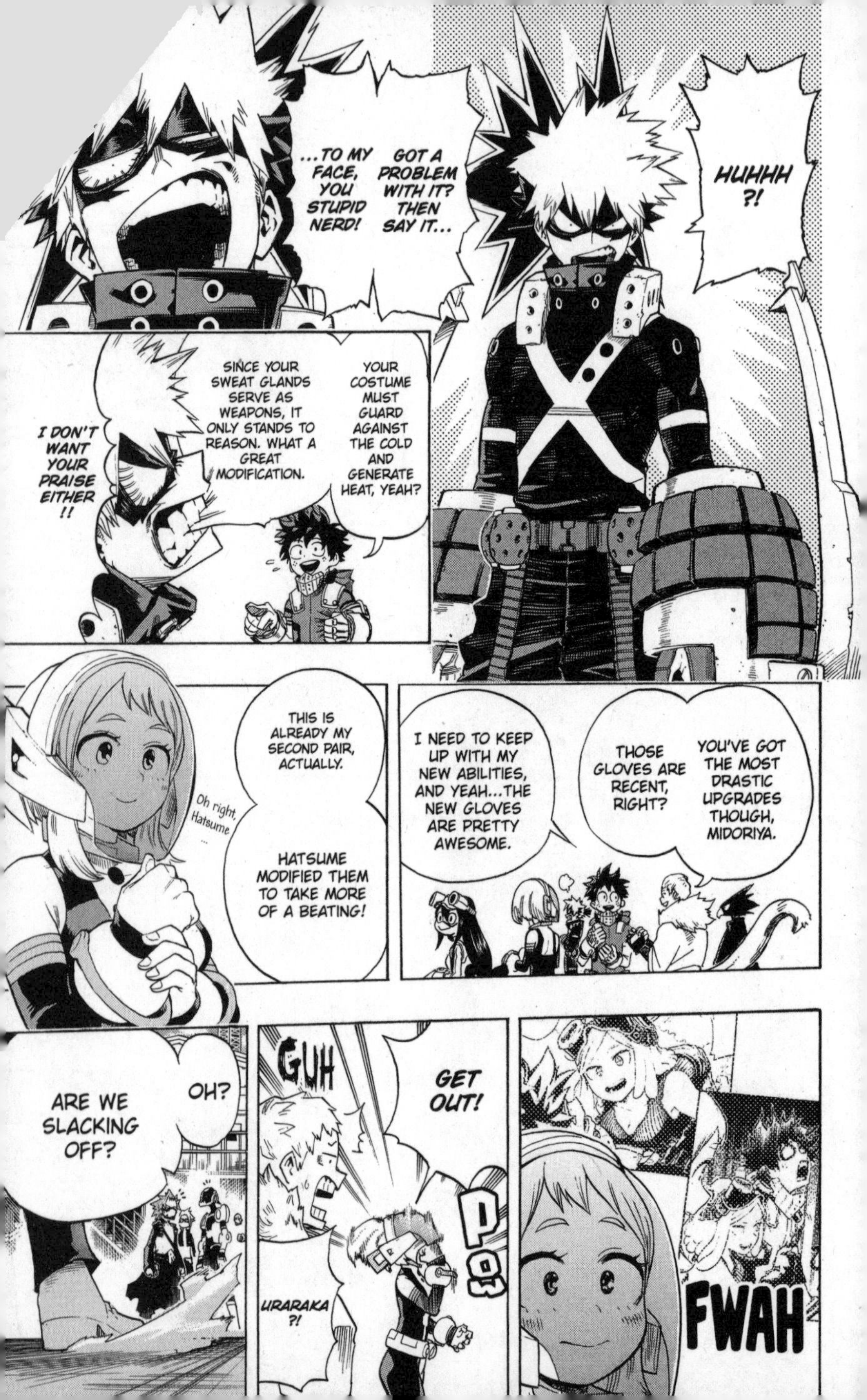
HUHHH ?!
GOT A PROBLEM WITH IT? THEN SAY IT...
...TO MY FACE, YOU STUPID NERD!
YOUR COSTUME MUST GUARD AGAINST THE COLD AND GENERATE HEAT, YEAH?
SINCE YOUR SWEAT GLANDS SERVE AS WEAPONS, IT ONLY STANDS TO REASON. WHAT A GREAT MODIFICATION.
I DON'T WANT YOUR PRAISE EITHER !!
YOU'VE GOT THE MOST DRASTIC UPGRADES THOUGH, MIDORIYA.
THOSE GLOVES ARE RECENT, RIGHT?
I NEED TO KEEP UP WITH MY NEW ABILITIES, AND YEAH...THE NEW GLOVES ARE PRETTY AWESOME.
THIS IS ALREADY MY SECOND PAIR, ACTUALLY.
HATSUME MODIFIED THEM TO TAKE MORE OF A BEATING!
Oh right, Hatsume...
FWAH
GET OUT!
GUH
Po
URARAKA ?!
OH?
ARE WE SLACKING OFF?

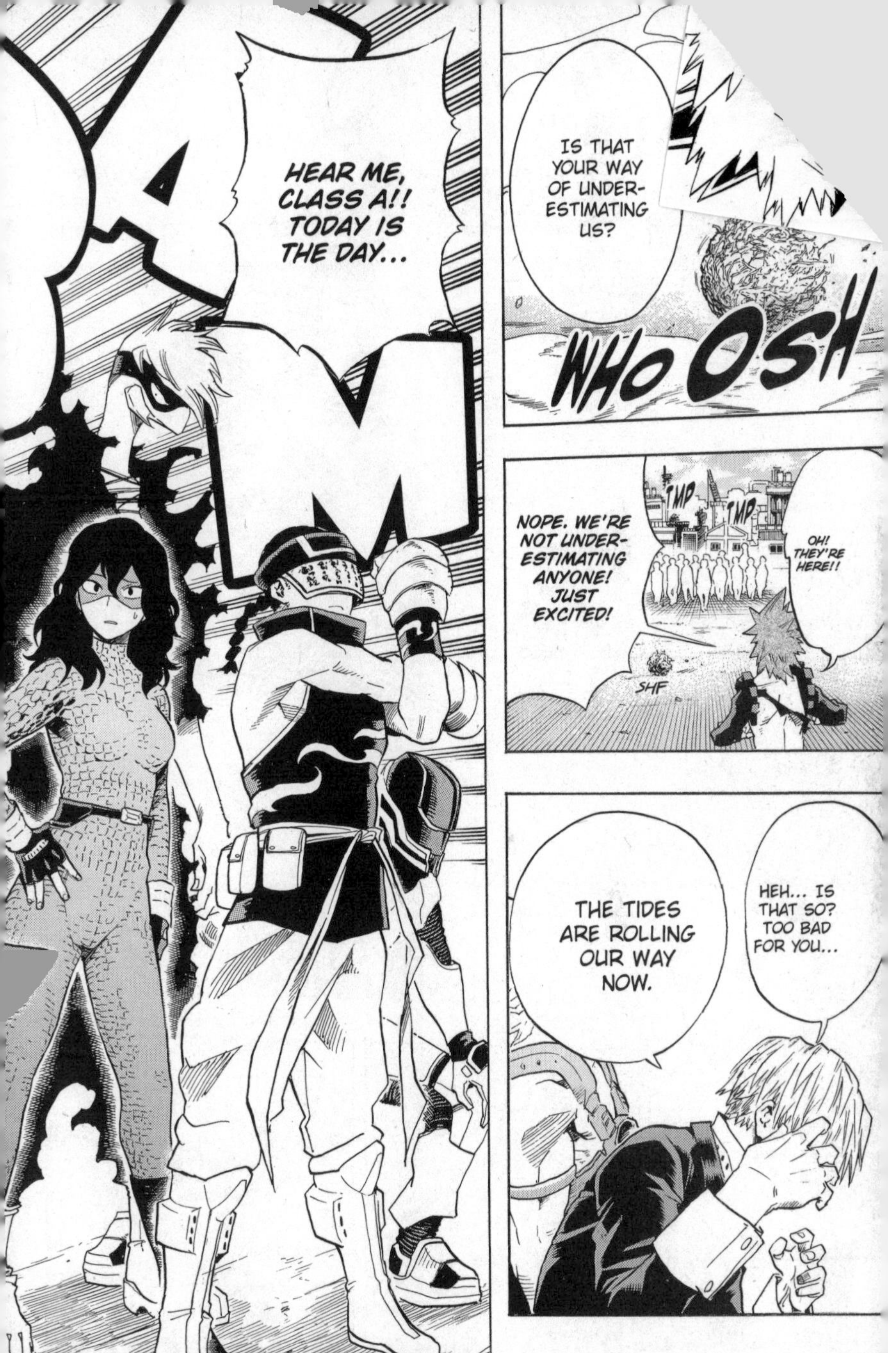
IS THAT YOUR WAY OF UNDER-ESTIMATING US?
WHOOSH
OH! THEY'RE HERE!!
TMP
TMP
NOPE. WE'RE NOT UNDER-ESTIMATING ANYONE! JUST EXCITED!
SHF
HEH... IS THAT SO? TOO BAD FOR YOU...
THE TIDES ARE ROLLING OUR WAY NOW.
HEAR ME, CLASS A!! TODAY IS THE DAY...

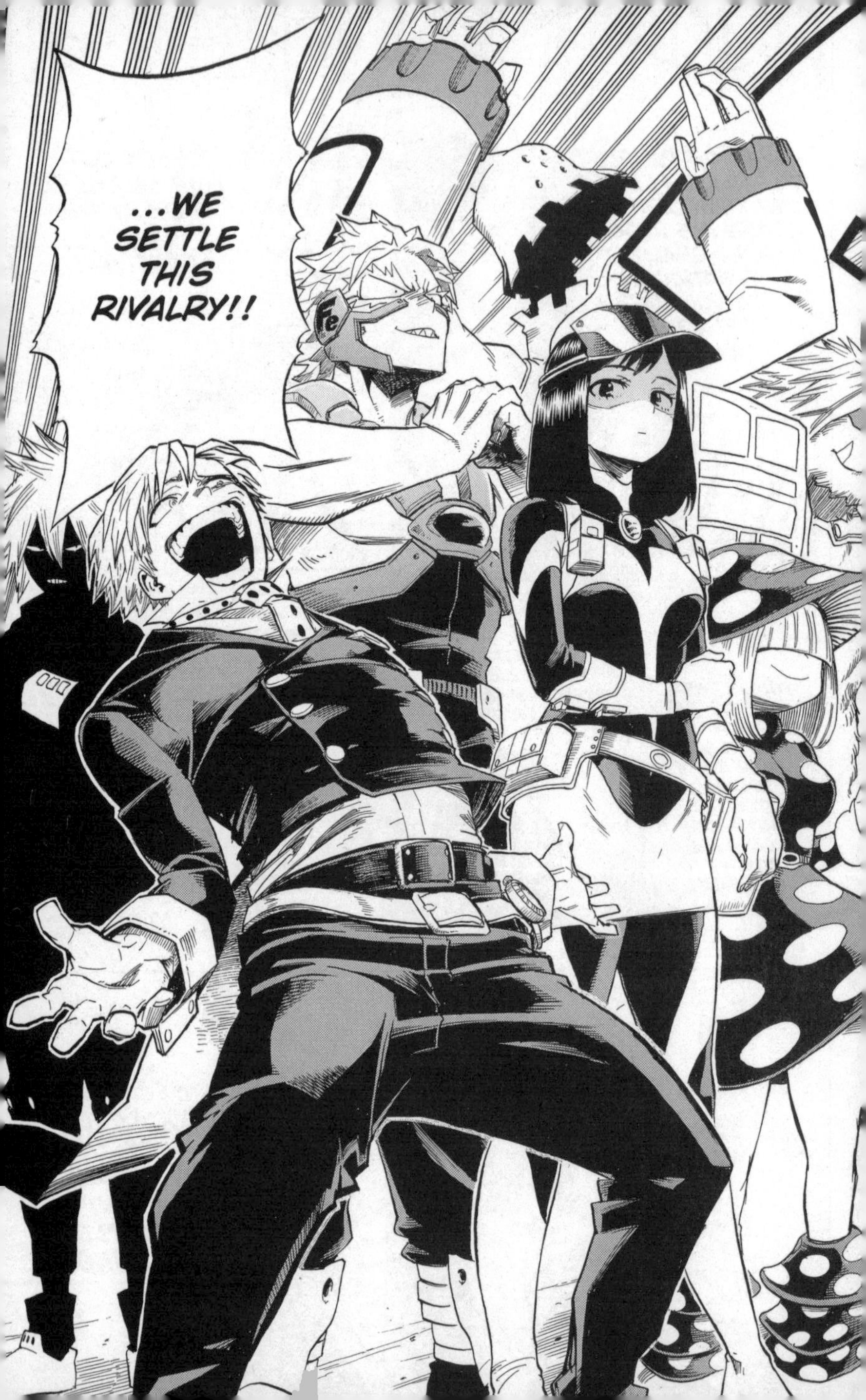
...WE SETTLE THIS RIVALRY!!

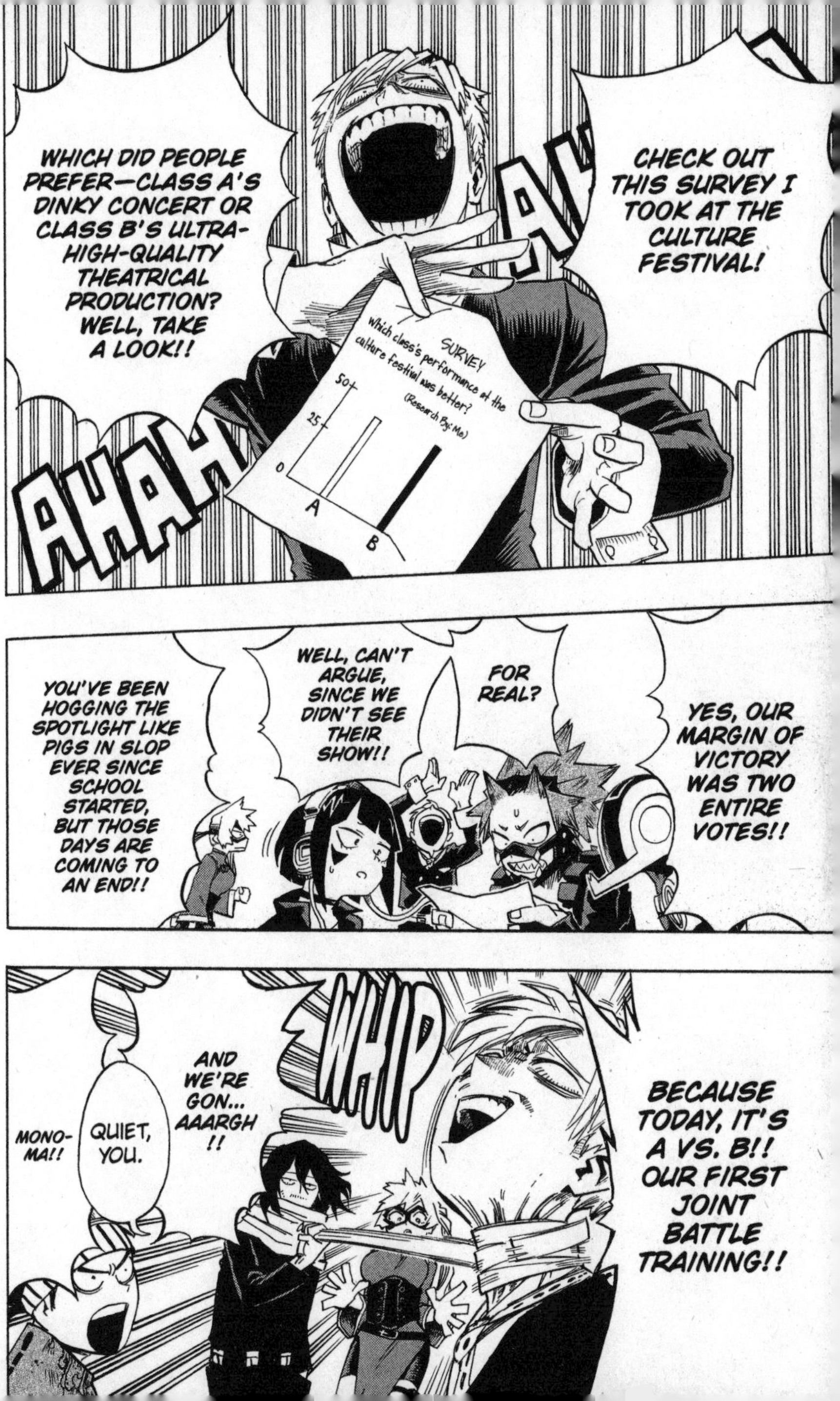
CHECK OUT THIS SURVEY I TOOK AT THE CULTURE FESTIVAL!
AH
WHICH DID PEOPLE PREFER—CLASS A'S DINKY CONCERT OR CLASS B'S ULTRA-HIGH-QUALITY THEATRICAL PRODUCTION? WELL, TAKE A LOOK!!
SURVEY
Which class's performance at the culture festival was better?
(Research By: Me)
50
25
0
A
B
AHAH
YES, OUR MARGIN OF VICTORY WAS TWO ENTIRE VOTES!!
FOR REAL?
WELL, CAN'T ARGUE, SINCE WE DIDN'T SEE THEIR SHOW!!
YOU'VE BEEN HOGGING THE SPOTLIGHT LIKE PIGS IN SLOP EVER SINCE SCHOOL STARTED, BUT THOSE DAYS ARE COMING TO AN END!!
BECAUSE TODAY, IT'S A VS. B!! OUR FIRST JOINT BATTLE TRAINING!!
WHIP
AND WE'RE GON... AAARGH!!
QUIET, YOU.
MONO-MA!!

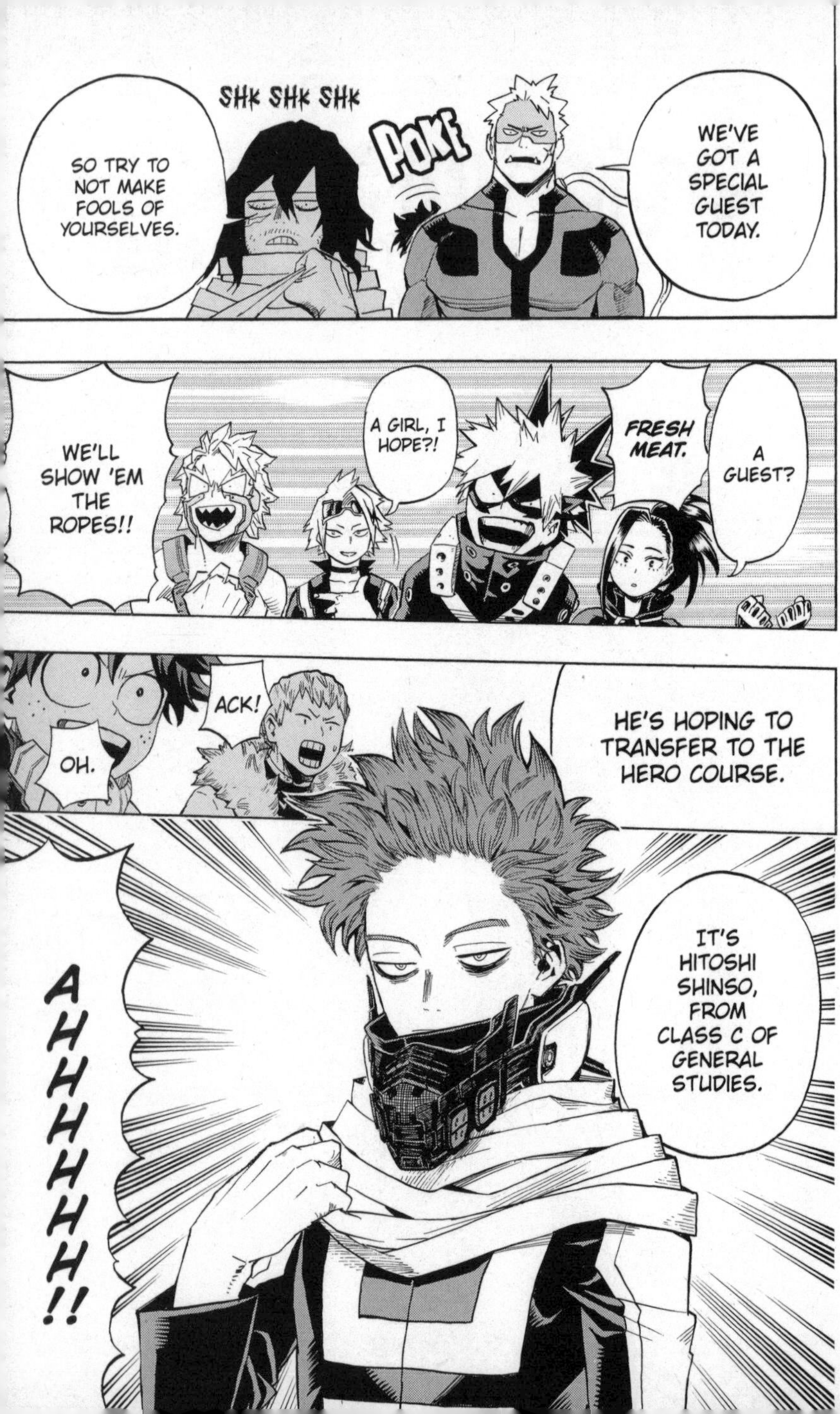
WE'VE GOT A SPECIAL GUEST TODAY.
POKE
SHK SHK SHK
SO TRY TO NOT MAKE FOOLS OF YOURSELVES.
A GUEST?
FRESH MEAT.
A GIRL, I HOPE?!
WE'LL SHOW 'EM THE ROPES!!
HE'S HOPING TO TRANSFER TO THE HERO COURSE.
ACK!
OH.
IT'S HITOSHI SHINSO, FROM CLASS C OF GENERAL STUDIES.
AHHHHHHH!!

THE WINTER COSTUME

Tsuyu isn't great at regulating her body temperature, so for winter, she's switched over to an insulated costume for a little extra protection!

The suit and the froggy neck wrap help keep her body temp right where it's meant to be!!

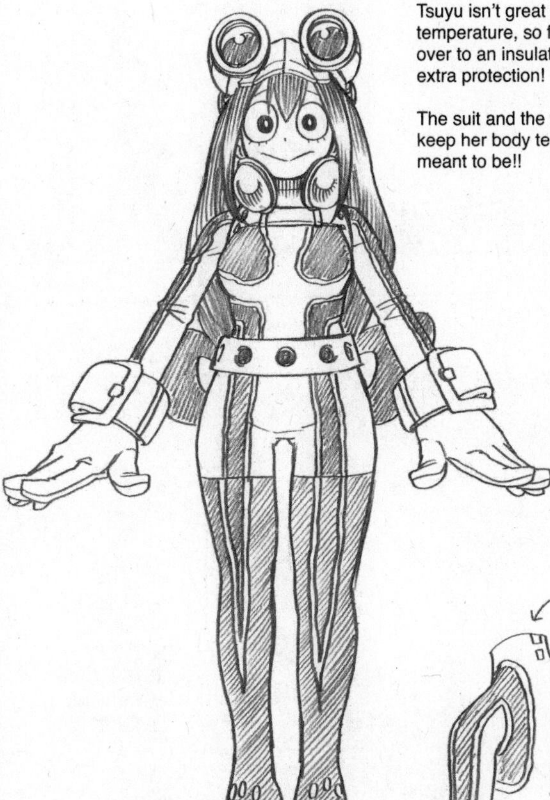

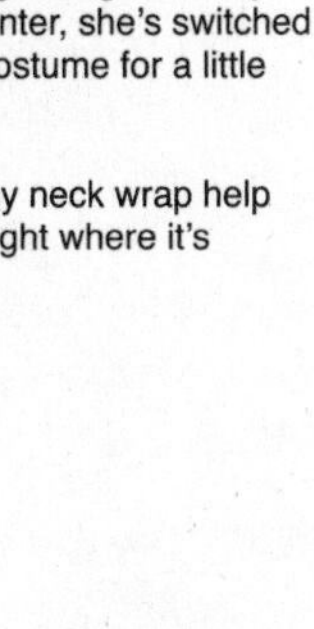

FROGGY CHEEK NECK WRAP
An accessory modeled after a frog's inflated cheeks. Equipped with a high-performance temperature-regulating function.

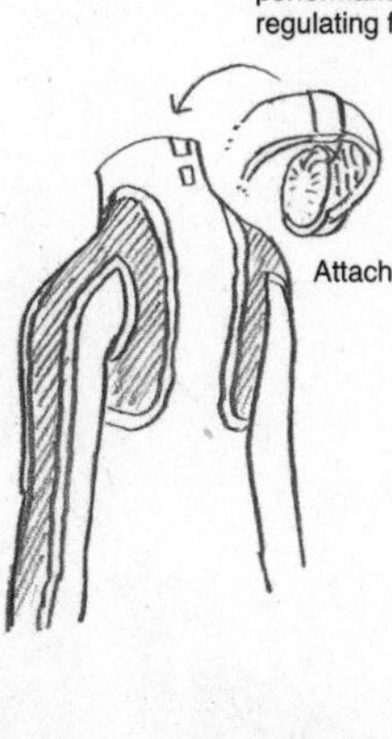

Attaches to the suit!

No. 195 - Clash! Class A vs. Class B!

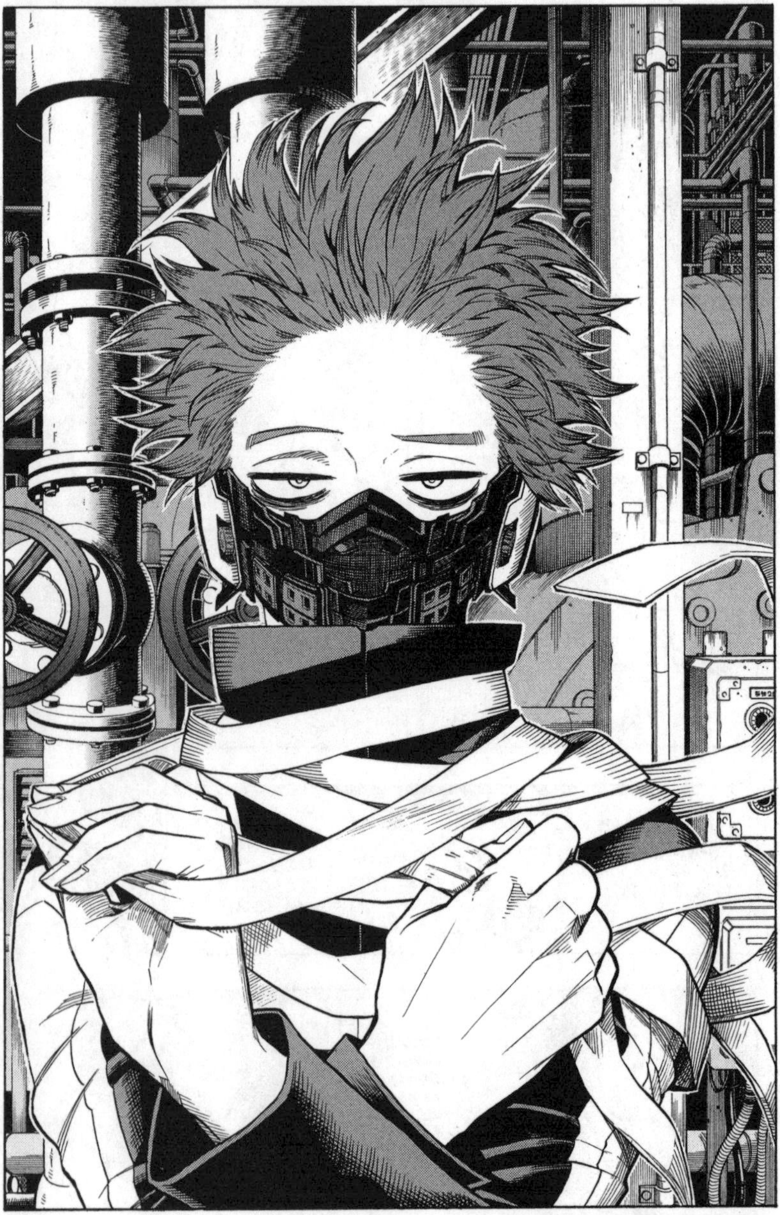

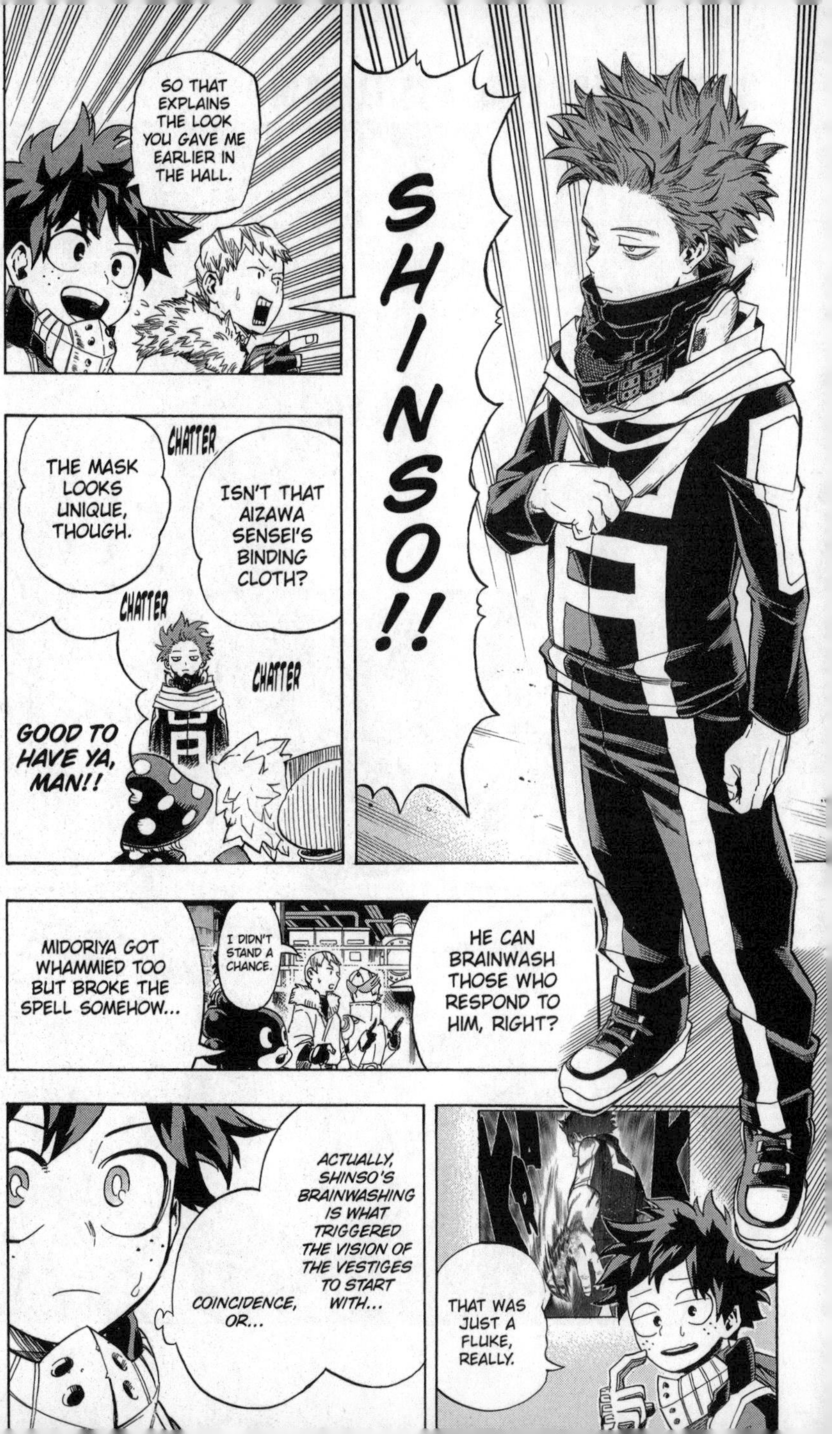
SHINSO!!
SO THAT EXPLAINS THE LOOK YOU GAVE ME EARLIER IN THE HALL.
CHATTER
ISN'T THAT AIZAWA SENSEI'S BINDING CLOTH?
THE MASK LOOKS UNIQUE, THOUGH.
CHATTER
CHATTER
GOOD TO HAVE YA, MAN!!
HE CAN BRAINWASH THOSE WHO RESPOND TO HIM, RIGHT?
I DIDN'T STAND A CHANCE.
MIDORIYA GOT WHAMMIED TOO BUT BROKE THE SPELL SOMEHOW...
THAT WAS JUST A FLUKE, REALLY.
ACTUALLY, SHINSO'S BRAINWASHING IS WHAT TRIGGERED THE VISION OF THE VESTIGES TO START WITH...
COINCIDENCE, OR...

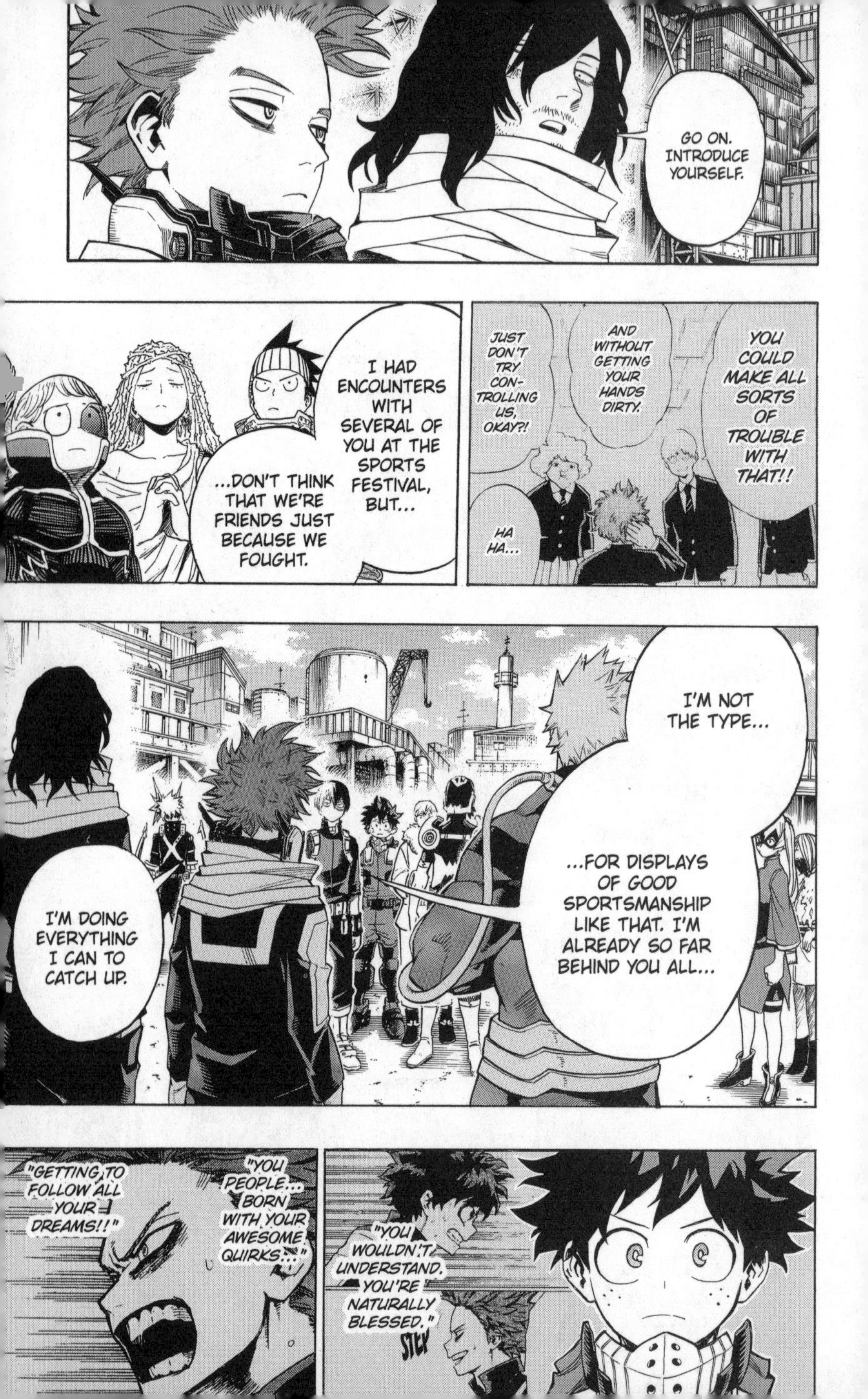
GO ON. INTRODUCE YOURSELF.
YOU COULD MAKE ALL SORTS OF TROUBLE WITH THAT!!
AND WITHOUT GETTING YOUR HANDS DIRTY.
JUST DON'T TRY CON-TROLLING US, OKAY?!
HA HA...
I HAD ENCOUNTERS WITH SEVERAL OF YOU AT THE SPORTS FESTIVAL, BUT...
...DON'T THINK THAT WE'RE FRIENDS JUST BECAUSE WE FOUGHT.
I'M NOT THE TYPE...
...FOR DISPLAYS OF GOOD SPORTSMANSHIP LIKE THAT. I'M ALREADY SO FAR BEHIND YOU ALL...
I'M DOING EVERYTHING I CAN TO CATCH UP.
"YOU WOULDN'T UNDERSTAND. YOU'RE NATURALLY BLESSED."
"YOU PEOPLE... BORN WITH YOUR AWESOME QUIRKS..."
"GETTING TO FOLLOW ALL YOUR DREAMS!!"

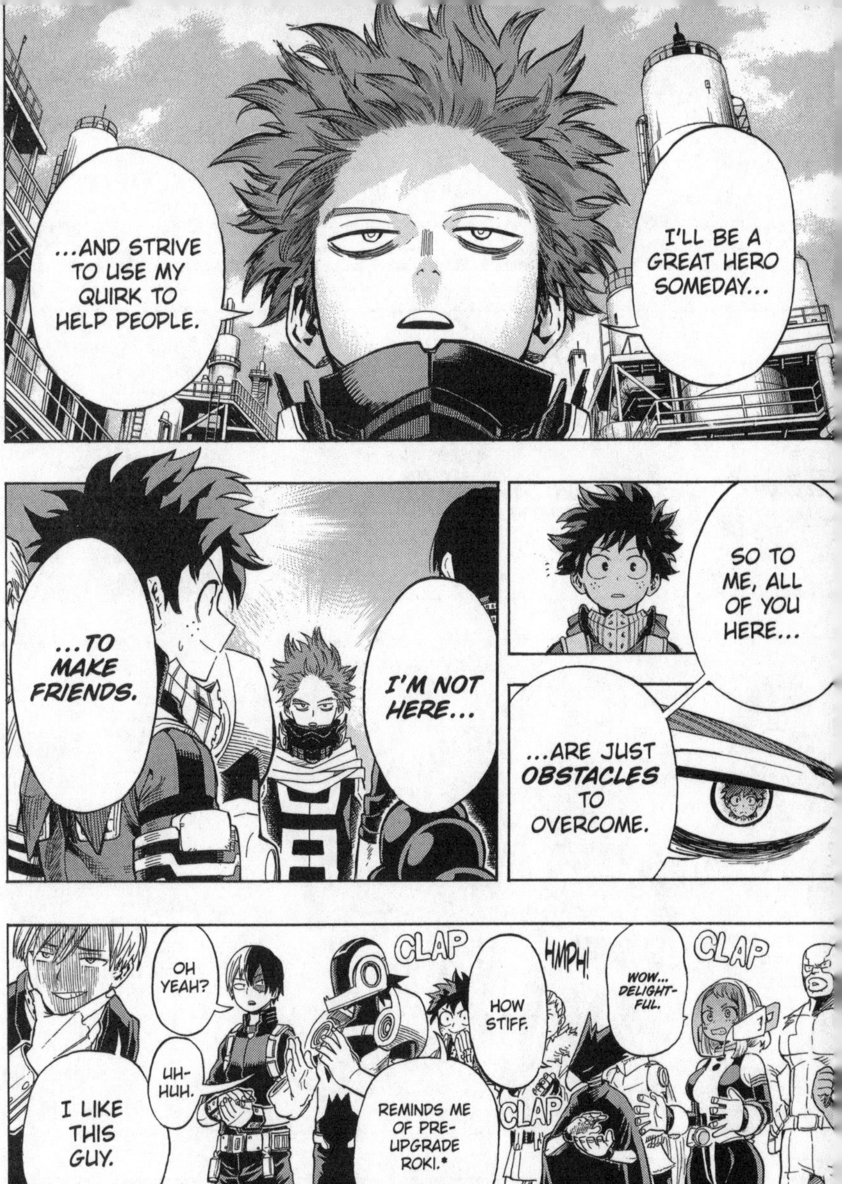
I'LL BE A GREAT HERO SOMEDAY...
...AND STRIVE TO USE MY QUIRK TO HELP PEOPLE.
SO TO ME, ALL OF YOU HERE...
...ARE JUST OBSTACLES TO OVERCOME.
I'M NOT HERE...
...TO MAKE FRIENDS.
CLAP
WOW... DELIGHT-FUL.
HMPH!
HOW STIFF.
CLAP
REMINDS ME OF PRE-UPGRADE ROKI.*
CLAP
OH YEAH?
UH-HUH.
I LIKE THIS GUY.

*THE WAY TODOROKI WAS PRIOR TO THE SPORTS FESTIVAL

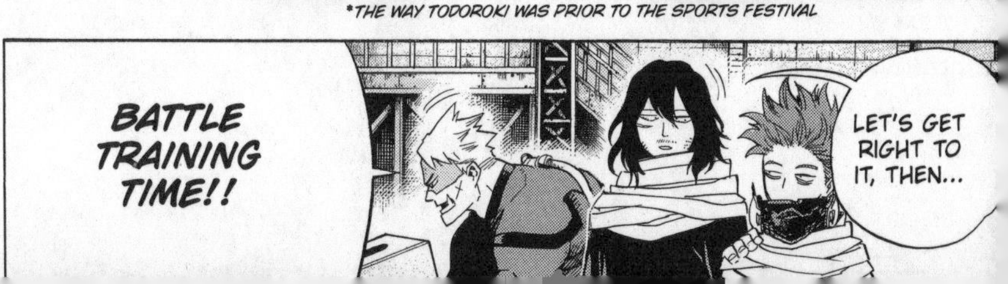
LET'S GET RIGHT TO IT, THEN...
BATTLE TRAINING TIME!!

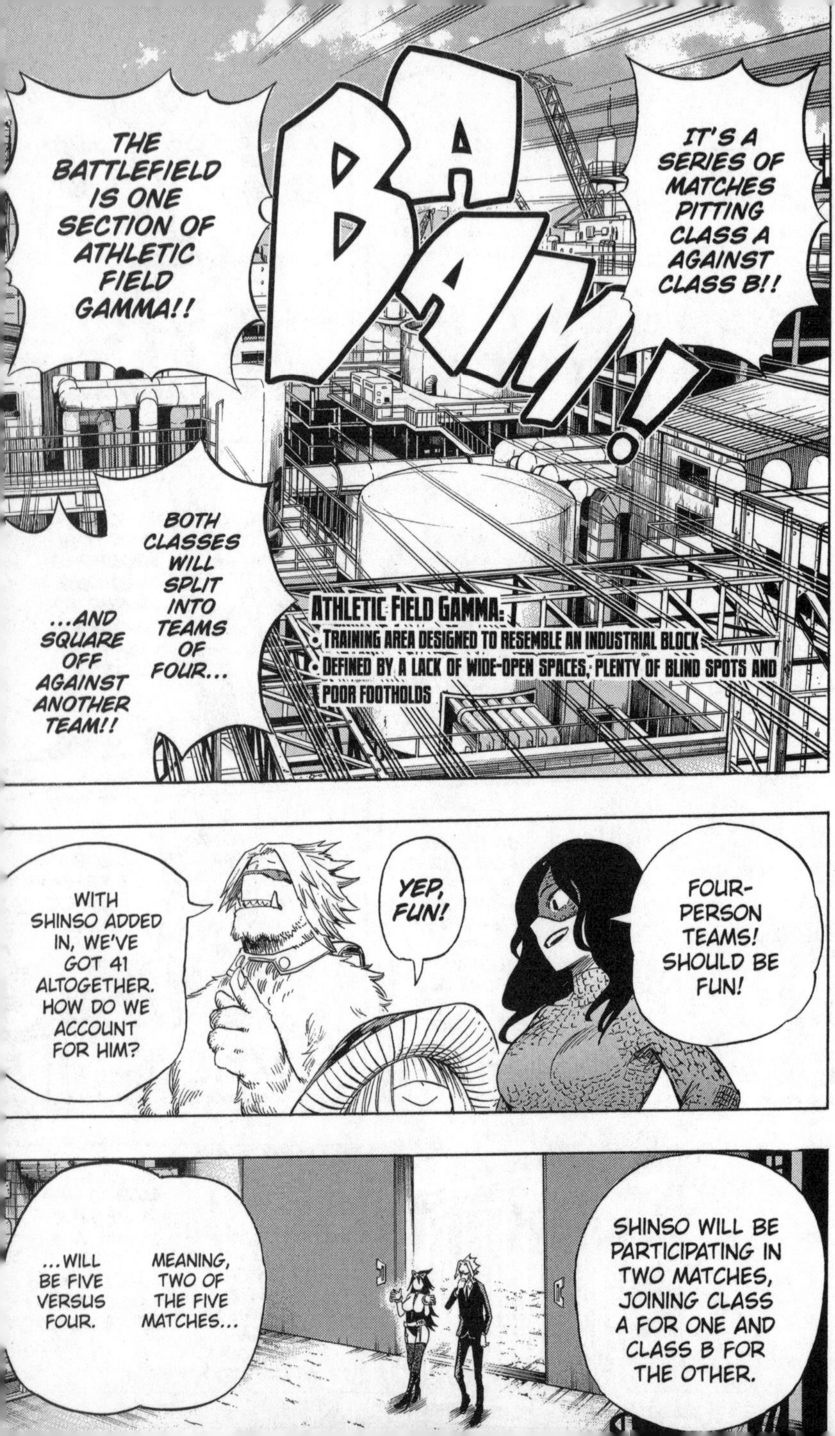
IT'S A SERIES OF MATCHES PITTING CLASS A AGAINST CLASS B!!
BA-BAM!
THE BATTLEFIELD IS ONE SECTION OF ATHLETIC FIELD GAMMA!!
ATHLETIC FIELD GAMMA:
• TRAINING AREA DESIGNED TO RESEMBLE AN INDUSTRIAL BLOCK
• DEFINED BY A LACK OF WIDE-OPEN SPACES, PLENTY OF BLIND SPOTS AND POOR FOOTHOLDS
BOTH CLASSES WILL SPLIT INTO TEAMS OF FOUR...
...AND SQUARE OFF AGAINST ANOTHER TEAM!!
FOUR-PERSON TEAMS! SHOULD BE FUN!
YEP, FUN!
WITH SHINSO ADDED IN, WE'VE GOT 41 ALTOGETHER. HOW DO WE ACCOUNT FOR HIM?
SHINSO WILL BE PARTICIPATING IN TWO MATCHES, JOINING CLASS A FOR ONE AND CLASS B FOR THE OTHER.
MEANING, TWO OF THE FIVE MATCHES...
...WILL BE FIVE VERSUS FOUR.

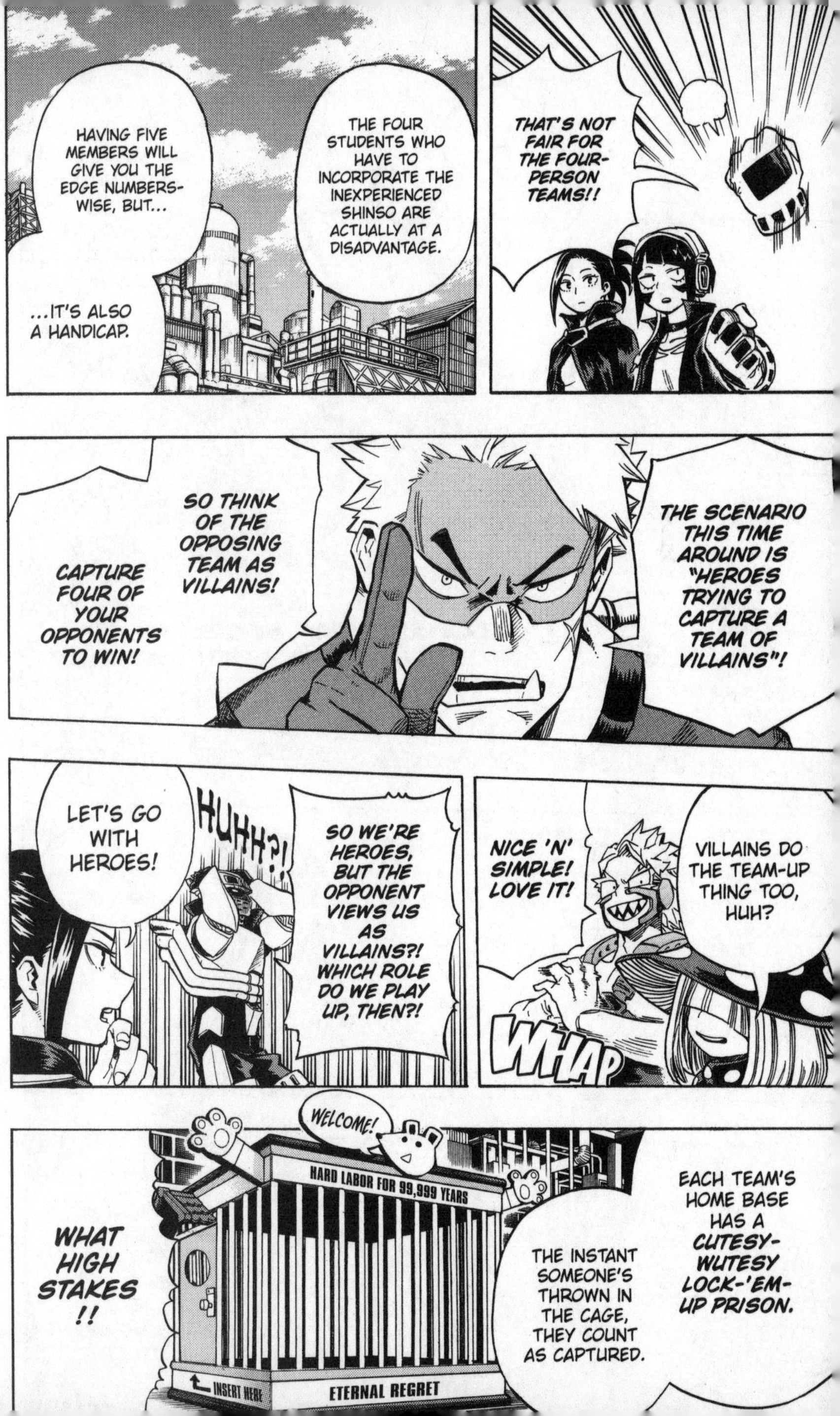
THAT'S NOT FAIR FOR THE FOUR-PERSON TEAMS!!
THE FOUR STUDENTS WHO HAVE TO INCORPORATE THE INEXPERIENCED SHINSO ARE ACTUALLY AT A DISADVANTAGE.
HAVING FIVE MEMBERS WILL GIVE YOU THE EDGE NUMBERS-WISE, BUT...
...IT'S ALSO A HANDICAP.
THE SCENARIO THIS TIME AROUND IS "HEROES TRYING TO CAPTURE A TEAM OF VILLAINS"!
SO THINK OF THE OPPOSING TEAM AS VILLAINS!
CAPTURE FOUR OF YOUR OPPONENTS TO WIN!
VILLAINS DO THE TEAM-UP THING TOO, HUH?
NICE 'N' SIMPLE! LOVE IT!
WHAP
SO WE'RE HEROES, BUT THE OPPONENT VIEWS US AS VILLAINS?! WHICH ROLE DO WE PLAY UP, THEN?!
HUHH?!
LET'S GO WITH HEROES!
WELCOME!
HARD LABOR FOR 99,999 YEARS
EACH TEAM'S HOME BASE HAS A CUTESY-WUTESY LOCK-'EM-UP PRISON.
THE INSTANT SOMEONE'S THROWN IN THE CAGE, THEY COUNT AS CAPTURED.
WHAT HIGH STAKES!!
INSERT HERE
ETERNAL REGRET

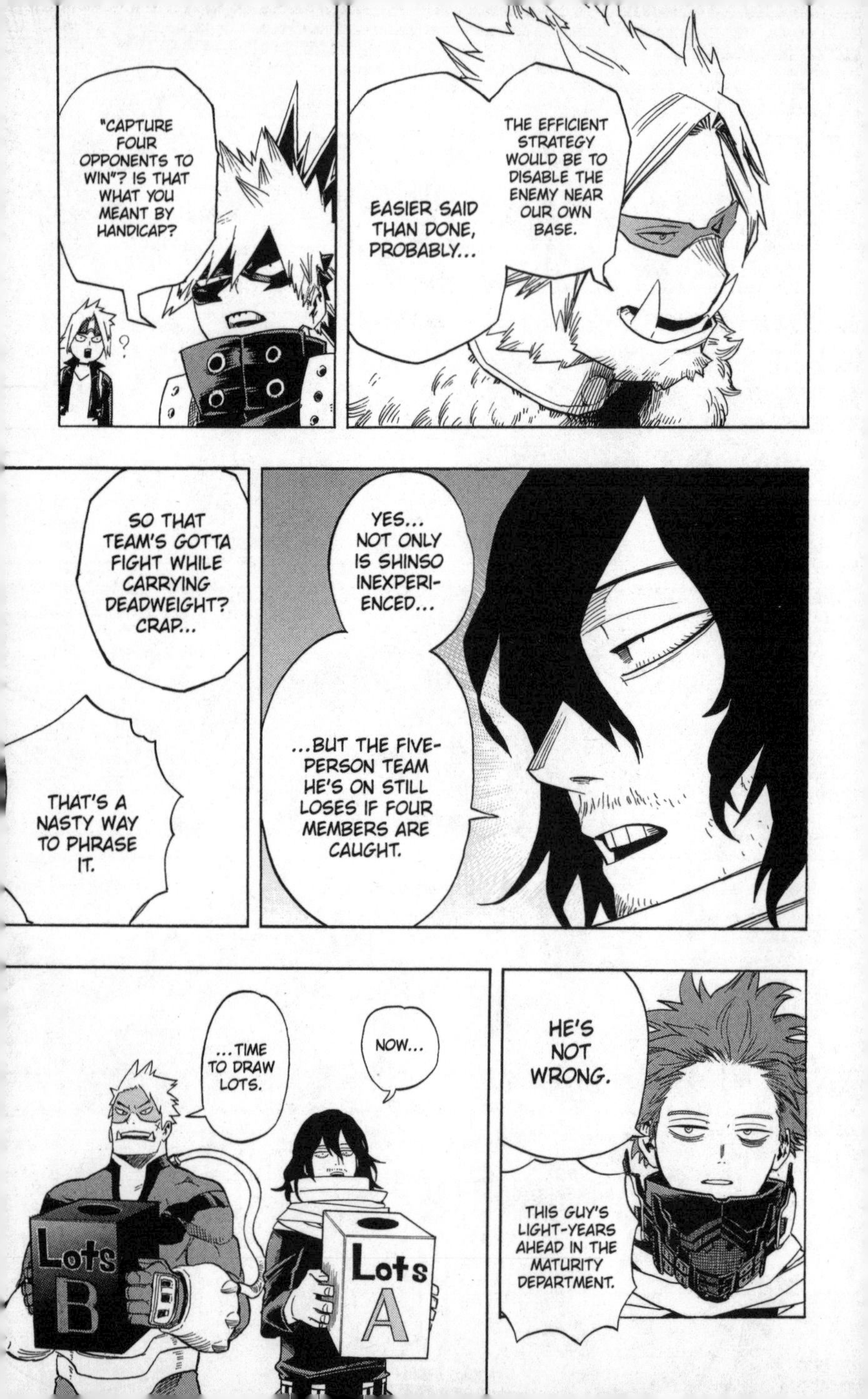
THE EFFICIENT STRATEGY WOULD BE TO DISABLE THE ENEMY NEAR OUR OWN BASE.
EASIER SAID THAN DONE, PROBABLY...
"CAPTURE FOUR OPPONENTS TO WIN"? IS THAT WHAT YOU MEANT BY HANDICAP?
?
YES... NOT ONLY IS SHINSO INEXPERI-ENCED...
...BUT THE FIVE-PERSON TEAM HE'S ON STILL LOSES IF FOUR MEMBERS ARE CAUGHT.
SO THAT TEAM'S GOTTA FIGHT WHILE CARRYING DEADWEIGHT? CRAP...
THAT'S A NASTY WAY TO PHRASE IT.
HE'S NOT WRONG.
THIS GUY'S LIGHT-YEARS AHEAD IN THE MATURITY DEPARTMENT.
NOW...
...TIME TO DRAW LOTS.
Lots A
Lots B

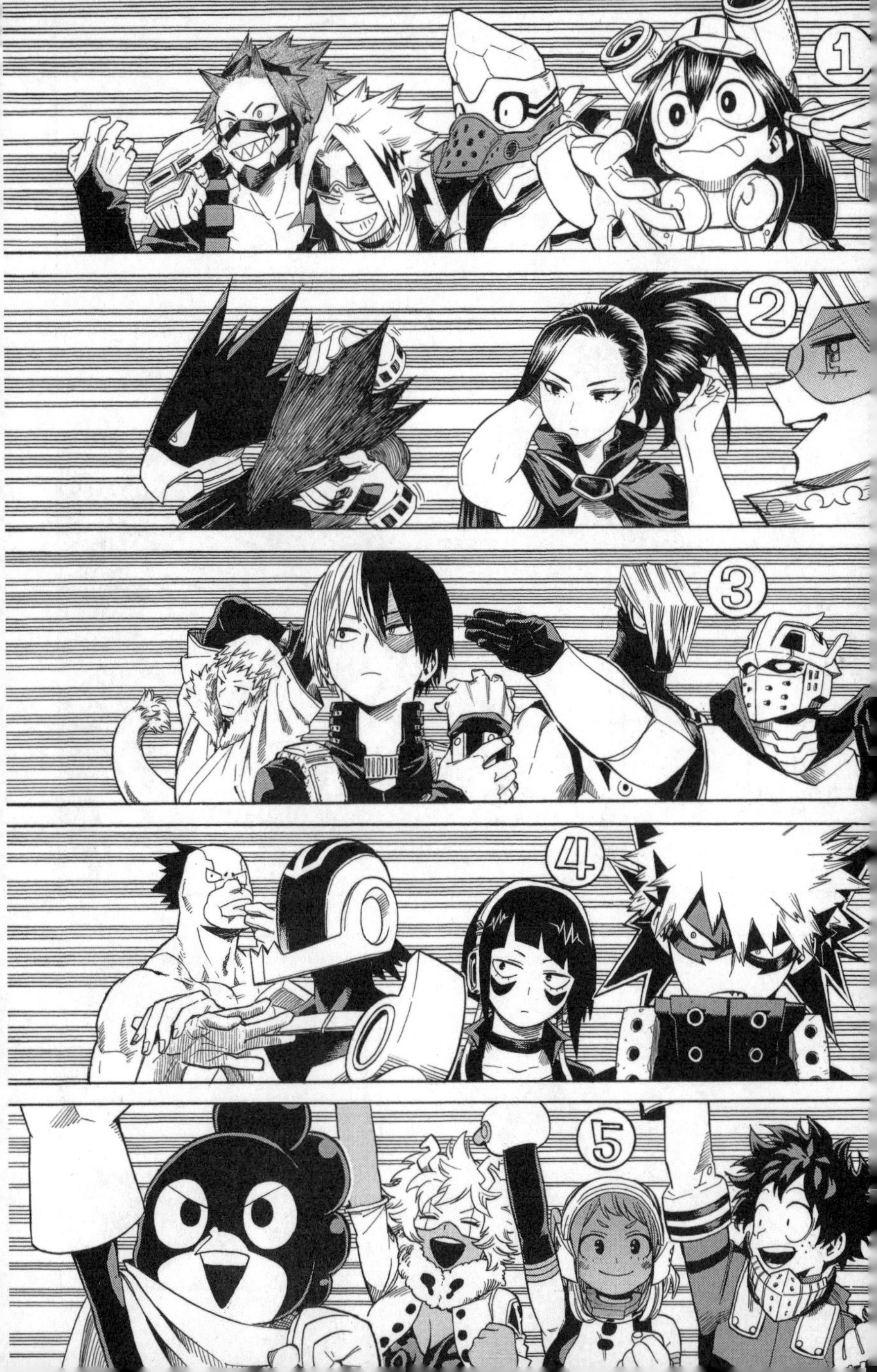
1
2
3
4
5

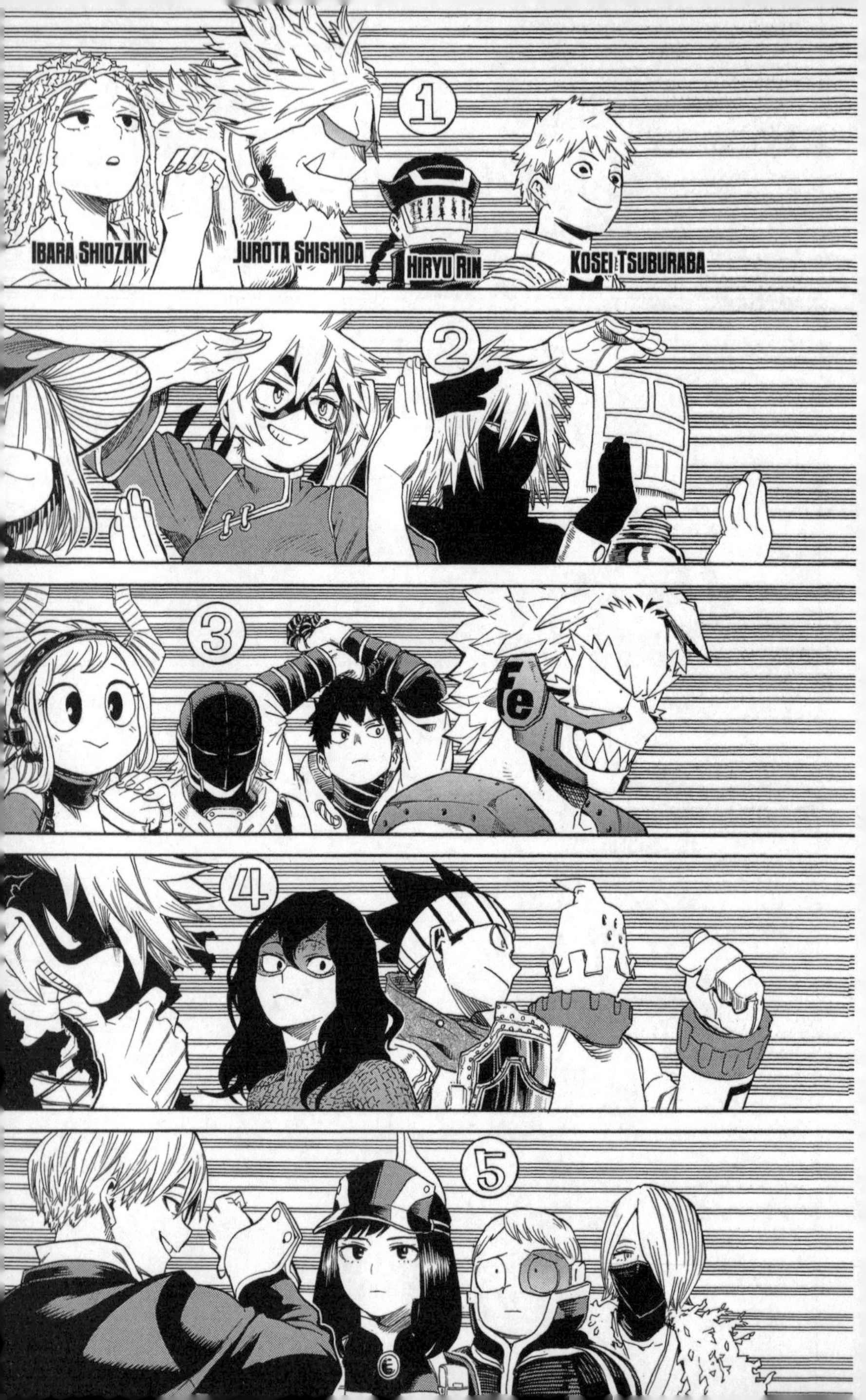
1
KOSEI TSUBURABA
HIRYU RIN
JUROTA SHISHIDA
IBARA SHIOZAKI
2
3
4
5

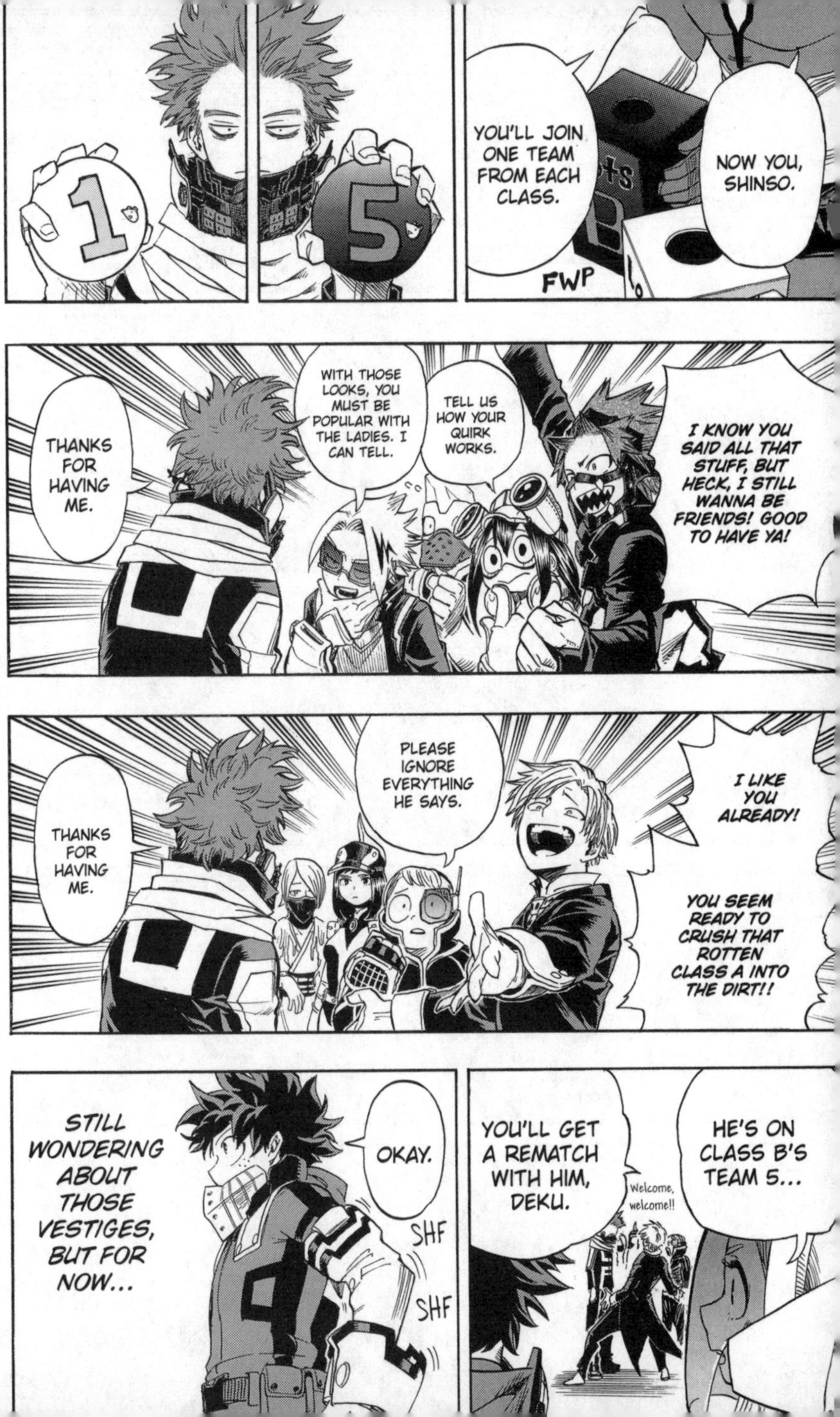
NOW YOU, SHINSO.
YOU'LL JOIN ONE TEAM FROM EACH CLASS.
FWP
I KNOW YOU SAID ALL THAT STUFF, BUT HECK, I STILL WANNA BE FRIENDS! GOOD TO HAVE YA!
TELL US HOW YOUR QUIRK WORKS.
WITH THOSE LOOKS, YOU MUST BE POPULAR WITH THE LADIES. I CAN TELL.
THANKS FOR HAVING ME.
I LIKE YOU ALREADY!
YOU SEEM READY TO CRUSH THAT ROTTEN CLASS A INTO THE DIRT!!
PLEASE IGNORE EVERYTHING HE SAYS.
THANKS FOR HAVING ME.
HE'S ON CLASS B'S TEAM 5...
Welcome, welcome!!
YOU'LL GET A REMATCH WITH HIM, DEKU.
OKAY.
SHF
SHF
STILL WONDERING ABOUT THOSE VESTIGES, BUT FOR NOW...

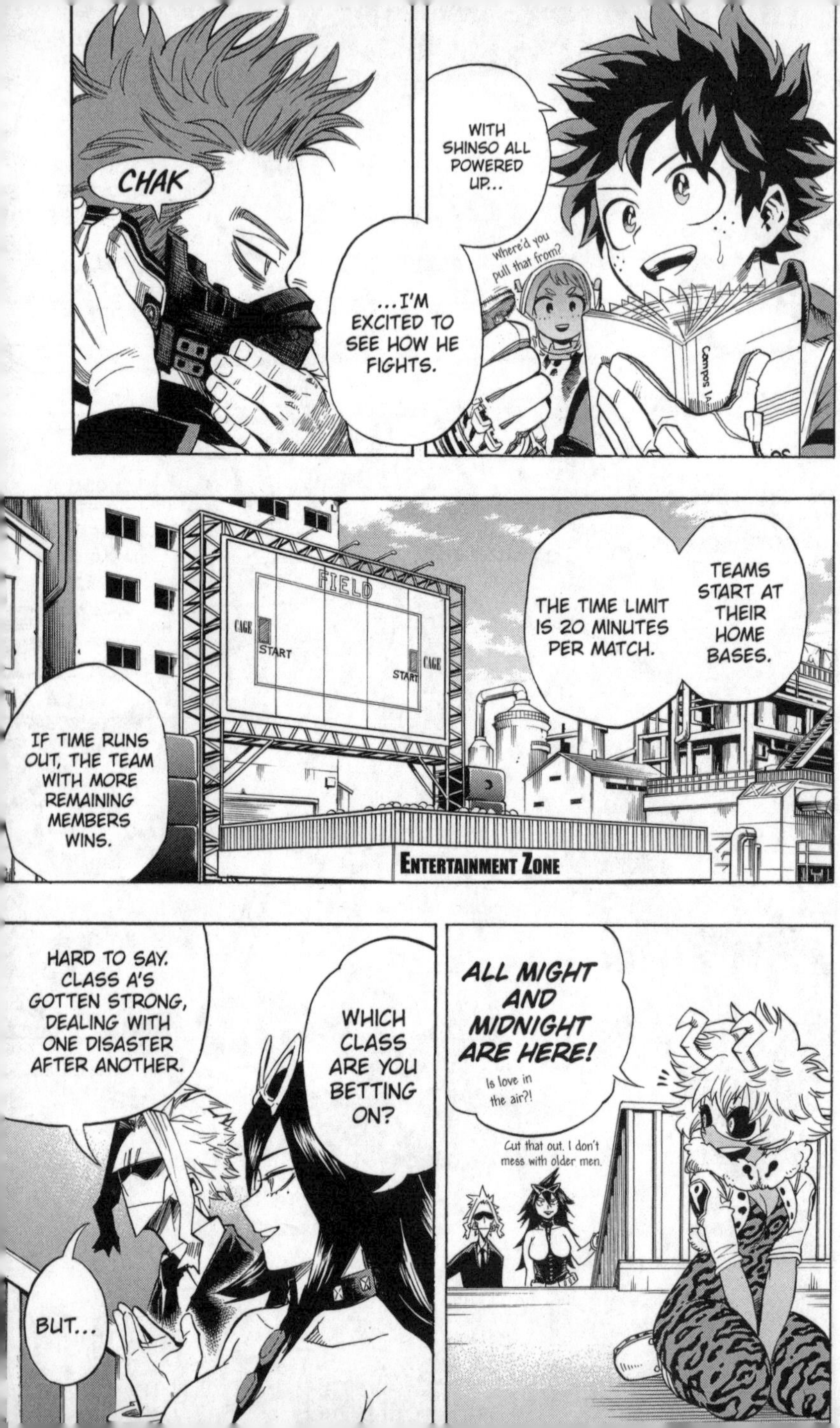

WITH SHINSO ALL POWERED UP...
...I'M EXCITED TO SEE HOW HE FIGHTS.
Where'd you pull that from?
CHAK
TEAMS START AT THEIR HOME BASES.
THE TIME LIMIT IS 20 MINUTES PER MATCH.
FIELD
CAGE
START
CAGE
START
IF TIME RUNS OUT, THE TEAM WITH MORE REMAINING MEMBERS WINS.
ENTERTAINMENT ZONE
ALL MIGHT AND MIDNIGHT ARE HERE!
Is love in the air?!
Cut that out. I don't mess with older men.
WHICH CLASS ARE YOU BETTING ON?
HARD TO SAY. CLASS A'S GOTTEN STRONG, DEALING WITH ONE DISASTER AFTER ANOTHER.
BUT...

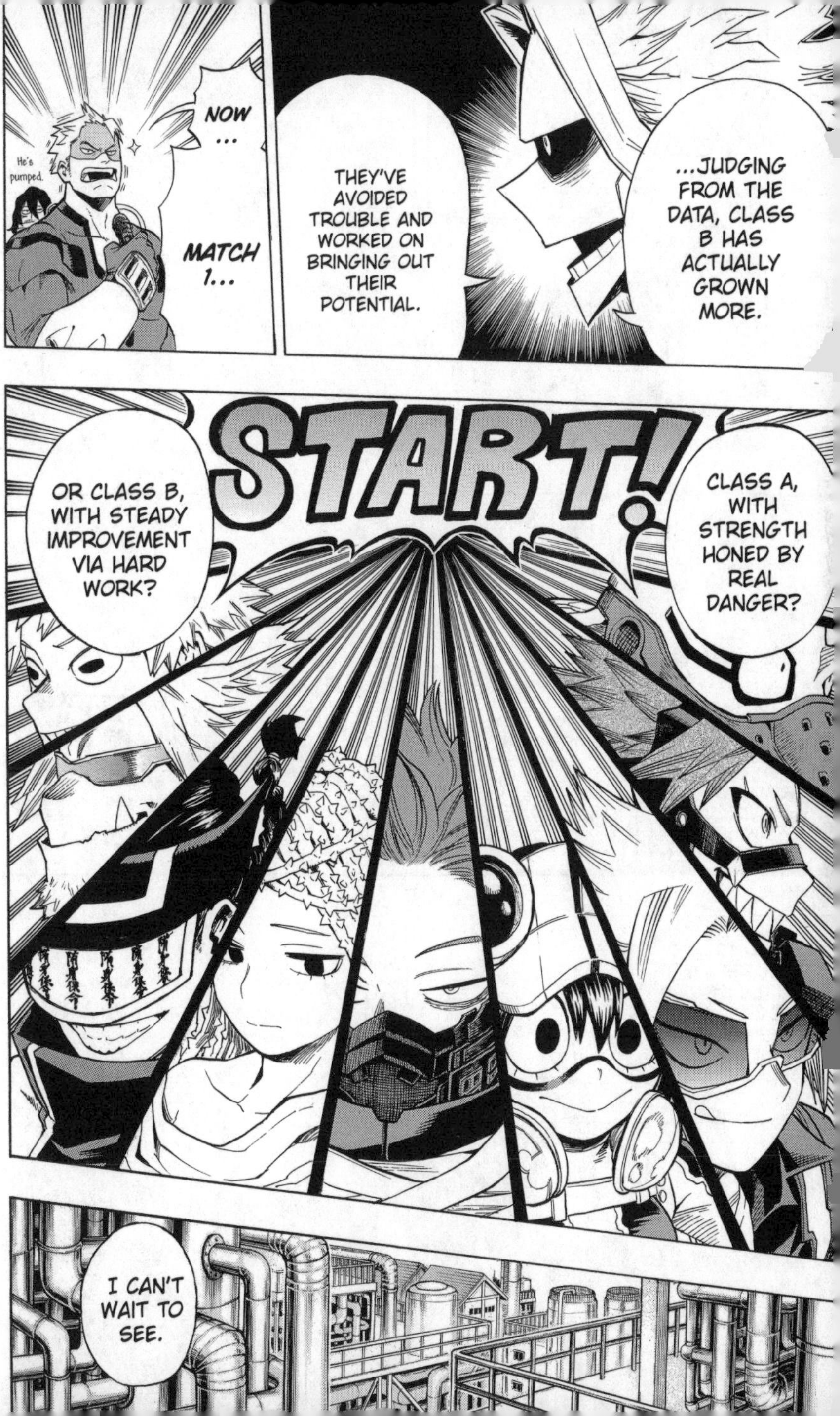
...JUDGING FROM THE DATA, CLASS B HAS ACTUALLY GROWN MORE.
THEY'VE AVOIDED TROUBLE AND WORKED ON BRINGING OUT THEIR POTENTIAL.
NOW ...
MATCH 1...
He's pumped.
START!
CLASS A, WITH STRENGTH HONED BY REAL DANGER?
OR CLASS B, WITH STEADY IMPROVEMENT VIA HARD WORK?
I CAN'T WAIT TO SEE.

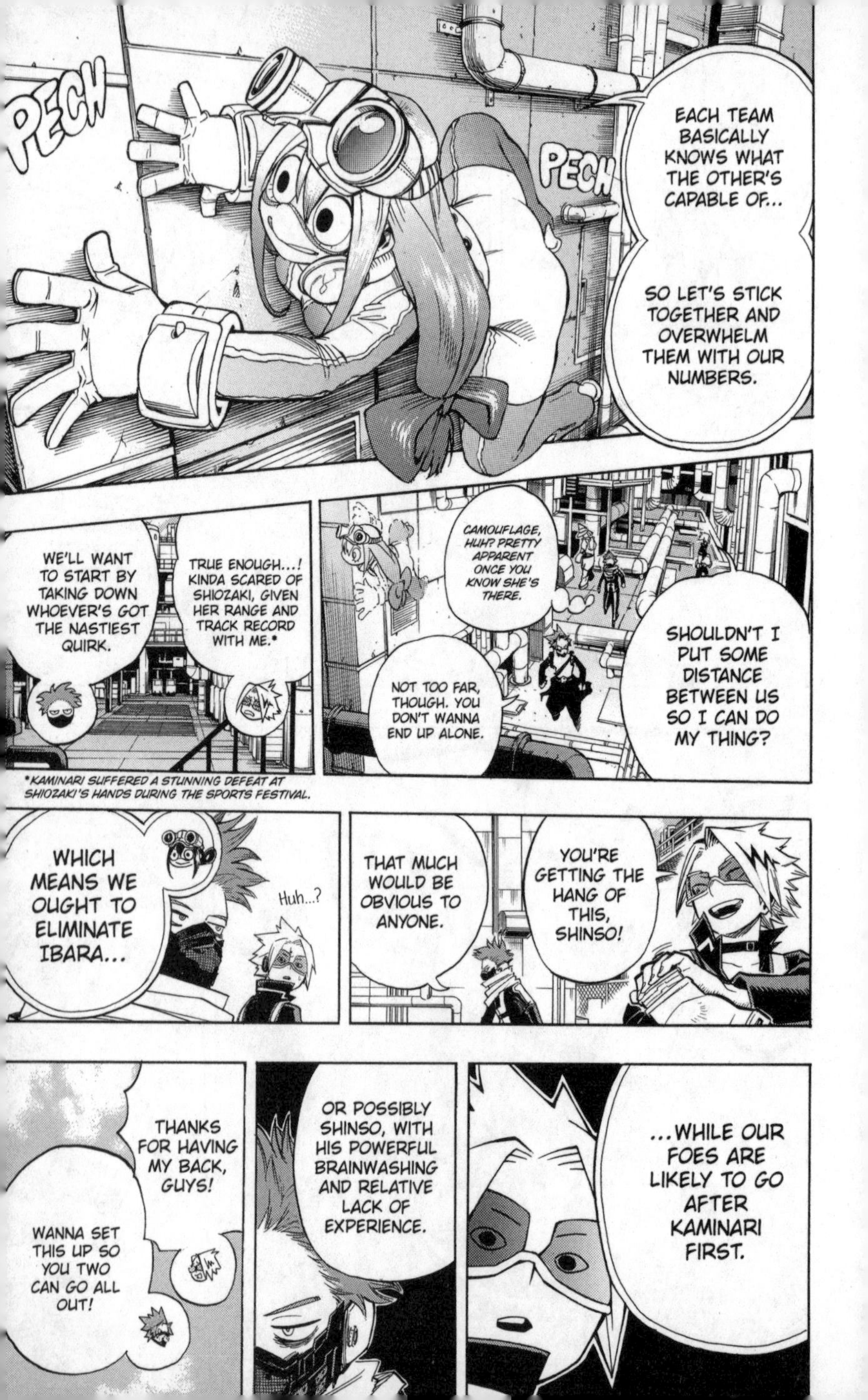
EACH TEAM BASICALLY KNOWS WHAT THE OTHER'S CAPABLE OF...
SO LET'S STICK TOGETHER AND OVERWHELM THEM WITH OUR NUMBERS.
PECH
PECH
CAMOUFLAGE, HUH? PRETTY APPARENT ONCE YOU KNOW SHE'S THERE.
SHOULDN'T I PUT SOME DISTANCE BETWEEN US SO I CAN DO MY THING?
NOT TOO FAR, THOUGH. YOU DON'T WANNA END UP ALONE.
TRUE ENOUGH...! KINDA SCARED OF SHIOZAKI, GIVEN HER RANGE AND TRACK RECORD WITH ME.*
WE'LL WANT TO START BY TAKING DOWN WHOEVER'S GOT THE NASTIEST QUIRK.
*KAMINARI SUFFERED A STUNNING DEFEAT AT SHIOZAKI'S HANDS DURING THE SPORTS FESTIVAL.
YOU'RE GETTING THE HANG OF THIS, SHINSO!
THAT MUCH WOULD BE OBVIOUS TO ANYONE.
WHICH MEANS WE OUGHT TO ELIMINATE IBARA...
Huh...?
...WHILE OUR FOES ARE LIKELY TO GO AFTER KAMINARI FIRST.
OR POSSIBLY SHINSO, WITH HIS POWERFUL BRAINWASHING AND RELATIVE LACK OF EXPERIENCE.
THANKS FOR HAVING MY BACK, GUYS!
WANNA SET THIS UP SO YOU TWO CAN GO ALL OUT!

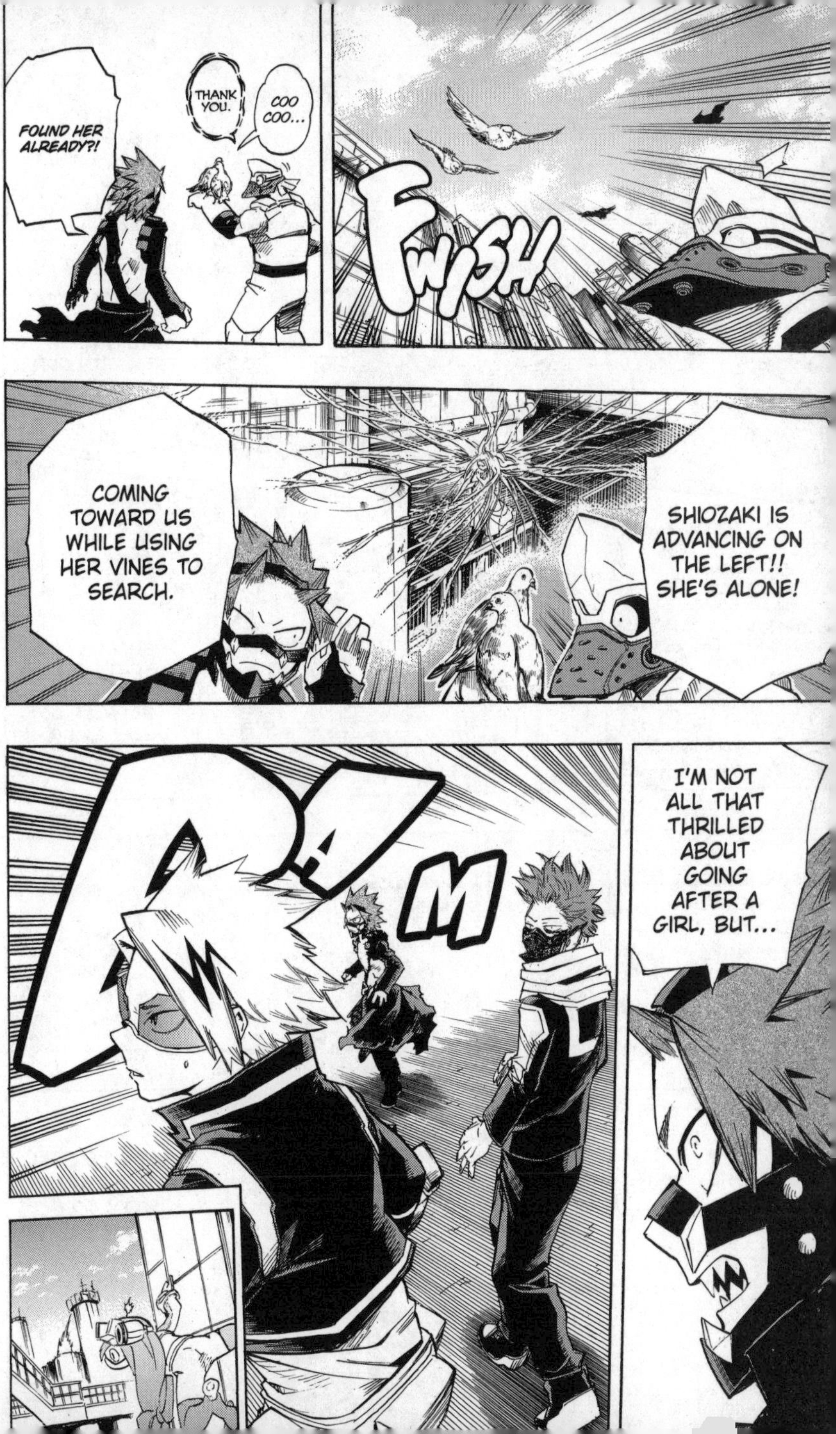
FWISH
COO COO...
THANK YOU.
FOUND HER ALREADY?!
SHIOZAKI IS ADVANCING ON THE LEFT!! SHE'S ALONE!
COMING TOWARD US WHILE USING HER VINES TO SEARCH.
I'M NOT ALL THAT THRILLED ABOUT GOING AFTER A GIRL, BUT...
BAM

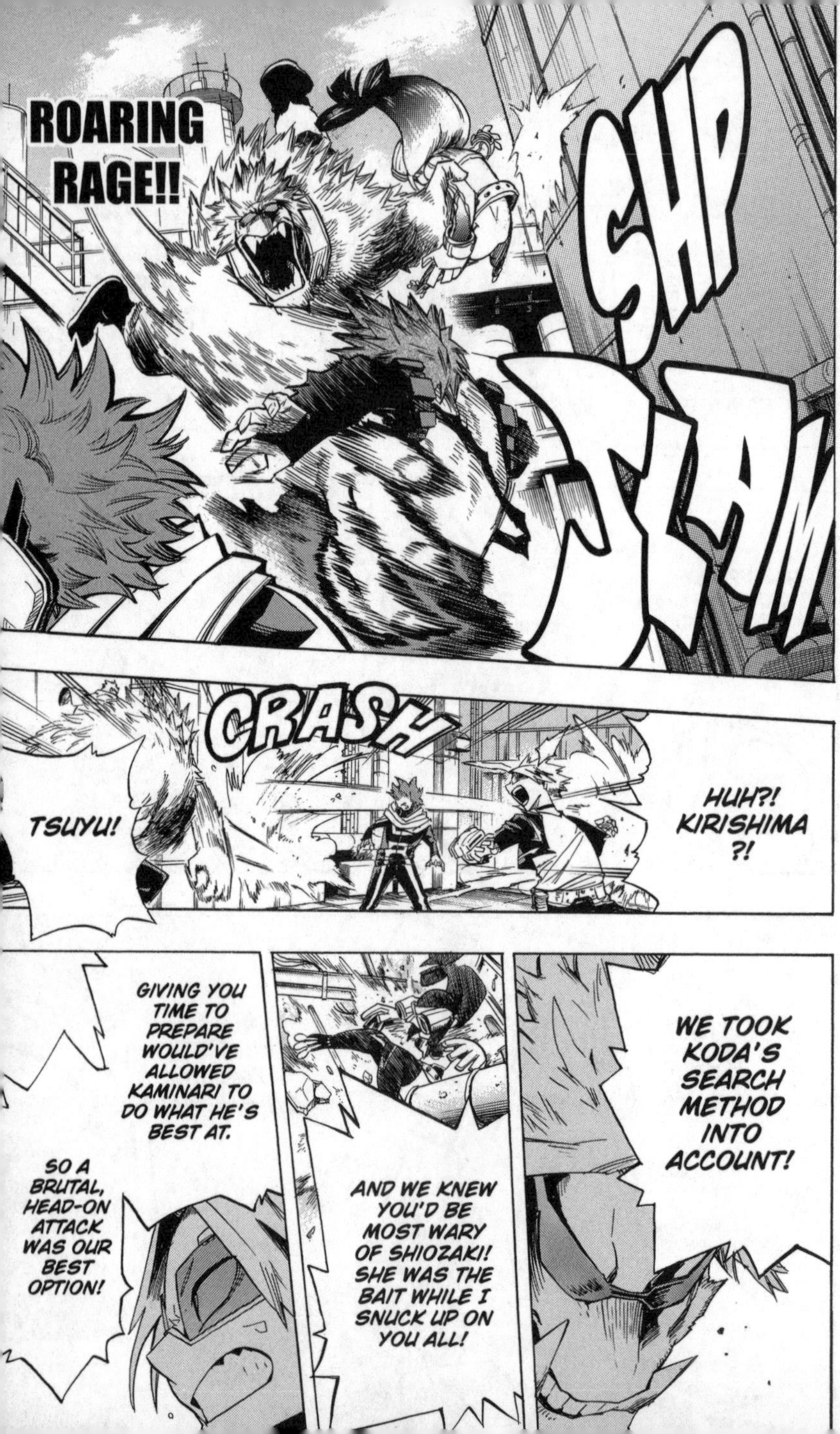
SHP
SLAM
ROARING RAGE!!
HUH?! KIRISHIMA ?!
CRASH
TSUYU!
WE TOOK KODA'S SEARCH METHOD INTO ACCOUNT!
AND WE KNEW YOU'D BE MOST WARY OF SHIOZAKI! SHE WAS THE BAIT WHILE I SNUCK UP ON YOU ALL!
GIVING YOU TIME TO PREPARE WOULD'VE ALLOWED KAMINARI TO DO WHAT HE'S BEST AT.
SO A BRUTAL, HEAD-ON ATTACK WAS OUR BEST OPTION!

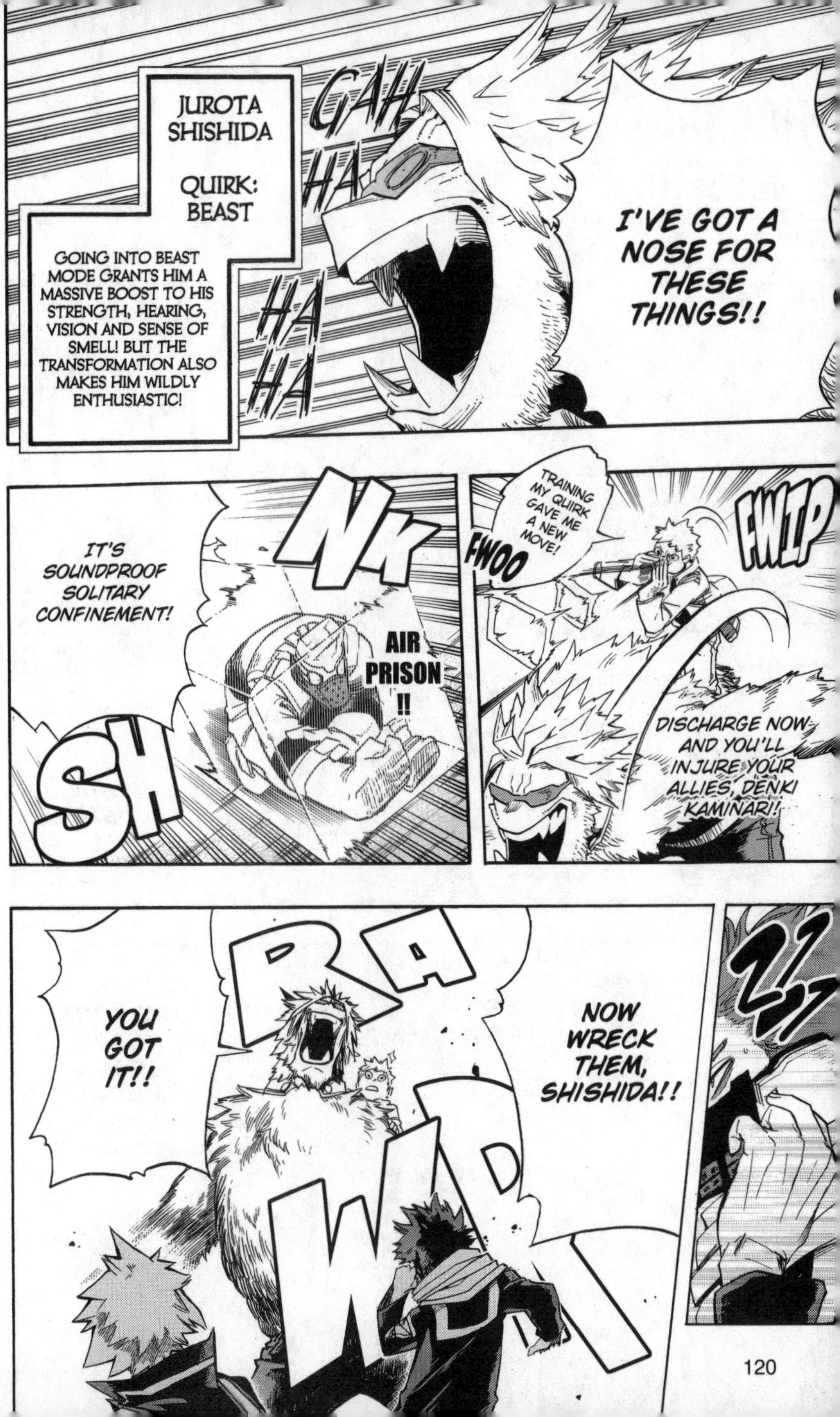
I'VE GOT A NOSE FOR THESE THINGS!!
GAH HA HA HA HA
JUROTA SHISHIDA
QUIRK: BEAST
GOING INTO BEAST MODE GRANTS HIM A MASSIVE BOOST TO HIS STRENGTH, HEARING, VISION AND SENSE OF SMELL! BUT THE TRANSFORMATION ALSO MAKES HIM WILDLY ENTHUSIASTIC!
FWIP
TRAINING MY QUIRK GAVE ME A NEW MOVE!
FWOO
DISCHARGE NOW AND YOU'LL INJURE YOUR ALLIES, DENKI KAMINARI!!
NK
IT'S SOUNDPROOF SOLITARY CONFINEMENT!
AIR PRISON!!
SH
RA
NOW WRECK THEM, SHISHIDA!!
YOU GOT IT!!

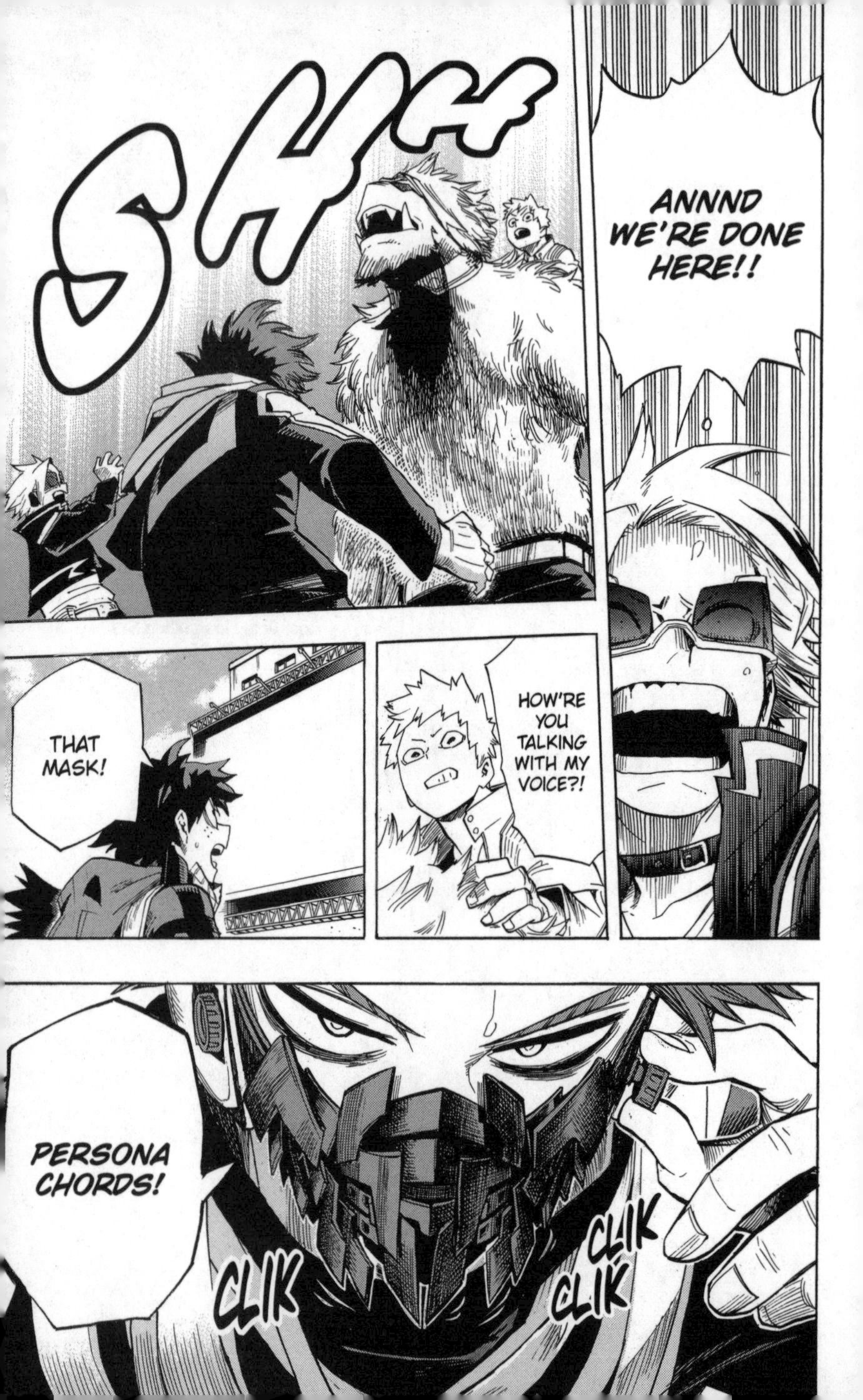
ANNND WE'RE DONE HERE!!
SHH
HOW'RE YOU TALKING WITH MY VOICE?!
THAT MASK!
PERSONA CHORDS!
CLIK CLIK
CLIK

JUROTA SHISHIDA (15)

STREET CLOTHES

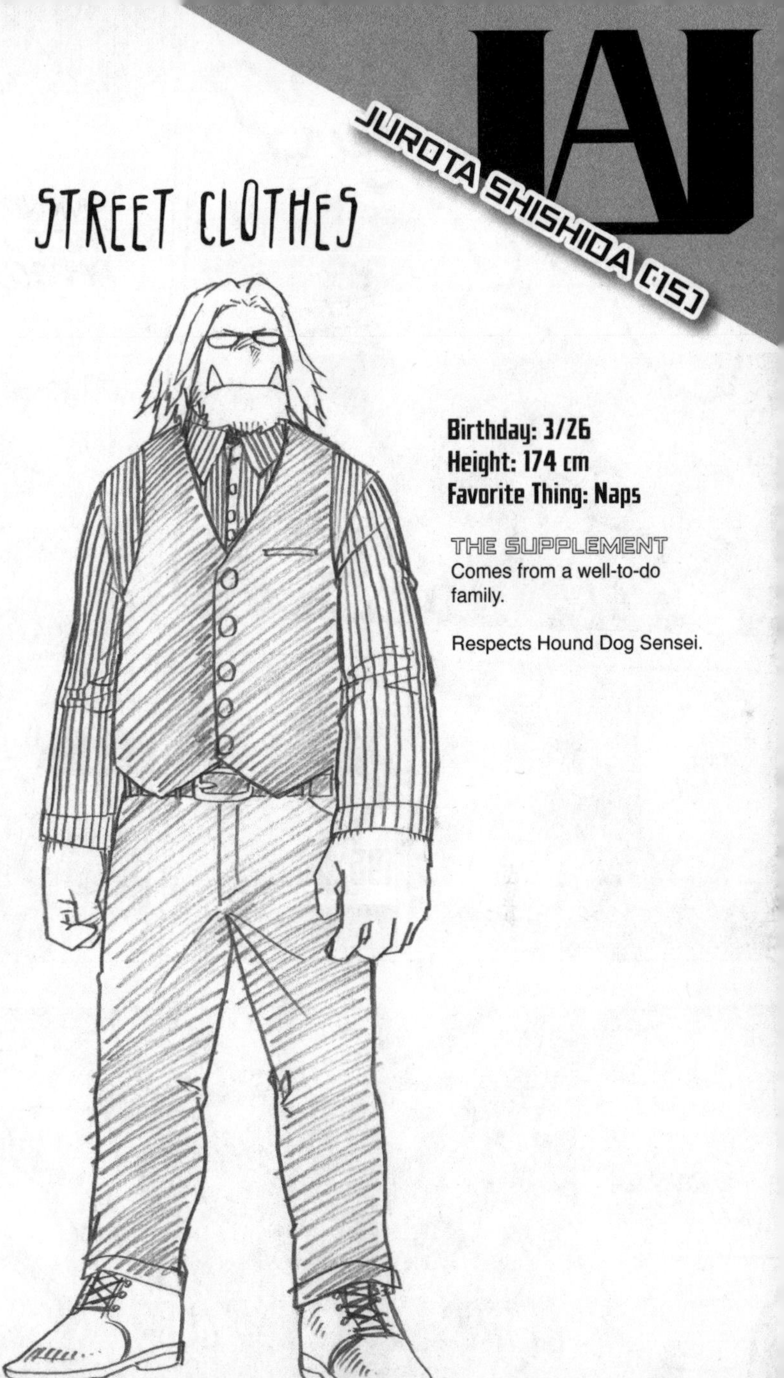

Birthday: 3/26
Height: 174 cm
Favorite Thing: Naps

THE SUPPLEMENT

Comes from a well-to-do family.

Respects Hound Dog Sensei.

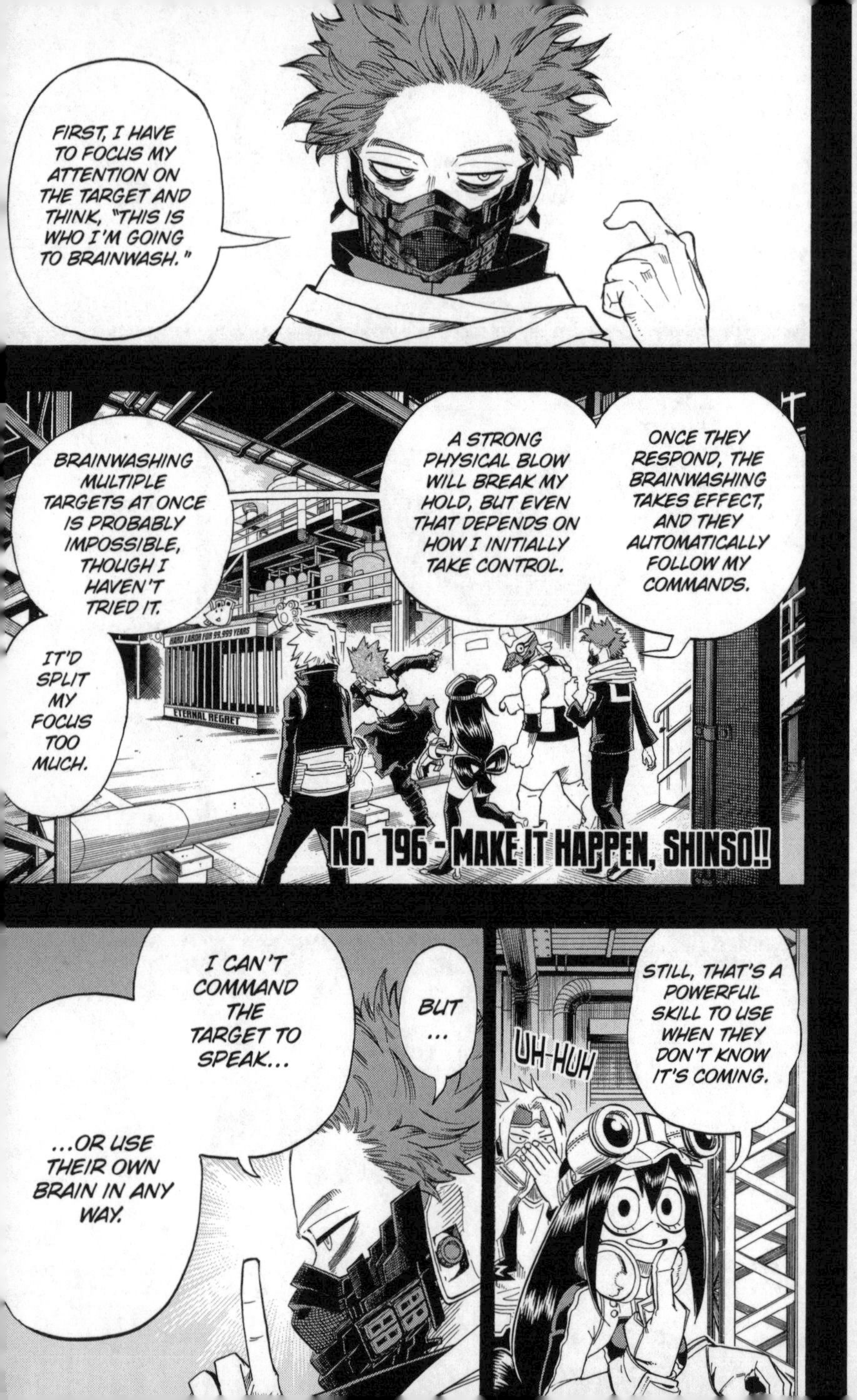
FIRST, I HAVE TO FOCUS MY ATTENTION ON THE TARGET AND THINK, "THIS IS WHO I'M GOING TO BRAINWASH."
ONCE THEY RESPOND, THE BRAINWASHING TAKES EFFECT, AND THEY AUTOMATICALLY FOLLOW MY COMMANDS.
A STRONG PHYSICAL BLOW WILL BREAK MY HOLD, BUT EVEN THAT DEPENDS ON HOW I INITIALLY TAKE CONTROL.
BRAINWASHING MULTIPLE TARGETS AT ONCE IS PROBABLY IMPOSSIBLE, THOUGH I HAVEN'T TRIED IT.
IT'D SPLIT MY FOCUS TOO MUCH.
HARD LABOR FOR 99,999 YEARS
ETERNAL REGRET
NO. 196 - MAKE IT HAPPEN, SHINSO!!
STILL, THAT'S A POWERFUL SKILL TO USE WHEN THEY DON'T KNOW IT'S COMING.
UH-HUH
BUT ...
I CAN'T COMMAND THE TARGET TO SPEAK...
...OR USE THEIR OWN BRAIN IN ANY WAY.

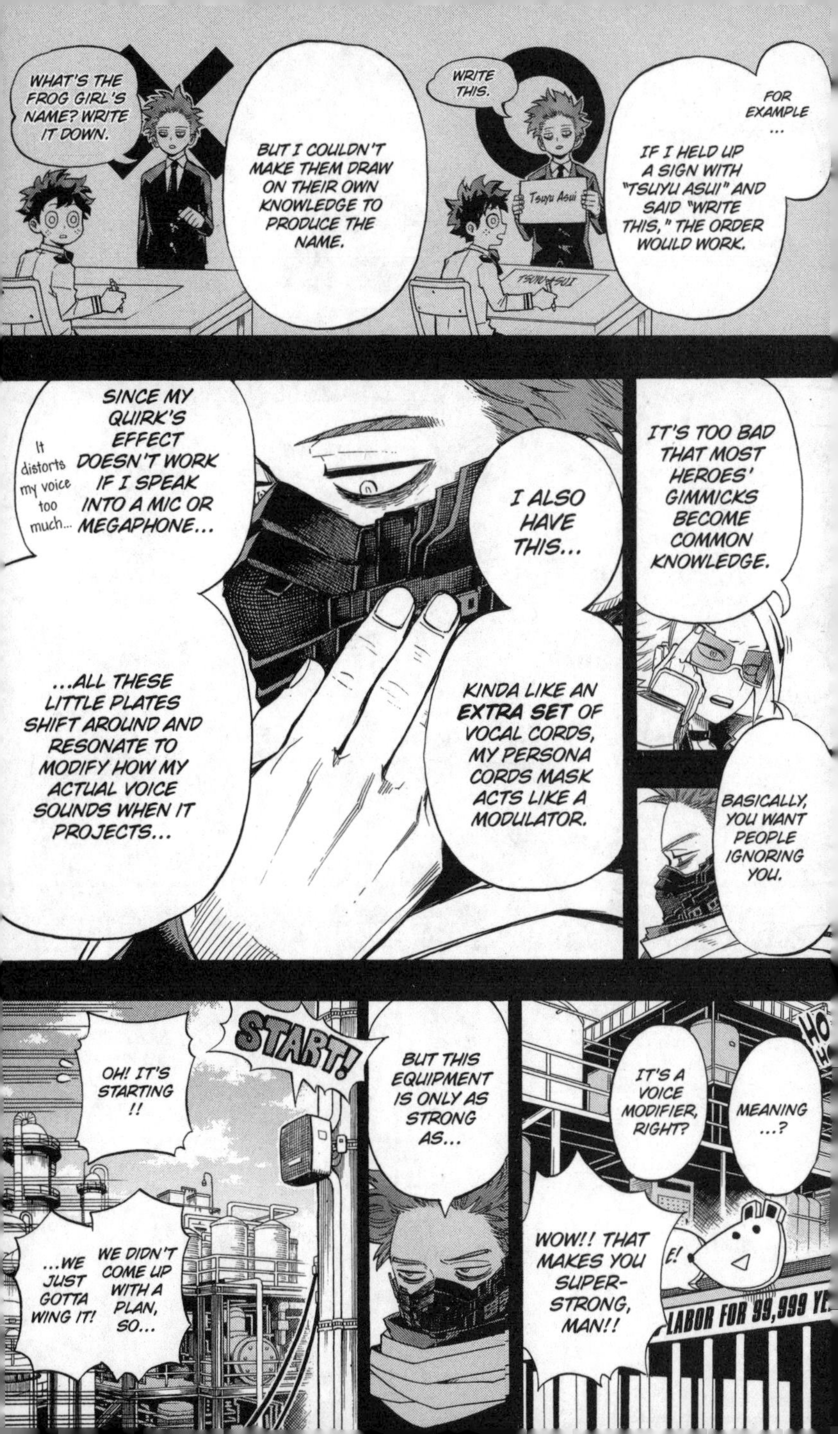

FOR EXAMPLE ...
IF I HELD UP A SIGN WITH "TSUYU ASUI" AND SAID "WRITE THIS," THE ORDER WOULD WORK.
WRITE THIS.
Tsuyu Asui
TSUYU ASUI
BUT I COULDN'T MAKE THEM DRAW ON THEIR OWN KNOWLEDGE TO PRODUCE THE NAME.
WHAT'S THE FROG GIRL'S NAME? WRITE IT DOWN.
IT'S TOO BAD THAT MOST HEROES' GIMMICKS BECOME COMMON KNOWLEDGE.
BASICALLY, YOU WANT PEOPLE IGNORING YOU.
I ALSO HAVE THIS...
KINDA LIKE AN **EXTRA SET** OF VOCAL CORDS, MY PERSONA CORDS MASK ACTS LIKE A MODULATOR.
SINCE MY QUIRK'S EFFECT DOESN'T WORK IF I SPEAK INTO A MIC OR MEGAPHONE...
It distorts my voice too much...
...ALL THESE LITTLE PLATES SHIFT AROUND AND RESONATE TO MODIFY HOW MY ACTUAL VOICE SOUNDS WHEN IT PROJECTS...
MEANING ...?
IT'S A VOICE MODIFIER, RIGHT?
WOW!! THAT MAKES YOU SUPER-STRONG, MAN!!
E!
LABOR FOR 99,999
BUT THIS EQUIPMENT IS ONLY AS STRONG AS...
START!
OH! IT'S STARTING !!
WE DIDN'T COME UP WITH A PLAN, SO...
...WE JUST GOTTA WING IT!

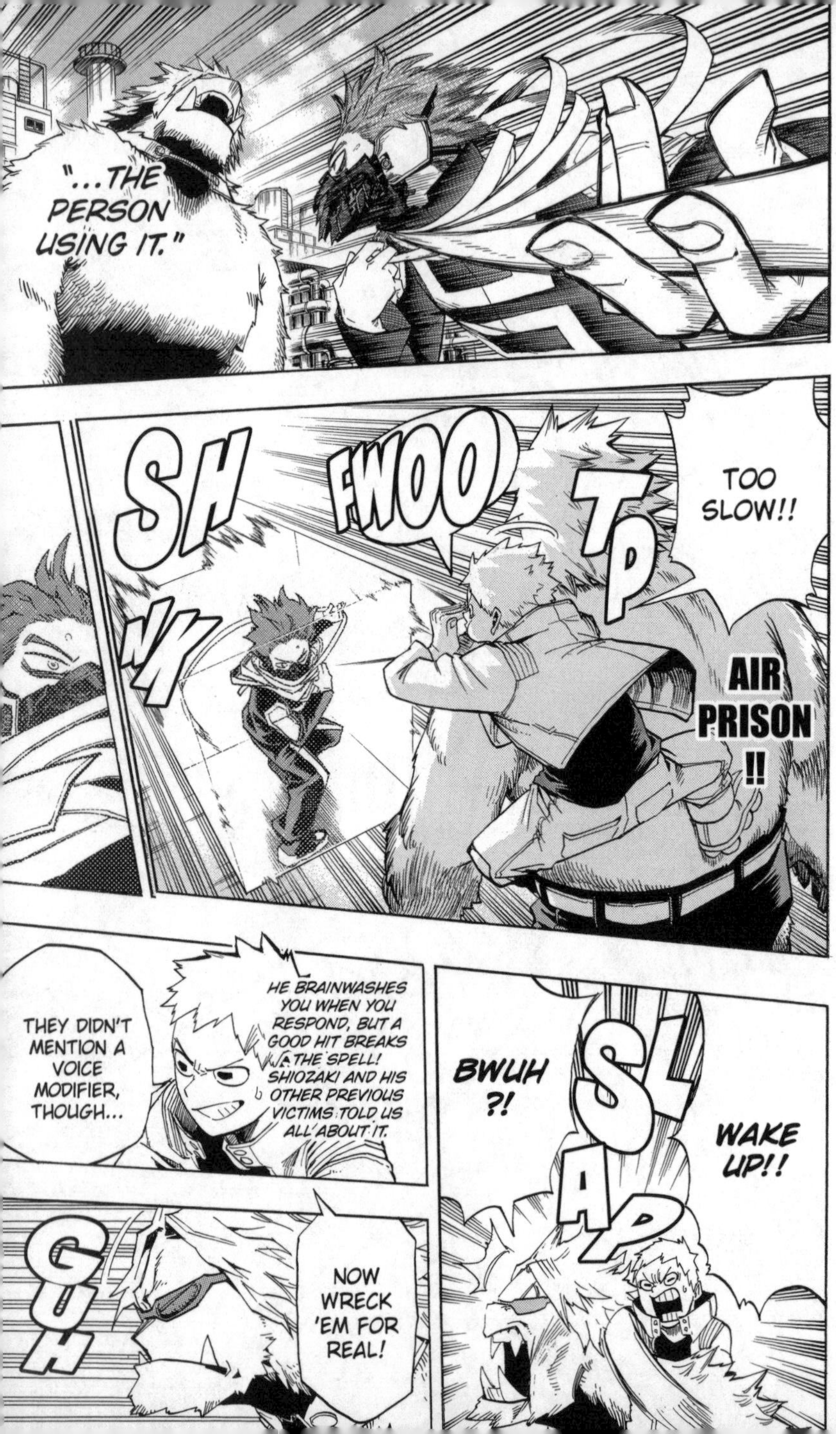
"...THE PERSON USING IT."
TOO SLOW!!
TP
FWOO
SH
AIR PRISON !!
NK
SL
BWUH ?!
WAKE UP!!
AP
HE BRAINWASHES YOU WHEN YOU RESPOND, BUT A GOOD HIT BREAKS THE SPELL! SHIOZAKI AND HIS OTHER PREVIOUS VICTIMS TOLD US ALL ABOUT IT.
THEY DIDN'T MENTION A VOICE MODIFIER, THOUGH...
NOW WRECK 'EM FOR REAL!
GUH

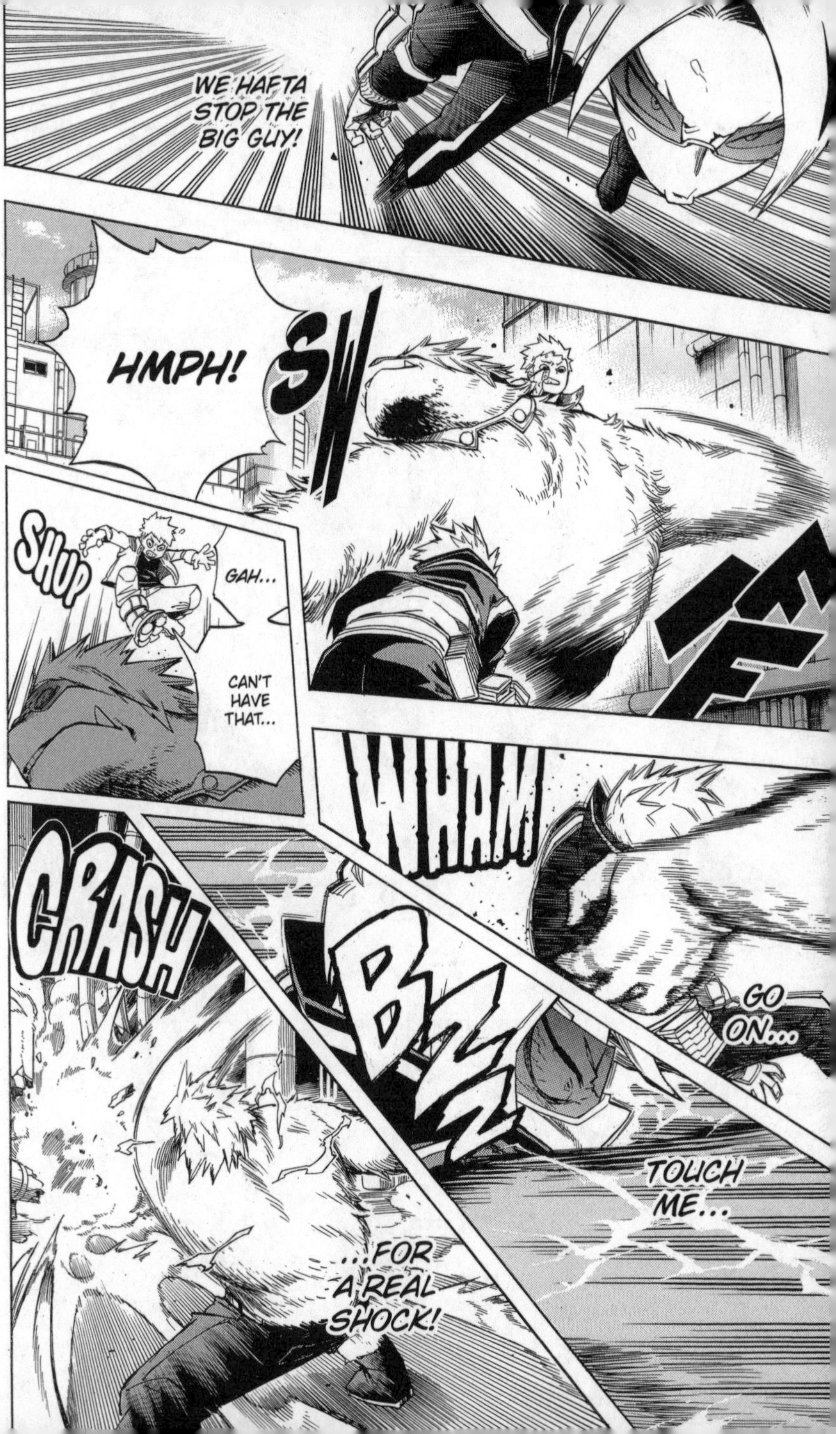
WE HAFTA STOP THE BIG GUY!
HMPH!
SW
SHUP
GAH...
CAN'T HAVE THAT...
WHAM
GO ON...
TOUCH ME...
...FOR A REAL SHOCK!
CRASH

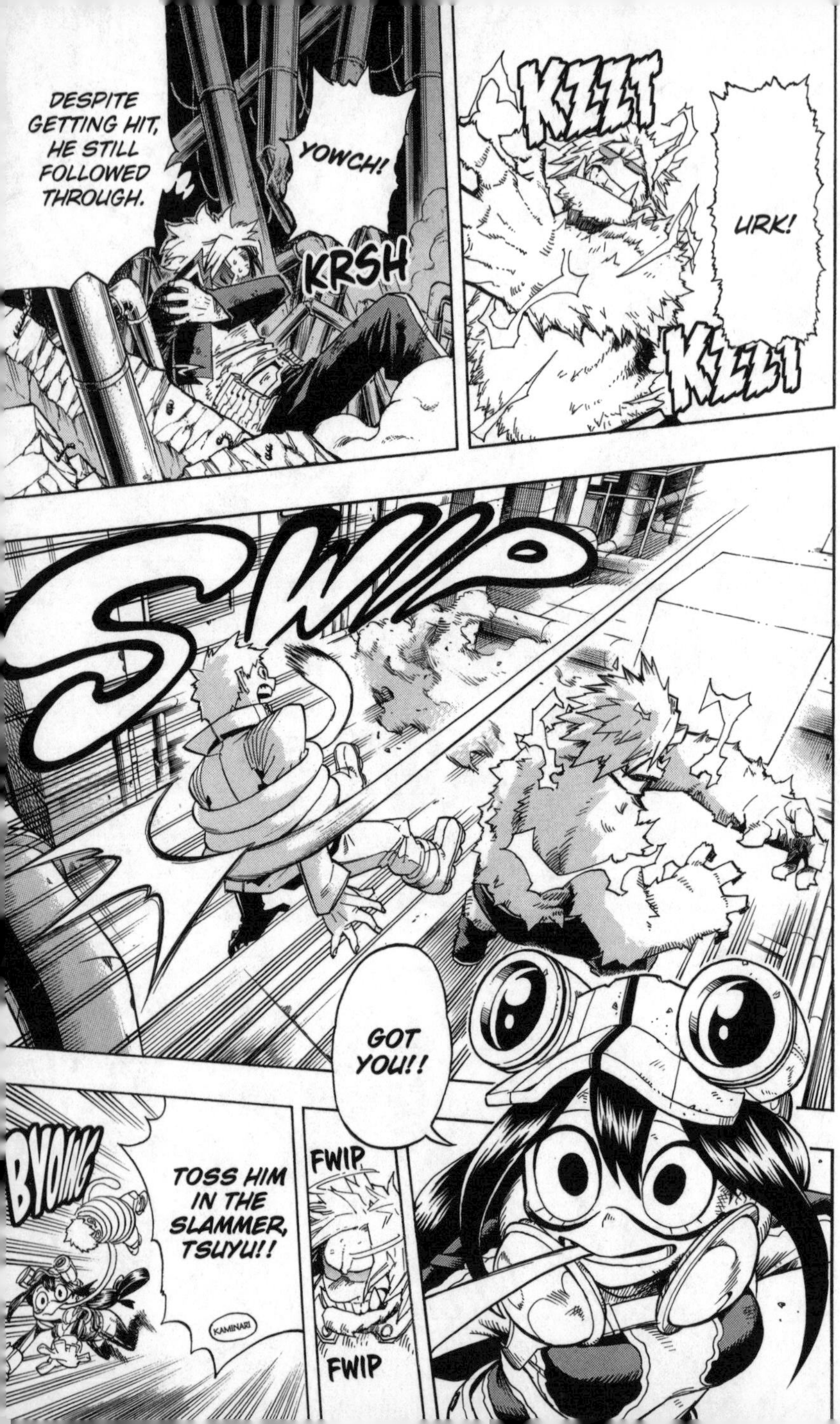
KZZZT
URK!
KZZZT
YOWCH!
DESPITE GETTING HIT, HE STILL FOLLOWED THROUGH.
KRSH
SWIP
GOT YOU!!
FWIP
FWIP
BYOING
TOSS HIM IN THE SLAMMER, TSUYU!!
KAMINARI

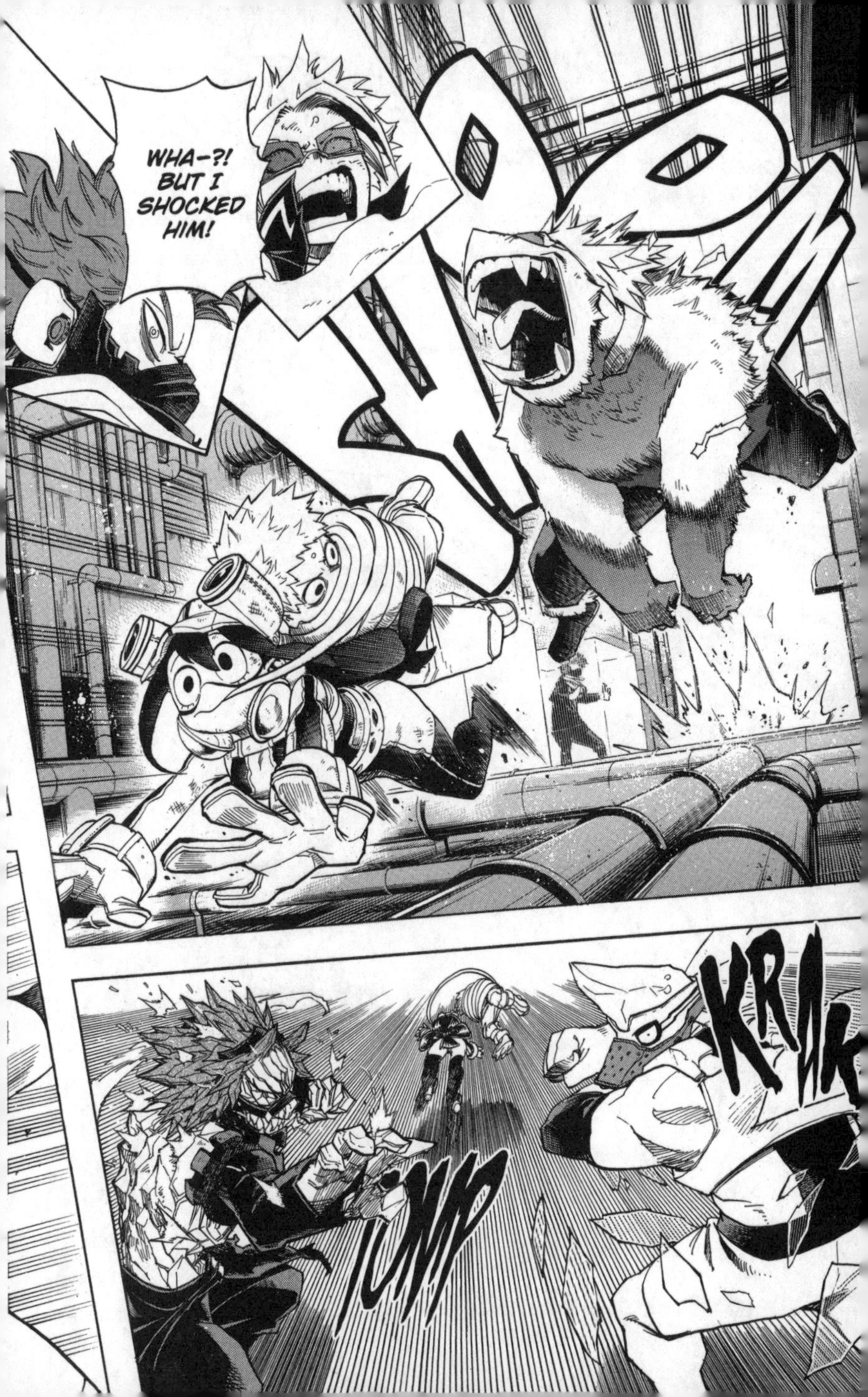
WHA-?! BUT I SHOCKED HIM!

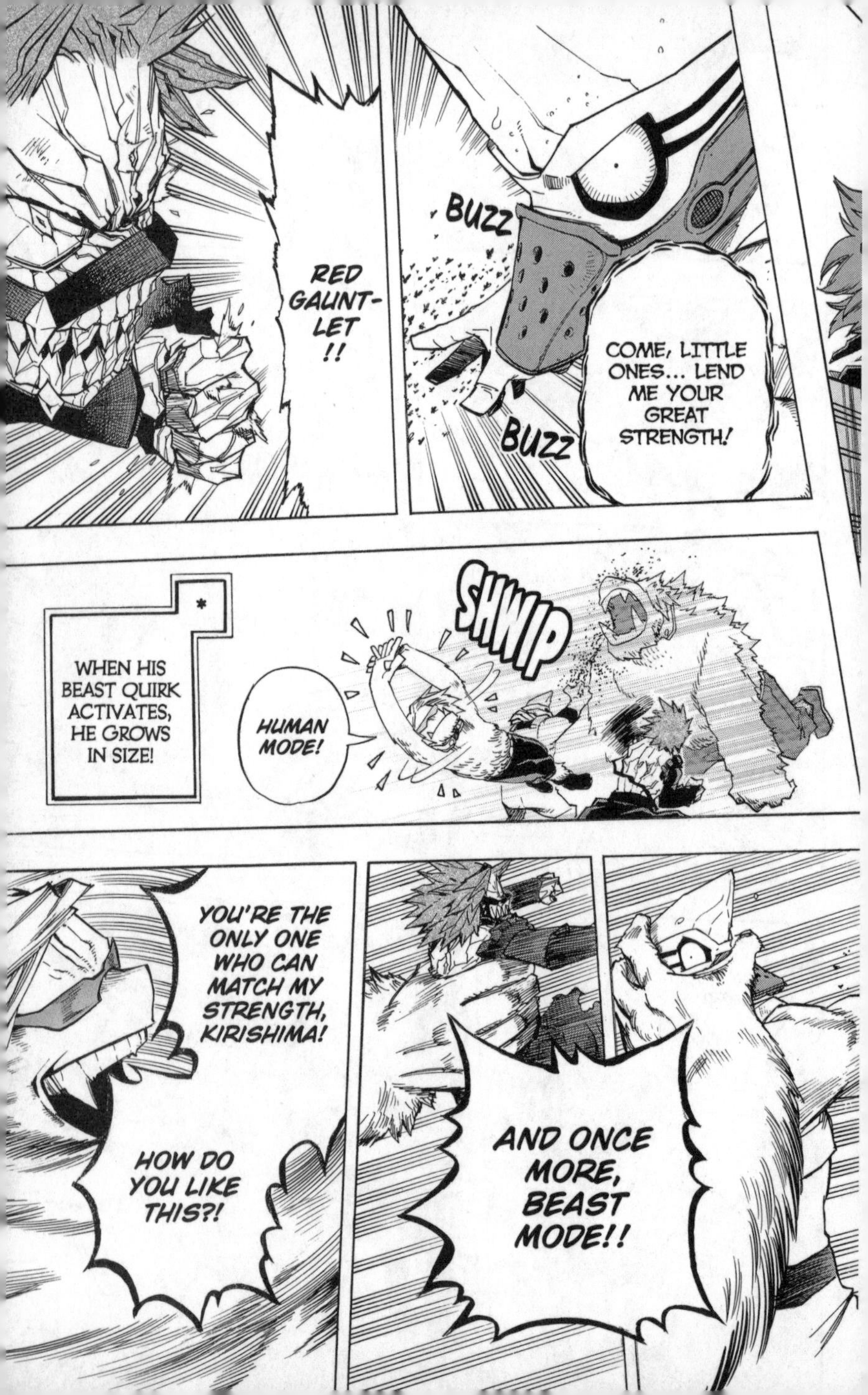
BUZZ
COME, LITTLE ONES... LEND ME YOUR GREAT STRENGTH!
BUZZ
RED GAUNT-LET!!
SHWIP
HUMAN MODE!
* WHEN HIS BEAST QUIRK ACTIVATES, HE GROWS IN SIZE!
AND ONCE MORE, BEAST MODE!!
YOU'RE THE ONLY ONE WHO CAN MATCH MY STRENGTH, KIRISHIMA!
HOW DO YOU LIKE THIS?!

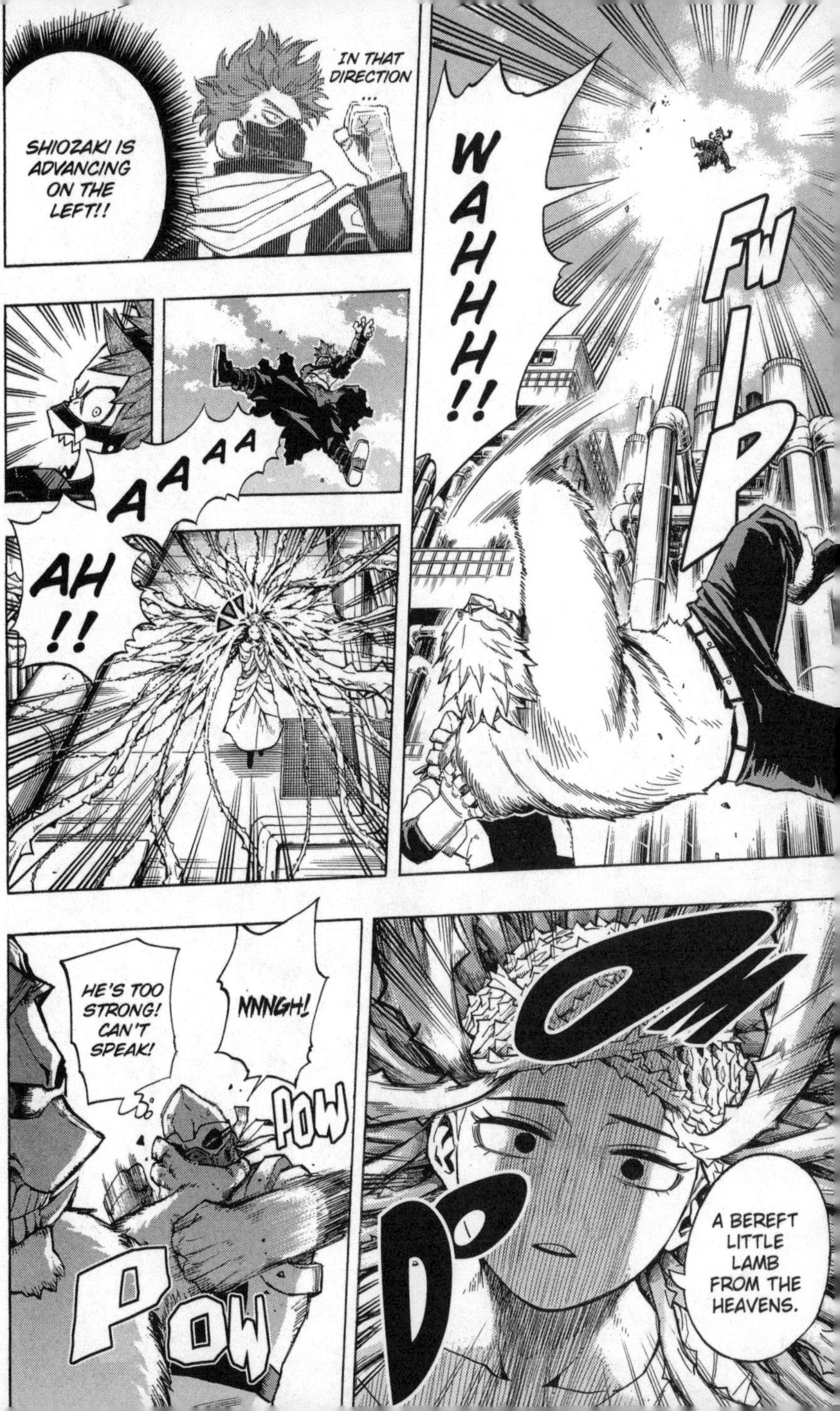
WAHHHH!!
FWIP
IN THAT DIRECTION ...
SHIOZAKI IS ADVANCING ON THE LEFT!!
AAAAA
AH!!
DOOM
A BEREFT LITTLE LAMB FROM THE HEAVENS.
NNNGH!
HE'S TOO STRONG! CAN'T SPEAK!
POW
POW

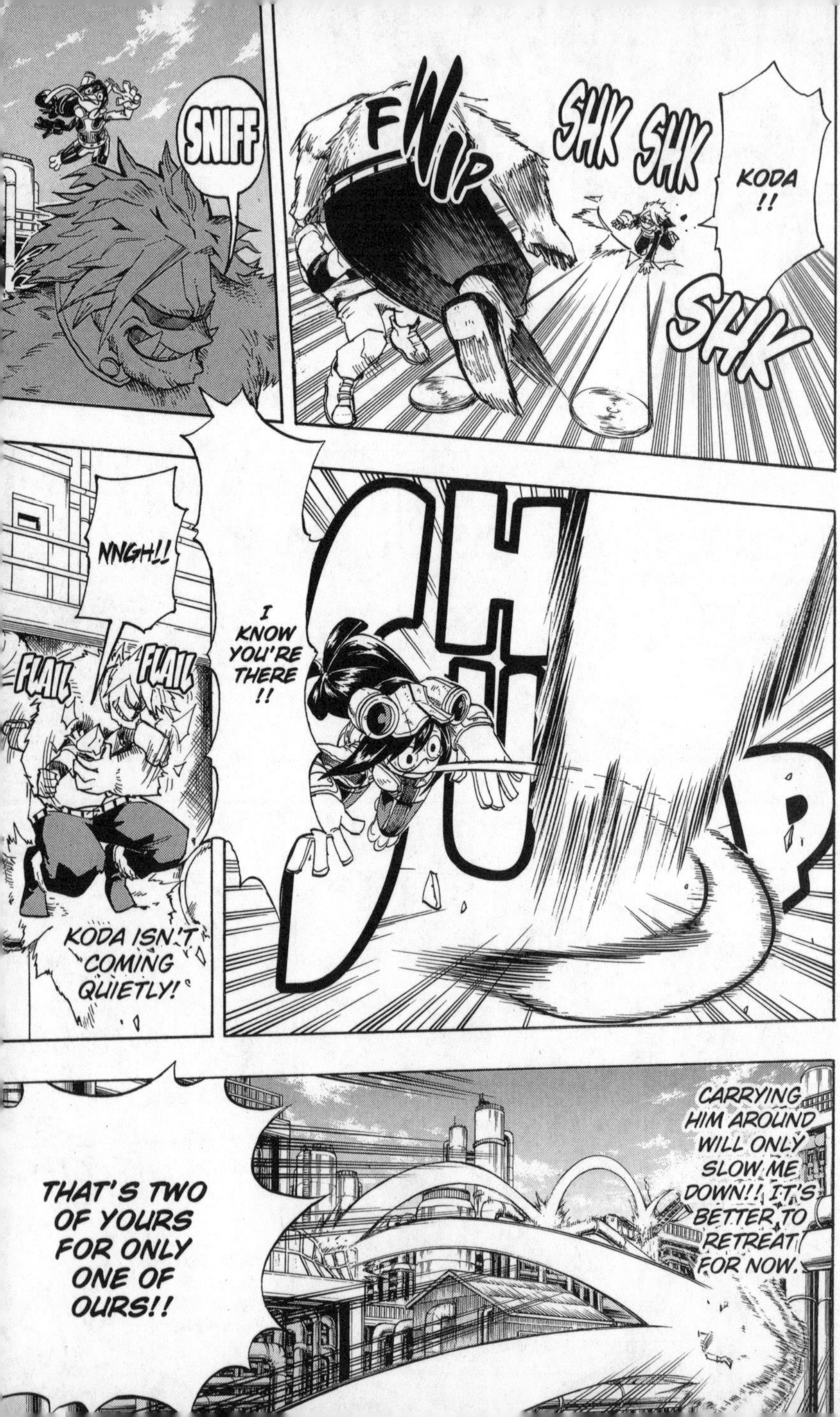
SHK SHK
KODA!!
FWIP
SHK
SNIFF
I KNOW YOU'RE THERE!!
NNGH!!
FLAIL
FLAIL
KODA ISN'T COMING QUIETLY!
CARRYING HIM AROUND WILL ONLY SLOW ME DOWN!! IT'S BETTER TO RETREAT FOR NOW.
THAT'S TWO OF YOURS FOR ONLY ONE OF OURS!!

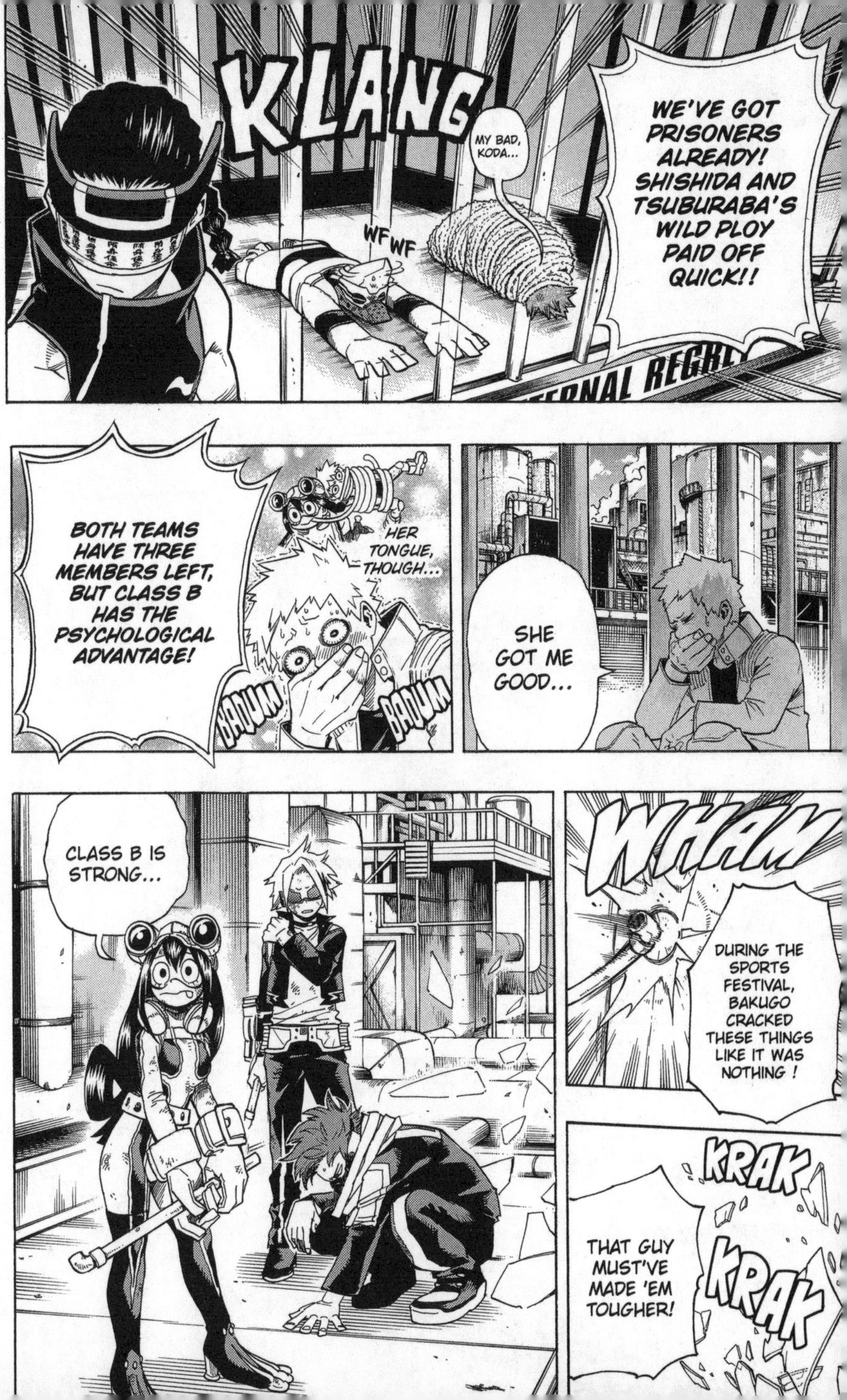

WE'VE GOT PRISONERS ALREADY! SHISHIDA AND TSUBURABA'S WILD PLOY PAID OFF QUICK!!
KLANG
MY BAD, KODA...
WF WF
SHE GOT ME GOOD...
HER TONGUE, THOUGH...
BOTH TEAMS HAVE THREE MEMBERS LEFT, BUT CLASS B HAS THE PSYCHOLOGICAL ADVANTAGE!
BADUM
BADUM
WHAM
DURING THE SPORTS FESTIVAL, BAKUGO CRACKED THESE THINGS LIKE IT WAS NOTHING !
KRAK
KRAK
THAT GUY MUST'VE MADE 'EM TOUGHER!
CLASS B IS STRONG...

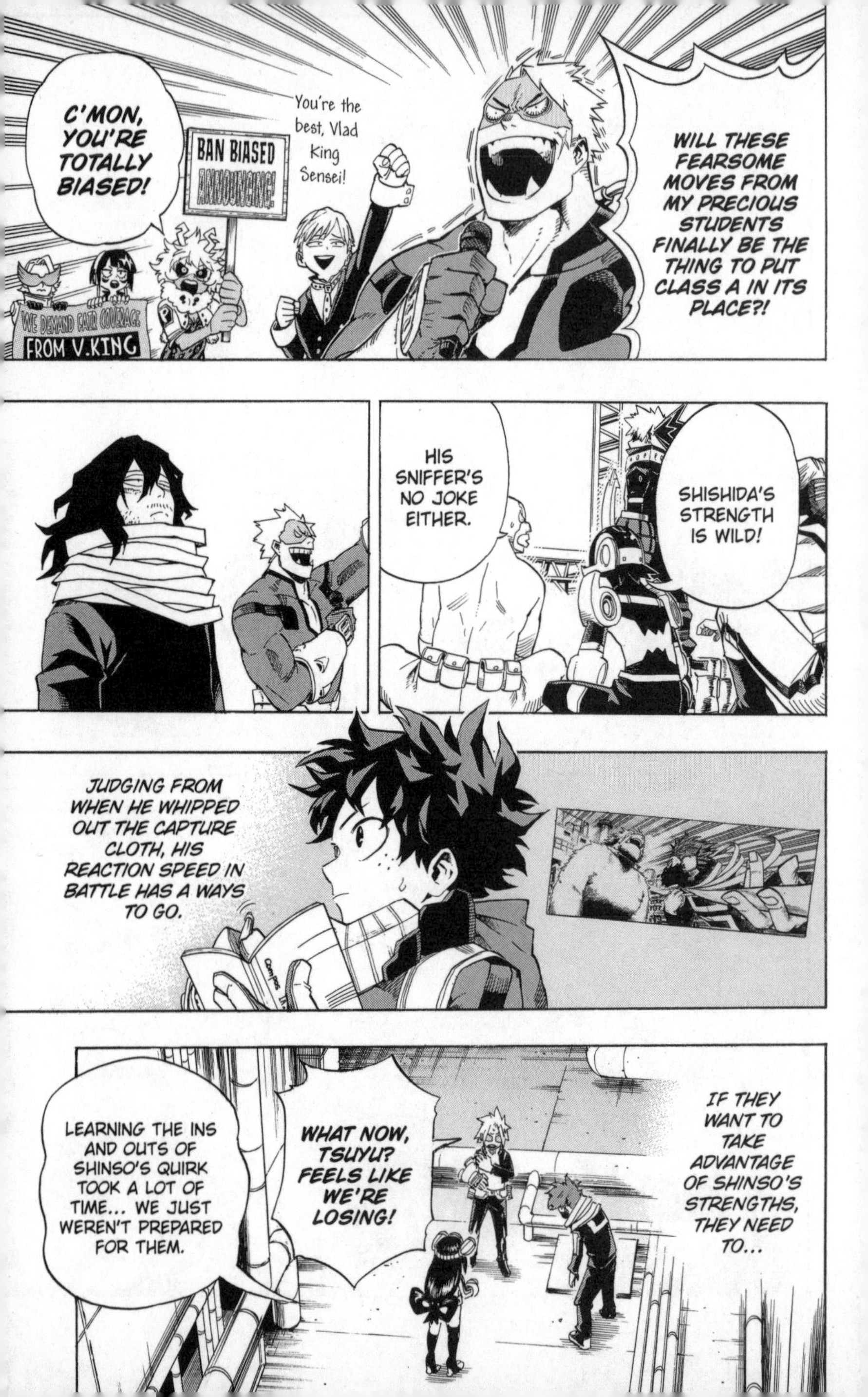
WILL THESE FEARSOME MOVES FROM MY PRECIOUS STUDENTS FINALLY BE THE THING TO PUT CLASS A IN ITS PLACE?!
You're the best, Vlad King Sensei!
BAN BIASED
C'MON, YOU'RE TOTALLY BIASED!
WE DEMAND FAIR COVERAGE FROM V.KING
SHISHIDA'S STRENGTH IS WILD!
HIS SNIFFER'S NO JOKE EITHER.
JUDGING FROM WHEN HE WHIPPED OUT THE CAPTURE CLOTH, HIS REACTION SPEED IN BATTLE HAS A WAYS TO GO.
IF THEY WANT TO TAKE ADVANTAGE OF SHINSO'S STRENGTHS, THEY NEED TO...
WHAT NOW, TSUYU? FEELS LIKE WE'RE LOSING!
LEARNING THE INS AND OUTS OF SHINSO'S QUIRK TOOK A LOT OF TIME... WE JUST WEREN'T PREPARED FOR THEM.

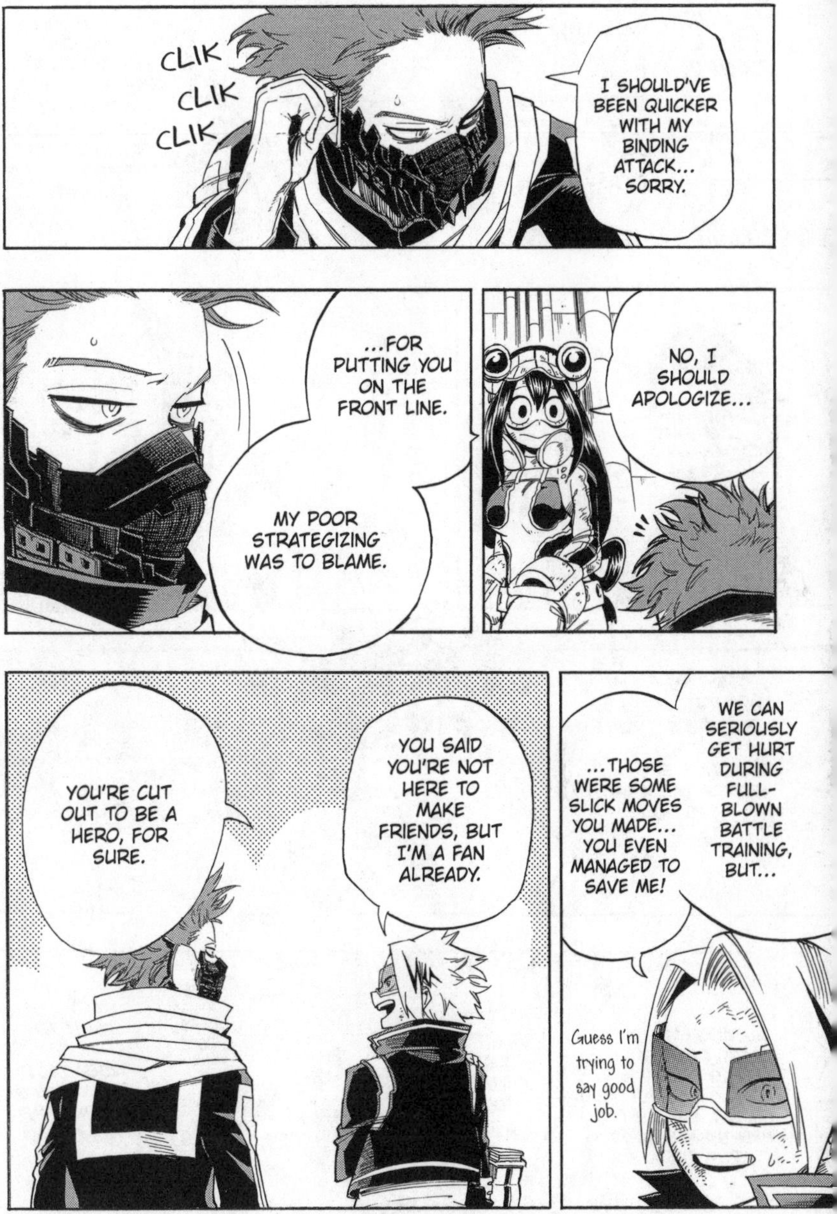
I SHOULD'VE BEEN QUICKER WITH MY BINDING ATTACK... SORRY.
CLIK
CLIK
CLIK
NO, I SHOULD APOLOGIZE...
...FOR PUTTING YOU ON THE FRONT LINE.
MY POOR STRATEGIZING WAS TO BLAME.
WE CAN SERIOUSLY GET HURT DURING FULL-BLOWN BATTLE TRAINING, BUT...
...THOSE WERE SOME SLICK MOVES YOU MADE... YOU EVEN MANAGED TO SAVE ME!
Guess I'm trying to say good job.
YOU SAID YOU'RE NOT HERE TO MAKE FRIENDS, BUT I'M A FAN ALREADY.
YOU'RE CUT OUT TO BE A HERO, FOR SURE.

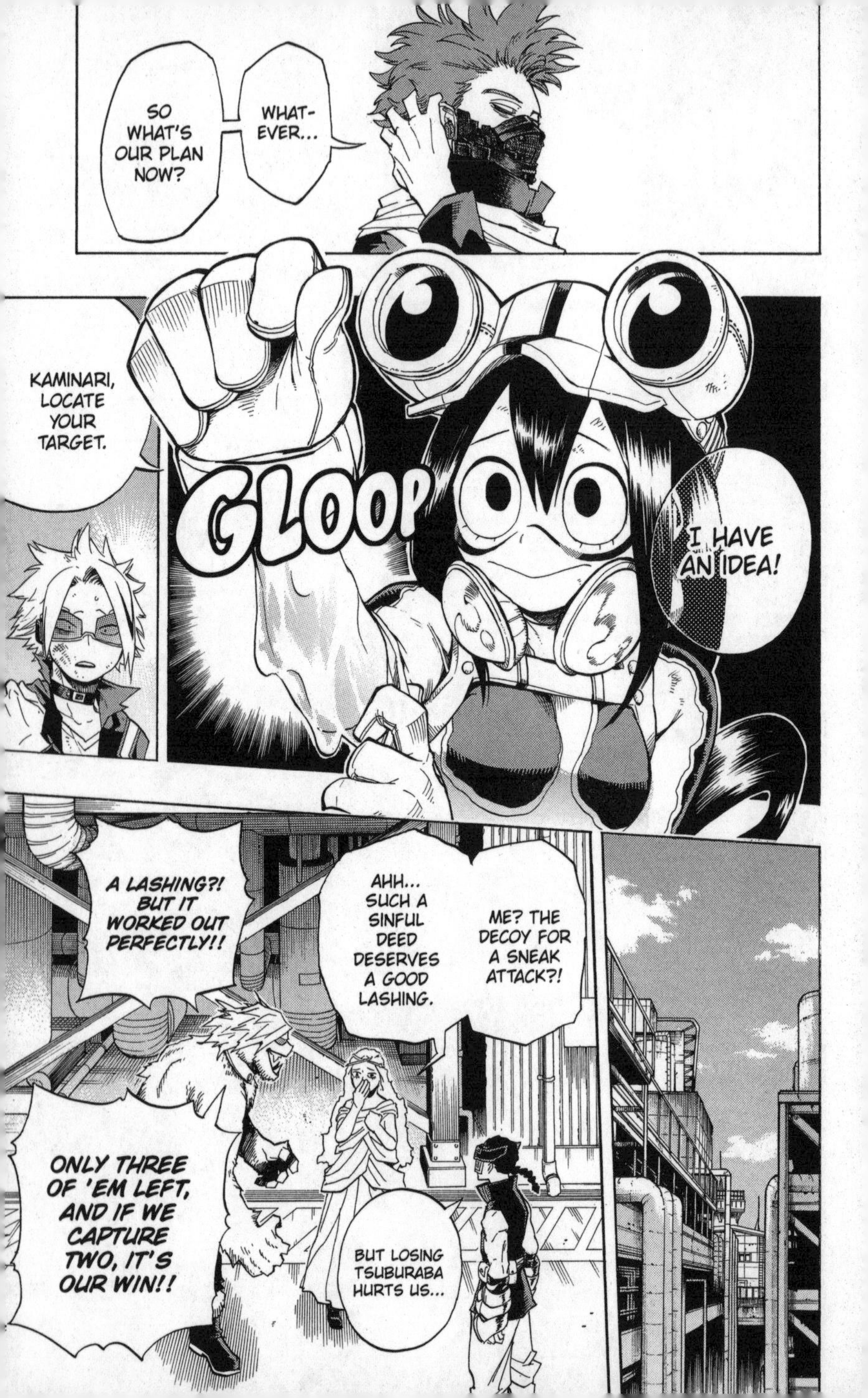
WHAT-EVER...
SO WHAT'S OUR PLAN NOW?
I HAVE AN IDEA!
GLOOP
KAMINARI, LOCATE YOUR TARGET.
ME? THE DECOY FOR A SNEAK ATTACK?!
AHH... SUCH A SINFUL DEED DESERVES A GOOD LASHING.
A LASHING?! BUT IT WORKED OUT PERFECTLY!!
ONLY THREE OF 'EM LEFT, AND IF WE CAPTURE TWO, IT'S OUR WIN!!
BUT LOSING TSUBURABA HURTS US...

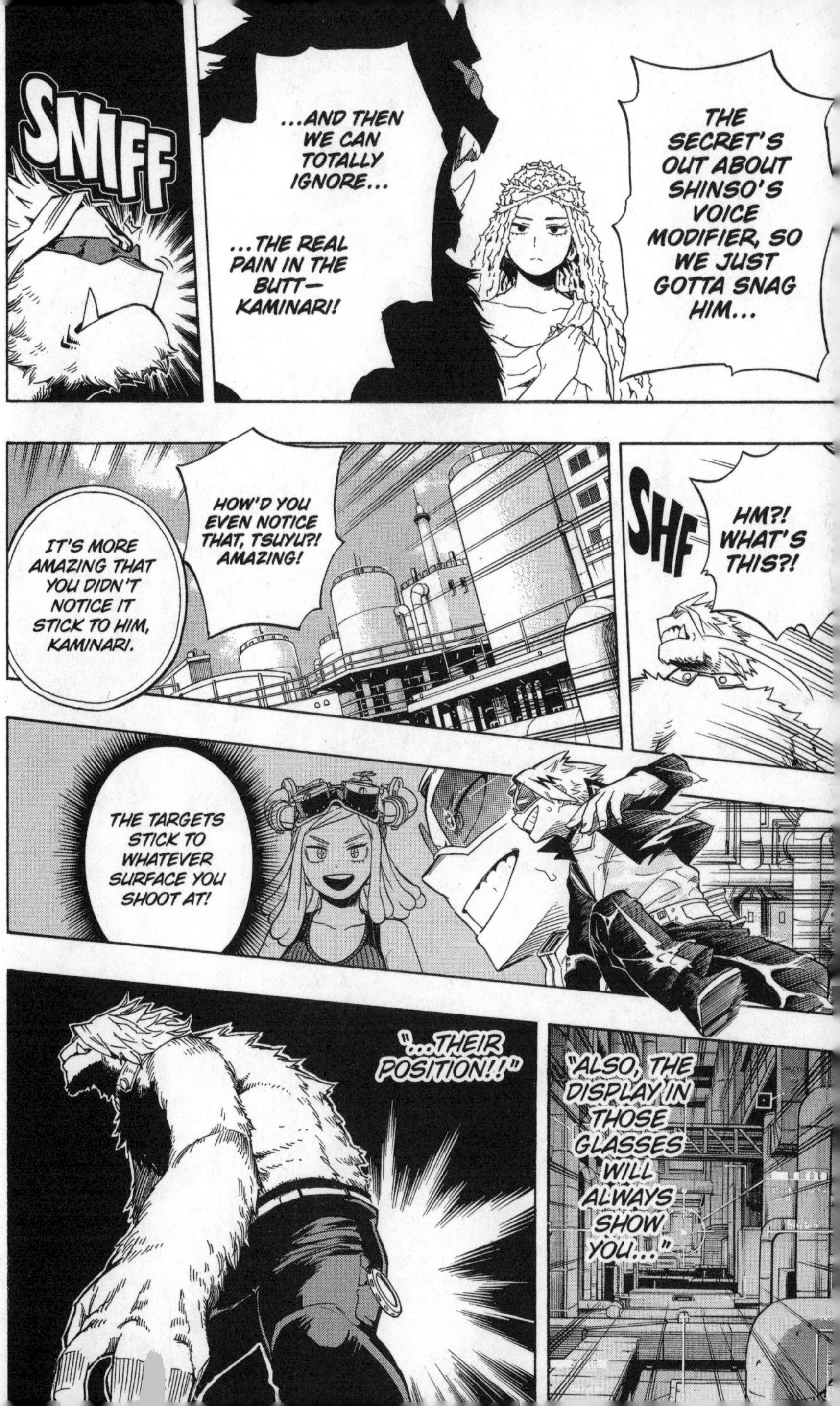
THE SECRET'S OUT ABOUT SHINSO'S VOICE MODIFIER, SO WE JUST GOTTA SNAG HIM...
...AND THEN WE CAN TOTALLY IGNORE...
...THE REAL PAIN IN THE BUTT— KAMINARI!
SNIFF
SHF
HM?! WHAT'S THIS?!
HOW'D YOU EVEN NOTICE THAT, TSUYU?! AMAZING!
IT'S MORE AMAZING THAT YOU DIDN'T NOTICE IT STICK TO HIM, KAMINARI.
THE TARGETS STICK TO WHATEVER SURFACE YOU SHOOT AT!
"ALSO, THE DISPLAY IN THOSE GLASSES WILL ALWAYS SHOW YOU..."
"...THEIR POSITION!!"

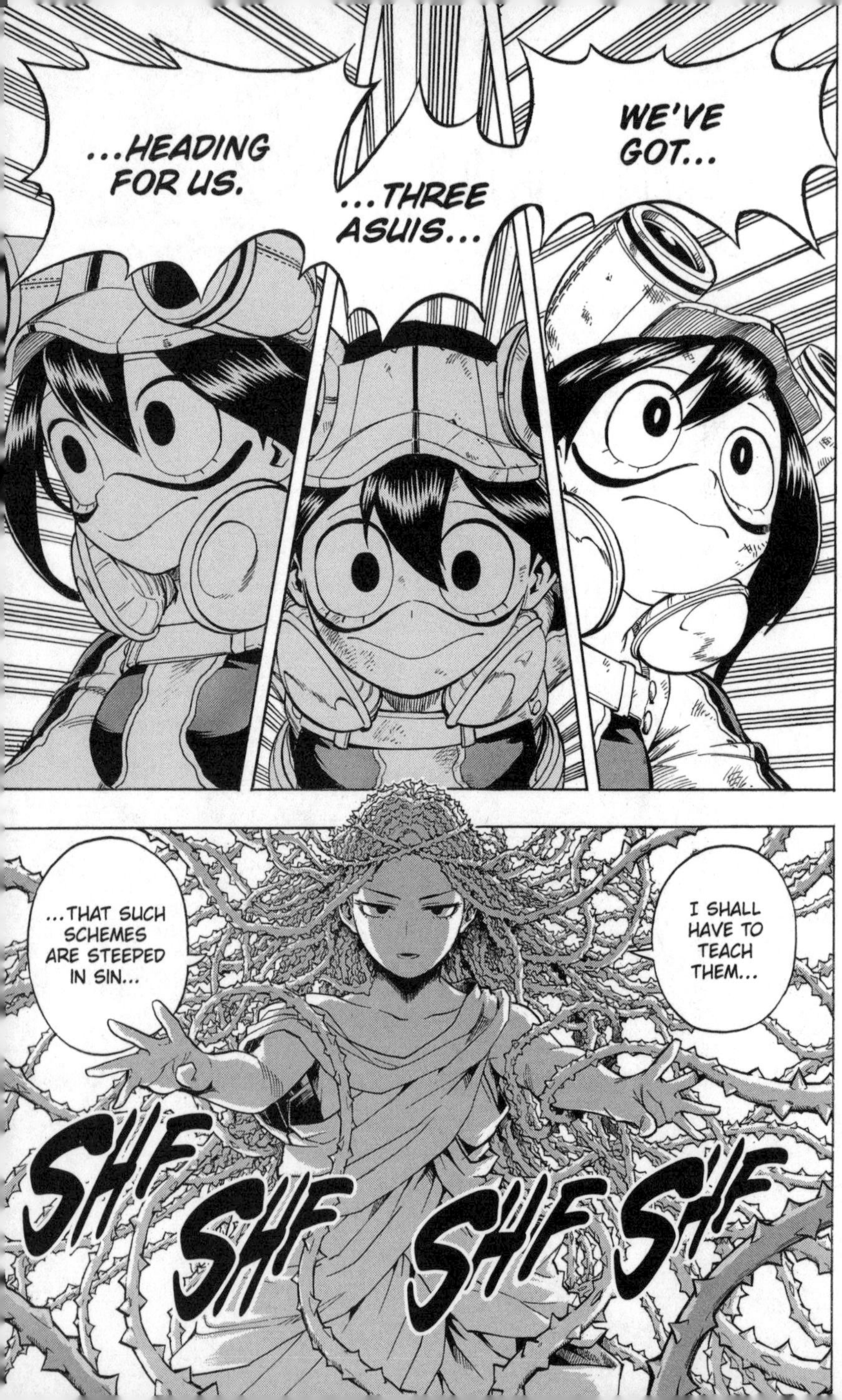
WE'VE GOT...
...THREE ASUIS...
...HEADING FOR US.
I SHALL HAVE TO TEACH THEM...
...THAT SUCH SCHEMES ARE STEEPED IN SIN...
SHF SHF SHF SHF SHF

KOSEI TSUBURABA (16)

STREET CLOTHES

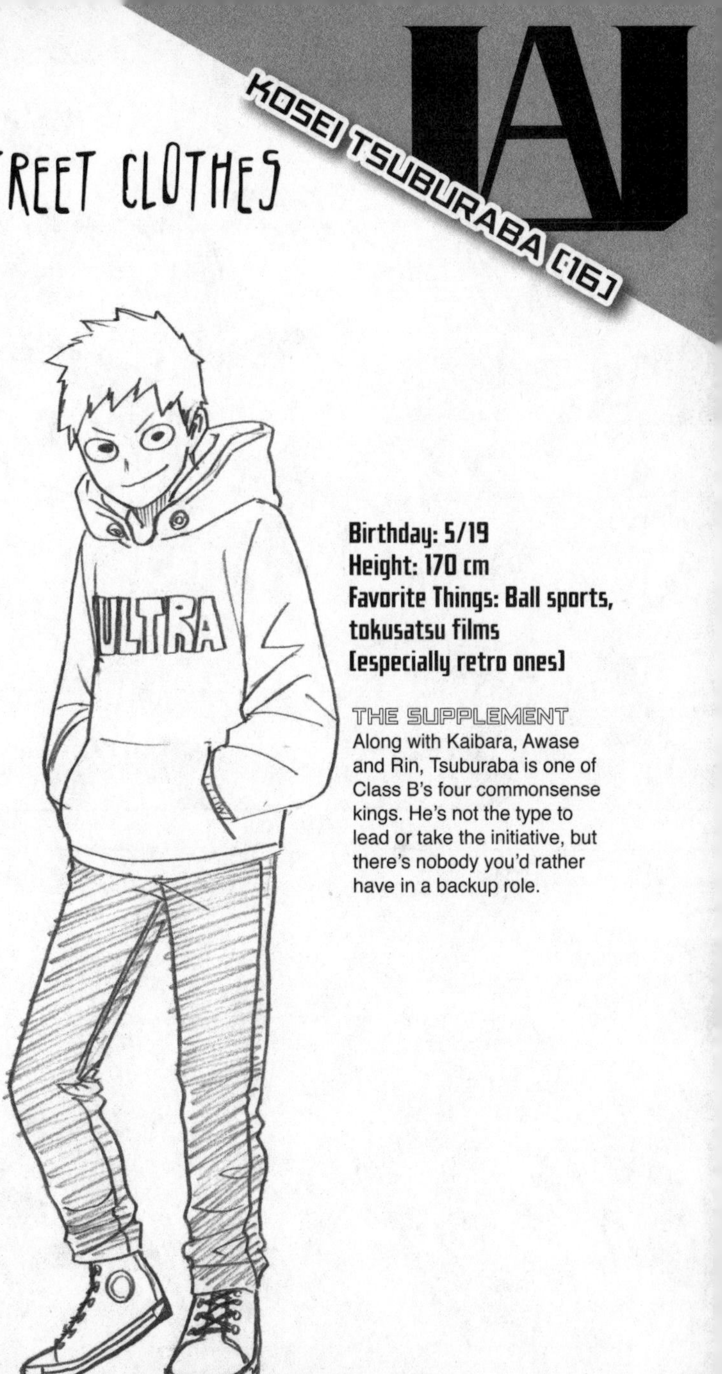
ULTRA

Birthday: 5/19
Height: 170 cm
Favorite Things: Ball sports, tokusatsu films (especially retro ones)

THE SUPPLEMENT

Along with Kaibara, Awase and Rin, Tsuburaba is one of Class B's four commonsense kings. He's not the type to lead or take the initiative, but there's nobody you'd rather have in a backup role.

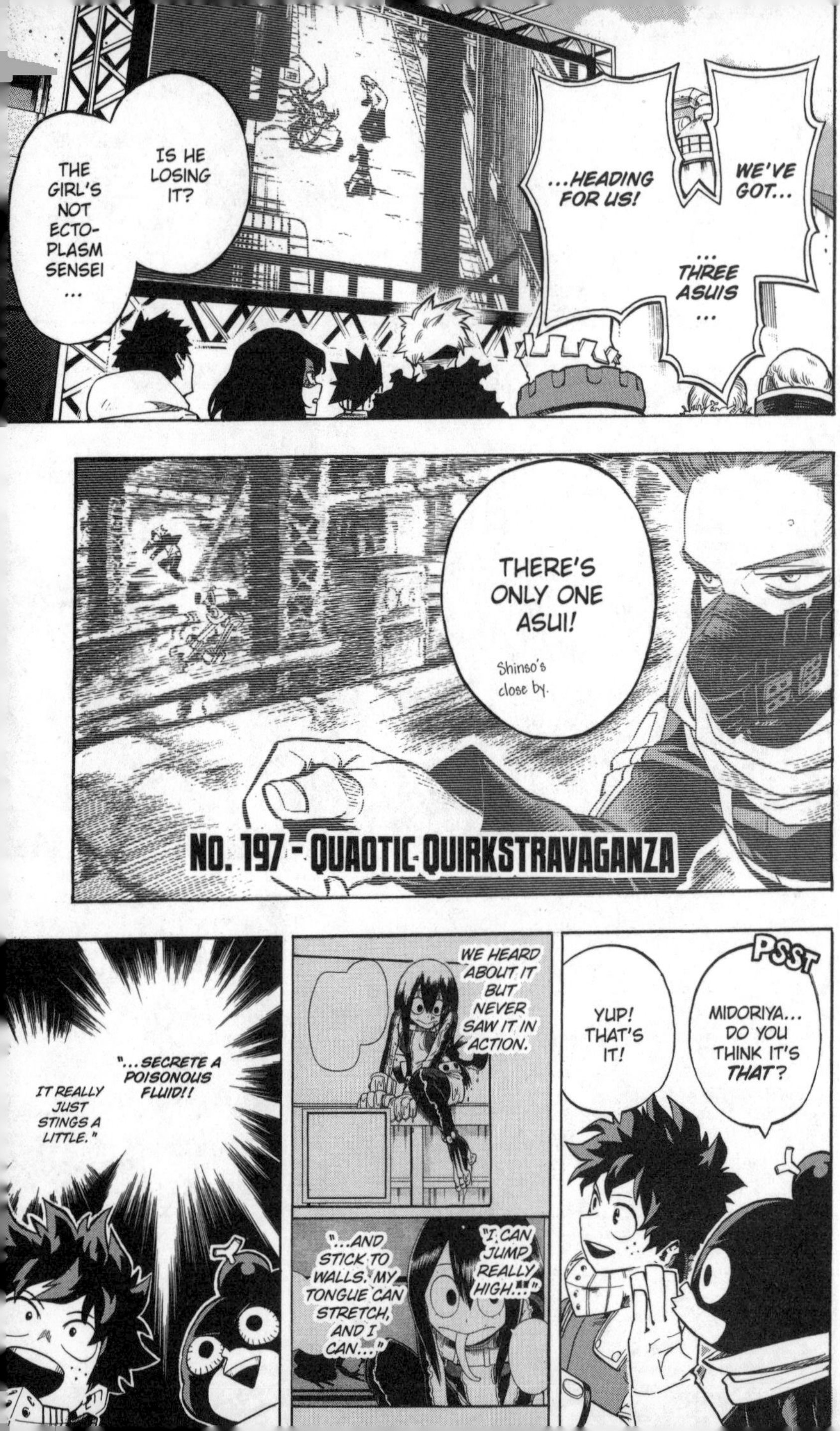
WE'VE GOT...
...THREE ASUIS...
...HEADING FOR US!
IS HE LOSING IT?
THE GIRL'S NOT ECTOPLASM SENSEI...
THERE'S ONLY ONE ASUI!
Shinso's close by.
NO. 197 - QUAOTIC QUIRKSTRAVAGANZA
PSST
MIDORIYA... DO YOU THINK IT'S THAT?
YUP! THAT'S IT!
WE HEARD ABOUT IT BUT NEVER SAW IT IN ACTION.
"I CAN JUMP REALLY HIGH!!"
"...AND STICK TO WALLS. MY TONGUE CAN STRETCH, AND I CAN..."
"...SECRETE A POISONOUS FLUID!!
IT REALLY JUST STINGS A LITTLE."

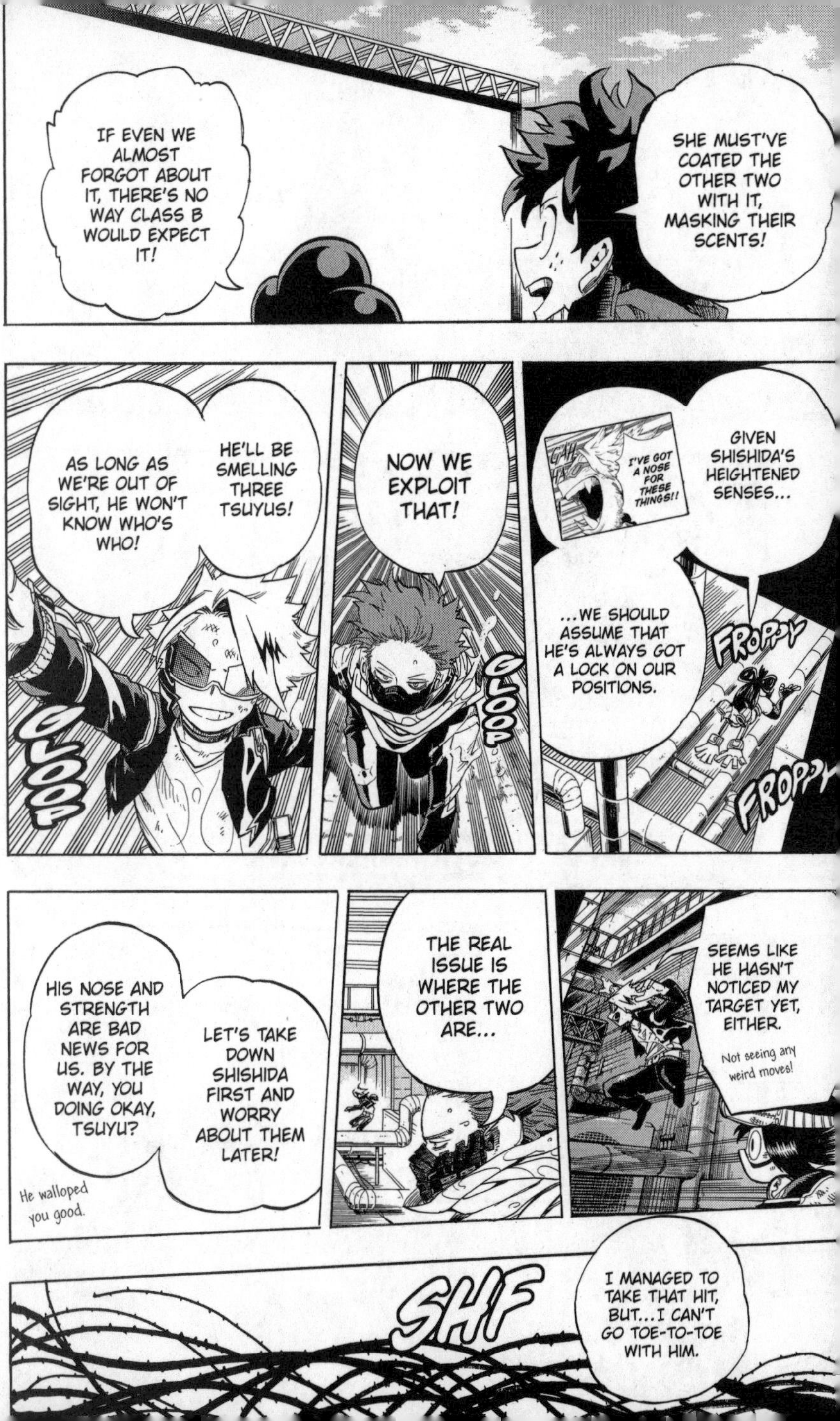
SHE MUST'VE COATED THE OTHER TWO WITH IT, MASKING THEIR SCENTS!
IF EVEN WE ALMOST FORGOT ABOUT IT, THERE'S NO WAY CLASS B WOULD EXPECT IT!
GIVEN SHISHIDA'S HEIGHTENED SENSES...
I'VE GOT A NOSE FOR THESE THINGS!!
...WE SHOULD ASSUME THAT HE'S ALWAYS GOT A LOCK ON OUR POSITIONS.
FROPPY
FROPPY
NOW WE EXPLOIT THAT!
GLOOP
HE'LL BE SMELLING THREE TSUYUS!
AS LONG AS WE'RE OUT OF SIGHT, HE WON'T KNOW WHO'S WHO!
GLOOP
SEEMS LIKE HE HASN'T NOTICED MY TARGET YET, EITHER.
Not seeing any weird moves!
THE REAL ISSUE IS WHERE THE OTHER TWO ARE...
LET'S TAKE DOWN SHISHIDA FIRST AND WORRY ABOUT THEM LATER!
HIS NOSE AND STRENGTH ARE BAD NEWS FOR US. BY THE WAY, YOU DOING OKAY, TSUYU?
He walloped you good.
I MANAGED TO TAKE THAT HIT, BUT...I CAN'T GO TOE-TO-TOE WITH HIM.
SHF

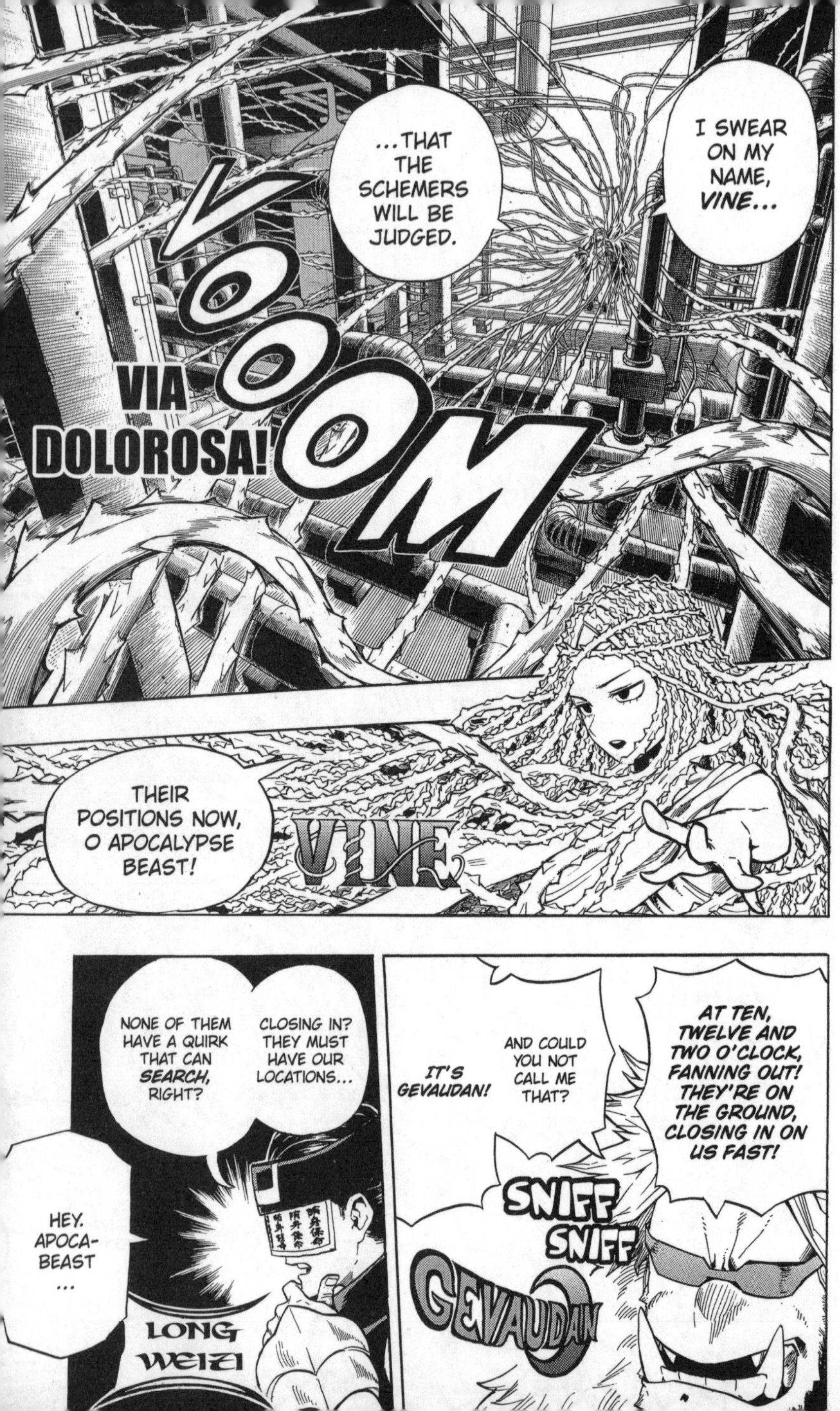
I SWEAR ON MY NAME, VINE...
...THAT THE SCHEMERS WILL BE JUDGED.
VOOOOM
VIA DOLOROSA!
THEIR POSITIONS NOW, O APOCALYPSE BEAST!
VINE
AT TEN, TWELVE AND TWO O'CLOCK, FANNING OUT! THEY'RE ON THE GROUND, CLOSING IN ON US FAST!
AND COULD YOU NOT CALL ME THAT?
IT'S GEVAUDAN!
SNIFF SNIFF
GEVAUDAN
CLOSING IN? THEY MUST HAVE OUR LOCATIONS...
NONE OF THEM HAVE A QUIRK THAT CAN SEARCH, RIGHT?
HEY. APOCA-BEAST...
LONG WEIZI

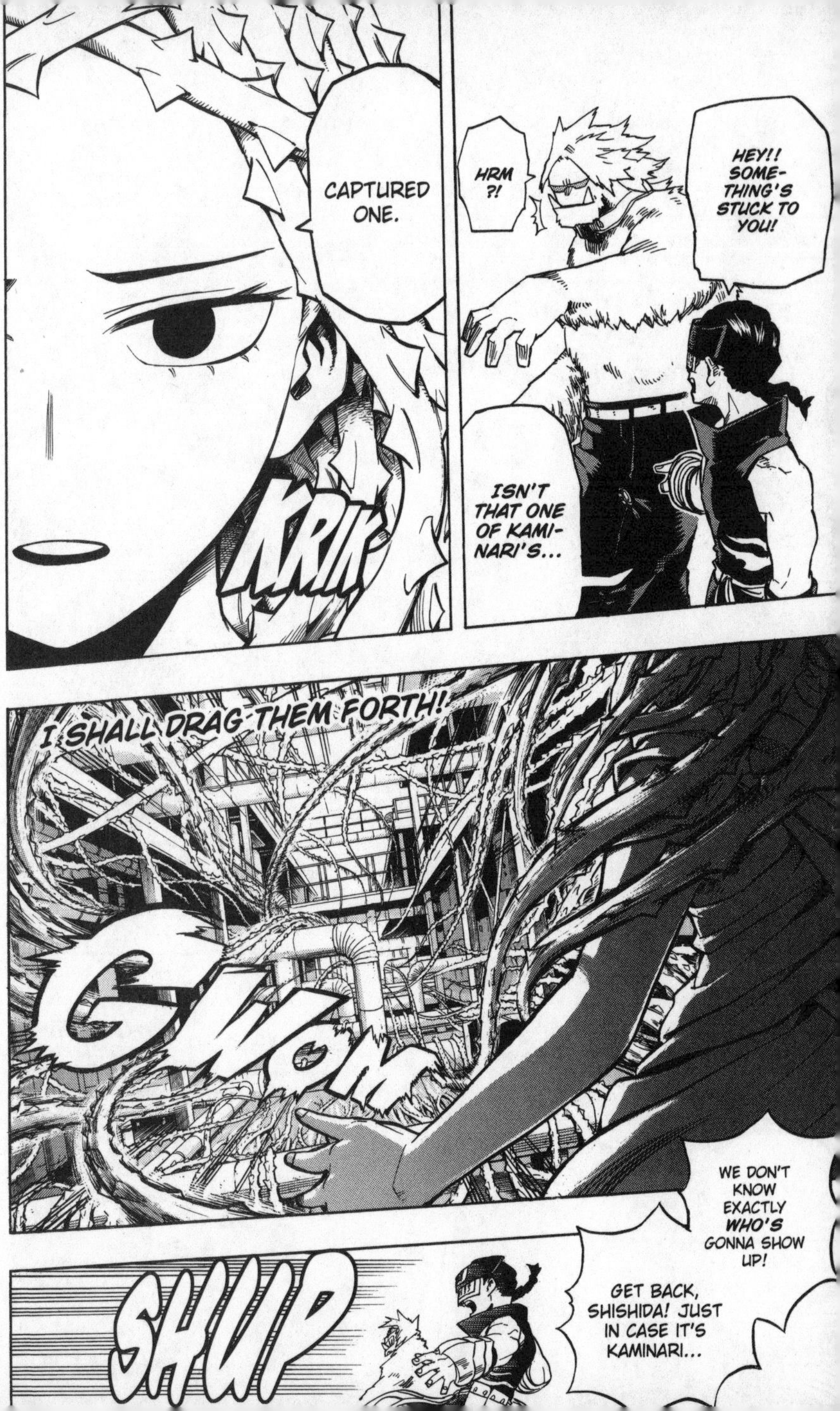
HEY!! SOME-THING'S STUCK TO YOU!
HRM ?!
ISN'T THAT ONE OF KAMI-NARI'S...
CAPTURED ONE.
KRIK
I SHALL DRAG THEM FORTH!
GWOM
WE DON'T KNOW EXACTLY WHO'S GONNA SHOW UP!
GET BACK, SHISHIDA! JUST IN CASE IT'S KAMINARI...
SHUP

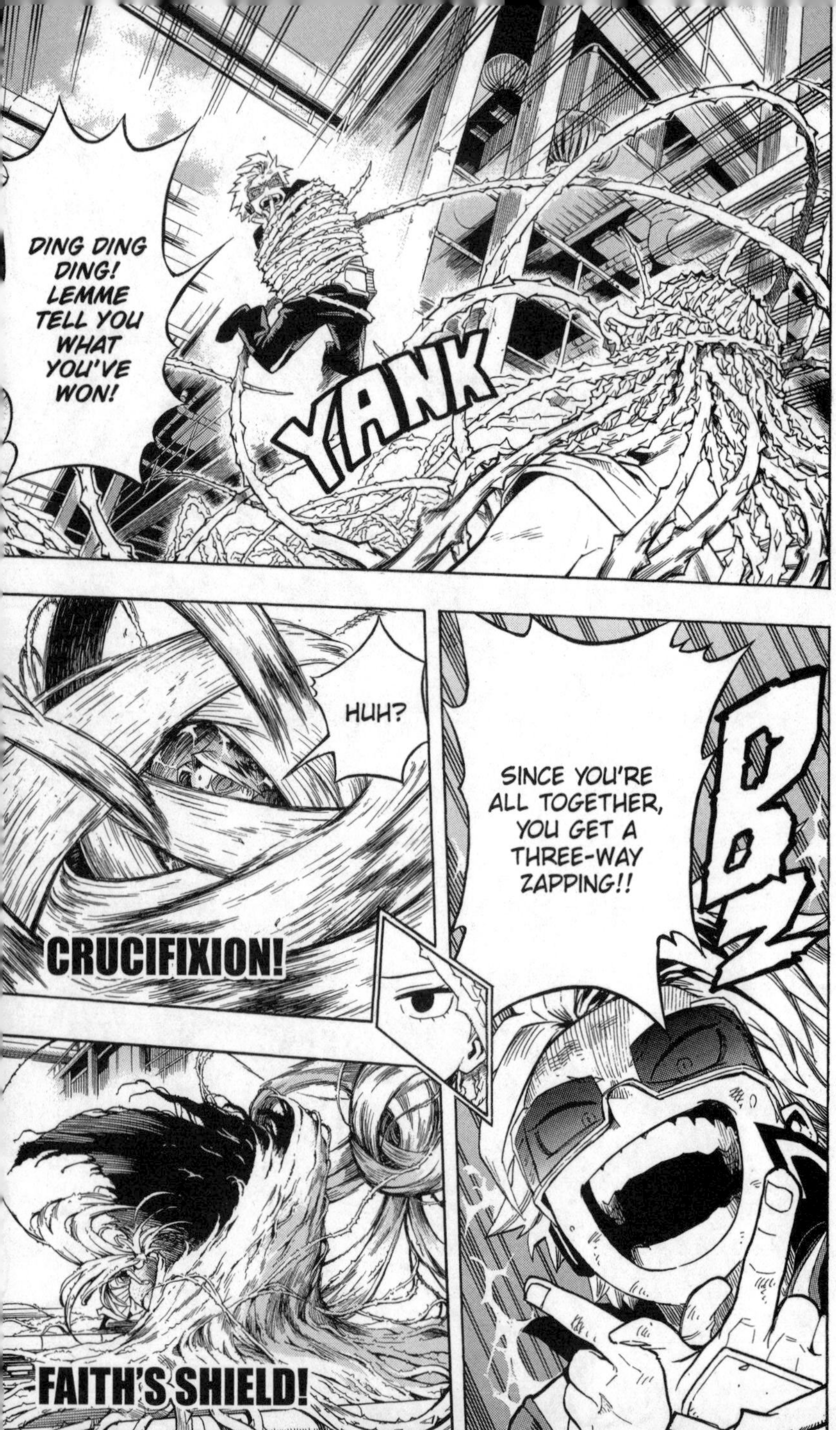
DING DING DING! LEMME TELL YOU WHAT YOU'VE WON!
YANK
SINCE YOU'RE ALL TOGETHER, YOU GET A THREE-WAY ZAPPING!!
B
HUH?
CRUCIFIXION!
FAITH'S SHIELD!

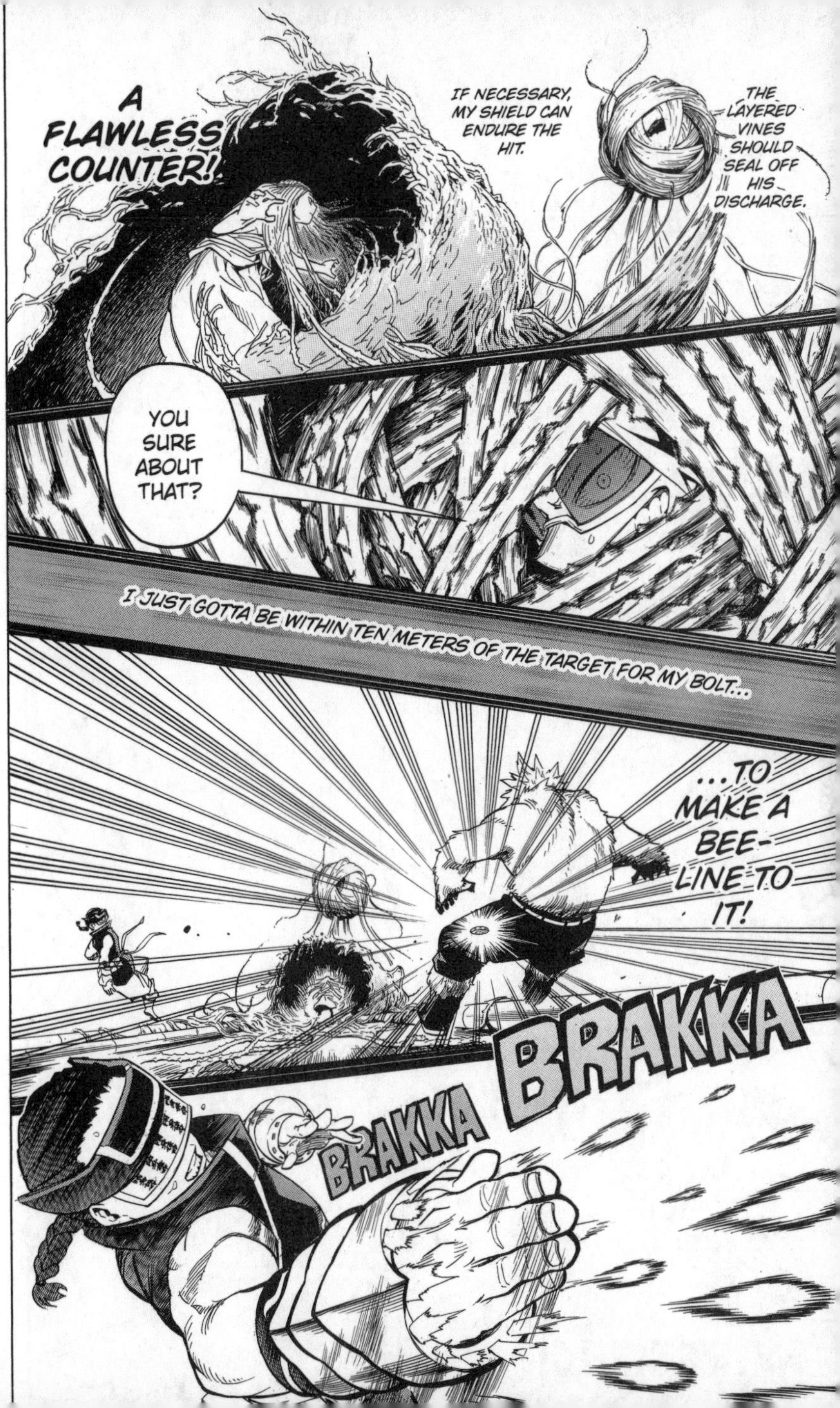
A FLAWLESS COUNTER!
IF NECESSARY, MY SHIELD CAN ENDURE THE HIT.
THE LAYERED VINES SHOULD SEAL OFF HIS DISCHARGE.
YOU SURE ABOUT THAT?
I JUST GOTTA BE WITHIN TEN METERS OF THE TARGET FOR MY BOLT...
...TO MAKE A BEE-LINE TO IT!
BRAKKA
BRAKKA

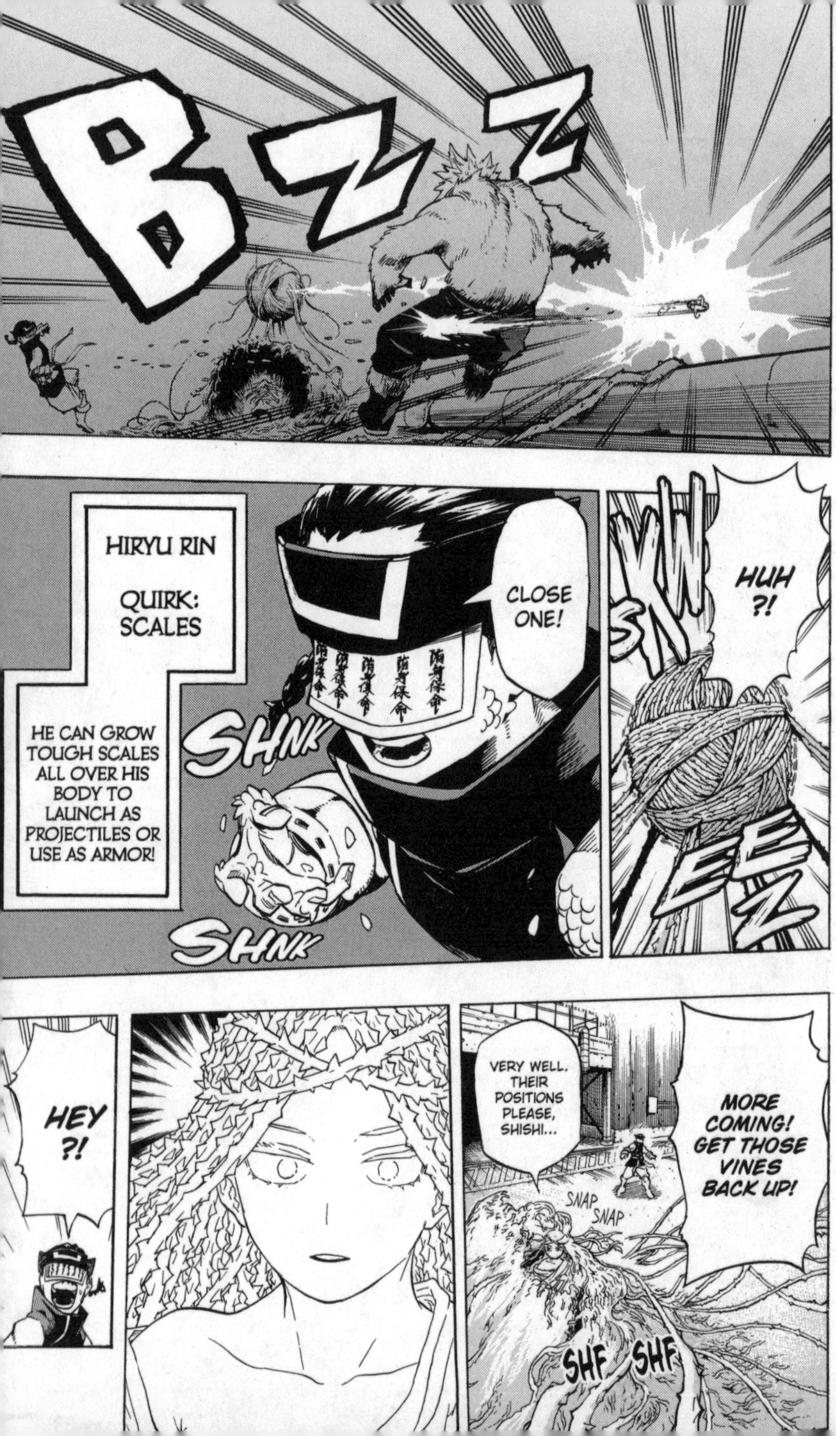

BZZ
HUH ?!
CLOSE ONE!
HIRYU RIN
QUIRK: SCALES
HE CAN GROW TOUGH SCALES ALL OVER HIS BODY TO LAUNCH AS PROJECTILES OR USE AS ARMOR!
SHNK
SHNK
MORE COMING! GET THOSE VINES BACK UP!
VERY WELL. THEIR POSITIONS PLEASE, SHISHI...
SNAP SNAP
SHF SHF
HEY ?!

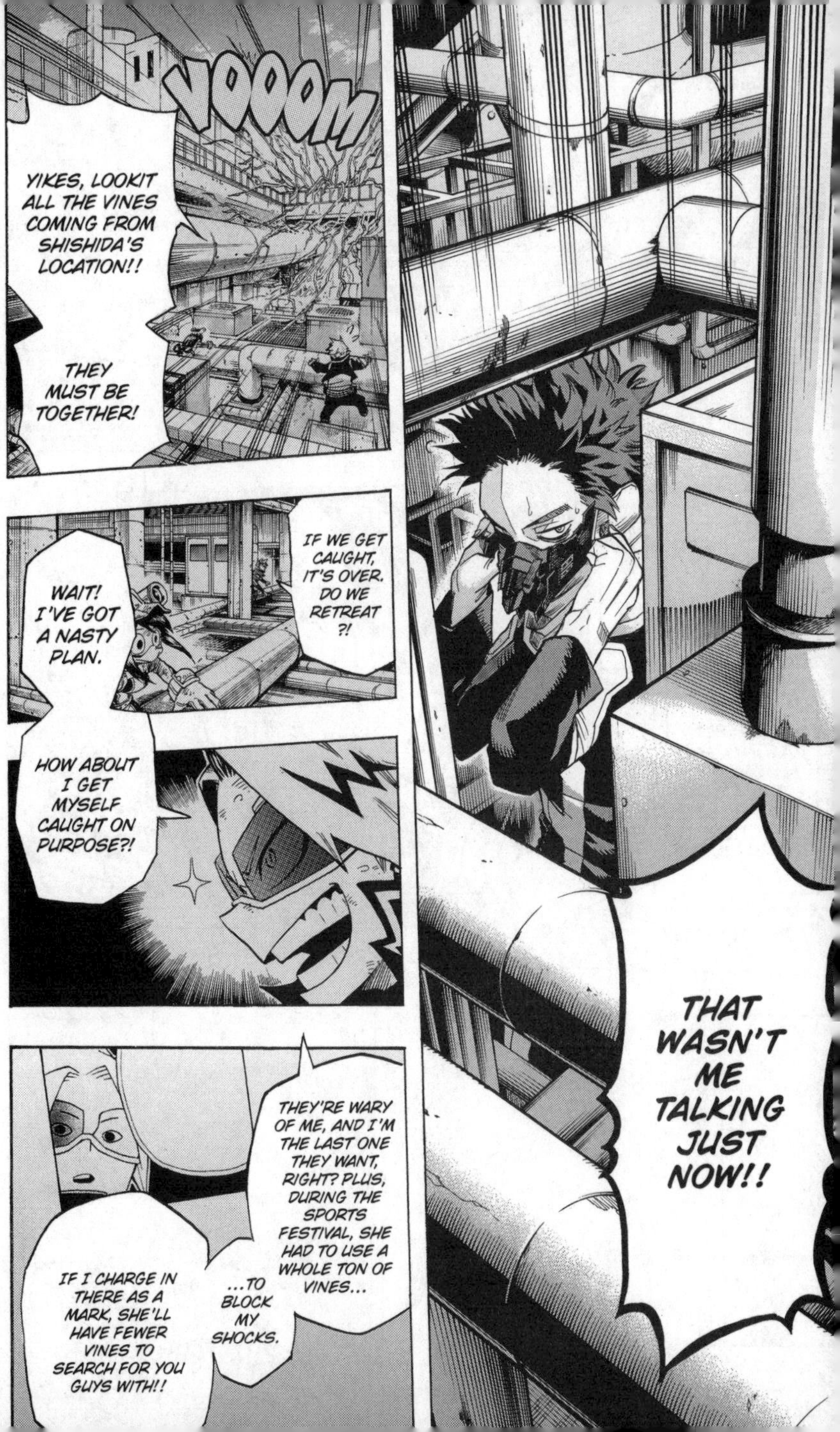
THAT WASN'T ME TALKING JUST NOW!!
VOOOM
YIKES, LOOKIT ALL THE VINES COMING FROM SHISHIDA'S LOCATION!!
THEY MUST BE TOGETHER!
IF WE GET CAUGHT, IT'S OVER. DO WE RETREAT?!
WAIT! I'VE GOT A NASTY PLAN.
HOW ABOUT I GET MYSELF CAUGHT ON PURPOSE?!
THEY'RE WARY OF ME, AND I'M THE LAST ONE THEY WANT, RIGHT? PLUS, DURING THE SPORTS FESTIVAL, SHE HAD TO USE A WHOLE TON OF VINES...
...TO BLOCK MY SHOCKS.
IF I CHARGE IN THERE AS A MARK, SHE'LL HAVE FEWER VINES TO SEARCH FOR YOU GUYS WITH!!

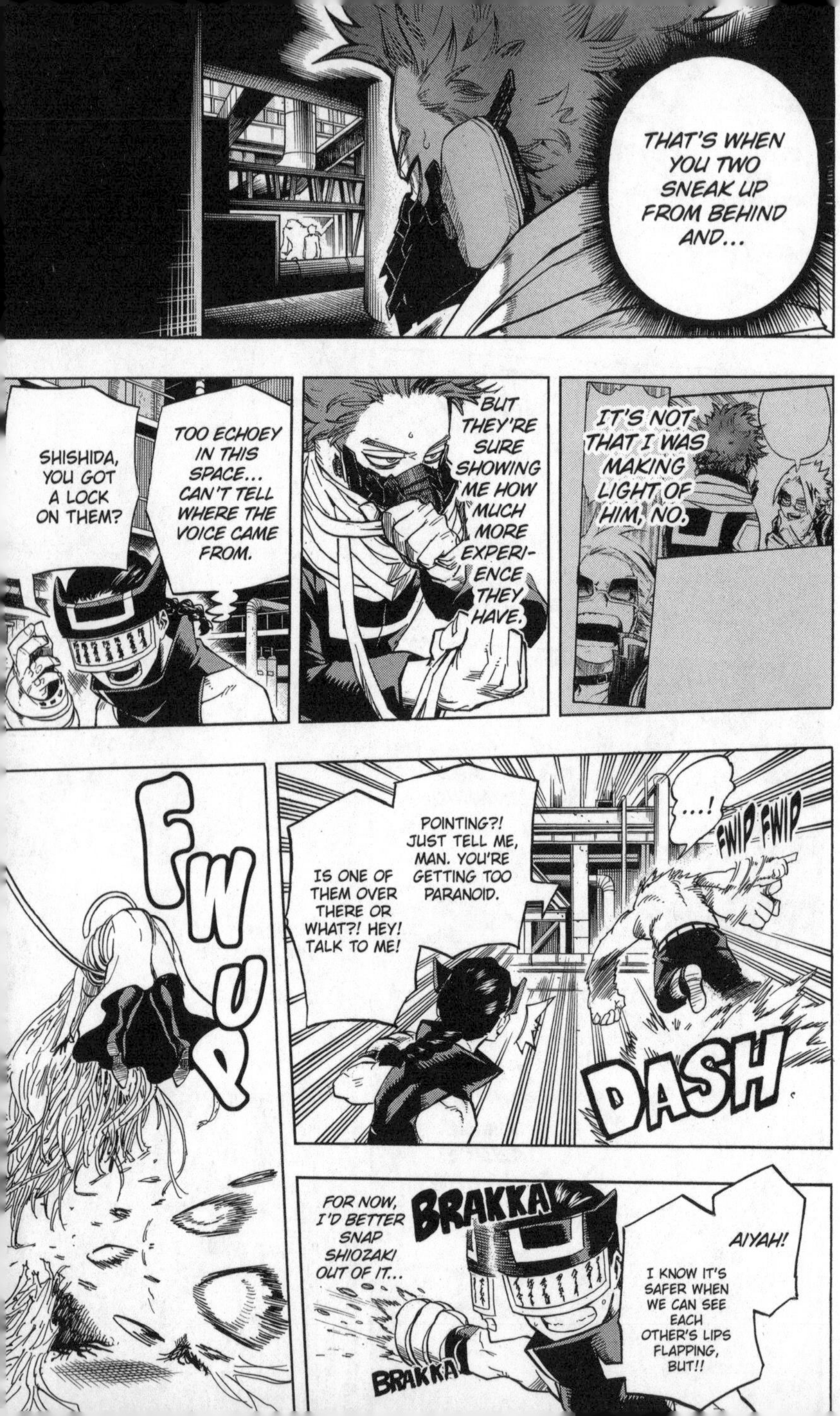
THAT'S WHEN YOU TWO SNEAK UP FROM BEHIND AND...
IT'S NOT THAT I WAS MAKING LIGHT OF HIM, NO.
BUT THEY'RE SURE SHOWING ME HOW MUCH MORE EXPERI-ENCE THEY HAVE.
TOO ECHOEY IN THIS SPACE... CAN'T TELL WHERE THE VOICE CAME FROM.
SHISHIDA, YOU GOT A LOCK ON THEM?
...!
FWIP FWIP
POINTING?! JUST TELL ME, MAN. YOU'RE GETTING TOO PARANOID.
IS ONE OF THEM OVER THERE OR WHAT?! HEY! TALK TO ME!
DASH
AIYAH!
I KNOW IT'S SAFER WHEN WE CAN SEE EACH OTHER'S LIPS FLAPPING, BUT!!
BRAKKA
FOR NOW, I'D BETTER SNAP SHIOZAKI OUT OF IT...
BRAKKA
FWUP

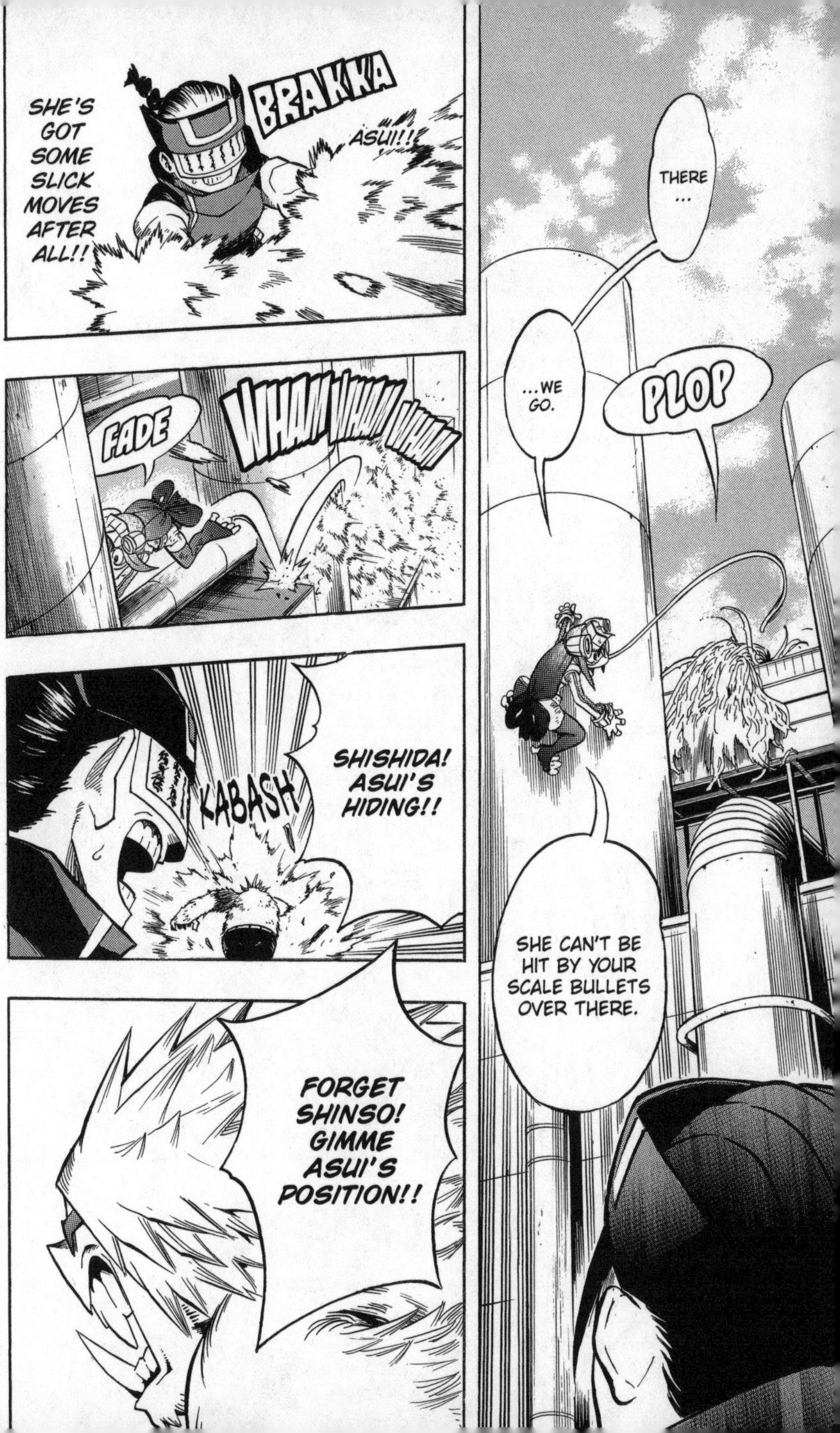
THERE ...
...WE GO.
PLOP
SHE CAN'T BE HIT BY YOUR SCALE BULLETS OVER THERE.
BRAKKA
ASUI!!!
SHE'S GOT SOME SLICK MOVES AFTER ALL!!
WHAM WHAM WHAM
FADE
SHISHIDA! ASUI'S HIDING!!
KABASH
FORGET SHINSO! GIMME ASUI'S POSITION!!

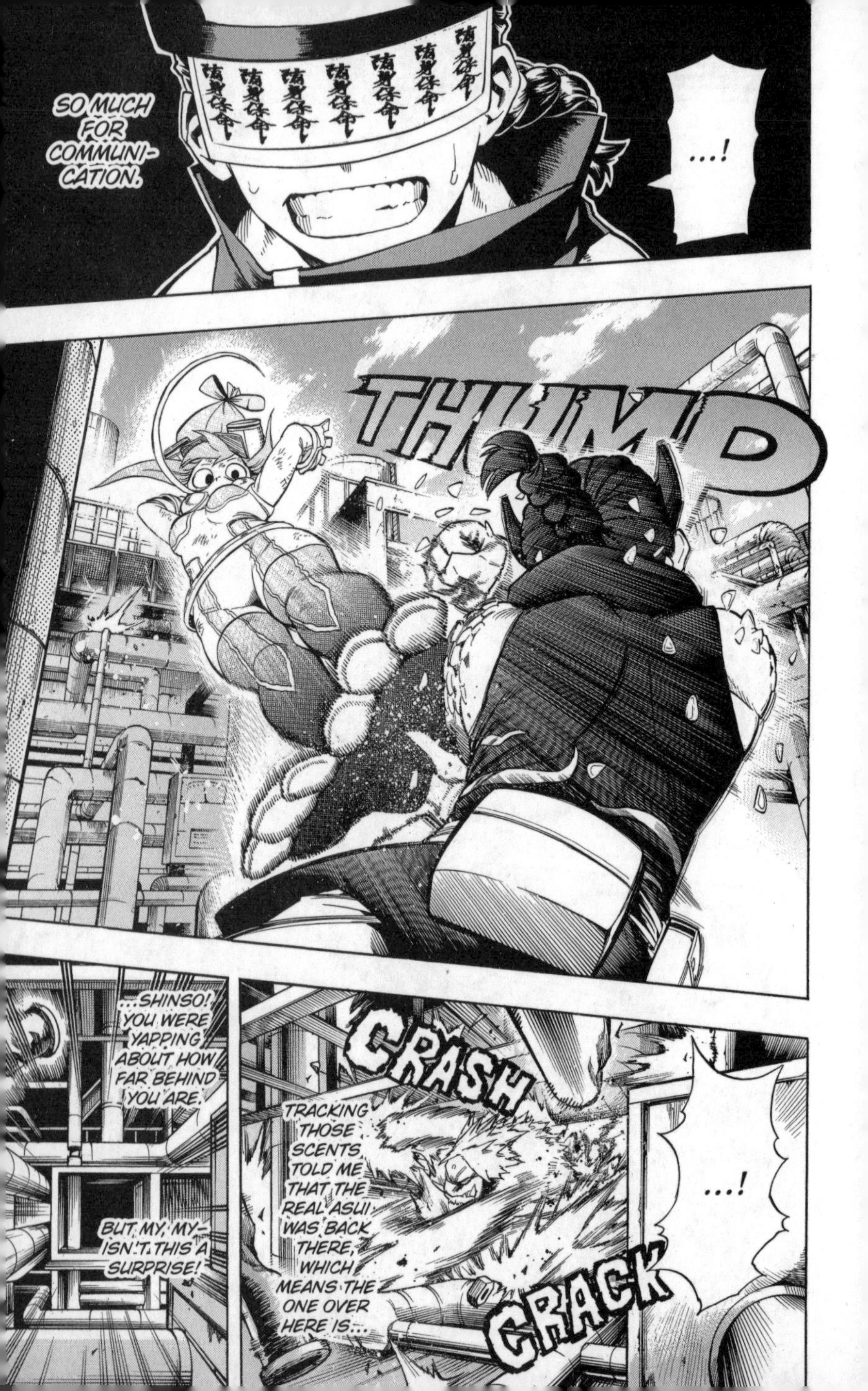

...!
SO MUCH FOR COMMUNICATION.
THUMP
CRASH
...!
TRACKING THOSE SCENTS TOLD ME THAT THE REAL ASUI WAS BACK THERE, WHICH MEANS THE ONE OVER HERE IS...
CRACK
...SHINSO! YOU WERE YAPPING ABOUT HOW FAR BEHIND YOU ARE.
BUT MY, MY-- ISN'T THIS A SURPRISE!

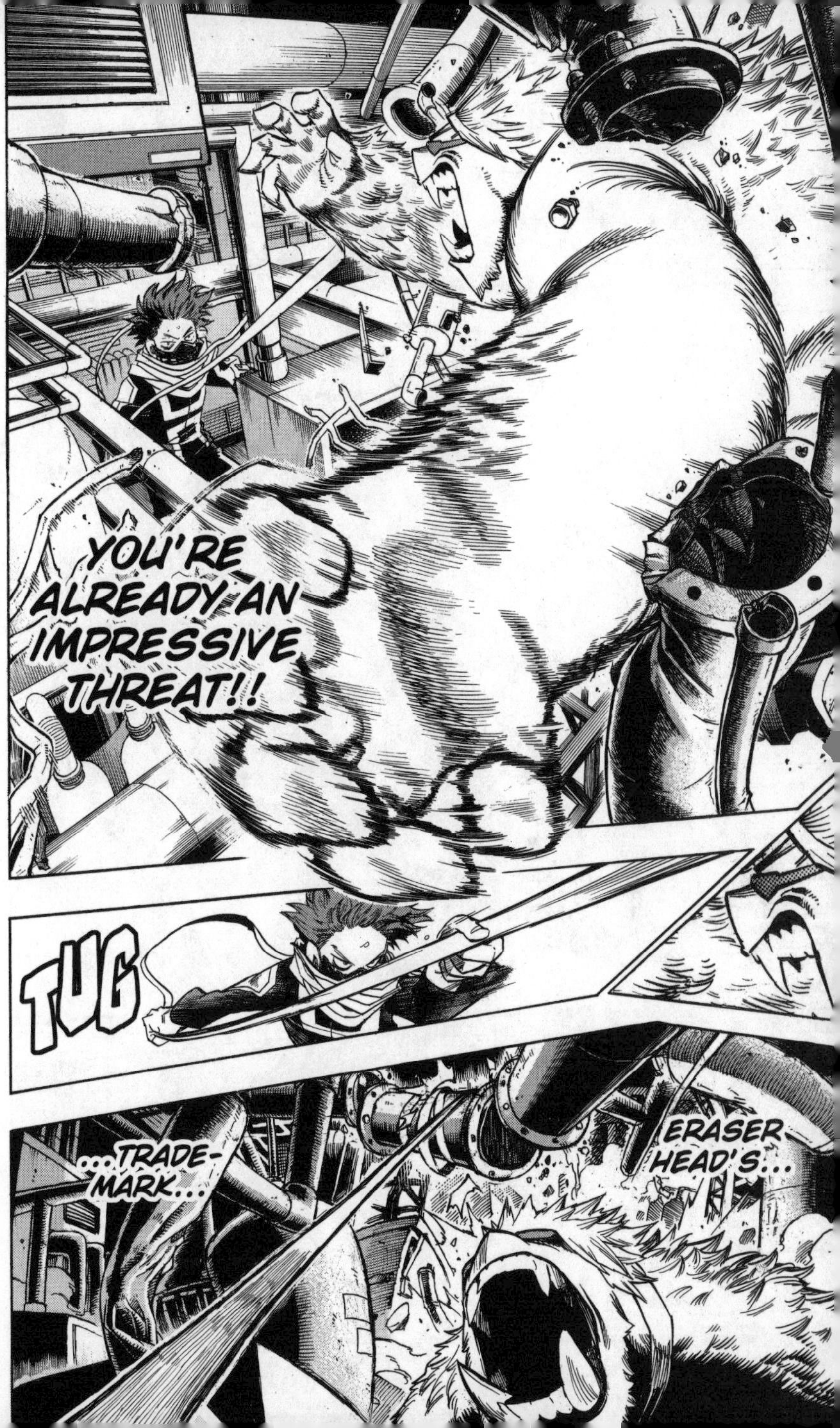
YOU'RE ALREADY AN IMPRESSIVE THREAT!!
TUG
ERASER HEAD'S...
...TRADE-MARK...

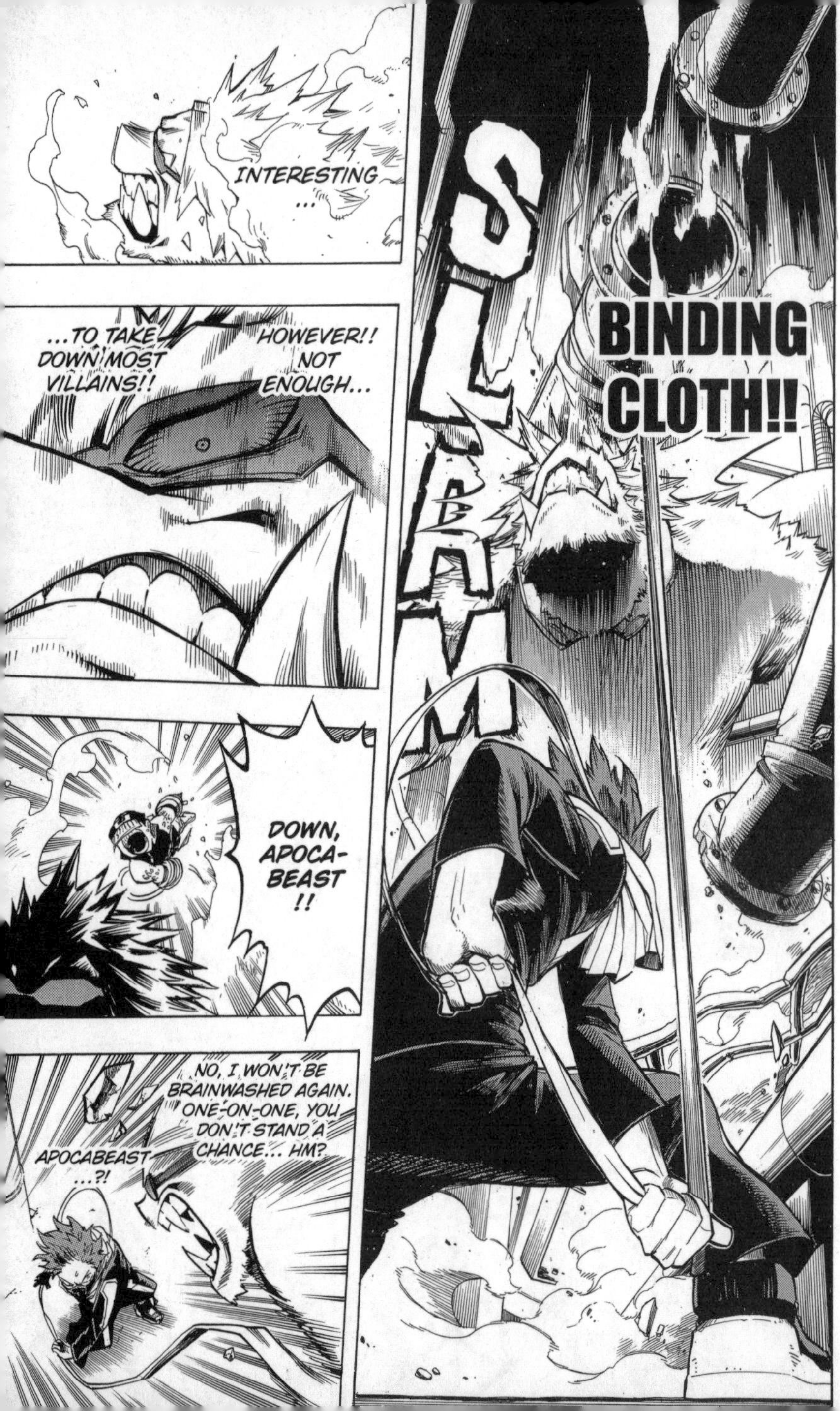
SLAM
BINDING CLOTH!!
INTERESTING ...
HOWEVER!! NOT ENOUGH...
...TO TAKE DOWN MOST VILLAINS!!
DOWN, APOCA-BEAST !!
NO, I WON'T BE BRAINWASHED AGAIN. ONE-ON-ONE, YOU DON'T STAND A CHANCE... HM?
APOCABEAST ...?!

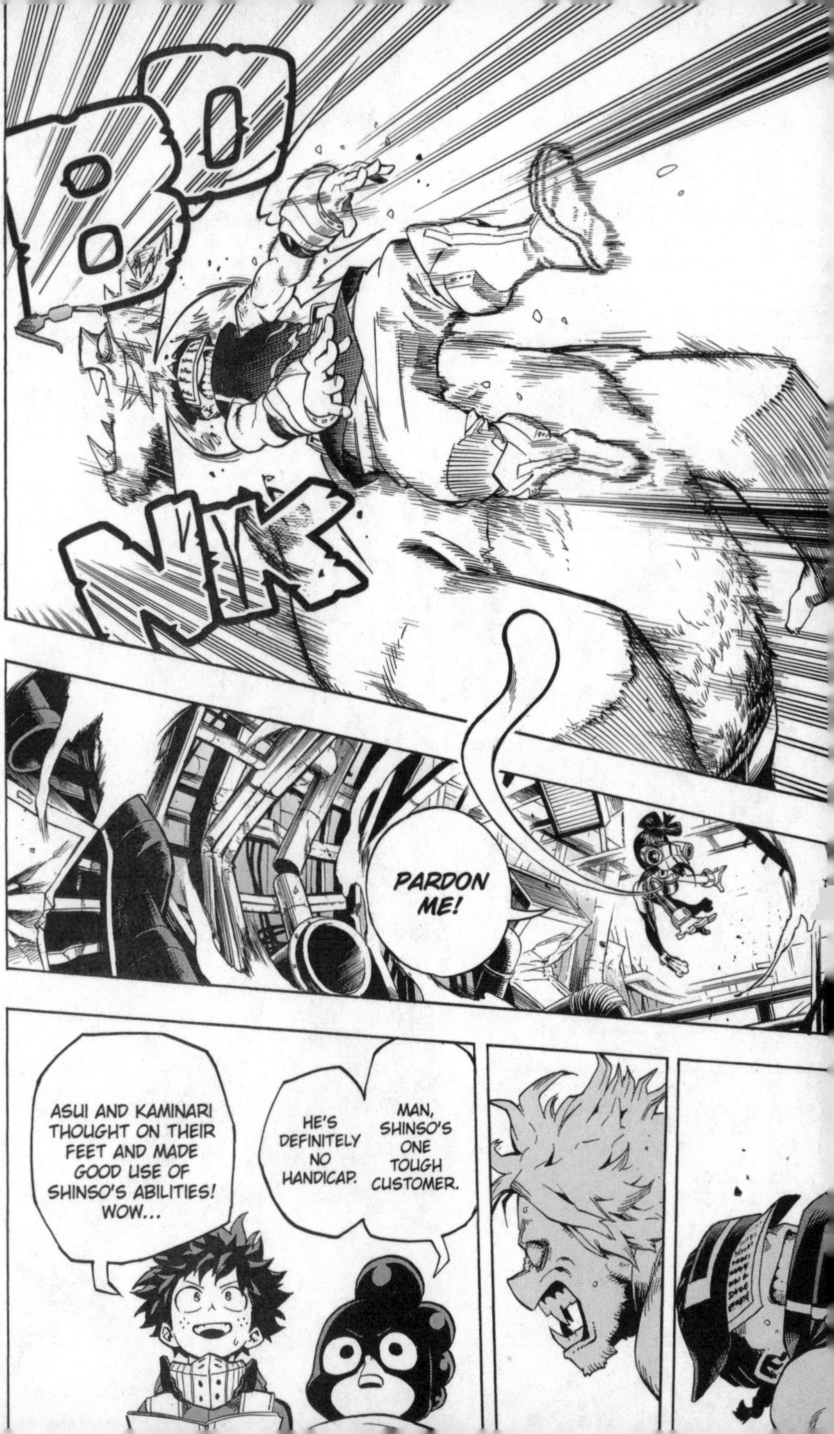
PARDON ME!
MAN, SHINSO'S ONE TOUGH CUSTOMER.
HE'S DEFINITELY NO HANDICAP.
ASUI AND KAMINARI THOUGHT ON THEIR FEET AND MADE GOOD USE OF SHINSO'S ABILITIES! WOW...

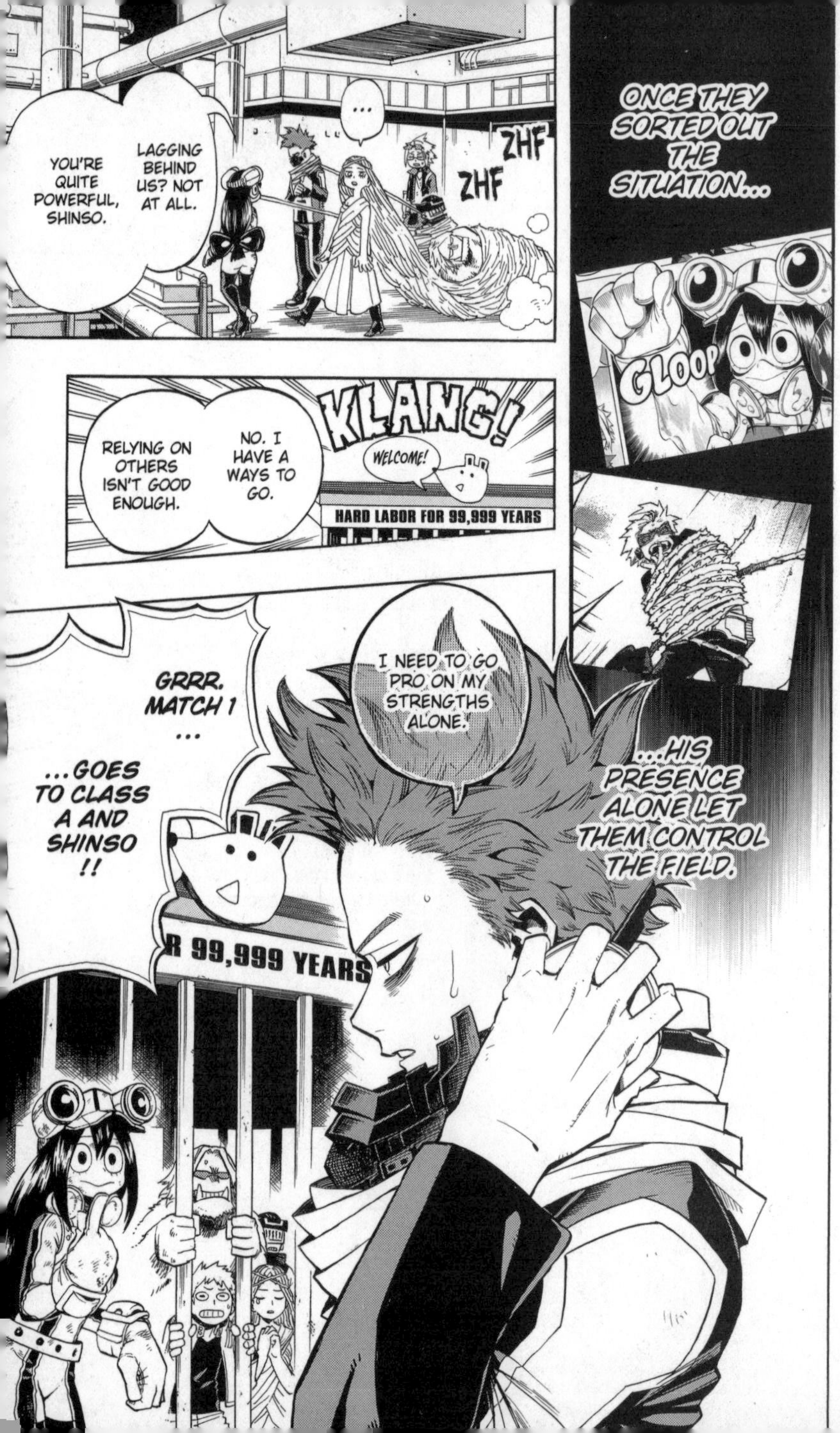
ONCE THEY SORTED OUT THE SITUATION...
GLOOP
...HIS PRESENCE ALONE LET THEM CONTROL THE FIELD.
...
ZHF
ZHF
LAGGING BEHIND US? NOT AT ALL.
YOU'RE QUITE POWERFUL, SHINSO.
KLANG!
WELCOME!
HARD LABOR FOR 99,999 YEARS
NO. I HAVE A WAYS TO GO.
RELYING ON OTHERS ISN'T GOOD ENOUGH.
I NEED TO GO PRO ON MY STRENGTHS ALONE.
GRRR. MATCH 1 ...
...GOES TO CLASS A AND SHINSO !!
R 99,999 YEARS

HIRYU RIN (16)

STREET CLOTHES

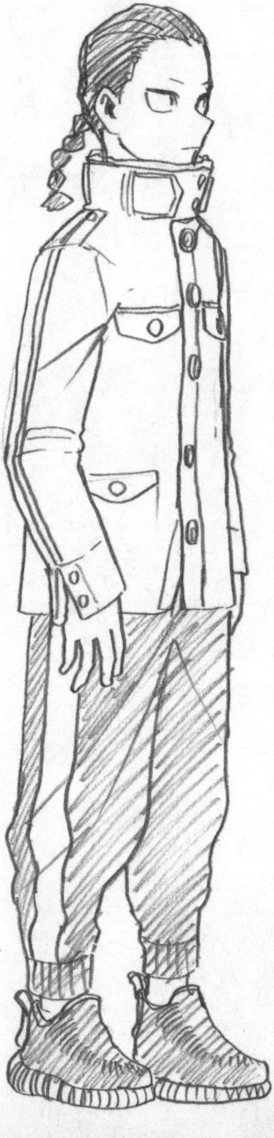

Birthday: 7/14
Height: 170 cm
Favorite Thing: Sushi

THE SUPPLEMENT

He moved to Japan from China when he was in elementary school.

Serious and studious. That queue braid is fantastic.

He's not a fan of winter, since the nature of his Quirk makes it hard for him to keep himself warm.

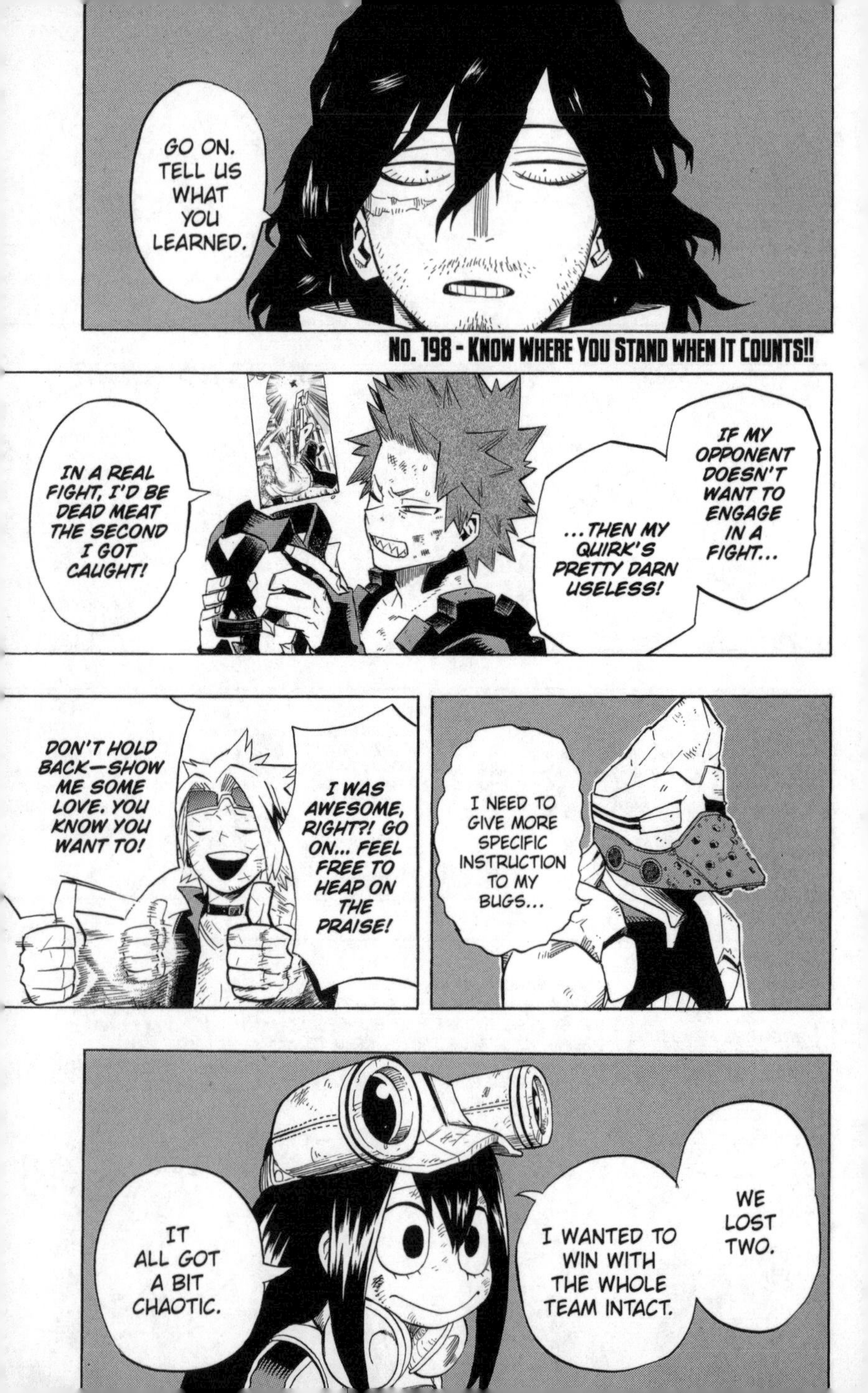
GO ON. TELL US WHAT YOU LEARNED.
NO. 198 - KNOW WHERE YOU STAND WHEN IT COUNTS!!
IF MY OPPONENT DOESN'T WANT TO ENGAGE IN A FIGHT...
...THEN MY QUIRK'S PRETTY DARN USELESS!
IN A REAL FIGHT, I'D BE DEAD MEAT THE SECOND I GOT CAUGHT!
I NEED TO GIVE MORE SPECIFIC INSTRUCTION TO MY BUGS...
I WAS AWESOME, RIGHT?! GO ON... FEEL FREE TO HEAP ON THE PRAISE!
DON'T HOLD BACK—SHOW ME SOME LOVE. YOU KNOW YOU WANT TO!
WE LOST TWO.
I WANTED TO WIN WITH THE WHOLE TEAM INTACT.
IT ALL GOT A BIT CHAOTIC.

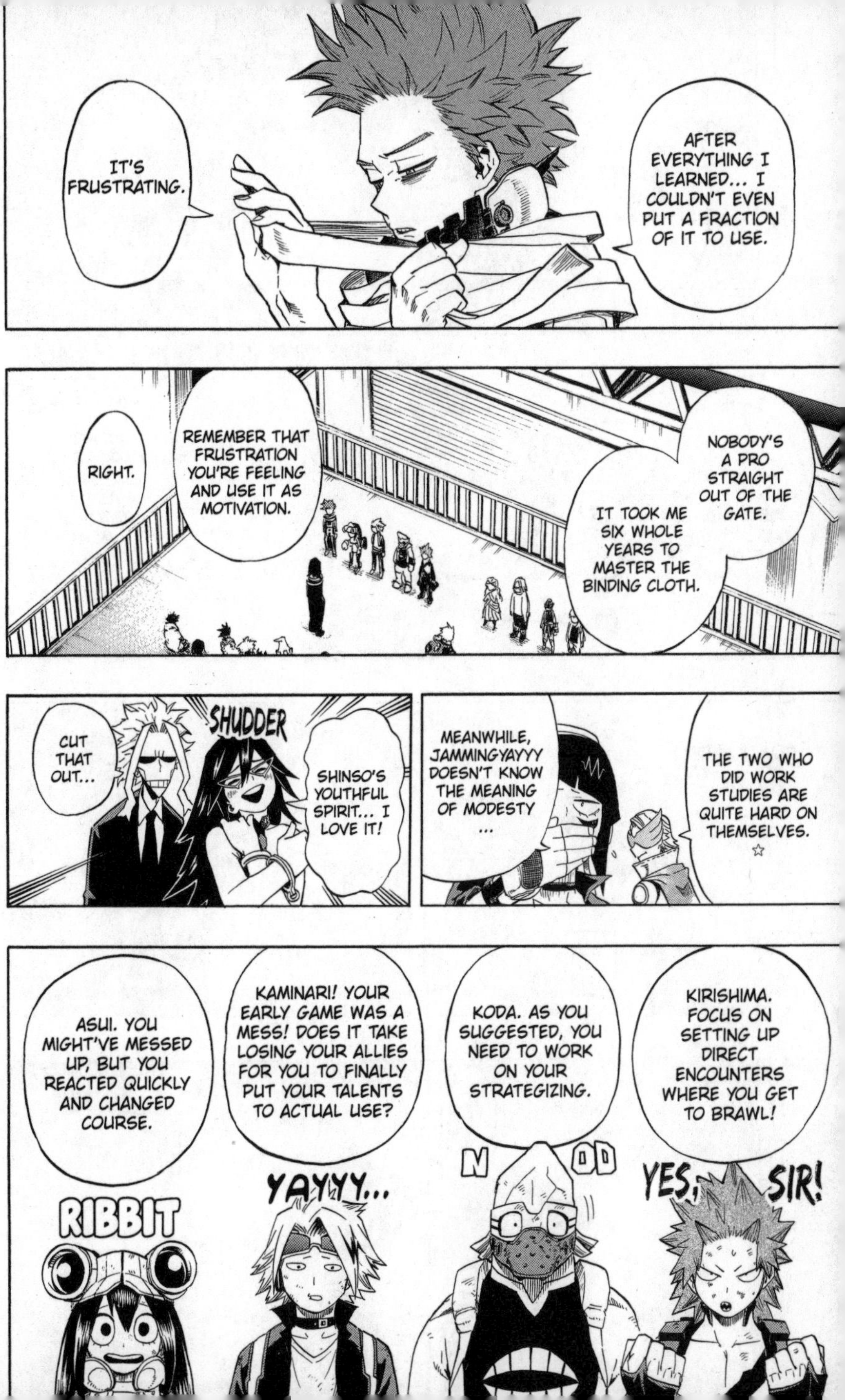
AFTER EVERYTHING I LEARNED... I COULDN'T EVEN PUT A FRACTION OF IT TO USE.
IT'S FRUSTRATING.
NOBODY'S A PRO STRAIGHT OUT OF THE GATE.
IT TOOK ME SIX WHOLE YEARS TO MASTER THE BINDING CLOTH.
REMEMBER THAT FRUSTRATION YOU'RE FEELING AND USE IT AS MOTIVATION.
RIGHT.
THE TWO WHO DID WORK STUDIES ARE QUITE HARD ON THEMSELVES. ☆
MEANWHILE, JAMMINGYAYYY DOESN'T KNOW THE MEANING OF MODESTY ...
SHINSO'S YOUTHFUL SPIRIT... I LOVE IT!
SHUDDER
CUT THAT OUT...
KIRISHIMA. FOCUS ON SETTING UP DIRECT ENCOUNTERS WHERE YOU GET TO BRAWL!
KODA. AS YOU SUGGESTED, YOU NEED TO WORK ON YOUR STRATEGIZING.
KAMINARI! YOUR EARLY GAME WAS A MESS! DOES IT TAKE LOSING YOUR ALLIES FOR YOU TO FINALLY PUT YOUR TALENTS TO ACTUAL USE?
ASUI. YOU MIGHT'VE MESSED UP, BUT YOU REACTED QUICKLY AND CHANGED COURSE.
YES, SIR!
NOD
YAYYY...
RIBBIT

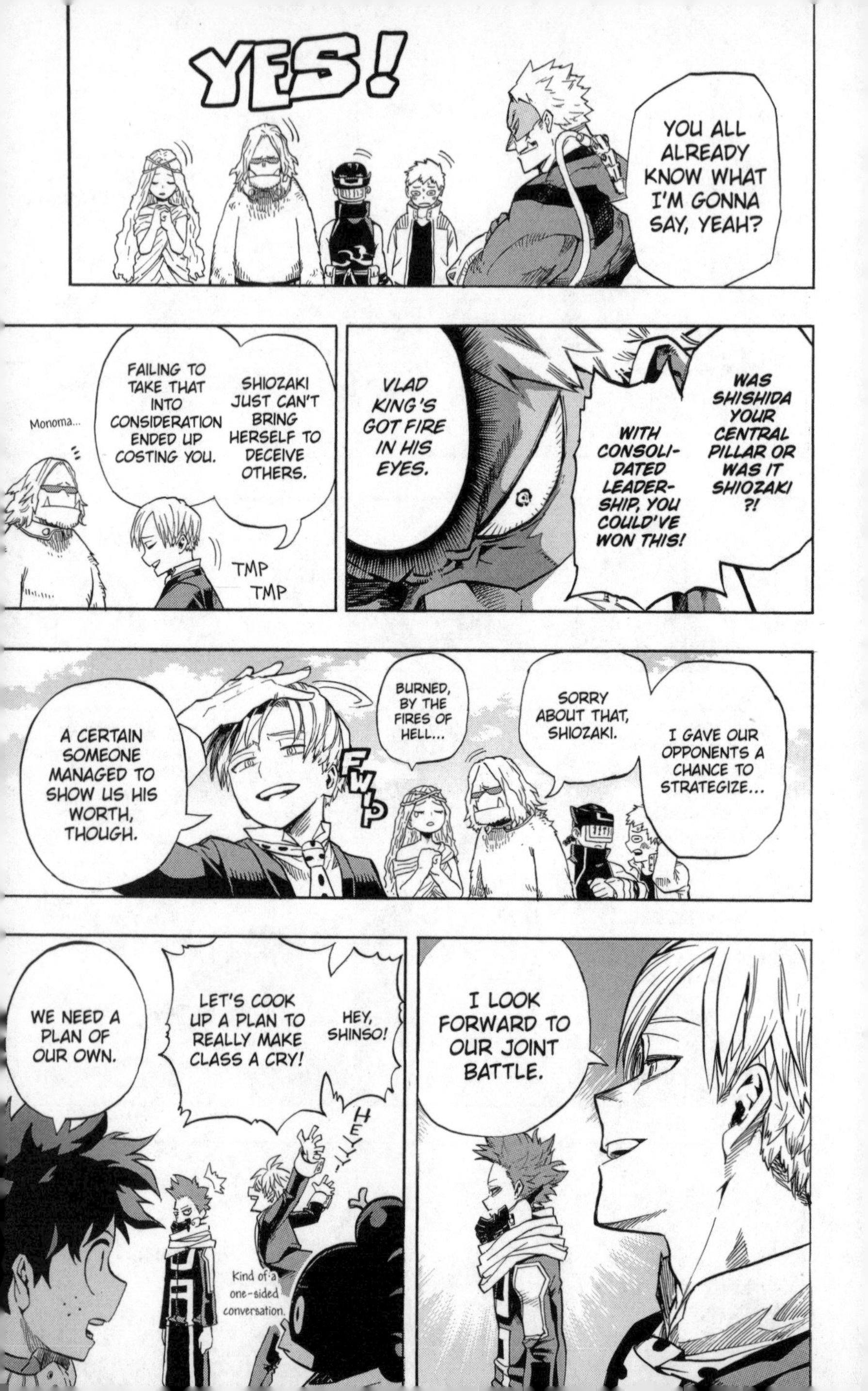
YOU ALL ALREADY KNOW WHAT I'M GONNA SAY, YEAH?
YES!
WAS SHISHIDA YOUR CENTRAL PILLAR OR WAS IT SHIOZAKI?!
WITH CONSOLIDATED LEADERSHIP, YOU COULD'VE WON THIS!
VLAD KING'S GOT FIRE IN HIS EYES.
SHIOZAKI JUST CAN'T BRING HERSELF TO DECEIVE OTHERS.
FAILING TO TAKE THAT INTO CONSIDERATION ENDED UP COSTING YOU.
Monoma...
TMP TMP
SORRY ABOUT THAT, SHIOZAKI.
I GAVE OUR OPPONENTS A CHANCE TO STRATEGIZE...
BURNED, BY THE FIRES OF HELL...
FWIP
A CERTAIN SOMEONE MANAGED TO SHOW US HIS WORTH, THOUGH.
I LOOK FORWARD TO OUR JOINT BATTLE.
HEY, SHINSO!
LET'S COOK UP A PLAN TO REALLY MAKE CLASS A CRY!
HEYYY
WE NEED A PLAN OF OUR OWN.
Kind of a one-sided conversation.

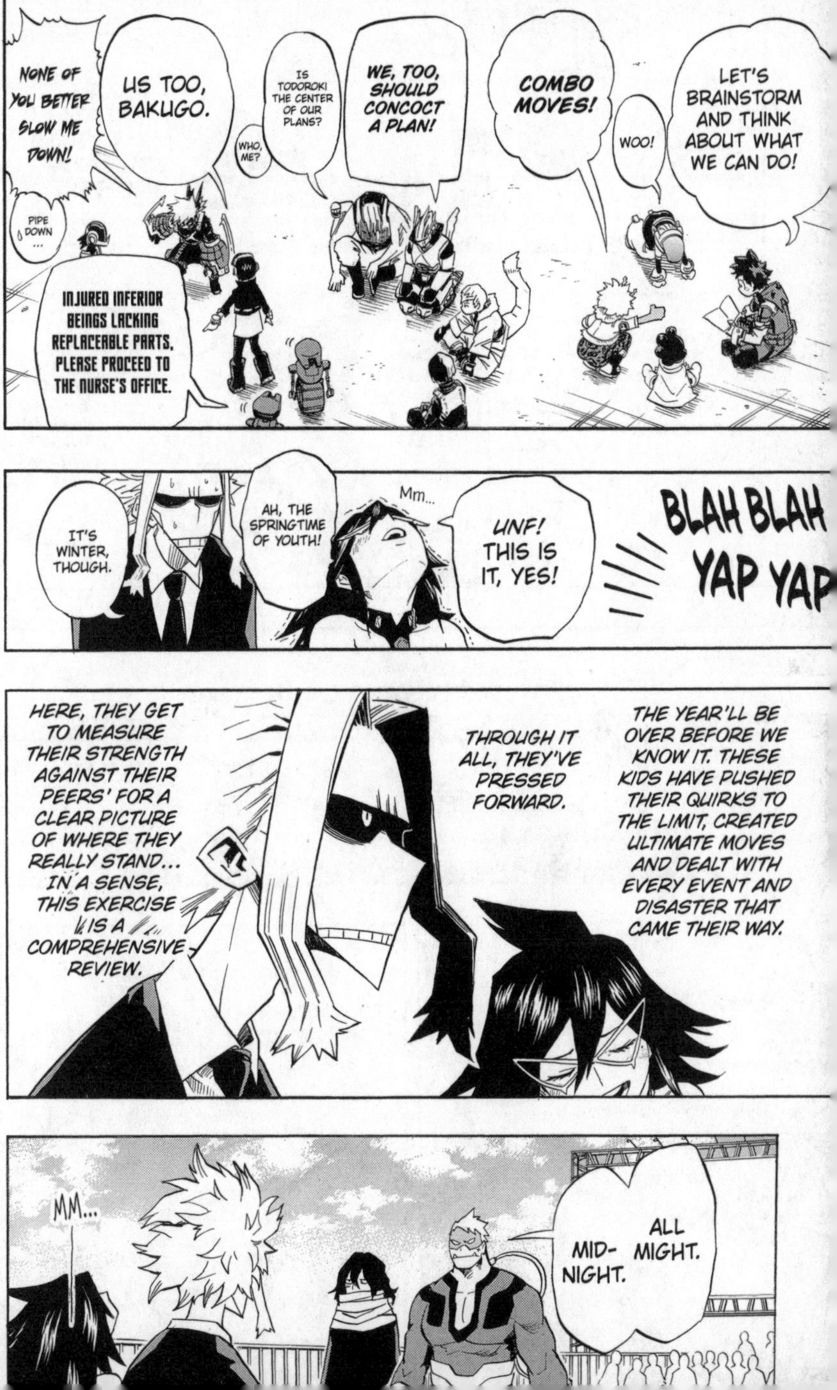
LET'S BRAINSTORM AND THINK ABOUT WHAT WE CAN DO!
WOO!
COMBO MOVES!
WE, TOO, SHOULD CONCOCT A PLAN!
IS TODOROKI THE CENTER OF OUR PLANS?
WHO, ME?
US TOO, BAKUGO.
NONE OF YOU BETTER SLOW ME DOWN!
PIPE DOWN...
INJURED INFERIOR BEINGS LACKING REPLACEABLE PARTS, PLEASE PROCEED TO THE NURSE'S OFFICE.
BLAH BLAH YAP YAP
UNF! THIS IS IT, YES!
Mm...
AH, THE SPRINGTIME OF YOUTH!
IT'S WINTER, THOUGH.
THE YEAR'LL BE OVER BEFORE WE KNOW IT. THESE KIDS HAVE PUSHED THEIR QUIRKS TO THE LIMIT, CREATED ULTIMATE MOVES AND DEALT WITH EVERY EVENT AND DISASTER THAT CAME THEIR WAY.
THROUGH IT ALL, THEY'VE PRESSED FORWARD.
HERE, THEY GET TO MEASURE THEIR STRENGTH AGAINST THEIR PEERS' FOR A CLEAR PICTURE OF WHERE THEY REALLY STAND... IN A SENSE, THIS EXERCISE IS A COMPREHENSIVE REVIEW.
ALL MIGHT.
MID-NIGHT.
MM...

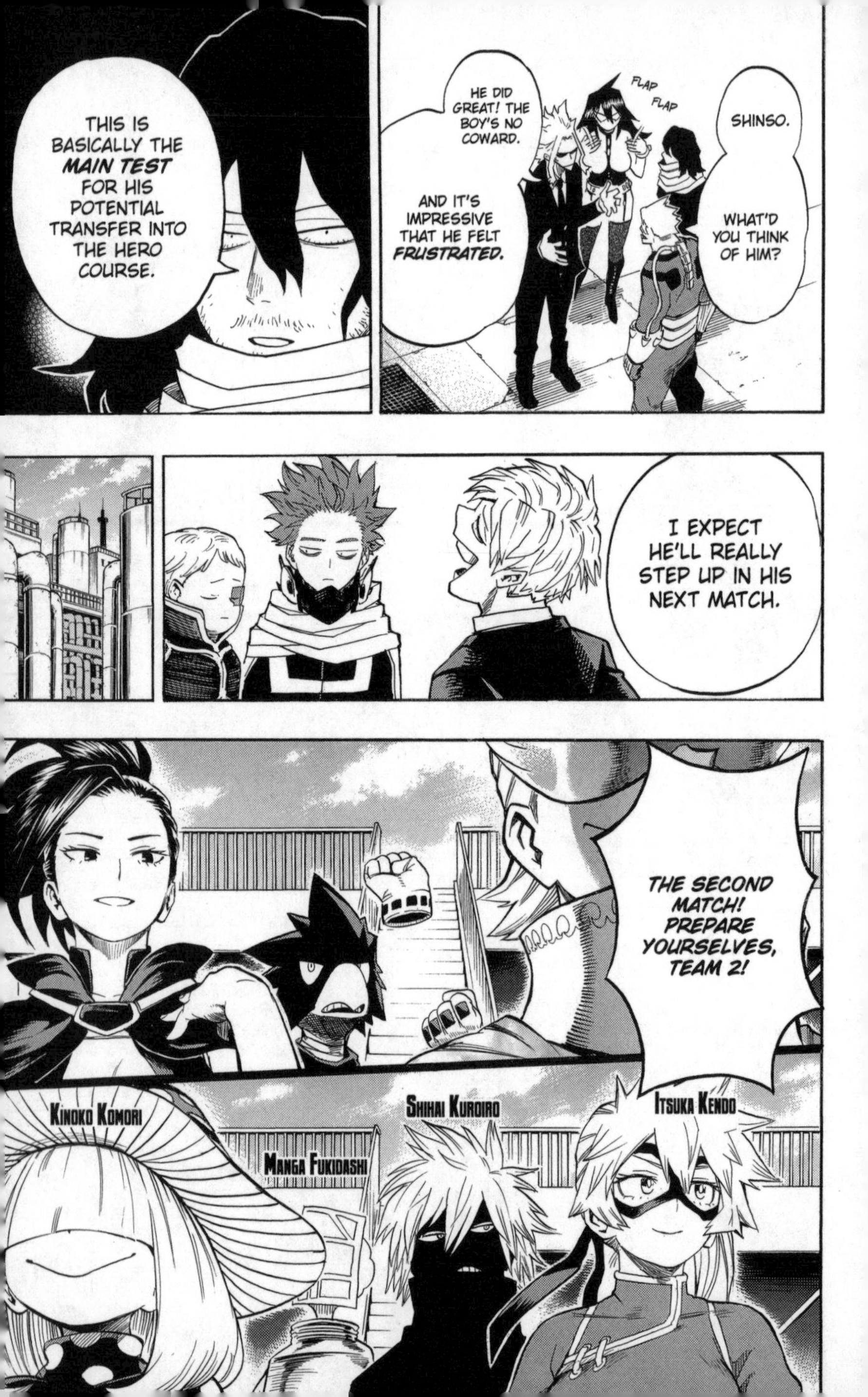

SHINSO.
FLAP FLAP
WHAT'D YOU THINK OF HIM?
HE DID GREAT! THE BOY'S NO COWARD.
AND IT'S IMPRESSIVE THAT HE FELT FRUSTRATED.
THIS IS BASICALLY THE MAIN TEST FOR HIS POTENTIAL TRANSFER INTO THE HERO COURSE.
I EXPECT HE'LL REALLY STEP UP IN HIS NEXT MATCH.
THE SECOND MATCH! PREPARE YOURSELVES, TEAM 2!
ITSUKA KENDO
SHIHAI KUROIRO
MANGA FUKIDASHI
KINOKO KOMORI

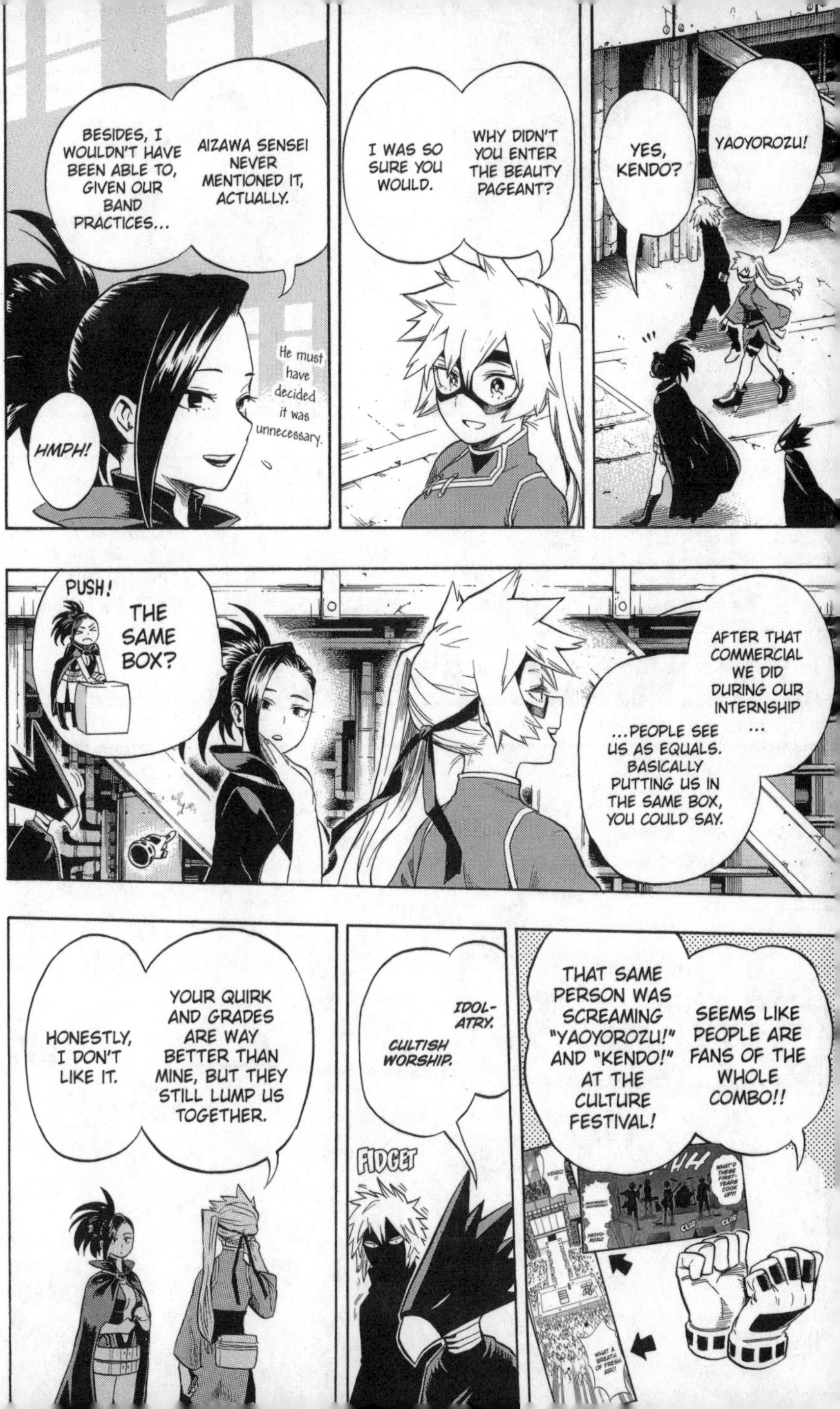
YAOYOROZU!
YES, KENDO?
WHY DIDN'T YOU ENTER THE BEAUTY PAGEANT?
I WAS SO SURE YOU WOULD.
AIZAWA SENSEI NEVER MENTIONED IT, ACTUALLY.
BESIDES, I WOULDN'T HAVE BEEN ABLE TO, GIVEN OUR BAND PRACTICES...
He must have decided it was unnecessary.
HMPH!
AFTER THAT COMMERCIAL WE DID DURING OUR INTERNSHIP ...
...PEOPLE SEE US AS EQUALS. BASICALLY PUTTING US IN THE SAME BOX, YOU COULD SAY.
THE SAME BOX?
PUSH!
SEEMS LIKE PEOPLE ARE FANS OF THE WHOLE COMBO!!
THAT SAME PERSON WAS SCREAMING "YAOYOROZU!" AND "KENDO!" AT THE CULTURE FESTIVAL!
WHAT'D THESE FIRST-YEARS COOK UP!?
CLAP
CLAP
WHAT A BREATH OF FRESH AIR!!
IDOLATRY.
CULTISH WORSHIP.
FIDGET
YOUR QUIRK AND GRADES ARE WAY BETTER THAN MINE, BUT THEY STILL LUMP US TOGETHER.
HONESTLY, I DON'T LIKE IT.

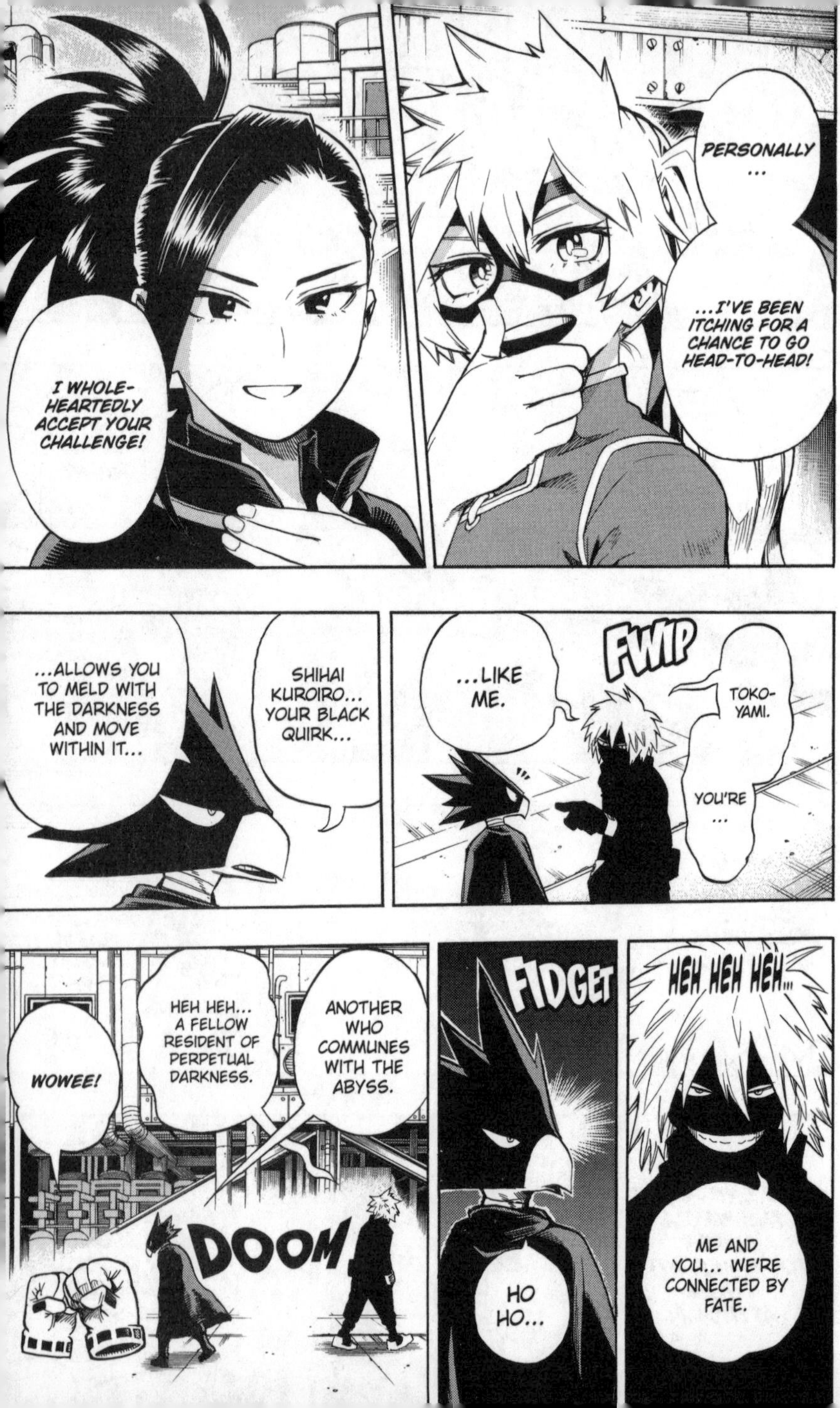
PERSONALLY ...
...I'VE BEEN ITCHING FOR A CHANCE TO GO HEAD-TO-HEAD!
I WHOLE-HEARTEDLY ACCEPT YOUR CHALLENGE!
FWIP
TOKO-YAMI.
YOU'RE ...
...LIKE ME.
SHIHAI KUROIRO... YOUR BLACK QUIRK...
...ALLOWS YOU TO MELD WITH THE DARKNESS AND MOVE WITHIN IT...
HEH HEH HEH...
ME AND YOU... WE'RE CONNECTED BY FATE.
FIDGET
HO HO...
ANOTHER WHO COMMUNES WITH THE ABYSS.
HEH HEH... A FELLOW RESIDENT OF PERPETUAL DARKNESS.
WOWEE!
DOOM

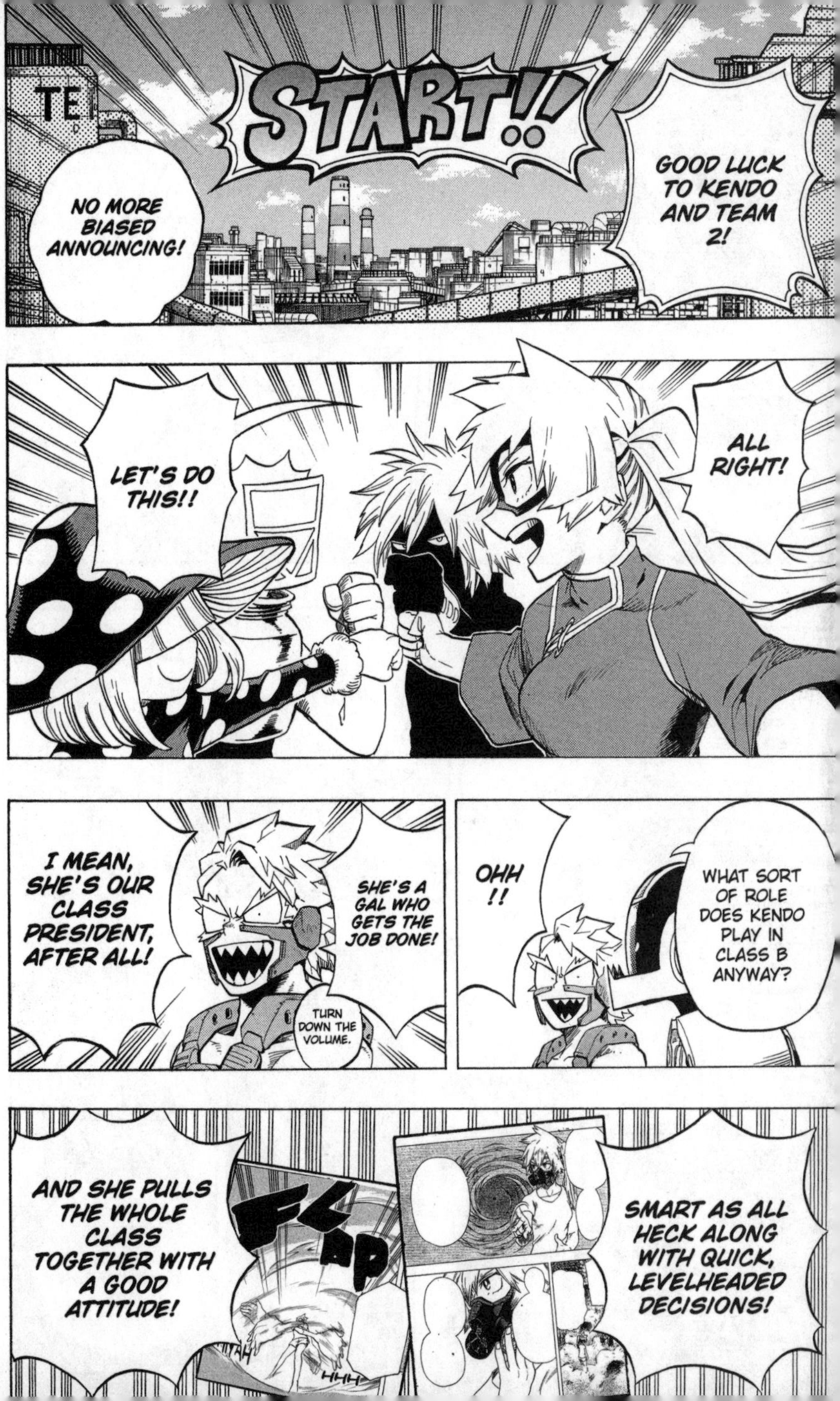
START!!
GOOD LUCK TO KENDO AND TEAM 2!
NO MORE BIASED ANNOUNCING!
ALL RIGHT!
LET'S DO THIS!!
WHAT SORT OF ROLE DOES KENDO PLAY IN CLASS B ANYWAY?
OHH !!
SHE'S A GAL WHO GETS THE JOB DONE!
I MEAN, SHE'S OUR CLASS PRESIDENT, AFTER ALL!
TURN DOWN THE VOLUME.
SMART AS ALL HECK ALONG WITH QUICK, LEVELHEADED DECISIONS!
AND SHE PULLS THE WHOLE CLASS TOGETHER WITH A GOOD ATTITUDE!

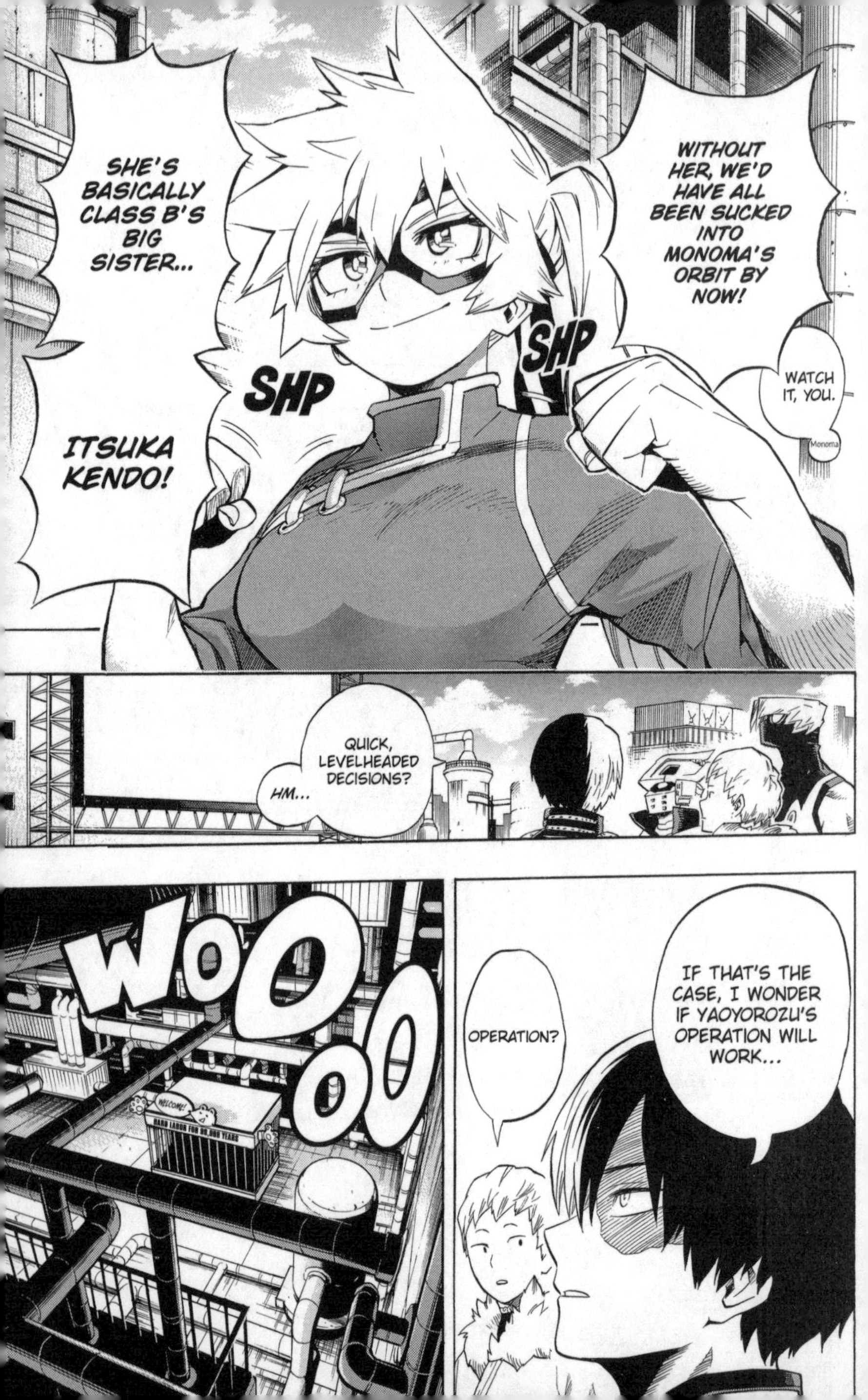
WITHOUT HER, WE'D HAVE ALL BEEN SUCKED INTO MONOMA'S ORBIT BY NOW!
SHE'S BASICALLY CLASS B'S BIG SISTER...
ITSUKA KENDO!
SHP
SHP
WATCH IT, YOU.
Monoma
QUICK, LEVELHEADED DECISIONS?
HM...
IF THAT'S THE CASE, I WONDER IF YAOYOROZU'S OPERATION WILL WORK...
OPERATION?
WOOOO
WELCOME!

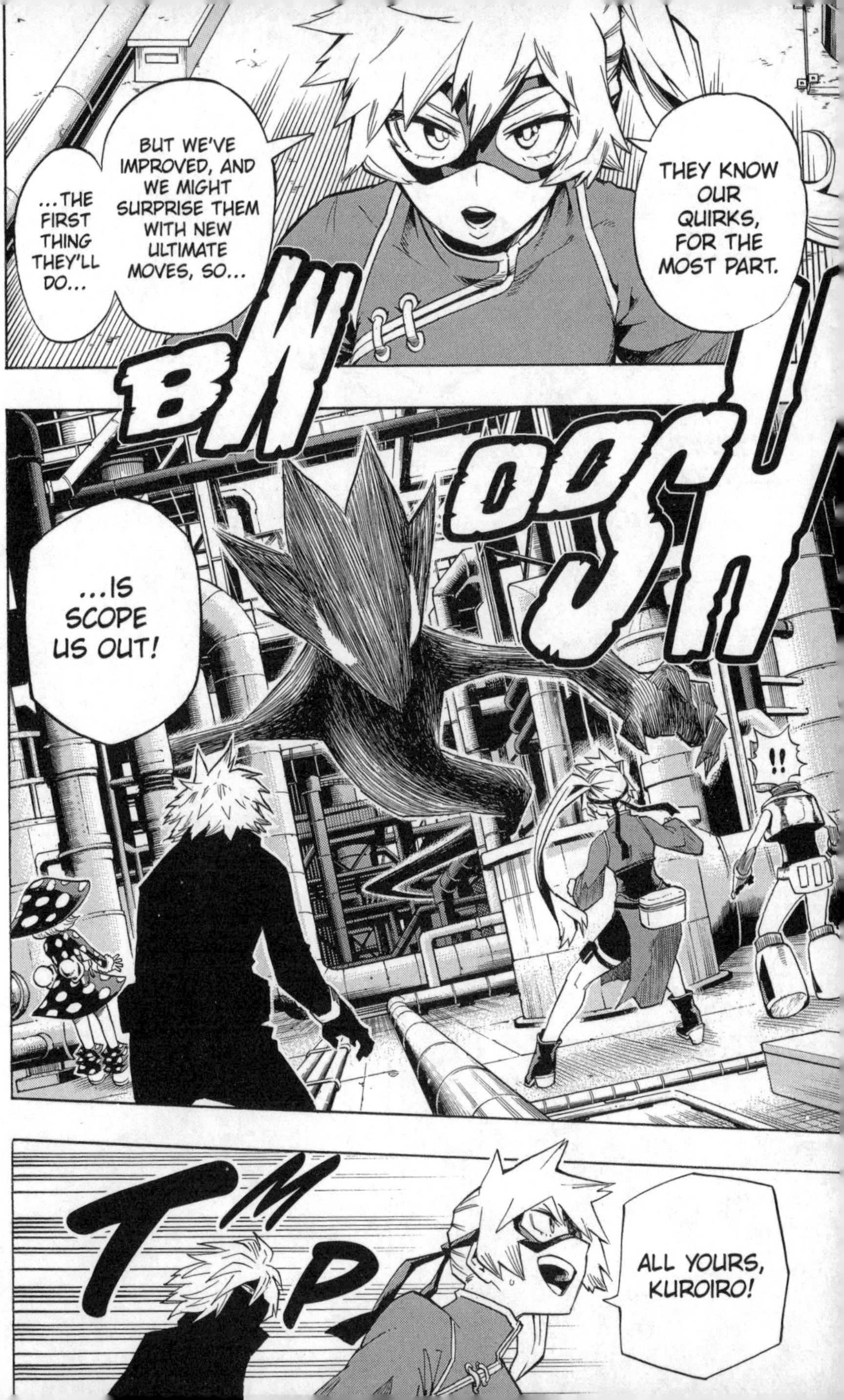
THEY KNOW OUR QUIRKS, FOR THE MOST PART.
BUT WE'VE IMPROVED, AND WE MIGHT SURPRISE THEM WITH NEW ULTIMATE MOVES, SO...
...THE FIRST THING THEY'LL DO...
BWOOSH
...IS SCOPE US OUT!
!!
ALL YOURS, KUROIRO!
TMP

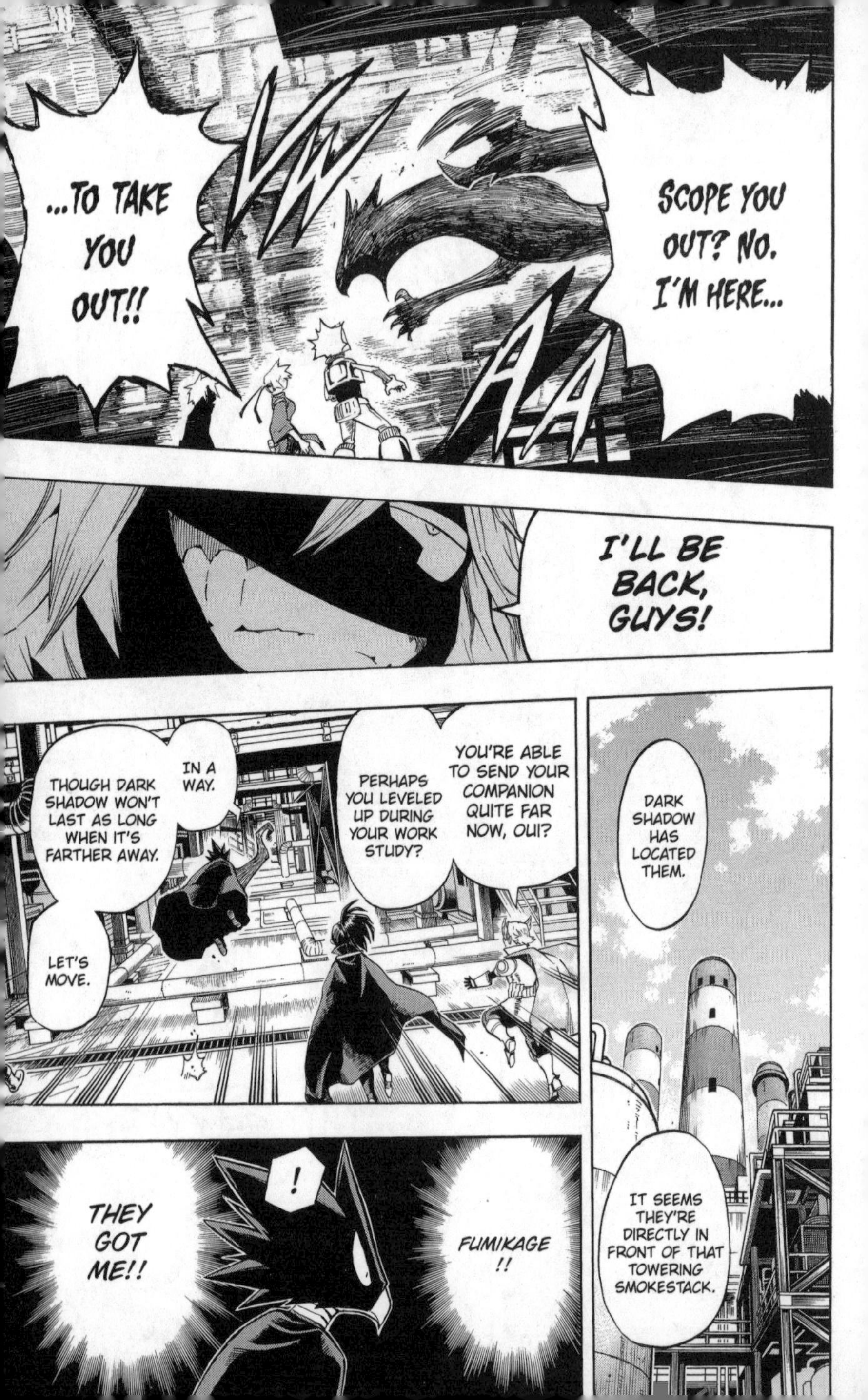
SCOPE YOU OUT? NO. I'M HERE...
...TO TAKE YOU OUT!!
I'LL BE BACK, GUYS!
DARK SHADOW HAS LOCATED THEM.
IT SEEMS THEY'RE DIRECTLY IN FRONT OF THAT TOWERING SMOKESTACK.
YOU'RE ABLE TO SEND YOUR COMPANION QUITE FAR NOW, OUI?
PERHAPS YOU LEVELED UP DURING YOUR WORK STUDY?
IN A WAY.
THOUGH DARK SHADOW WON'T LAST AS LONG WHEN IT'S FARTHER AWAY.
LET'S MOVE.
!
FUMIKAGE !!
THEY GOT ME!!

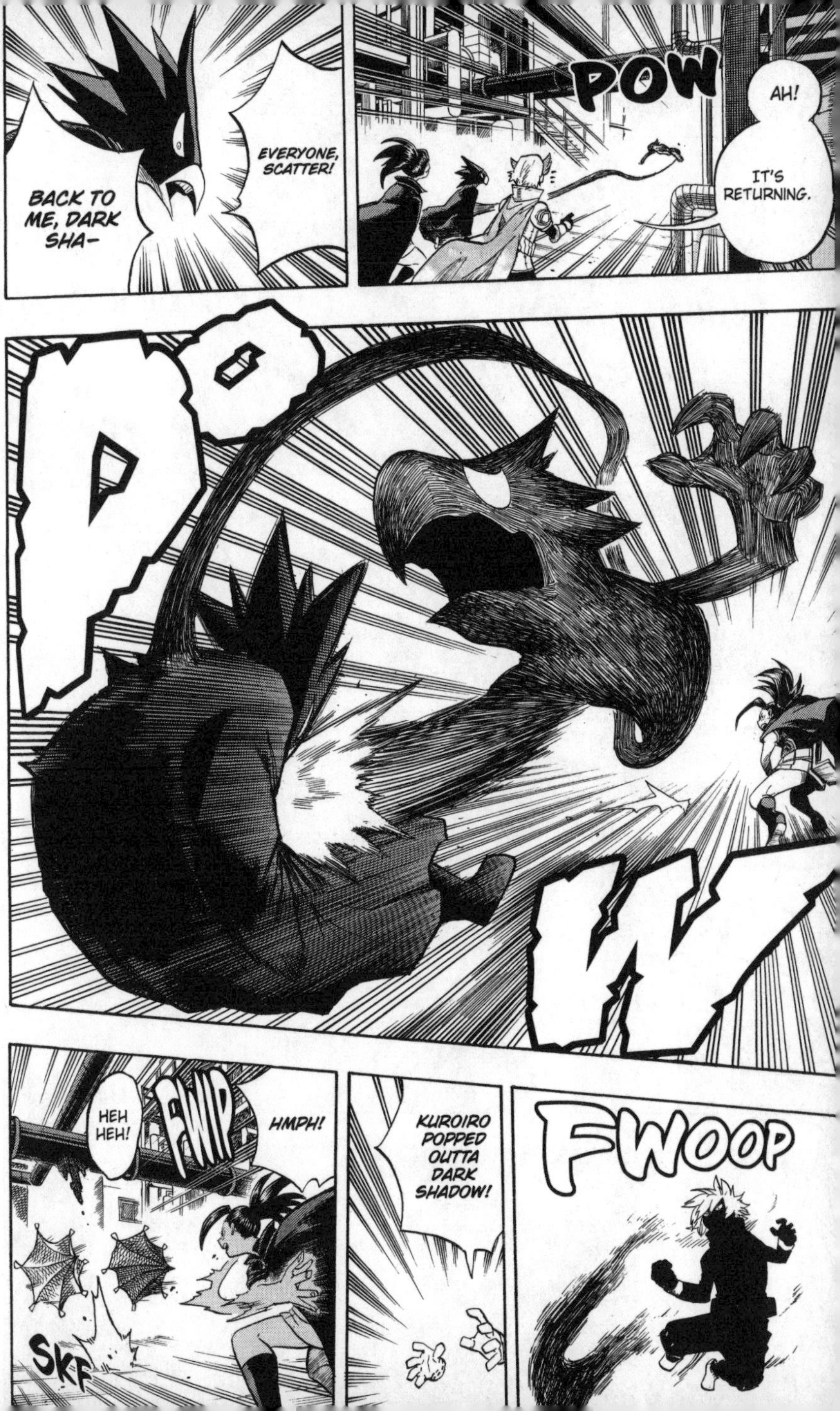
POW
AH!
IT'S RETURNING.
EVERYONE, SCATTER!
BACK TO ME, DARK SHA-
POW
FWOOP
KUROIRO POPPED OUTTA DARK SHADOW!
HMPH!
FWIP
HEH HEH!
SKF

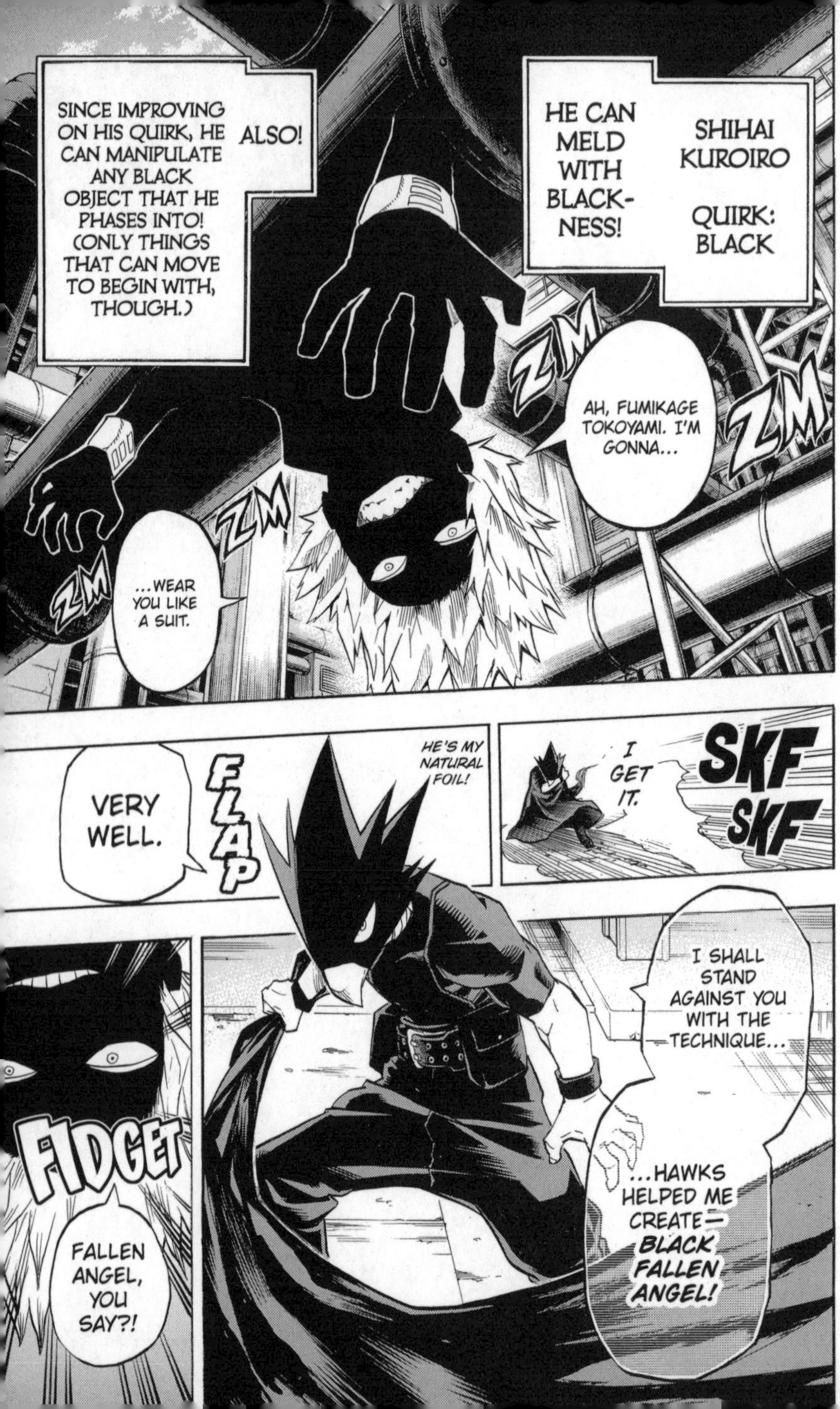
SHIHAI KUROIRO
QUIRK: BLACK
HE CAN MELD WITH BLACKNESS!
ALSO!
SINCE IMPROVING ON HIS QUIRK, HE CAN MANIPULATE ANY BLACK OBJECT THAT HE PHASES INTO! (ONLY THINGS THAT CAN MOVE TO BEGIN WITH, THOUGH.)
ZM
AH, FUMIKAGE TOKOYAMI. I'M GONNA...
ZM
ZM
ZM
...WEAR YOU LIKE A SUIT.
SKF
SKF
I GET IT.
HE'S MY NATURAL FOIL!
FLAP
VERY WELL.
I SHALL STAND AGAINST YOU WITH THE TECHNIQUE...
...HAWKS HELPED ME CREATE— BLACK FALLEN ANGEL!
FIDGET
FALLEN ANGEL, YOU SAY?!

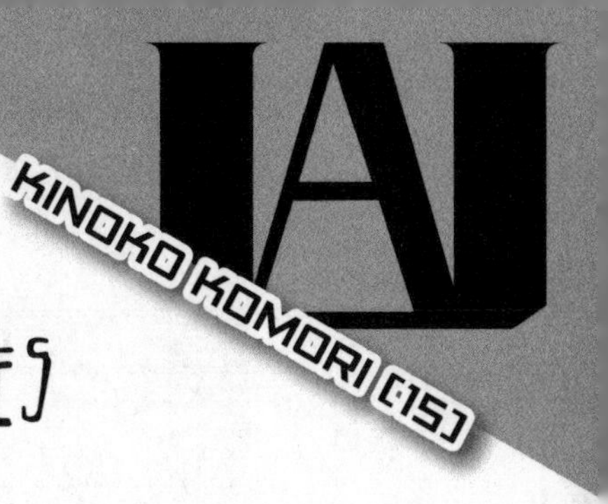
KINOKO KOMORI (15)

STREET CLOTHES

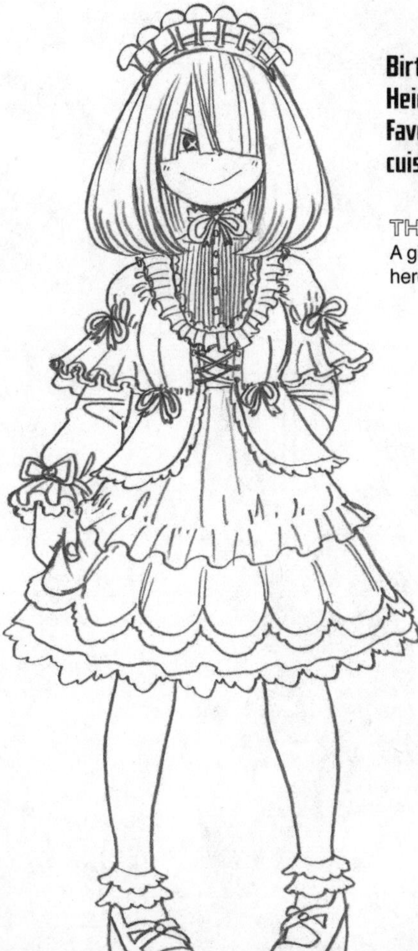

Birthday: 12/2
Height: 152 cm
Favorite Thing: Mushroom-based cuisine

THE SUPPLEMENT
A girl who wants to be an idol hero. Loves mushrooms.

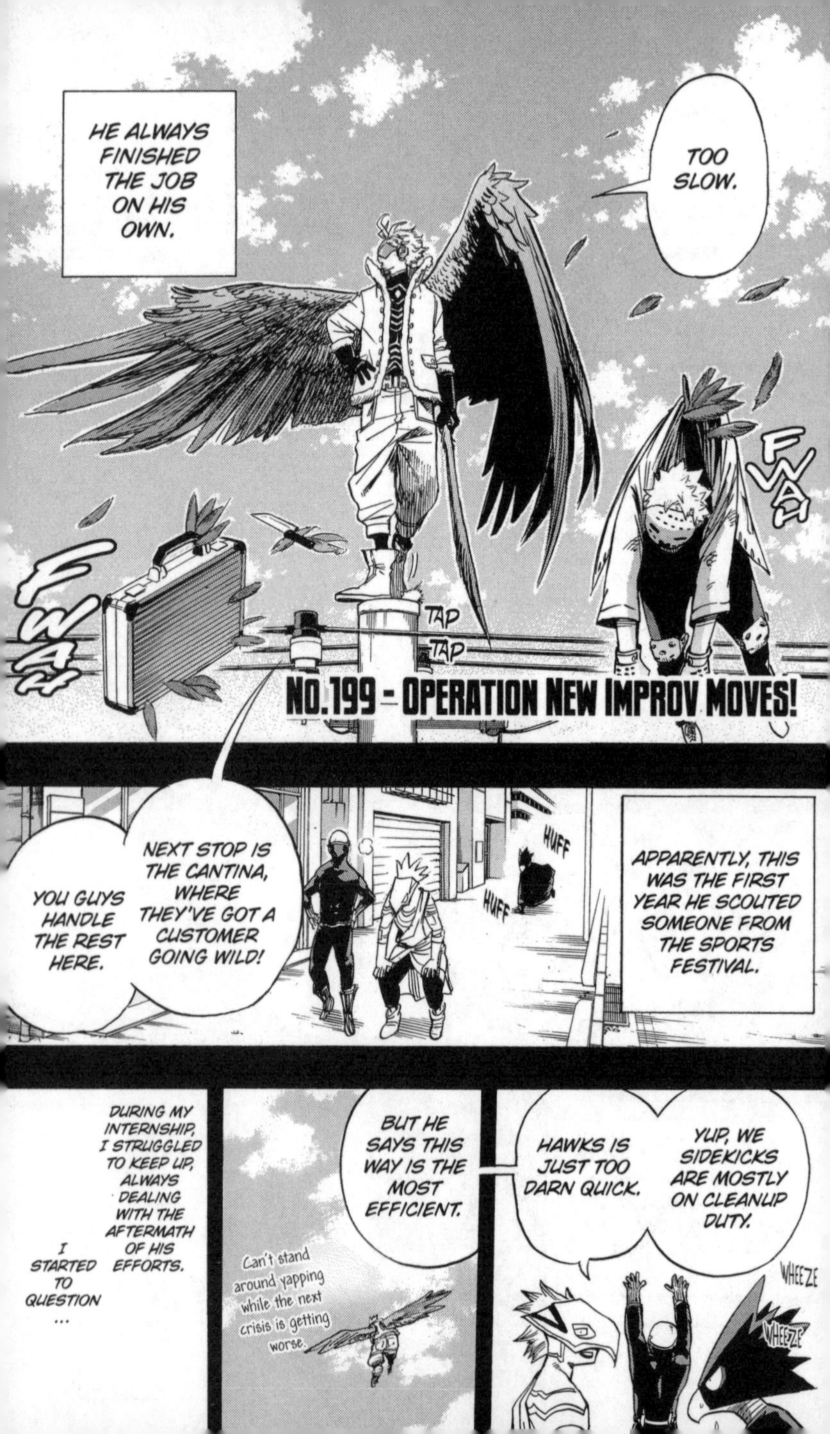
TOO SLOW.
HE ALWAYS FINISHED THE JOB ON HIS OWN.
FWAH
TAP TAP
FWAH
NO.199 - OPERATION NEW IMPROV MOVES!
APPARENTLY, THIS WAS THE FIRST YEAR HE SCOUTED SOMEONE FROM THE SPORTS FESTIVAL.
HUFF
HUFF
NEXT STOP IS THE CANTINA, WHERE THEY'VE GOT A CUSTOMER GOING WILD!
YOU GUYS HANDLE THE REST HERE.
YUP, WE SIDEKICKS ARE MOSTLY ON CLEANUP DUTY.
HAWKS IS JUST TOO DARN QUICK.
BUT HE SAYS THIS WAY IS THE MOST EFFICIENT.
WHEEZE
WHEEZE
Can't stand around yapping while the next crisis is getting worse.
DURING MY INTERNSHIP, I STRUGGLED TO KEEP UP, ALWAYS DEALING WITH THE AFTERMATH OF HIS EFFORTS.
I STARTED TO QUESTION ...

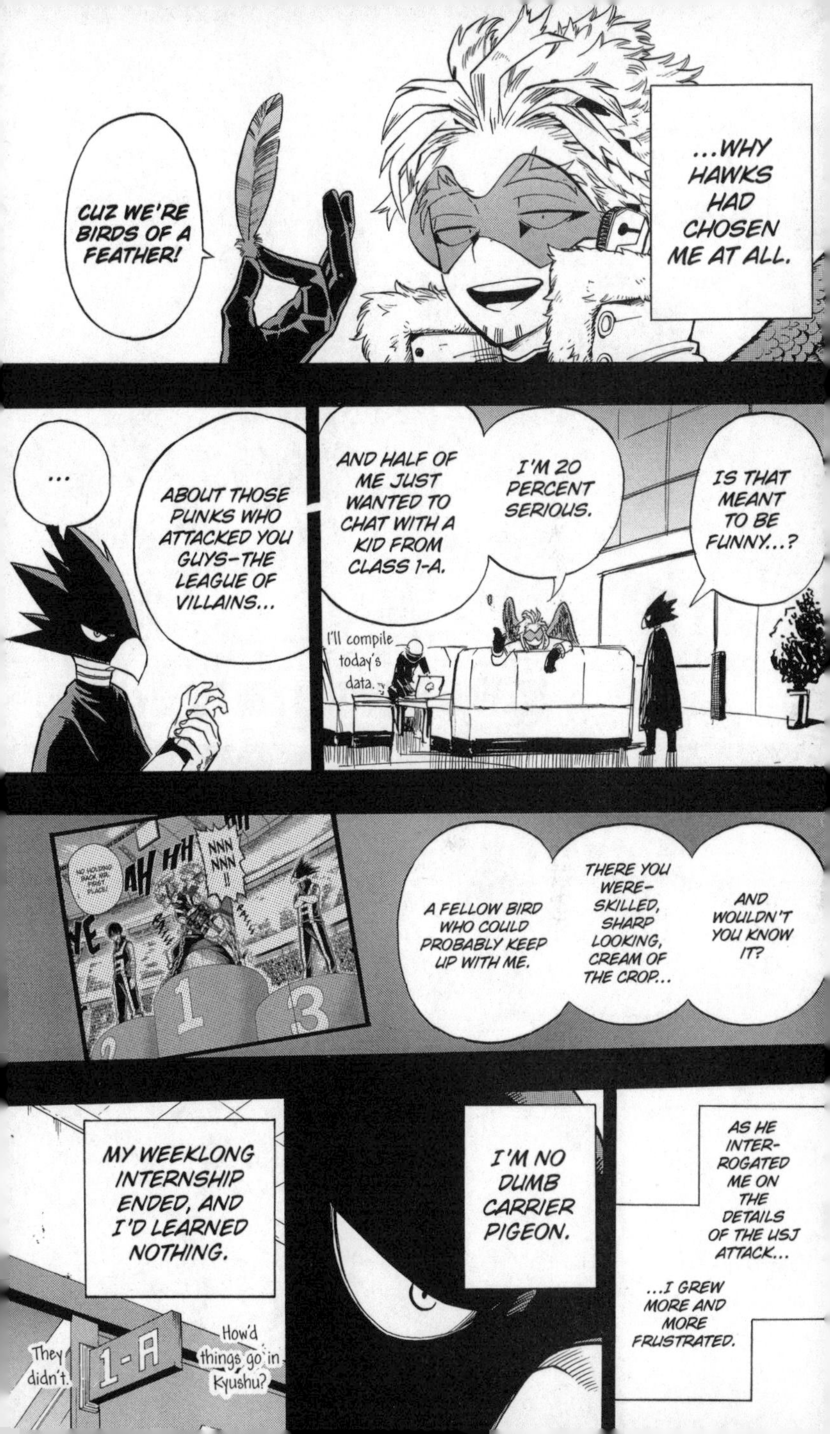
...WHY HAWKS HAD CHOSEN ME AT ALL.
CUZ WE'RE BIRDS OF A FEATHER!
IS THAT MEANT TO BE FUNNY...?
I'M 20 PERCENT SERIOUS.
AND HALF OF ME JUST WANTED TO CHAT WITH A KID FROM CLASS 1-A.
I'll compile today's data.
ABOUT THOSE PUNKS WHO ATTACKED YOU GUYS—THE LEAGUE OF VILLAINS...
...
AND WOULDN'T YOU KNOW IT?
THERE YOU WERE—SKILLED, SHARP LOOKING, CREAM OF THE CROP...
A FELLOW BIRD WHO COULD PROBABLY KEEP UP WITH ME.
AS HE INTER-ROGATED ME ON THE DETAILS OF THE USJ ATTACK...
...I GREW MORE AND MORE FRUSTRATED.
I'M NO DUMB CARRIER PIGEON.
MY WEEKLONG INTERNSHIP ENDED, AND I'D LEARNED NOTHING.
How'd things go in Kyushu?
1-A
They didn't.

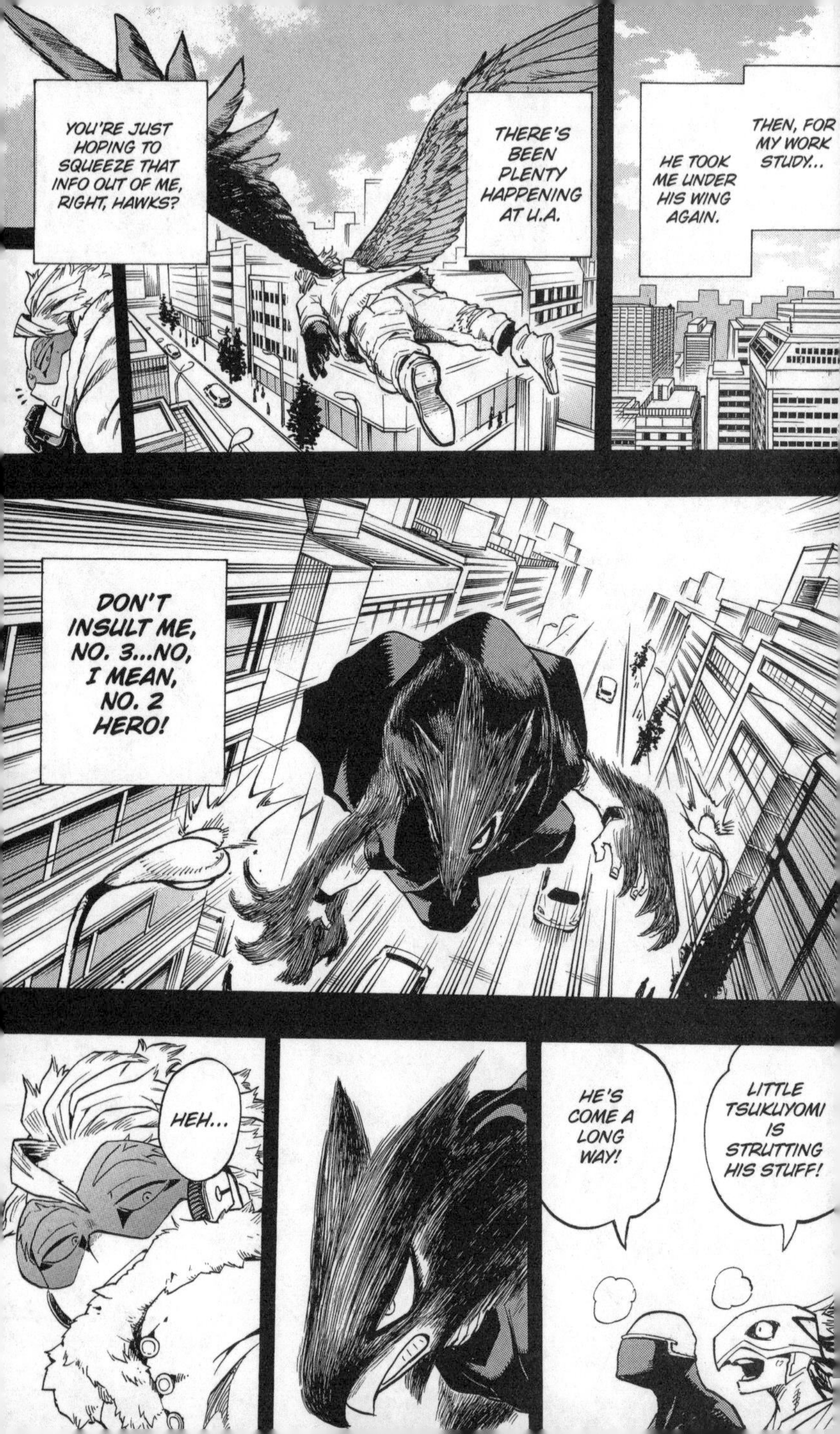
THEN, FOR MY WORK STUDY...
HE TOOK ME UNDER HIS WING AGAIN.
THERE'S BEEN PLENTY HAPPENING AT U.A.
YOU'RE JUST HOPING TO SQUEEZE THAT INFO OUT OF ME, RIGHT, HAWKS?
DON'T INSULT ME, NO. 3...NO, I MEAN, NO. 2 HERO!
LITTLE TSUKUYOMI IS STRUTTING HIS STUFF!
HE'S COME A LONG WAY!
HEH...

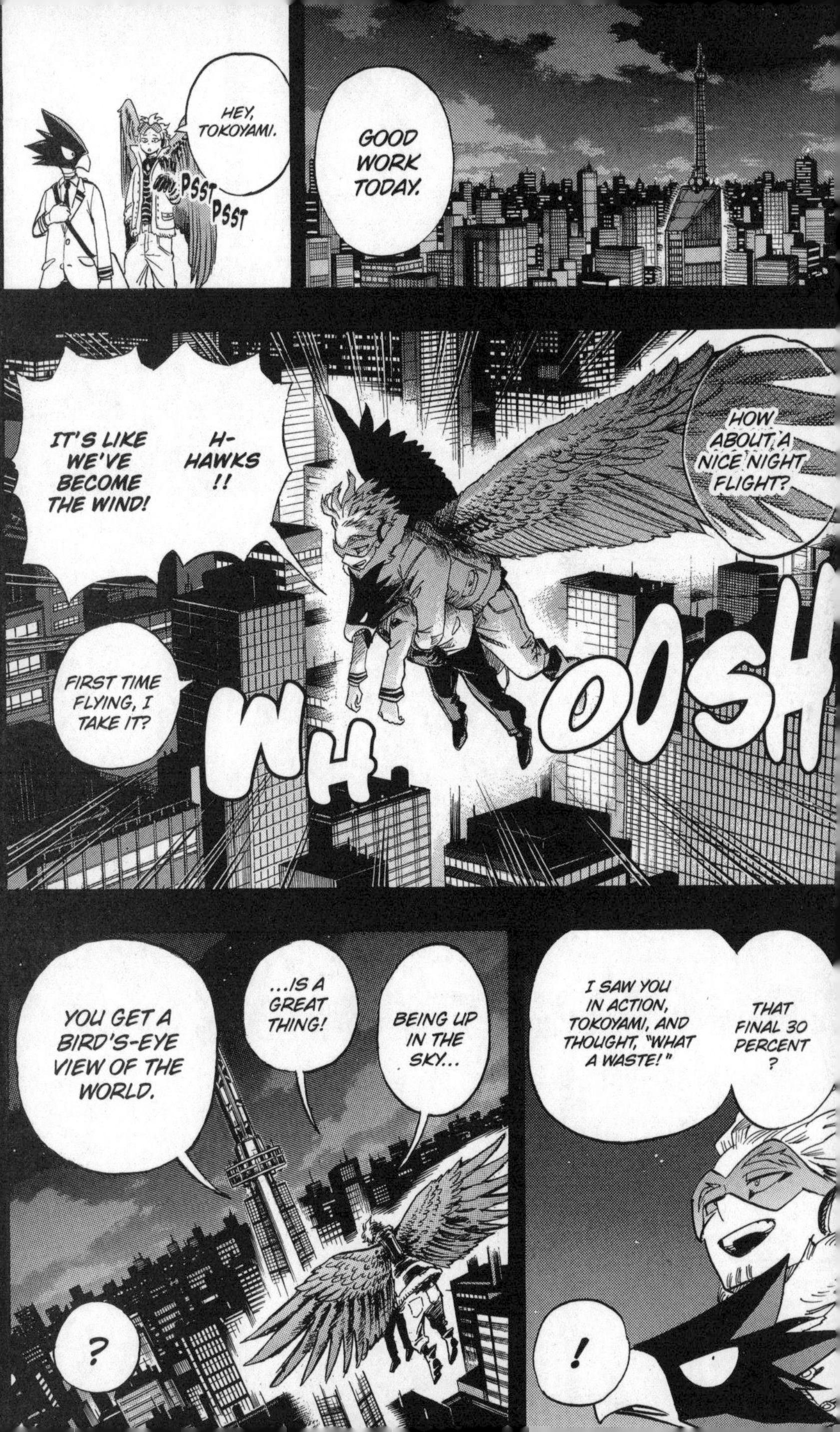
GOOD WORK TODAY.
HEY, TOKOYAMI.
PSST PSST
HOW ABOUT A NICE NIGHT FLIGHT?
WHOOSH
H-HAWKS!!
IT'S LIKE WE'VE BECOME THE WIND!
FIRST TIME FLYING, I TAKE IT?
THAT FINAL 30 PERCENT?
I SAW YOU IN ACTION, TOKOYAMI, AND THOUGHT, "WHAT A WASTE!"
!
BEING UP IN THE SKY...
...IS A GREAT THING!
YOU GET A BIRD'S-EYE VIEW OF THE WORLD.
?

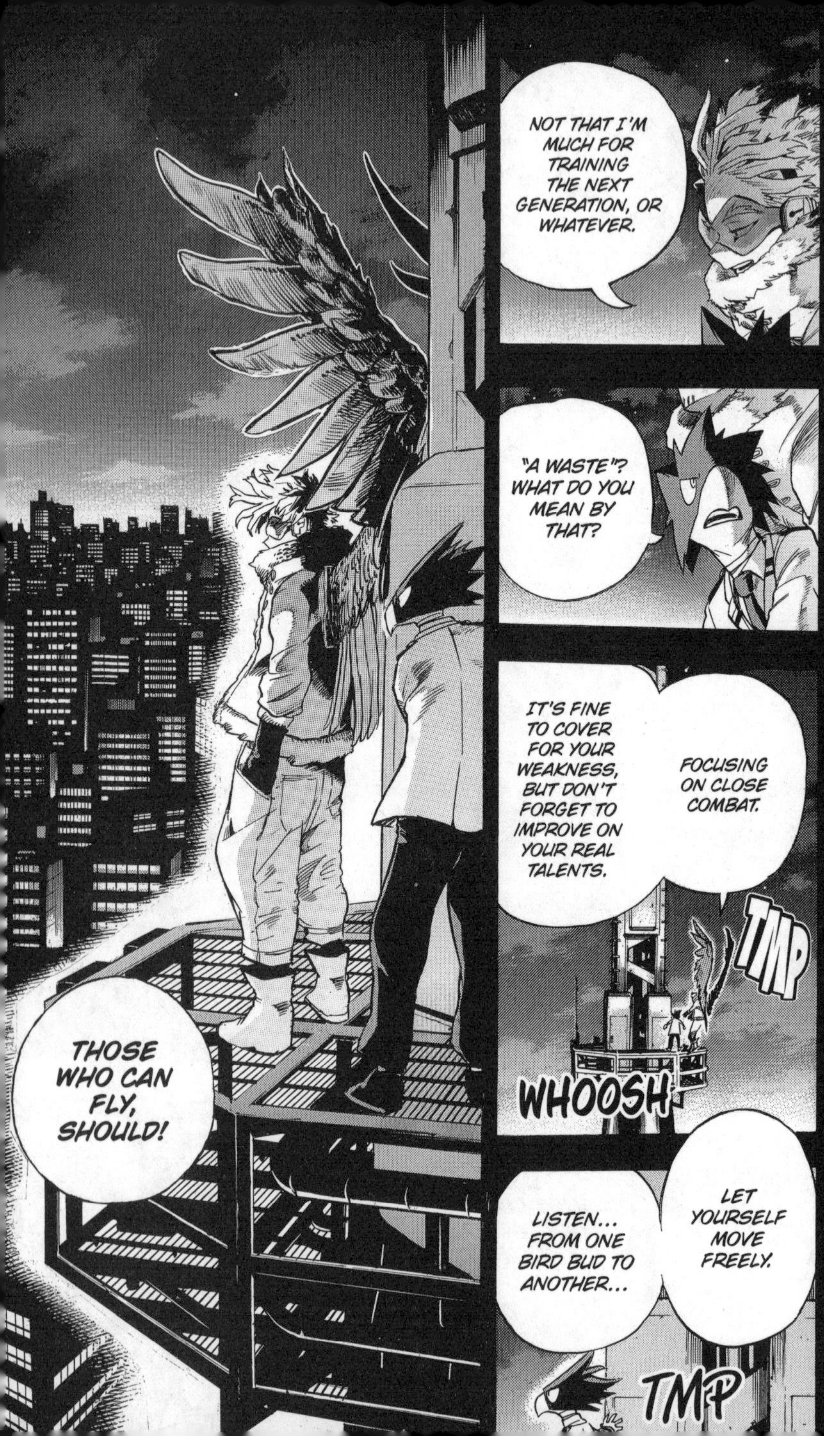
NOT THAT I'M MUCH FOR TRAINING THE NEXT GENERATION, OR WHATEVER.
"A WASTE"? WHAT DO YOU MEAN BY THAT?
FOCUSING ON CLOSE COMBAT.
IT'S FINE TO COVER FOR YOUR WEAKNESS, BUT DON'T FORGET TO IMPROVE ON YOUR REAL TALENTS.
TMP
WHOOSH
LET YOURSELF MOVE FREELY.
LISTEN... FROM ONE BIRD BUD TO ANOTHER...
TMP
THOSE WHO CAN FLY, SHOULD!

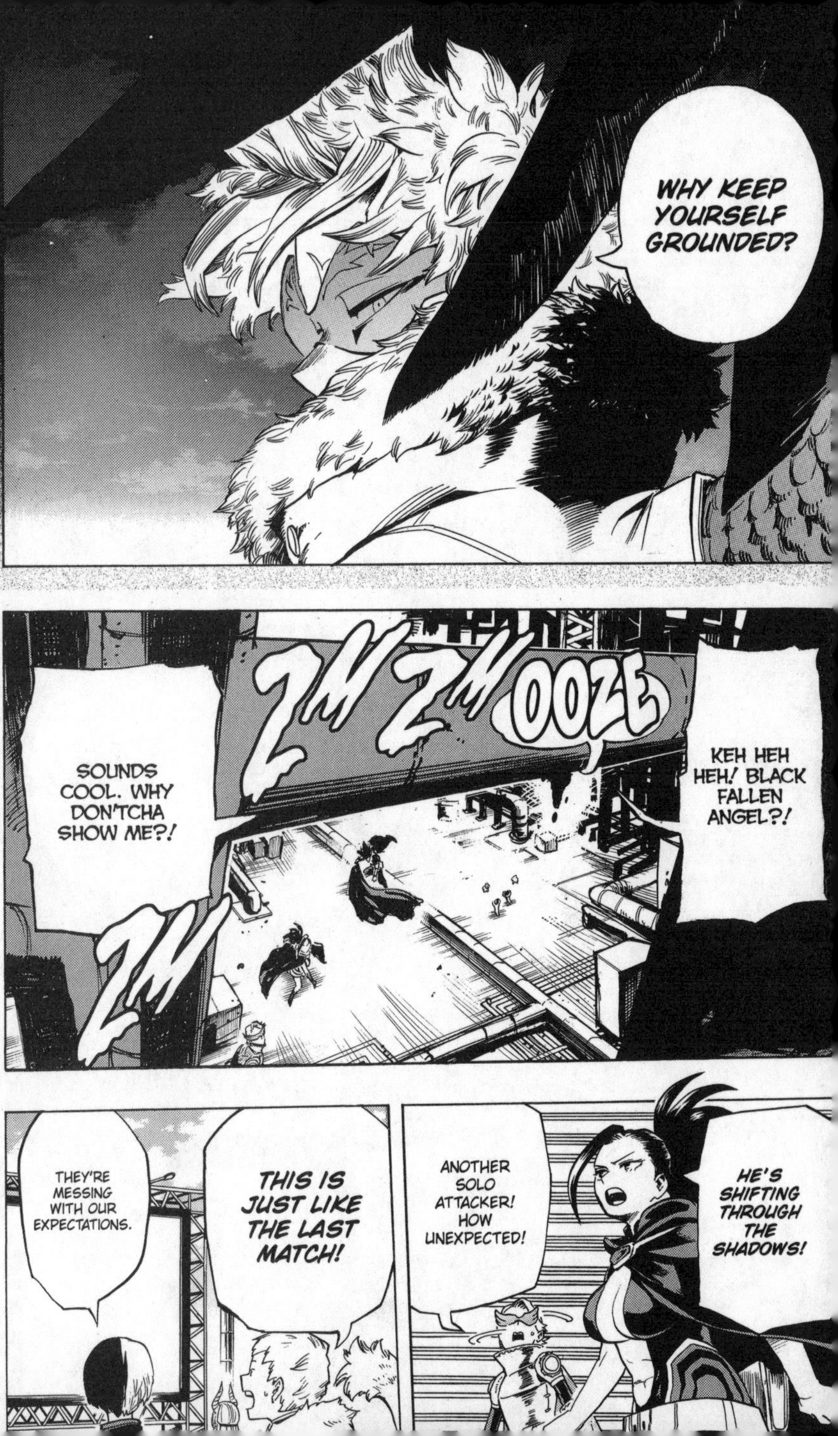
WHY KEEP YOURSELF GROUNDED?
KEH HEH HEH! BLACK FALLEN ANGEL?!
ZM ZM OOZE
SOUNDS COOL. WHY DON'TCHA SHOW ME?!
ZM
HE'S SHIFTING THROUGH THE SHADOWS!
ANOTHER SOLO ATTACKER! HOW UNEXPECTED!
THIS IS JUST LIKE THE LAST MATCH!
THEY'RE MESSING WITH OUR EXPECTATIONS.

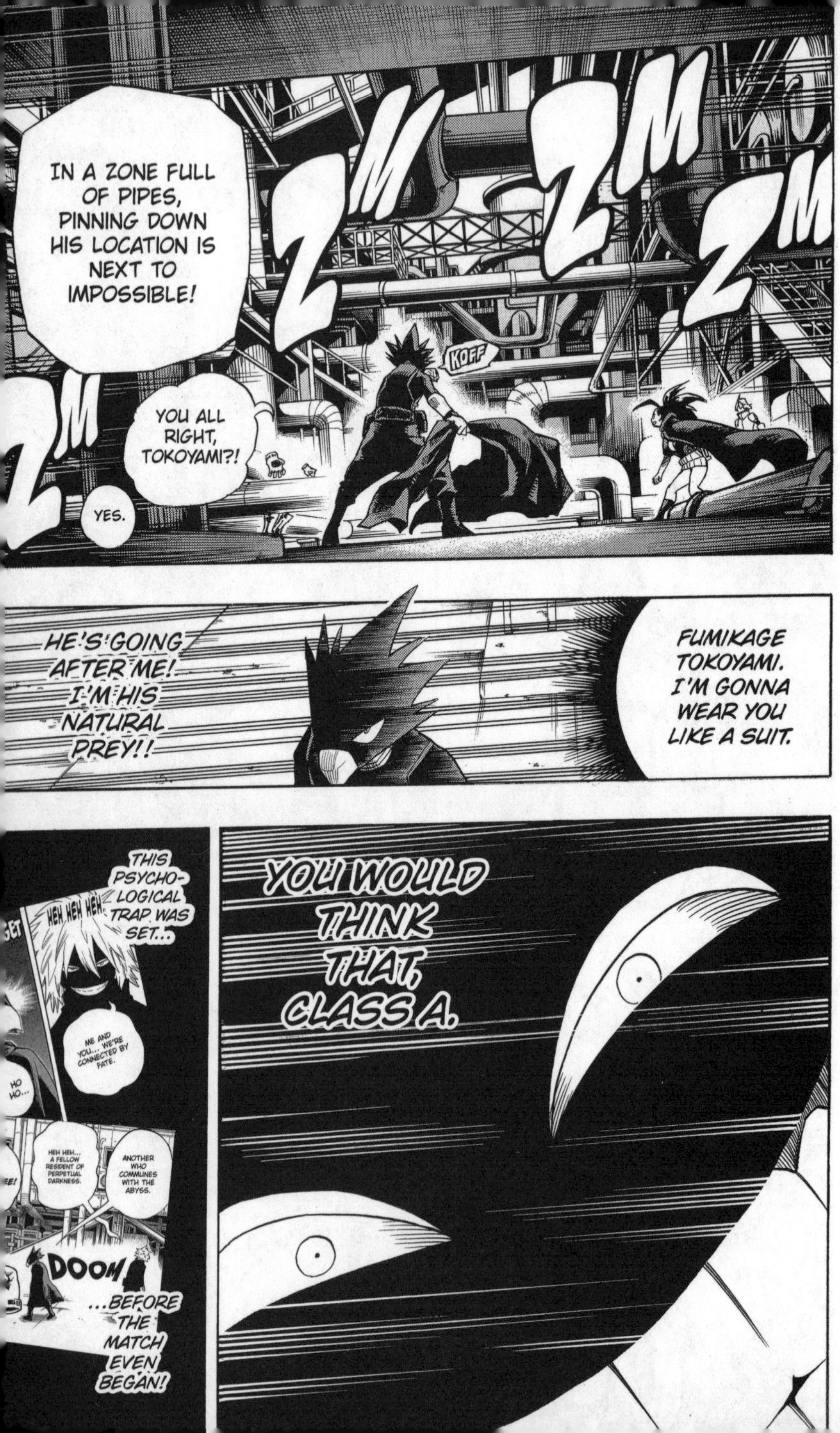
ZM ZM ZM
IN A ZONE FULL OF PIPES, PINNING DOWN HIS LOCATION IS NEXT TO IMPOSSIBLE!
KOFF
YOU ALL RIGHT, TOKOYAMI?!
YES.
FUMIKAGE TOKOYAMI. I'M GONNA WEAR YOU LIKE A SUIT.
HE'S GOING AFTER ME! I'M HIS NATURAL PREY!!
YOU WOULD THINK THAT, CLASS A.
THIS PSYCHOLOGICAL TRAP WAS SET...
HEH HEH HEH
ME AND YOU... WE'RE CONNECTED BY FATE.
HO HO...
ANOTHER WHO COMMUNES WITH THE ABYSS.
HEH HEH... A FELLOW RESIDENT OF PERPETUAL DARKNESS.
DOOM
...BEFORE THE MATCH EVEN BEGAN!

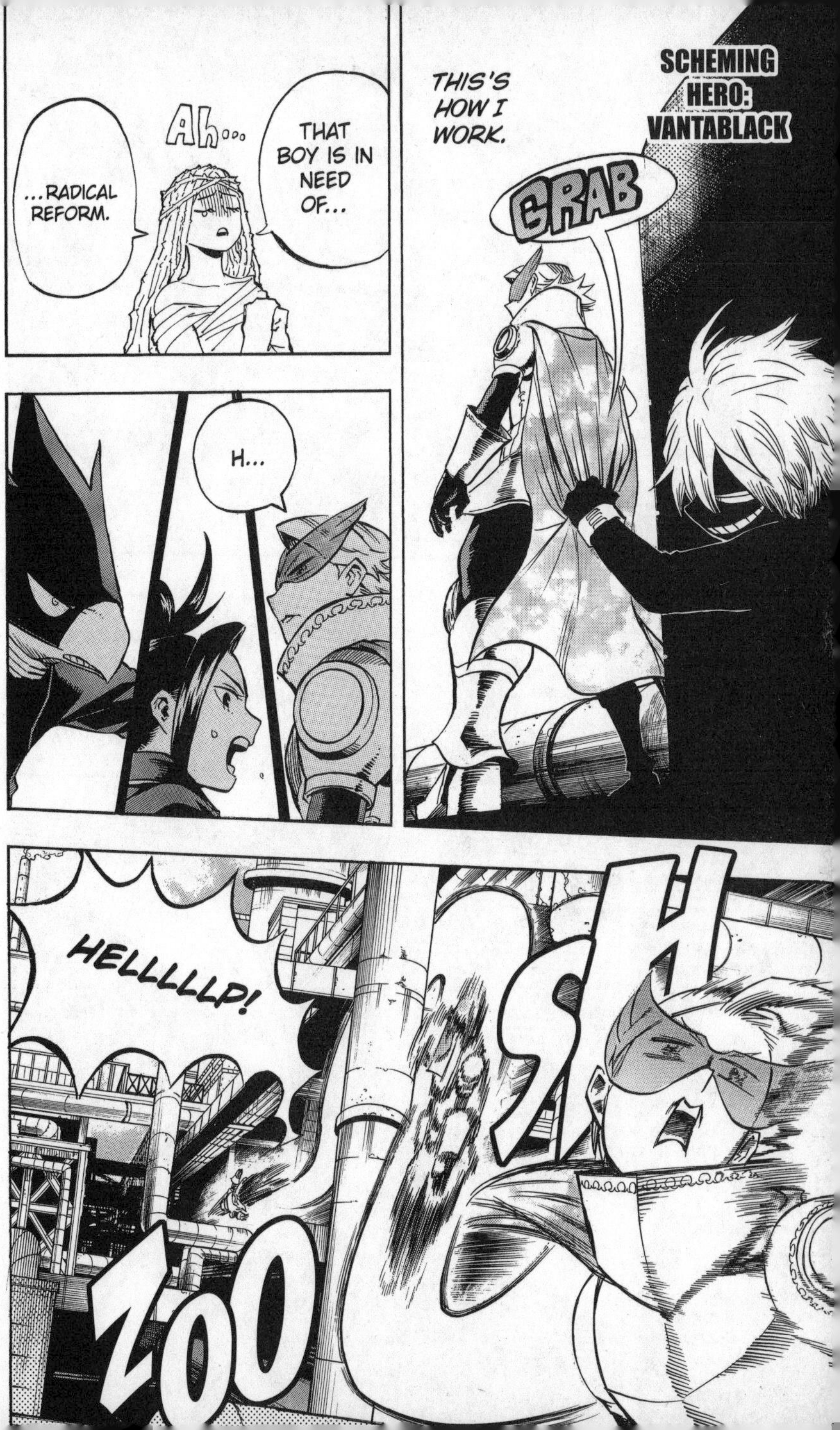
SCHEMING HERO: VANTABLACK
THIS'S HOW I WORK.
GRAB
THAT BOY IS IN NEED OF...
Ah...
...RADICAL REFORM.
H...
SH
HELLLLLP!
ZOO

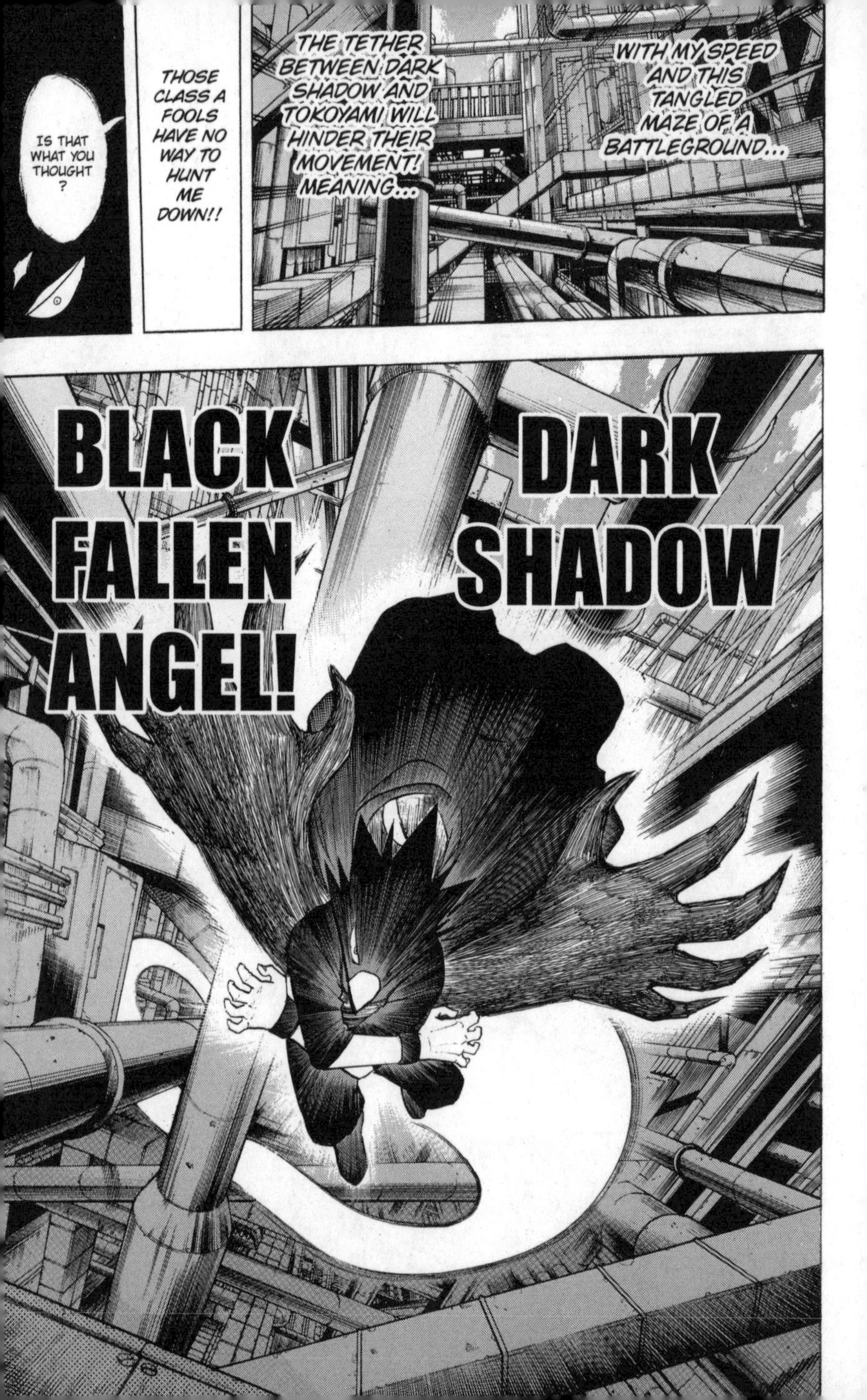
WITH MY SPEED AND THIS TANGLED MAZE OF A BATTLEGROUND...
THE TETHER BETWEEN DARK SHADOW AND TOKOYAMI WILL HINDER THEIR MOVEMENT! MEANING...
THOSE CLASS A FOOLS HAVE NO WAY TO HUNT ME DOWN!!
IS THAT WHAT YOU THOUGHT ?
DARK SHADOW
BLACK FALLEN ANGEL!

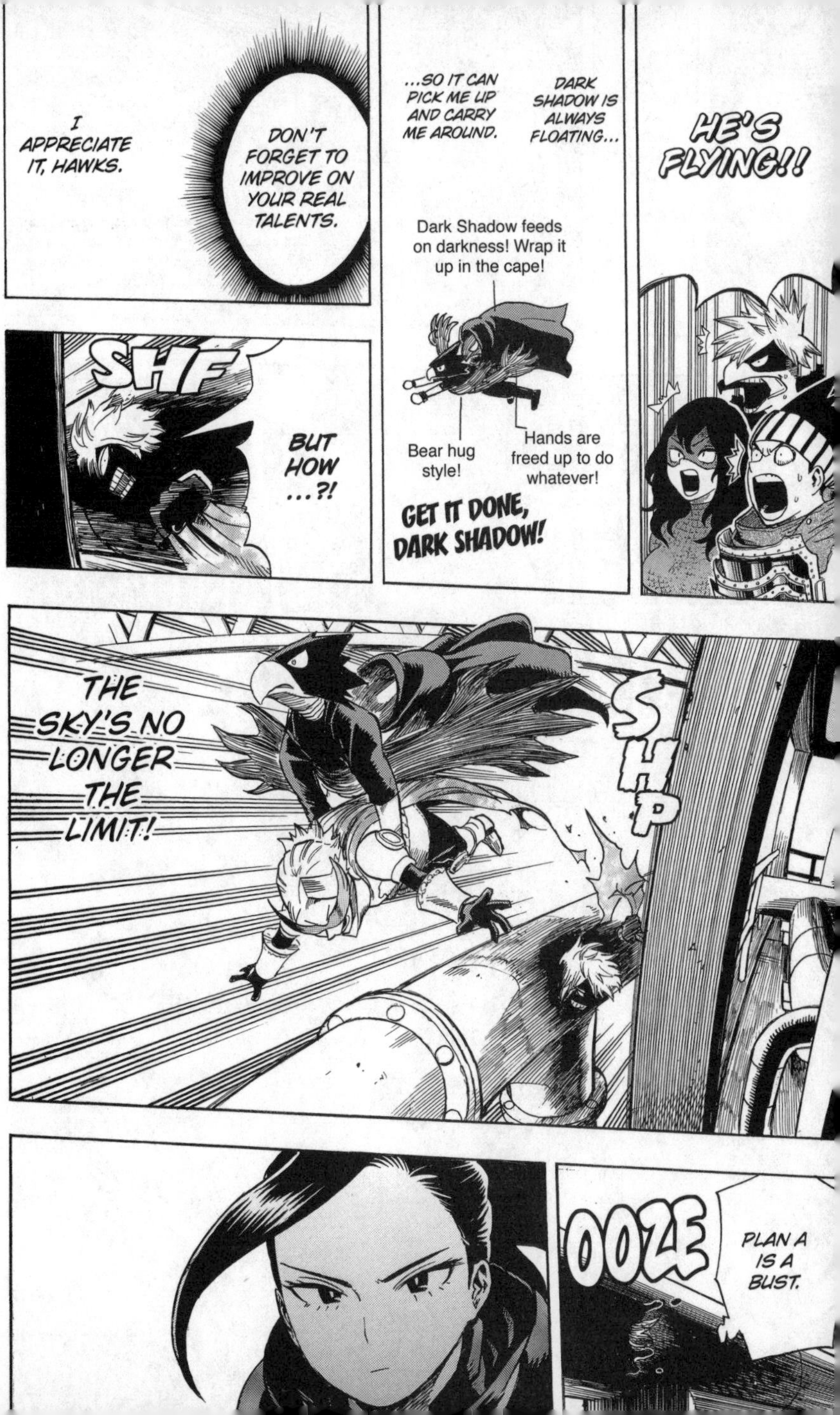

HE'S FLYING!!
DARK SHADOW IS ALWAYS FLOATING...
...SO IT CAN PICK ME UP AND CARRY ME AROUND.
Dark Shadow feeds on darkness! Wrap it up in the cape!
Hands are freed up to do whatever!
Bear hug style!
GET IT DONE, DARK SHADOW!
DON'T FORGET TO IMPROVE ON YOUR REAL TALENTS.
I APPRECIATE IT, HAWKS.
SHF
BUT HOW ...?!
SHP
THE SKY'S NO LONGER THE LIMIT!
PLAN A IS A BUST.
OOZE

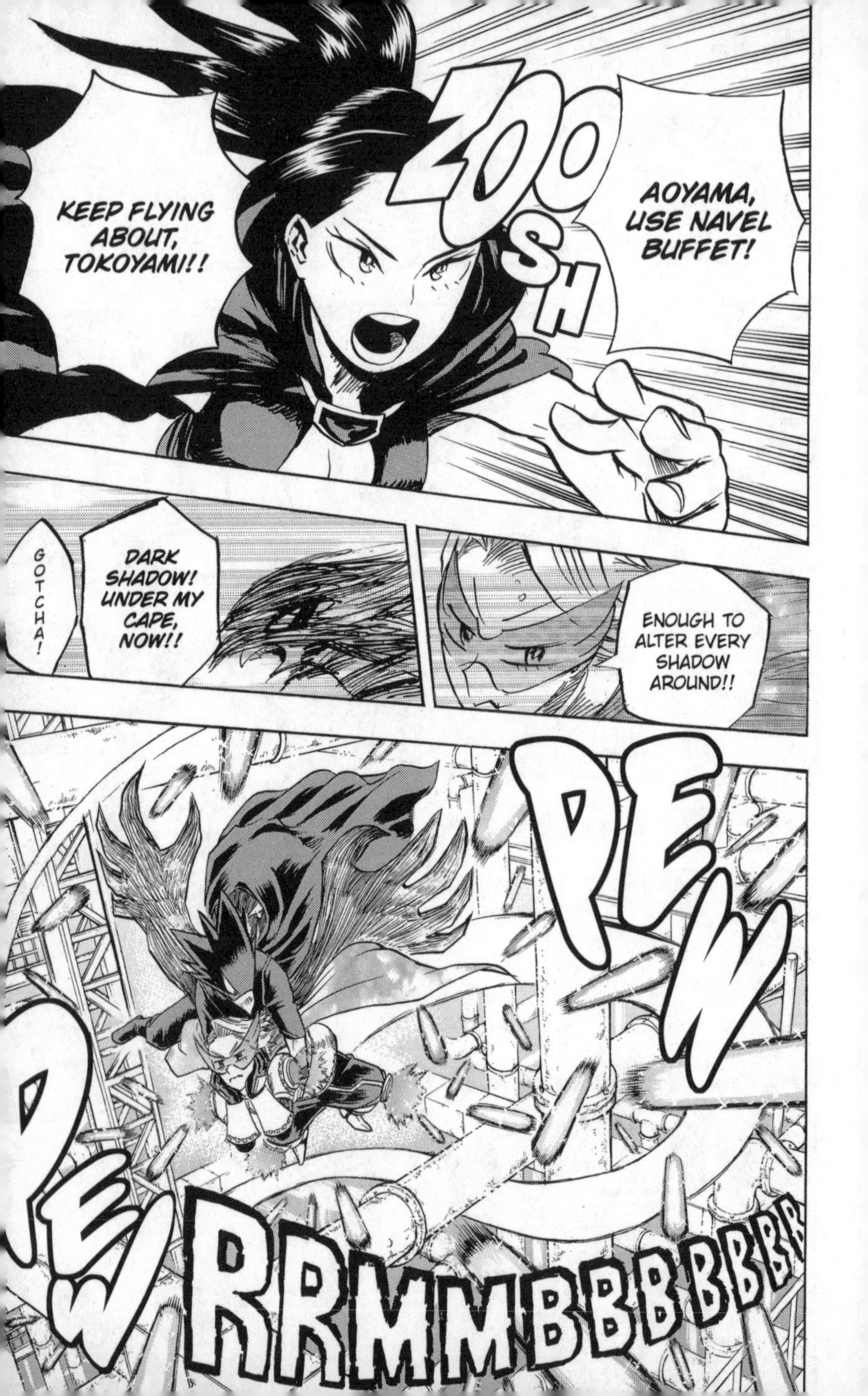
AOYAMA, USE NAVEL BUFFET!
ZOOOSH
KEEP FLYING ABOUT, TOKOYAMI!!
ENOUGH TO ALTER EVERY SHADOW AROUND!!
DARK SHADOW! UNDER MY CAPE, NOW!!
GOTCHA!
PEW
PEW
RRMMBBBBBB

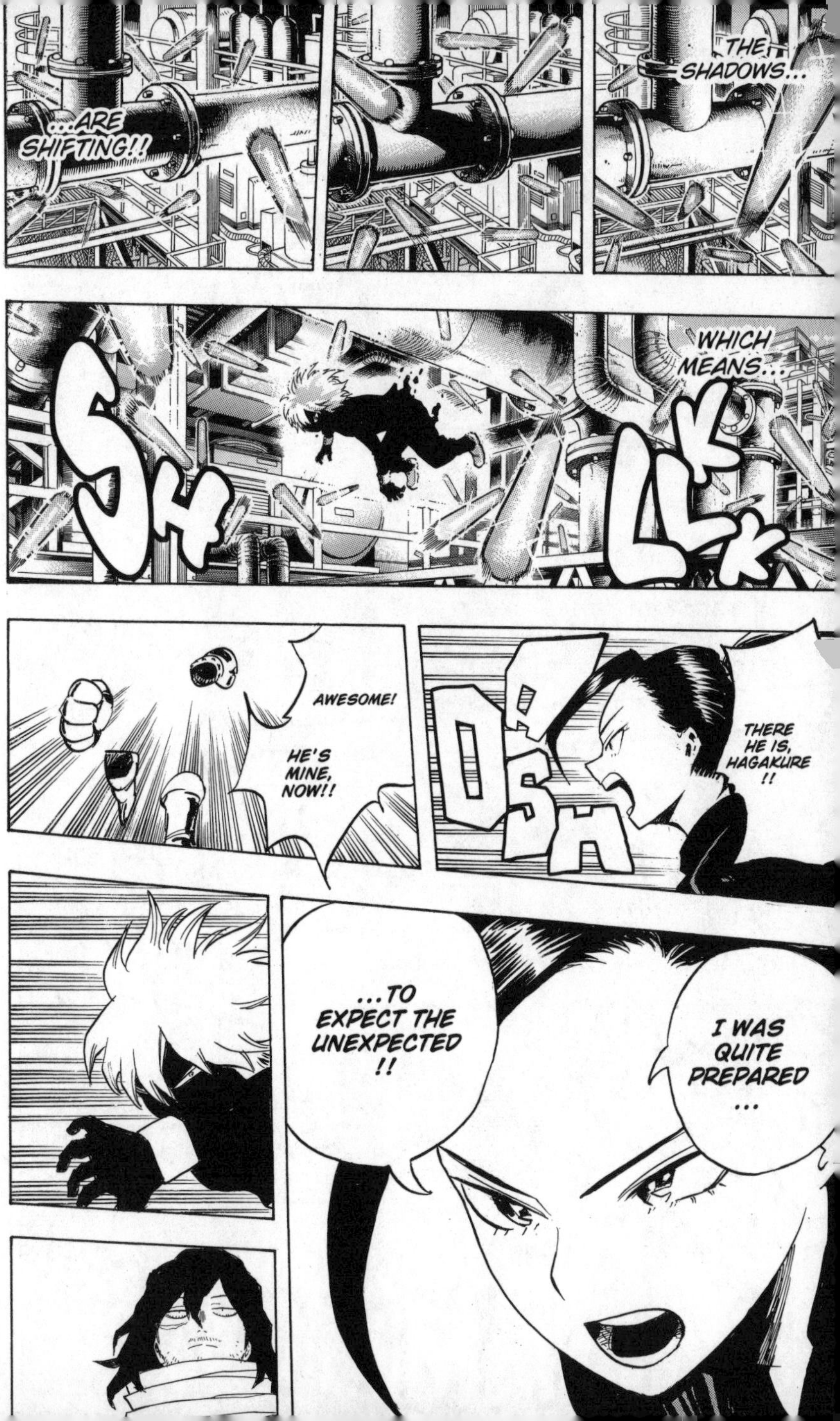
THE SHADOWS...
...ARE SHIFTING!!
WHICH MEANS...
SH
LLK
DASH
THERE HE IS, HAGAKURE !!
AWESOME!
HE'S MINE, NOW!!
I WAS QUITE PREPARED ...
...TO EXPECT THE UNEXPECTED !!

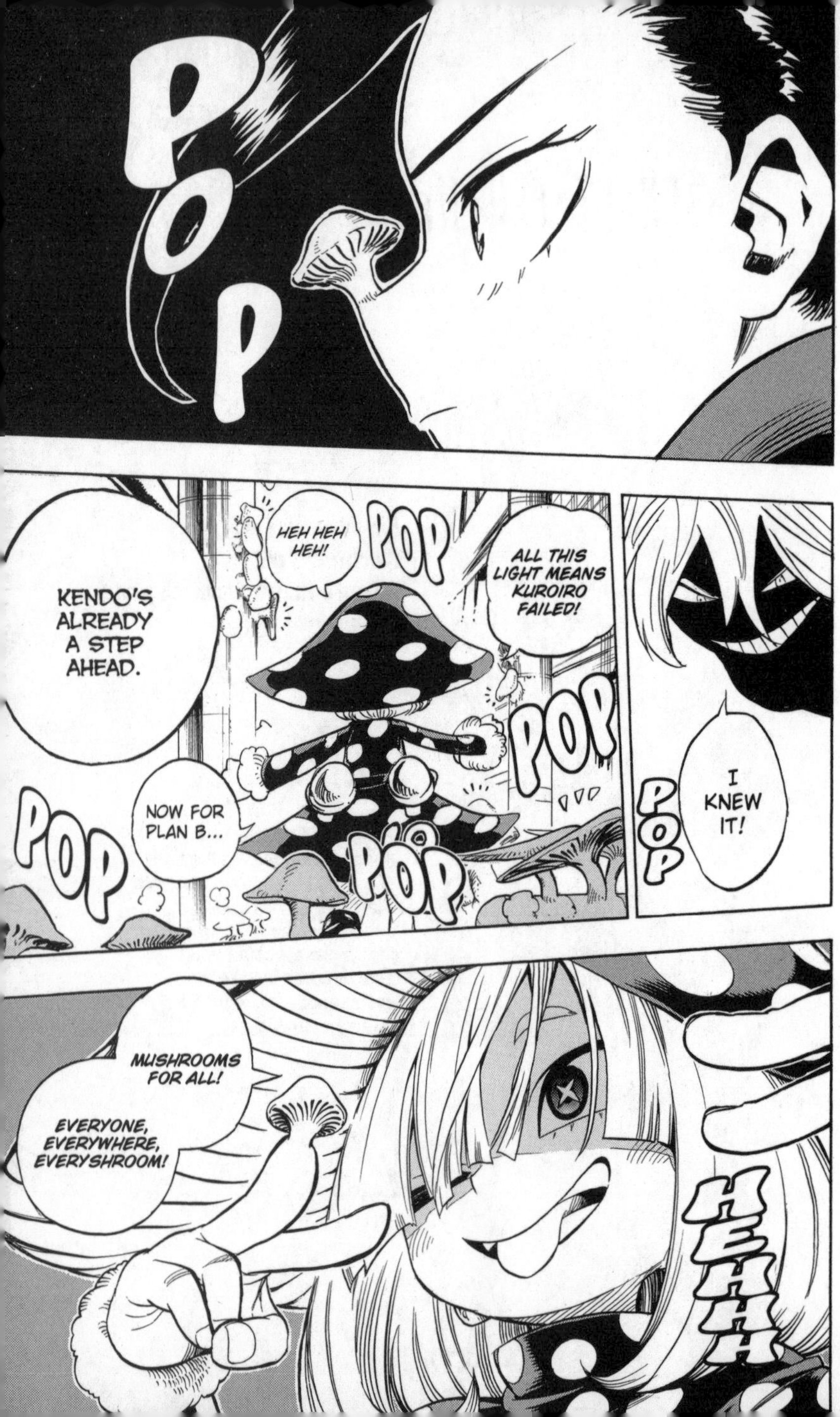
POP
POP
POP
I KNEW IT!
ALL THIS LIGHT MEANS KUROIRO FAILED!
POP
HEH HEH HEH!
POP
KENDO'S ALREADY A STEP AHEAD.
POP
NOW FOR PLAN B...
POP
HEHHH
MUSHROOMS FOR ALL!
EVERYONE, EVERYWHERE, EVERYSHROOM!

SHIHAI KUROIRO (16)

STREET CLOTHES

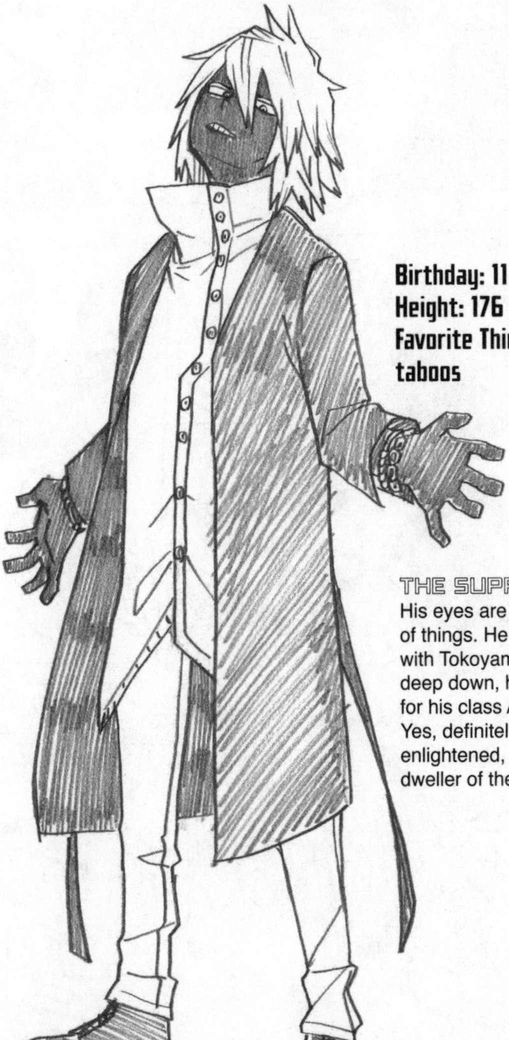

Birthday: 11/1
Height: 176 cm
Favorite Things: Squid-ink pasta, taboos

THE SUPPLEMENT

His eyes are open to the truth of things. He says stuff to mess with Tokoyami's head, but deep down, he feels an affinity for his class A counterpart. Yes, definitely awakened, enlightened, etc. And/or a dweller of the abyss.

No. 200 - Clever Commander!

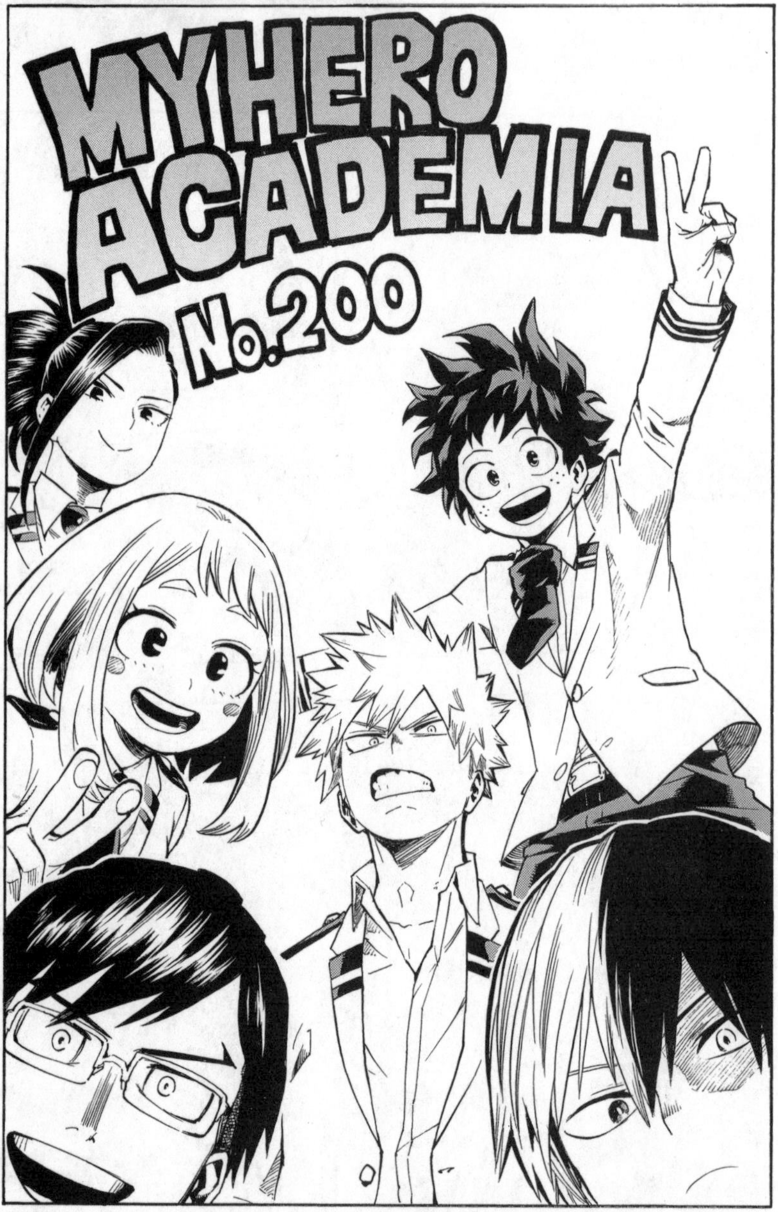
MY HERO ACADEMIA
No.200

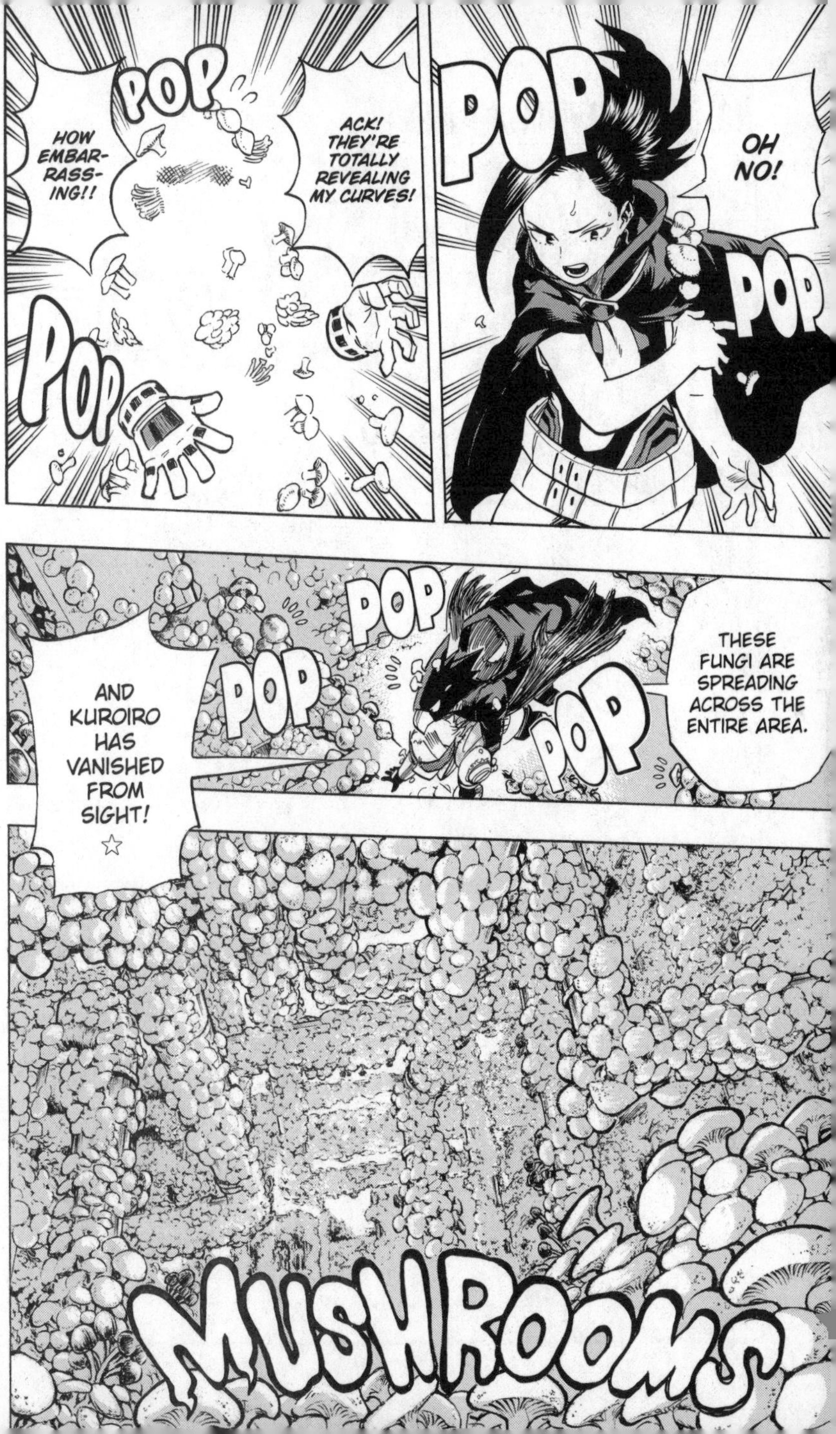
POP
OH NO!
POP
ACK! THEY'RE TOTALLY REVEALING MY CURVES!
POP
HOW EMBARRASSING!!
POP
THESE FUNGI ARE SPREADING ACROSS THE ENTIRE AREA.
POP
POP
POP
AND KUROIRO HAS VANISHED FROM SIGHT! ☆
MUSHROOMS

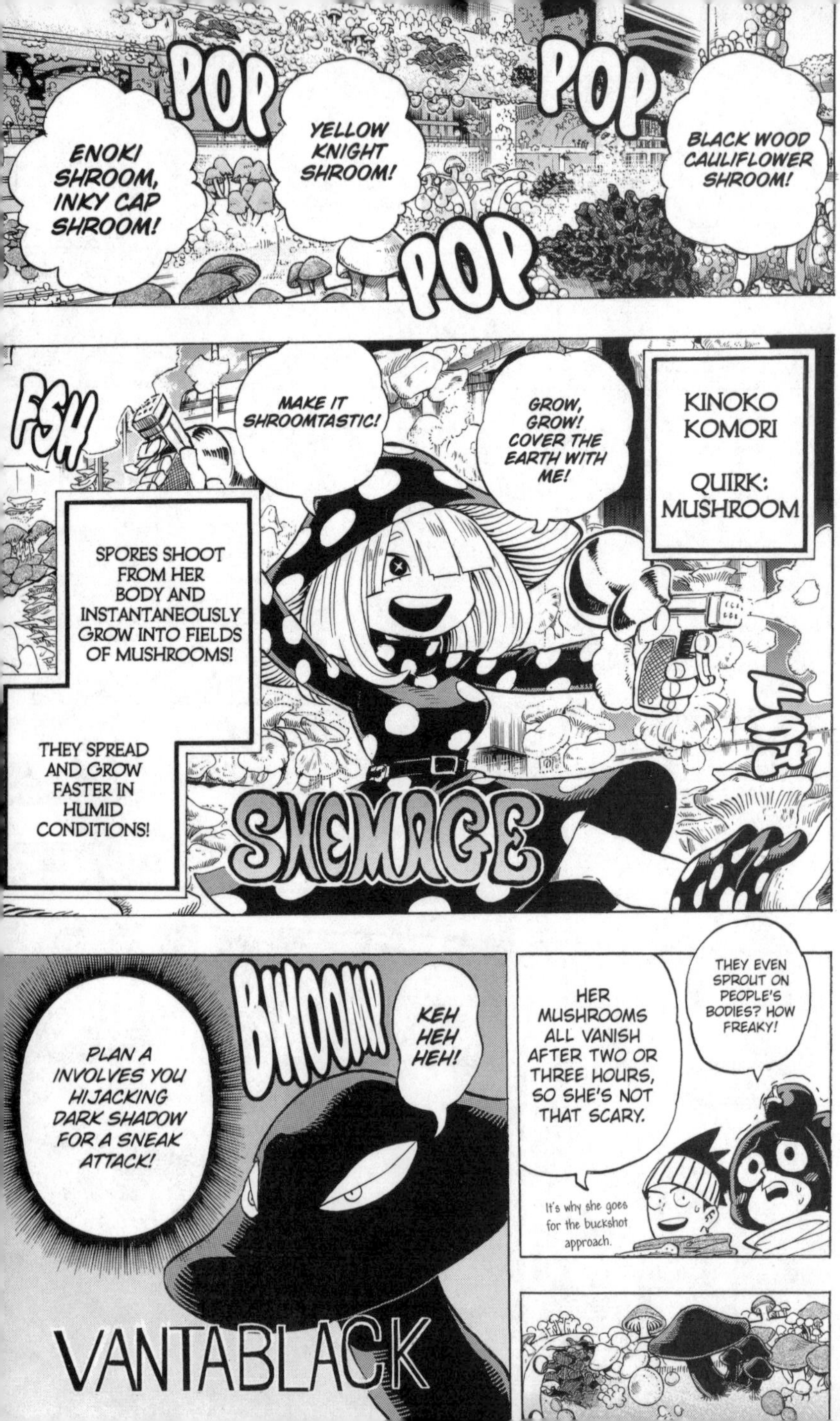
POP
BLACK WOOD CAULIFLOWER SHROOM!
POP
YELLOW KNIGHT SHROOM!
ENOKI SHROOM, INKY CAP SHROOM!
POP
KINOKO KOMORI
QUIRK: MUSHROOM
GROW, GROW! COVER THE EARTH WITH ME!
MAKE IT SHROOMTASTIC!
FSH
FSH
SPORES SHOOT FROM HER BODY AND INSTANTANEOUSLY GROW INTO FIELDS OF MUSHROOMS!
THEY SPREAD AND GROW FASTER IN HUMID CONDITIONS!
SHEMAGE
THEY EVEN SPROUT ON PEOPLE'S BODIES? HOW FREAKY!
HER MUSHROOMS ALL VANISH AFTER TWO OR THREE HOURS, SO SHE'S NOT THAT SCARY.
It's why she goes for the buckshot approach.
BWOOMP
KEH HEH HEH!
PLAN A INVOLVES YOU HIJACKING DARK SHADOW FOR A SNEAK ATTACK!
VANTABLACK

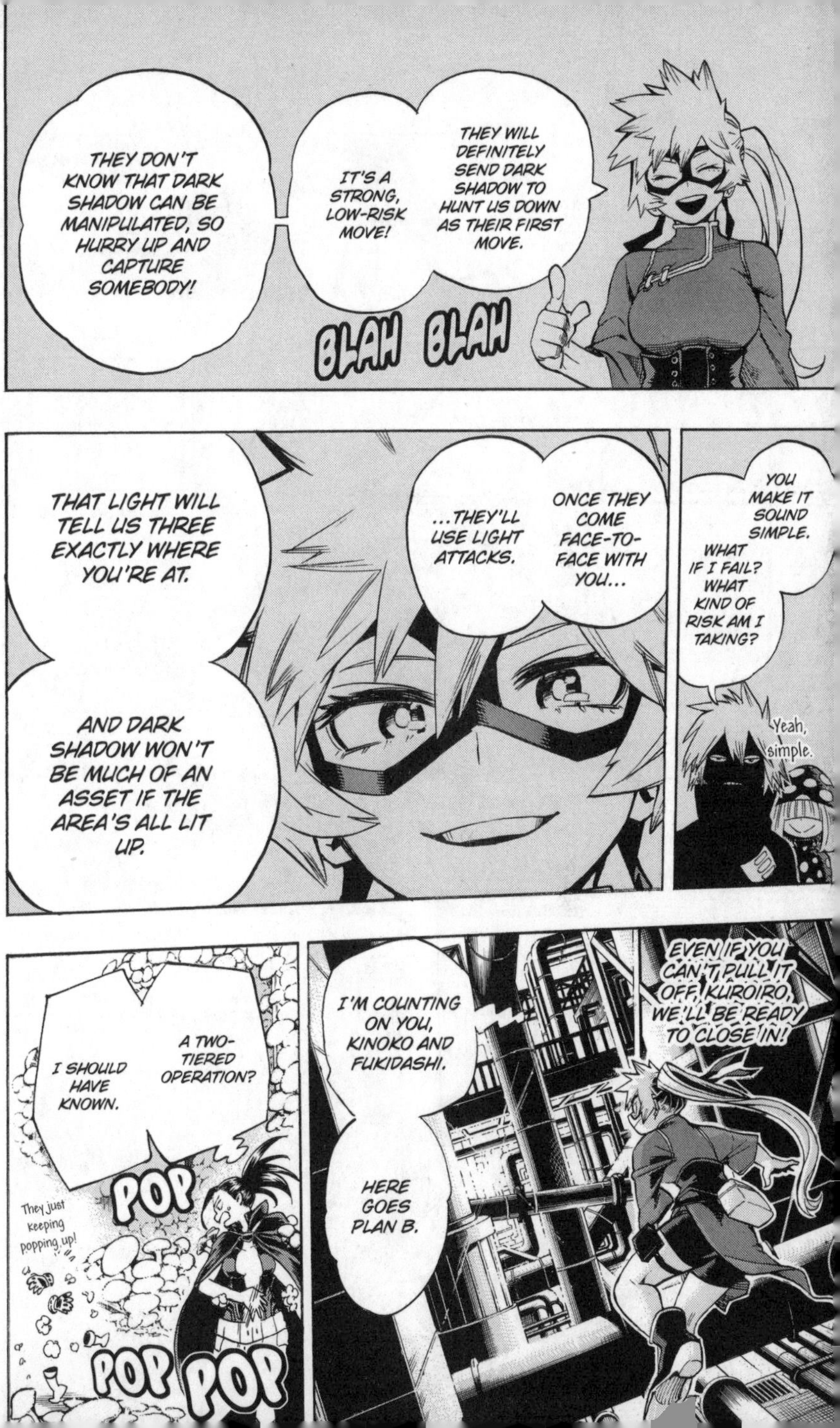
THEY WILL DEFINITELY SEND DARK SHADOW TO HUNT US DOWN AS THEIR FIRST MOVE.
IT'S A STRONG, LOW-RISK MOVE!
THEY DON'T KNOW THAT DARK SHADOW CAN BE MANIPULATED, SO HURRY UP AND CAPTURE SOMEBODY!
BLAH BLAH
YOU MAKE IT SOUND SIMPLE.
WHAT IF I FAIL? WHAT KIND OF RISK AM I TAKING?
Yeah, simple.
ONCE THEY COME FACE-TO-FACE WITH YOU...
...THEY'LL USE LIGHT ATTACKS.
THAT LIGHT WILL TELL US THREE EXACTLY WHERE YOU'RE AT.
AND DARK SHADOW WON'T BE MUCH OF AN ASSET IF THE AREA'S ALL LIT UP.
EVEN IF YOU CAN'T PULL IT OFF, KUROIRO, WE'LL BE READY TO CLOSE IN!
I'M COUNTING ON YOU, KINOKO AND FUKIDASHI.
HERE GOES PLAN B.
A TWO-TIERED OPERATION?
I SHOULD HAVE KNOWN.
POP
They just keeping popping up!
POP POP

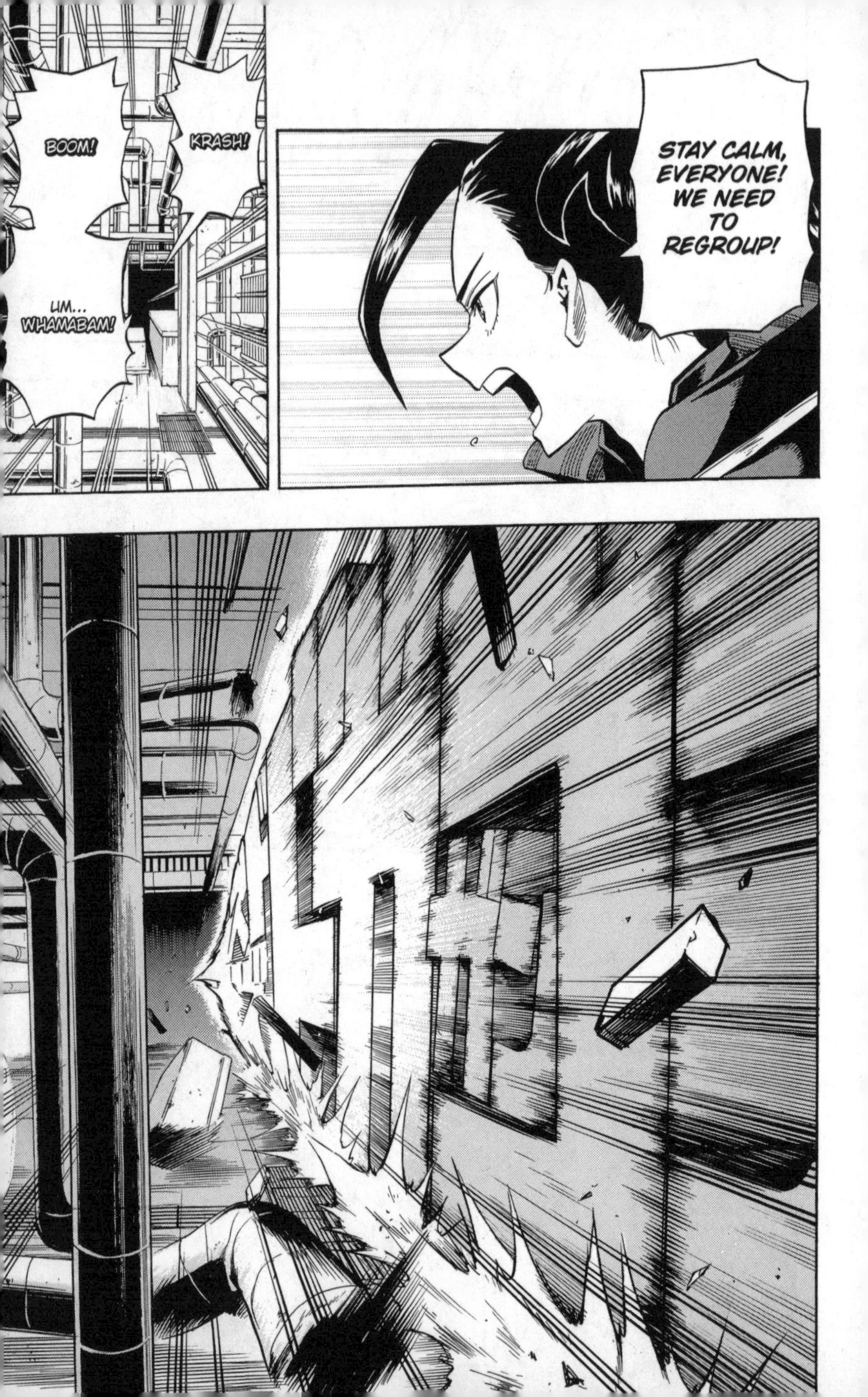
STAY CALM, EVERYONE! WE NEED TO REGROUP!
KRASH!
BOOM!
UM... WHAMABAM!

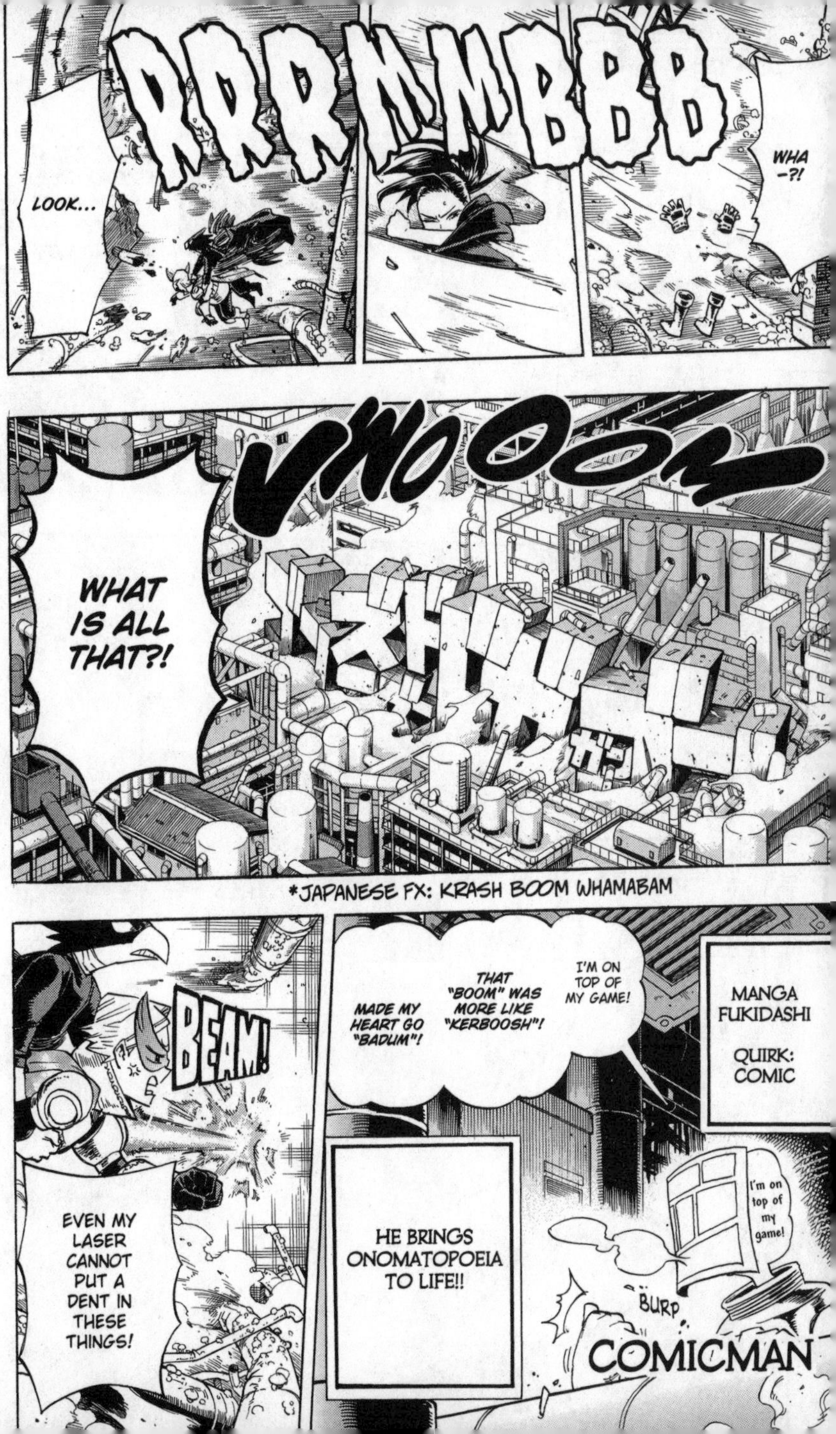
RRRMMBBB
WHA-?!
LOOK...
VWOOOM
WHAT IS ALL THAT?!
*JAPANESE FX: KRASH BOOM WHAMABAM
MANGA FUKIDASHI
QUIRK: COMIC
I'M ON TOP OF MY GAME!
THAT "BOOM" WAS MORE LIKE "KERBOOSH"!
MADE MY HEART GO "BADUM"!
I'm on top of my game!
BURP
COMICMAN
HE BRINGS ONOMATOPOEIA TO LIFE!!
BEAM!
EVEN MY LASER CANNOT PUT A DENT IN THESE THINGS!

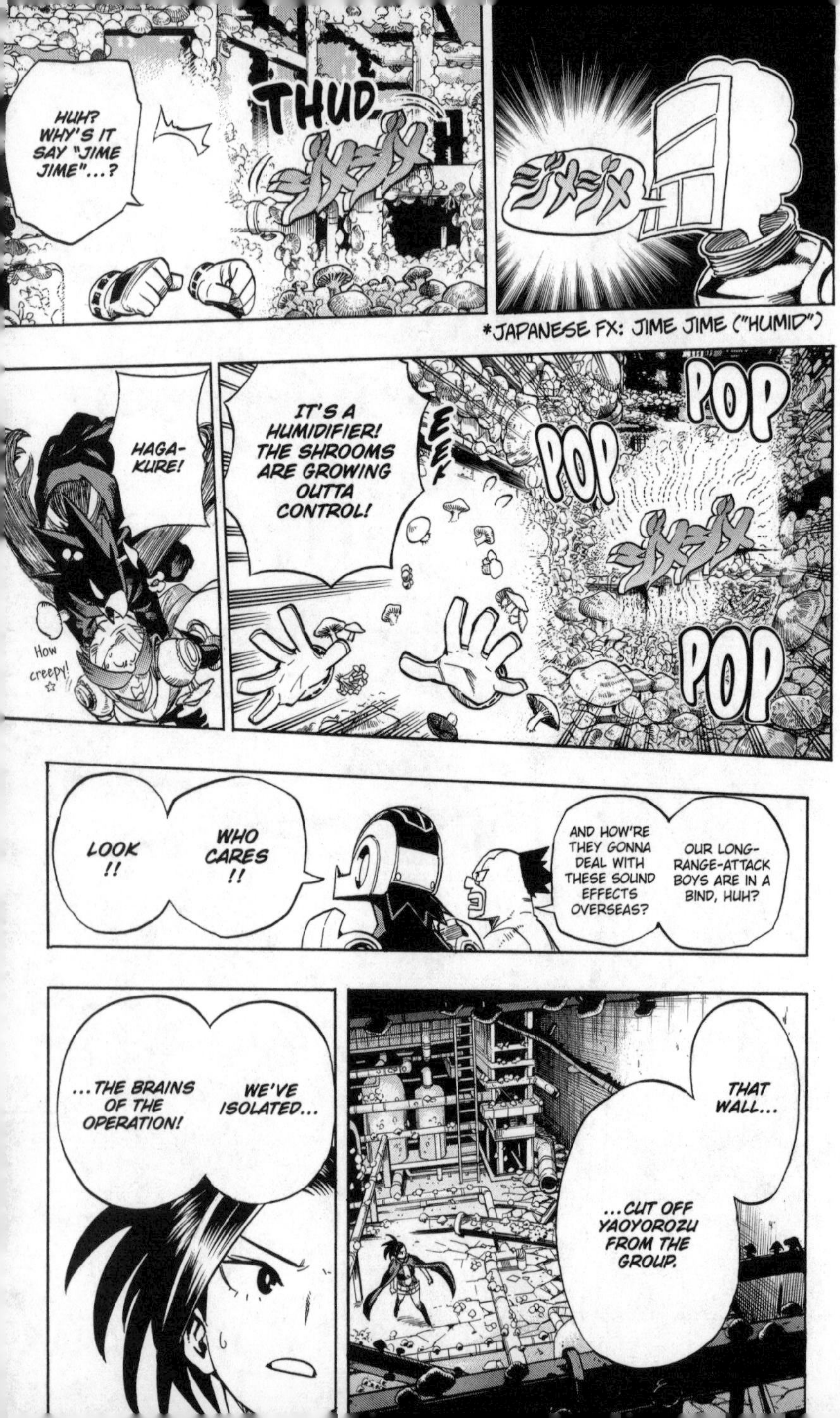
ジメジメ
THUD
ジメジメ
HUH? WHY'S IT SAY "JIME JIME"...?
*JAPANESE FX: JIME JIME ("HUMID")
POP
POP
ジメジメ
EEK
IT'S A HUMIDIFIER! THE SHROOMS ARE GROWING OUTTA CONTROL!
POP
HAGA-KURE!
How creepy! ☆
OUR LONG-RANGE-ATTACK BOYS ARE IN A BIND, HUH?
AND HOW'RE THEY GONNA DEAL WITH THESE SOUND EFFECTS OVERSEAS?
WHO CARES !!
LOOK !!
THAT WALL...
...CUT OFF YAOYOROZU FROM THE GROUP.
WE'VE ISOLATED...
...THE BRAINS OF THE OPERATION!

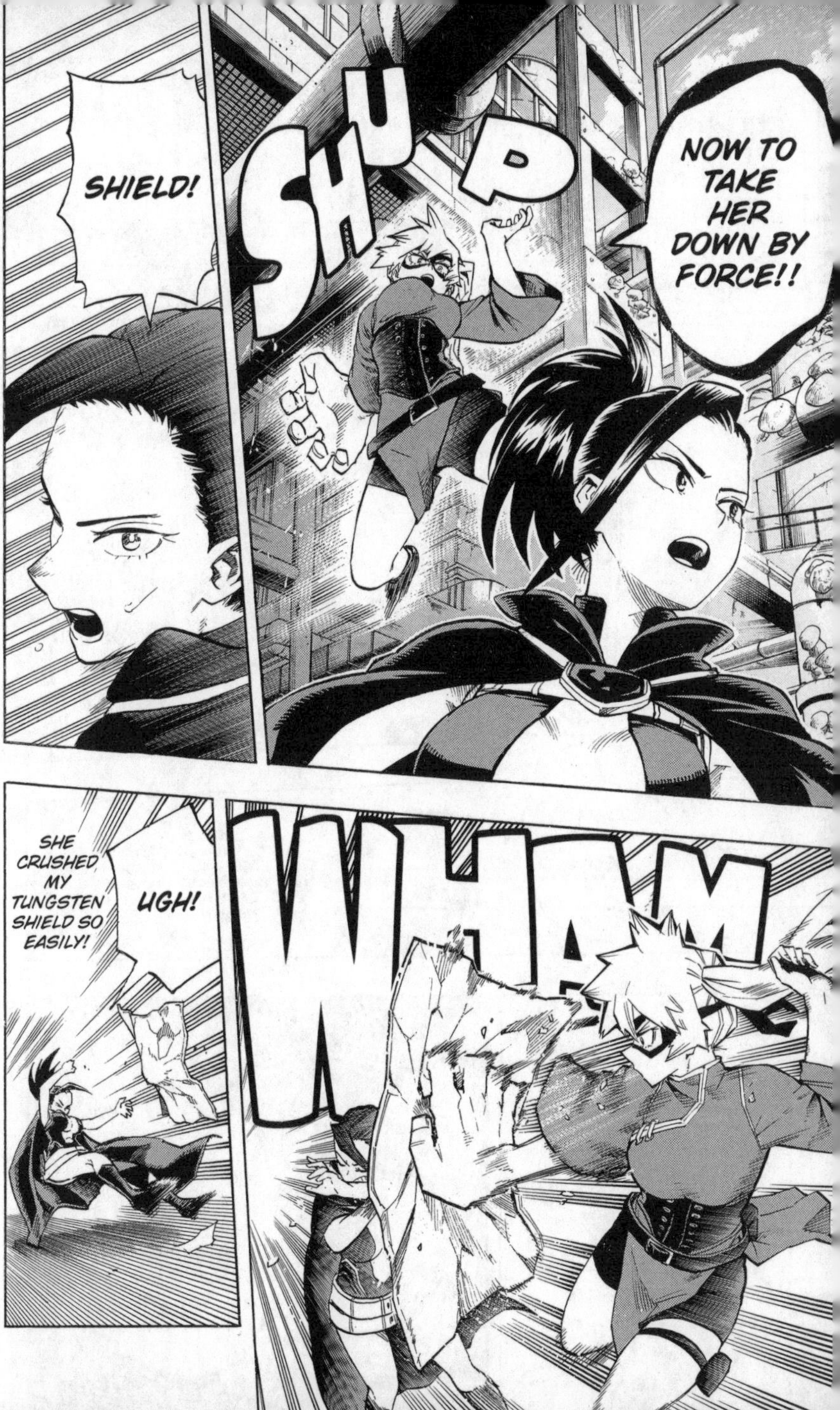
SHUP
NOW TO TAKE HER DOWN BY FORCE!!
SHIELD!
WHAM
UGH!
SHE CRUSHED MY TUNGSTEN SHIELD SO EASILY!

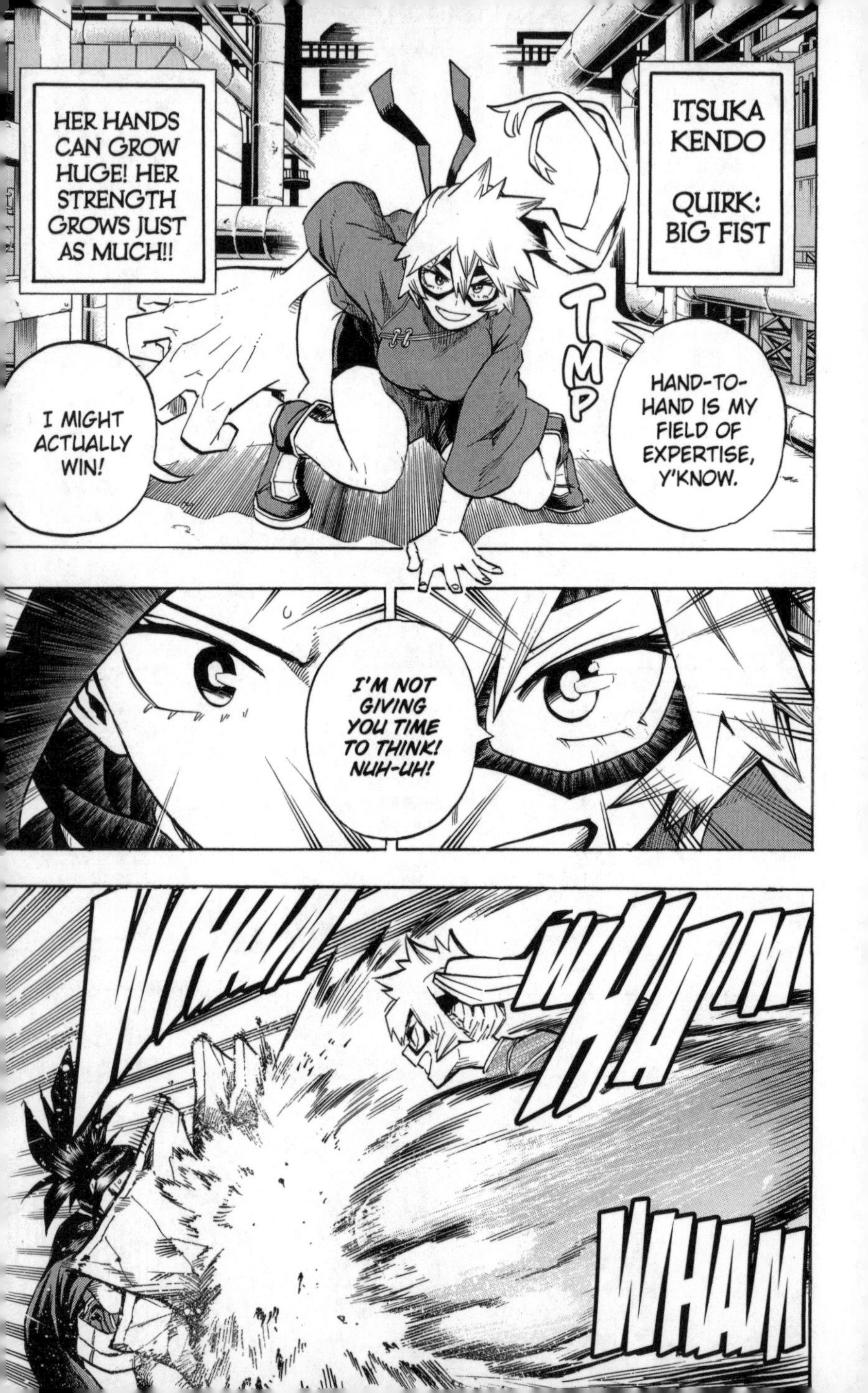
ITSUKA KENDO

QUIRK: BIG FIST
TMP
HAND-TO-HAND IS MY FIELD OF EXPERTISE, Y'KNOW.
HER HANDS CAN GROW HUGE! HER STRENGTH GROWS JUST AS MUCH!!
I MIGHT ACTUALLY WIN!
I'M NOT GIVING YOU TIME TO THINK! NUH-UH!
WHAM
WHAM
WHAM

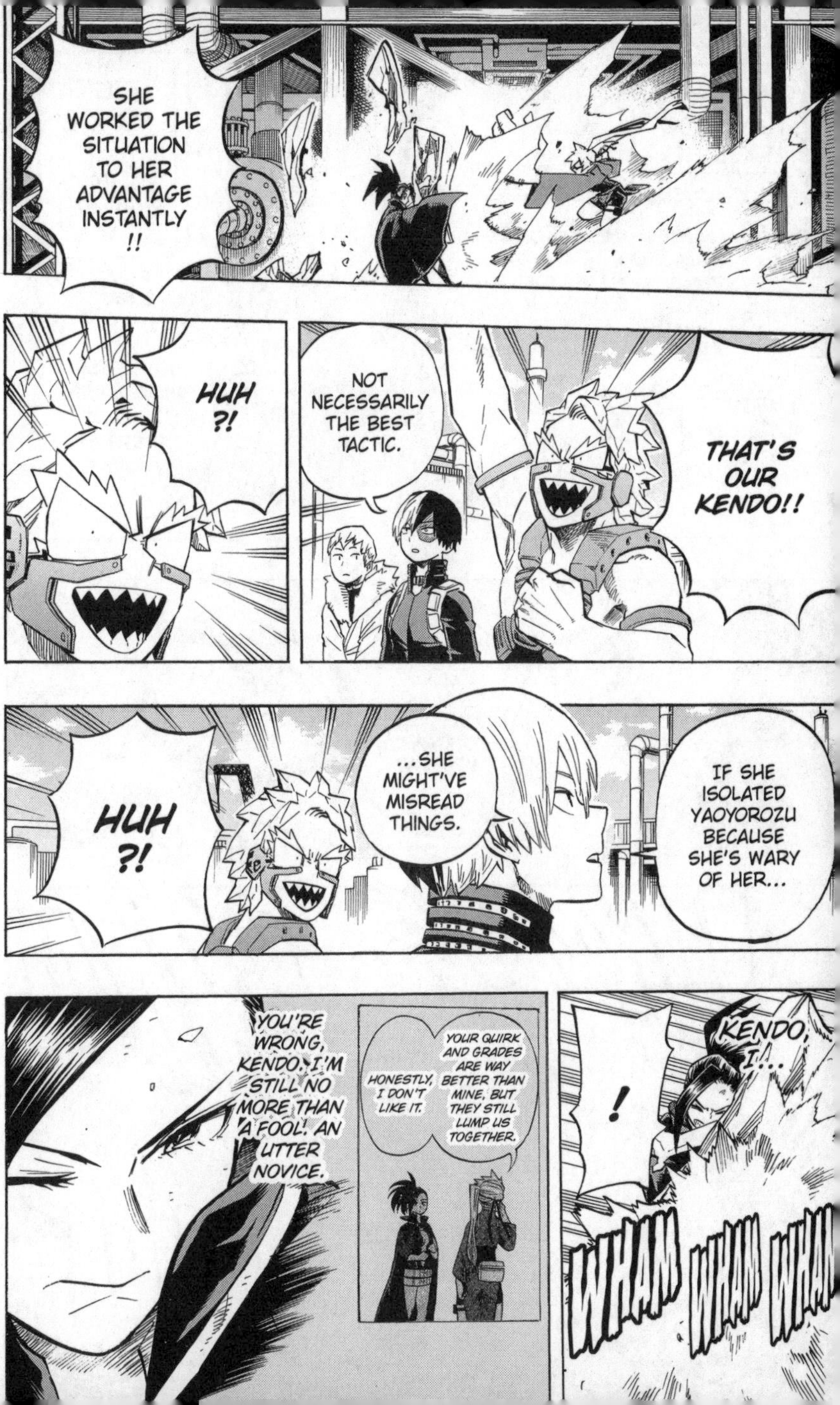
SHE WORKED THE SITUATION TO HER ADVANTAGE INSTANTLY !!
THAT'S OUR KENDO!!
NOT NECESSARILY THE BEST TACTIC.
HUH ?!
IF SHE ISOLATED YAOYOROZU BECAUSE SHE'S WARY OF HER...
...SHE MIGHT'VE MISREAD THINGS.
HUH ?!
KENDO, I...
!
WHAM WHAM WHAM
YOUR QUIRK AND GRADES ARE WAY BETTER THAN MINE, BUT THEY STILL LUMP US TOGETHER.
HONESTLY, I DON'T LIKE IT.
YOU'RE WRONG, KENDO. I'M STILL NO MORE THAN A FOOL. AN UTTER NOVICE.

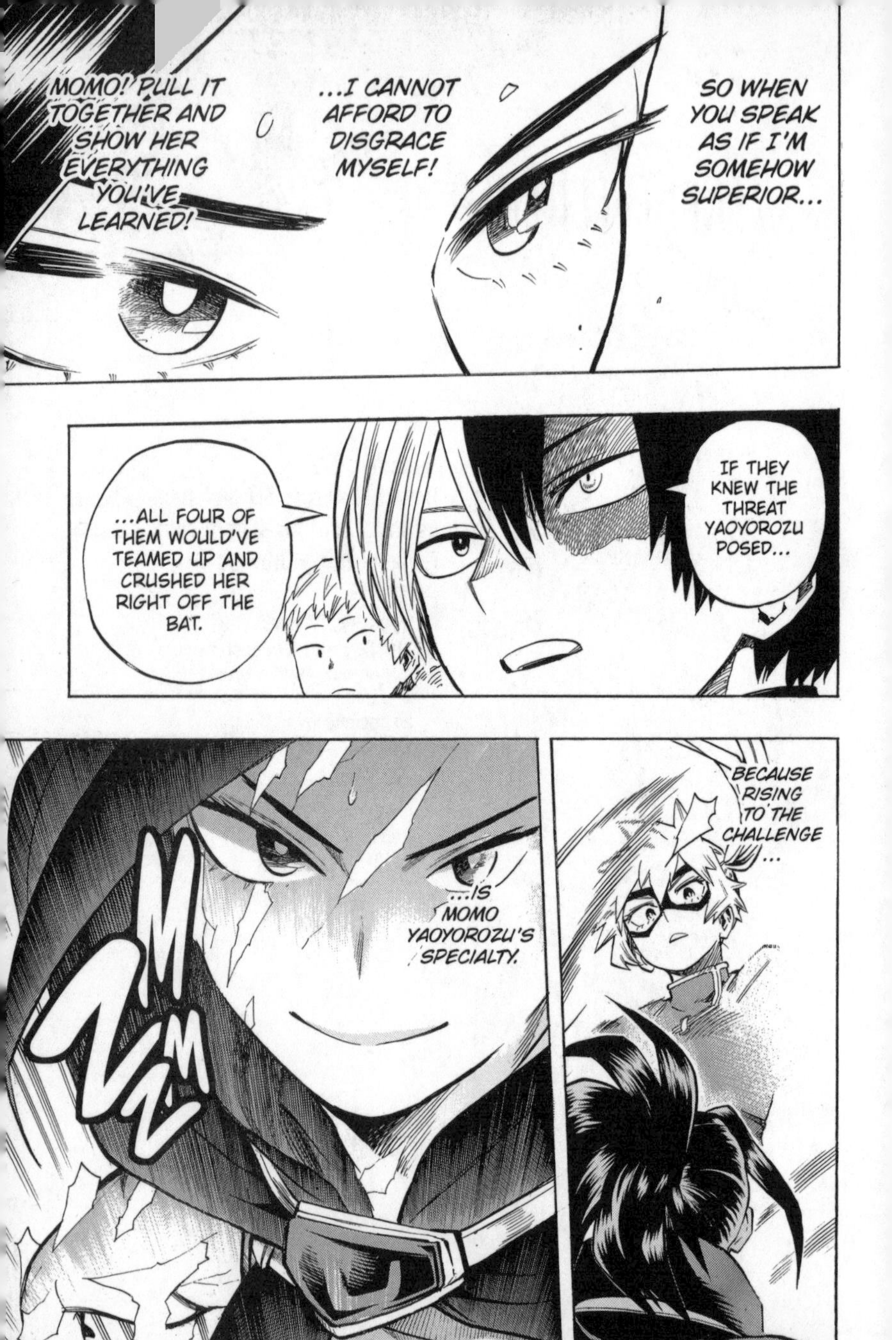
SO WHEN YOU SPEAK AS IF I'M SOMEHOW SUPERIOR...
...I CANNOT AFFORD TO DISGRACE MYSELF!
MOMO! PULL IT TOGETHER AND SHOW HER EVERYTHING YOU'VE LEARNED!
IF THEY KNEW THE THREAT YAOYOROZU POSED...
...ALL FOUR OF THEM WOULD'VE TEAMED UP AND CRUSHED HER RIGHT OFF THE BAT.
BECAUSE RISING TO THE CHALLENGE...
...IS MOMO YAOYOROZU'S SPECIALTY.

VOLUME 21 - WHY HE GETS BACK UP (END)

STREET CLOTHES

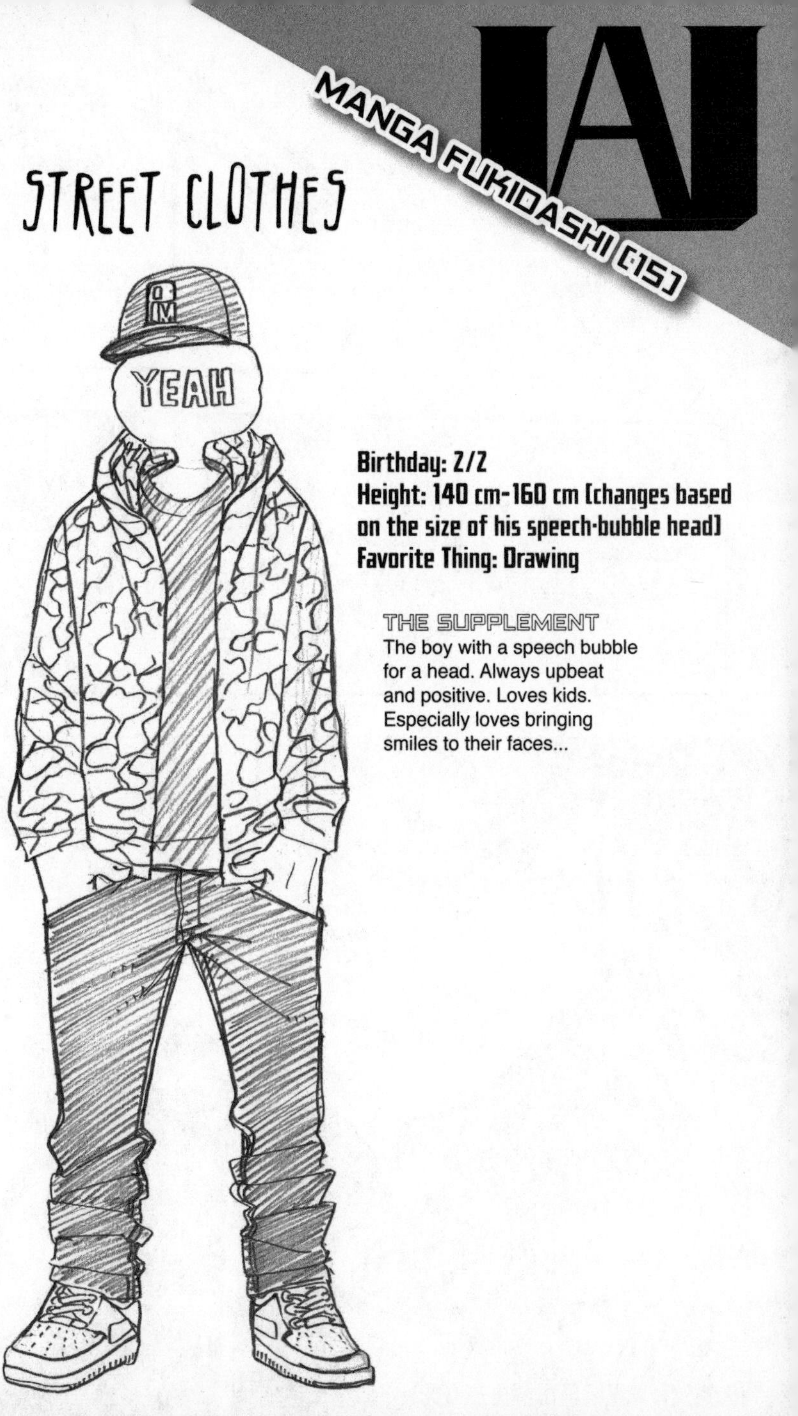
YEAH

Birthday: 2/2
Height: 140 cm-160 cm [changes based on the size of his speech-bubble head]
Favorite Thing: Drawing

THE SUPPLEMENT

The boy with a speech bubble for a head. Always upbeat and positive. Loves kids. Especially loves bringing smiles to their faces...

THE MEGA FAN

HIROSHI TAMEDA (18)

"CAN'TCHA SEE?!"

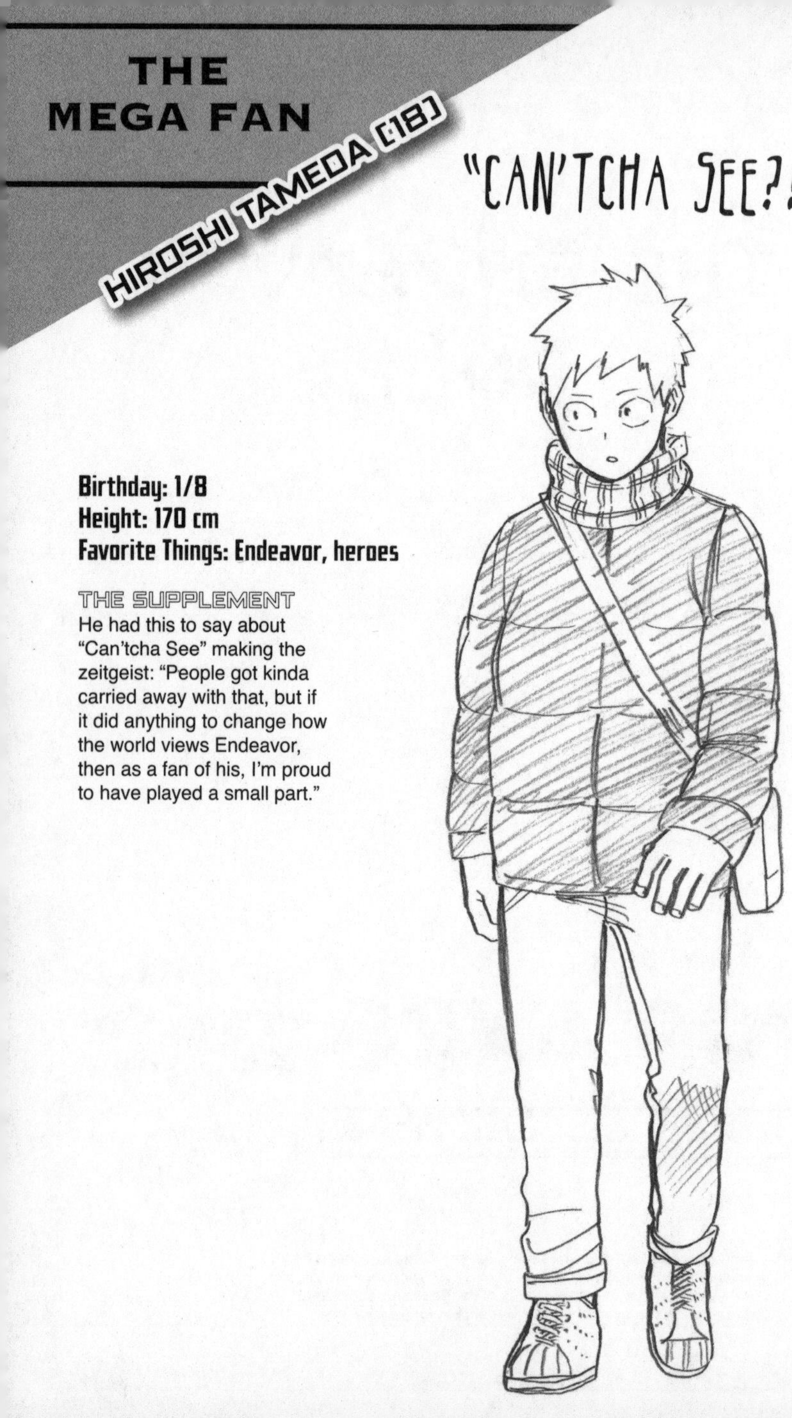

Birthday: 1/8
Height: 170 cm
Favorite Things: Endeavor, heroes

THE SUPPLEMENT

He had this to say about "Can'tcha See" making the zeitgeist: "People got kinda carried away with that, but if it did anything to change how the world views Endeavor, then as a fan of his, I'm proud to have played a small part."

THE ENDEAVOR DOLL

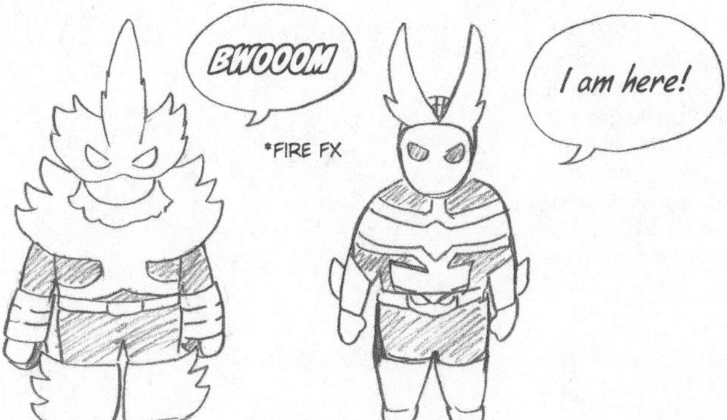
BWOOOM
*FIRE FX
I am here!

TOP HERO

★☆★☆★☆★☆★☆★☆★☆★☆★☆★☆★☆★☆

PUFFY COLLECTION

PRESS THEIR TUMMIES FOR SOUND!!

3,000 Yen
(tax not included)

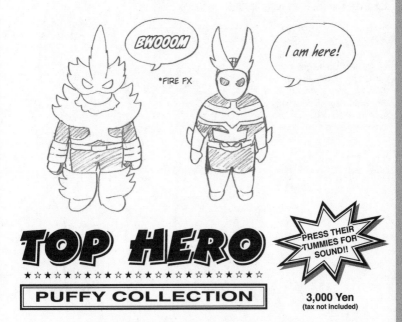

While the All Might doll was selling out and being scooped up by scalpers who would later charge a premium, vendors were left to deal with huge leftover inventories of the Endeavor doll. They ended up throwing him into the bargain bin for just 500 yen.

Momoyao's cape is very warm. It kind of makes her look like a sorceress.

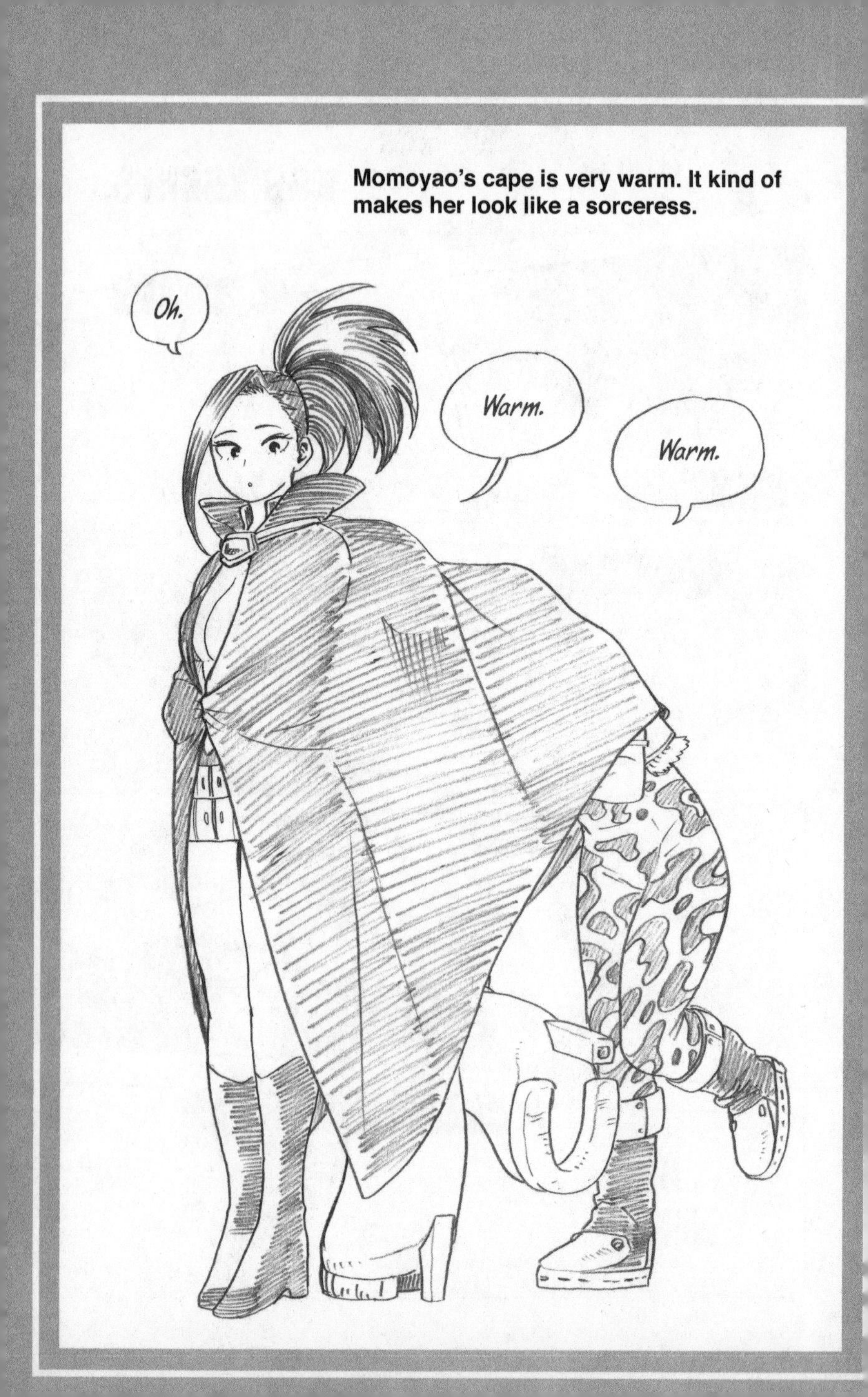
Oh.
Warm.
Warm.

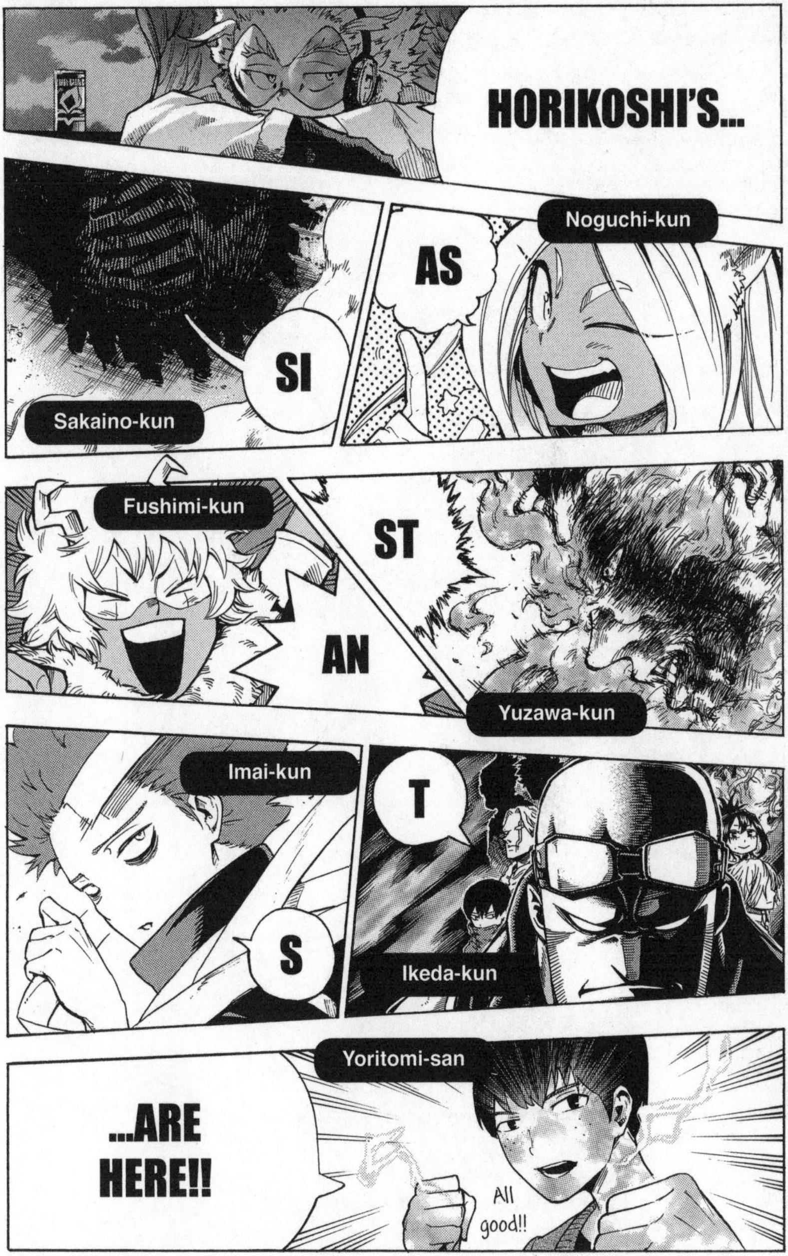
HORIKOSHI'S...
Noguchi-kun
AS
SI
Sakaino-kun
ST
Yuzawa-kun
Fushimi-kun
AN
T
Ikeda-kun
Imai-kun
S
Yoritomi-san
...ARE HERE!!
All good!!

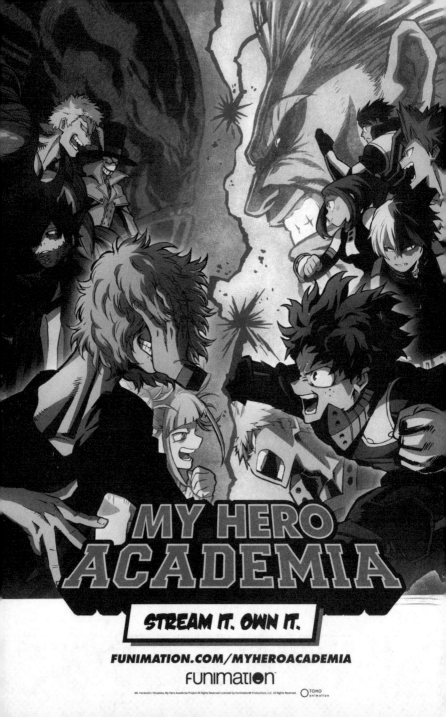

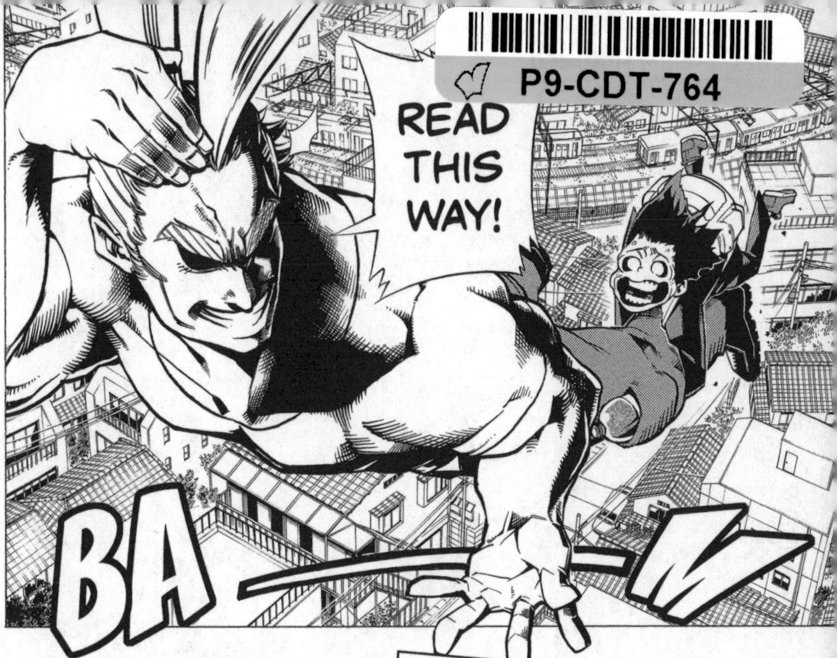
READ THIS WAY!
BA—M

MY HERO ACADEMIA

reads from right to left, starting in the upper-right corner. Japanese is read from right to left, meaning that action, sound effects and word-balloon order are completely reversed from English order.

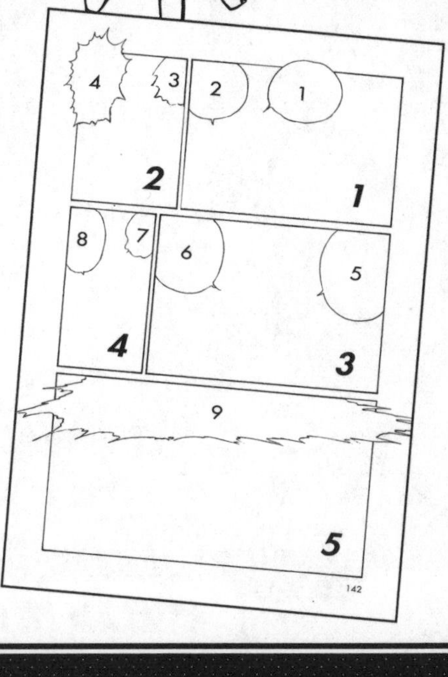
1
2
3
4
1
2
5
6
7
8
3
4
9
5
142